"In her new book, *Social Justice Handbook,* Mae Elise Cannon provides a comprehensive, historical overview of individuals and organizations that have effectively influenced others to take action on issues of social justice. There should be no question about the role and responsibility of the body of Christ to care for the poor and needy, as over two thousand Scripture references clearly indicate the heart of God and his mandate to us as believers. As well as providing the historical background of many life-changing causes, Cannon lists small steps that we can each take to actively live out our faith in tangible, practical ways as advocates for Christ and his work here on earth."

DR. WESS STAFFORD, president and CEO, Compassion International

"People often ask me for resources on what they can do about injustice in the world. Now I can point them to Mae Cannon's *Social Justice Handbook.* This guide is packed full of resources and ideas for following the God of justice both at home and around the globe."

GARY A. HAUGEN, president and CEO, International Justice Mission, author, *Good News About Injustice* and *Just Courage*

"'The LORD . . . was displeased that there was no justice. . . . He was appalled that there was no one to intervene' (Isaiah 59:15-16). Churches have engaged in evangelism, teaching and compassion for years, while we have sat on the sidelines of justice. Mae moves us . . . from feet that are frozen to walking, from a framework to a path, and from inspiration to hard work and action. This is the most comprehensive and compelling work I've read on justice. This book has the potential to make our churches into the unstoppable forces God intended them to be, with justice for all."

NANCY ORTBERG, author of *Looking for God: An Unexpected Journey Through Tattoos, Tofu and Pronouns*

"Mae Cannon's passion, compassion and theological strength of calling as an advocate for the 'least of these' leaps off of every page of the *Social Justice Handbook.* This book informs the average follower of Christ and the Christian leader alike to act as Jesus would in the face of injustice. Mae's call for action convicts us all to do something for Christ's sake. Every Christian needs this book within arm's reach."

DR. DAVID ANDERSON, senior pastor, Bridgeway Community Church, and author of *Gracism*

"This is a cookbook for plotting goodness and stirring up holy mischief. Take a look and find a recipe for revolution. Then let us take it to the streets—interrupting injustice with grace, surprising the world with joy and whispering God's love to a broken world."

SHANE CLAIBORNE, activist, author and lover, www.thesimpleway.org

"*Social Justice Handbook* is a long overdue work. Despite the resurgence of interest in justice by many churches, there has been a noticeable lack of available resources on this topic. Mae Cannon gives us the biblical framework that can spur churches to action as well as giving us practical tips and real-life models and examples of how justice can be lived out in our world. For any individual, Christian fellowship or church wanting to grow in the area of biblical social justice, this is the book you want to get."

SOONG-CHAN RAH, Milton B. Engebretson Assistant Professor of Church Growth and Evangelism, North Park Theological Seminary, and author of *The Next Evangelicalism*

"*Social Justice Handbook* is more than a manual for public discipleship; it is a comprehensive account of Christian social conviction that reads like an apologetics of the faith. I am in awe of this book!"

CHARLES MARSH, author of *The Beloved Community: How Faith Shapes Social Justice, from the Civil Rights Movement to Today,* and professor of religious studies and director of the Project on Lived Theology, University of Virginia

"Mae Cannon has done what many would deem impossible: she has developed a solid introduction to social justice rooted in Scripture, she has given churches concrete steps for becoming agents of social justice, and she has provided an amazingly comprehensive overview of justice-related issues that we face in our world today. And she has done so in a clear, readable, accessible style that people in your church will appreciate. Through her work and the work of many others like her, what seemed impossible even a few years ago may be happening soon—thousands of American churches growing beyond an 'it's all about me' spirituality to a more mature identity as communities of integral mission."

BRIAN MCLAREN, author of *Everything Must Change*

"Jesus was about the justification of souls and justice for every soul and society. The church when at its best has been devoted to both. This is a hands-on book on how to understand issues of justice and tangible ways to pursue it through local churches. Thank you, Mae."

LON ALLISON, executive director, Billy Graham Center, Wheaton College

"*Social Justice Handbook* is a highly valuable aid to every pastor and church leader. This book tells us how to get started on social justice causes and where to find the groups that support the causes we believe in."

ALVERA MICKELSEN, writer, editor and educator

"The moment you open *Social Justice Handbook,* it will vibrate in your hands with the heart-passion that inspired its making, a passion generated by him who described his life-mission as bringing good news to the poor, release to captives, sight to the blind, freedom to the oppressed and the time of God's grace. This book will simply not allow all those great intentions to become lost in theory. It will take you by the hand and lead you step by step into their glorious implementation."

GILBERT BILEZIKIAN, Professor Emeritus, Wheaton College, and a founding leader of Willow Creek Community Church

"*Social Justice Handbook* serves as a veritable, global, ecclesial terminal, a launching off point to the myriad ways that the shalom of Christ has gloriously broken forth in, and through, his rebellious and needy creation. Mae Cannon does this with the unequivocal passion of one who cares deeply about what the church is called to be. Through the *Handbook,* Cannon generously offers Christians tangible points of access to taste, and enter into, what God is doing in his world."

CRAIG WONG, Executive Director, Grace Urban Ministries, San Francisco, CA

# Social Justice Handbook

## SMALL STEPS TO A BETTER WORLD

## Mae Elise Cannon

FOREWORD BY John Perkins

IVP Books

An imprint of InterVarsity Press
Downers Grove, Illinois

InterVarsity Press
P.O. Box 1400, Downers Grove, IL 60515-1426
World Wide Web: www.ivpress.com
E-mail: email@ivpress.com

InterVarsity Press® is the book publishing division of InterVarsity Christian Fellowship/USA®, a movement of students and faculty active on campus at hundreds of universities, colleges and schools of nursing in the United States of America, and a member movement of the International Fellowship of Evangelical Students. For information about local and regional activities, write Public Relations Dept., InterVarsity Christian Fellowship/USA, 6400 Schroeder Rd., P.O. Box 7895, Madison, WI 53707 7895, or visit the IVCF website at <www.intervarsity.org>.

All Scripture quotations, unless otherwise indicated, are taken from the Holy Bible, Today's New International Version™ Copyright © 2001 by International Bible Society. All rights reserved.

Design: Cindy Kiple

Cover images:   houses on a hill: Kevin Cooley/Getty Images
                abandoned shoes: Tomek Sikora/Getty Images
Interior images: worn shoes: Andreas Gradin/Shutterstock
                 row homes: Andrea Gingerich/iStockphoto

ISBN 978-0-8308-3715-1

Printed in the United States of America ∞

**Library of Congress Cataloging-in-Publication Data**

Cannon, Mae Elise, 1976-
 Social justice handbook: small steps for a better world / Mae Elise
Cannon.
    p. cm.
 Includes bibliographical references.
 ISBN 978-0-8308-3715-1 (pbk.: alk. paper)
 1. Christian sociology. 2. Church and social problems. 3. Social
justice—Religious aspects—Christianity. 4. Christianity and
justice. I. Title.
 BT738.C345 2009
 261.8—dc22

                                                                        2009021602

| P | 23 | 22 | 21 | 20 | 19 | 18 | 17 | 16 | 15 | 14 | 13 | 12 | 11 | 10 | 9 | 8 | 7 | 6 | 5 | 4 |
| Y | 28 | 27 | 26 | 25 | 24 | 23 | 22 | 21 | 20 | 19 | 18 | 17 | 16 | 15 | 14 | 13 | 12 | 11 |

*To my husband, Roby,*

*with love, as we learn*

*how to live this out together.*


*To my parents,*

*one day may you fully know*

*the justice and mercy of God.*

# Contents

# PROFILES AND SIDEBARS

# Foreword

Small steps to a better world . . . that is all that Christ calls us to do. Many believers who have come to know Christ live not in fear, but rather put their faith into action by expressing the love of Jesus, sharing the truth of the gospel, and pursuing the justice of God. The love of God is manifested in both his righteousness and his justice. When people stand up on the side of the oppressed and of justice, they decide to trade comfort for concern, apathy for action, violence for nonviolence, and hate for love. *Social Justice Handbook* is a call for all believers to move from apathy to advocacy for the sake of the gospel of Christ.

I first met Mae when I was the teacher in residence in 2004 for Willow Creek's Justice Journey experience that she was helping to lead. The mission of the trip was to "experience the past, understand the present, and embrace hope for the future." In many ways, *Social Justice Handbook* is just such an experience—looking at past history of injustices in the United States and around the world, attempting to understand what they mean for us today, and embracing hope for the future that comes because of the presence of the Holy Spirit and the work of Christ through his people.

Our understanding of the gospel makes us ready for Christian social action. As we enter into the lives of our neighbors, in their hearts and into their homes, we come face to face with their needs and are compelled because of the love of Christ to respond. It is the responsibility of the body of Christ to live out his life on earth and to make the love of God visible in our time. That's why I highly recommend this book. This book is an attempt to give practical tools and valuable information to help individuals, churches and other groups take small steps toward making a difference in the lives of people in their surrounding communities and around the world.

This handbook will help you find your place in God's global work of social justice. The first half provides a biblical and historical overview of what the God of justice has been doing throughout Scripture and church history. The second part highlights dozens of specific topics in handy alphabetical order, explaining what you need to know and what you can do about them. The issues might be as personal as domestic abuse or as global as genocide. But in every case, we have hope for the oppressed and good news for the world, because God cares about justice and works through his people to make things right. I pray that this book will give you ideas for living out God's call on your life in ways that are surprising and unexpected.

I am encouraged that a new generation is joining God on this courageous adventure of transforming a fallen and hurting world. Many are joining Jesus in preaching good news to the poor, proclaiming freedom for the prisoners and releasing the oppressed (Luke 4:18). May this book be a companion on your journey, and may you discover new frontiers of justice and service that previous generations have never imagined.

*John Perkins*

# Introduction

During the past several years of my ministry at both Willow Creek Community Church and Hillside Covenant Church, I continually come into contact with the needs of the poor. Time and again I am amazed at the material needs present. I am also amazed at the wealth of Christian life and experience found by faithful believers who were serving others, living faithfully and trying to overcome the challenges of poverty.

My ministry experience has provided me with personal encounters and a glimpse of problems and struggles that are outside of my normal everyday paradigm: a little boy who suffers from such severe asthma that his medicine takes more space in his home than all of his other material possessions; a young mother who continually struggles to hold down a job without having the resources to provide childcare for her three young children; a grandfather who lives in the basement of an abandoned building because he isn't able to garnish enough social security to pay for rent. These encounters propelled me on a journey of trying to grasp what it means to respond to these kinds of needs through Christian ministry. The church so often has solid theology and teaching, but sometimes neglects to respond to the physical needs that present themselves right on our doorstep and beyond.

In January 2005, I began a ministry at Willow Creek Community Church that focused on social justice. Of course there had been and were others at Willow who were knowledgeable about and valued social justice, but I wanted there to be an organized movement within the church that not only extended compassion but started to get at the root of the issues that cause poverty, oppression and injustice.

At the same time there seemed to be a movement sweeping through the evangelical church on a national, if not global, front. I began to notice articles on social justice appearing in Christian magazines. Other partner churches were beginning to ask similar questions about the church's role in shaping society and leading reform. Over and over I heard talk in Christian circles about what it means to live out Matthew 25, what it means to put faith in action as described in James 2 and Isaiah 58. Everywhere I turned it seemed people were asking what it means to respond to the poor and the oppressed in society. I was caught up in the excitement, but deep in my soul I also believed that there was an impending need not yet being met by the church.

Of course, this conversation wasn't really new. Believers in the early church (Acts 2) were attentive to the needs of the orphans and the widows. From early antiquity the church often carried the responsibility of meeting the needs of society's most unfortunate. As I began this journey in pursuit of social justice, I longed to understand the deeper meaning of biblical justice and its relationship to the more familiar concepts of compassion, mercy and charity.

I began to search. I read books. I went to seminars. I met individuals who will be crowned with many jewels in heaven because of their activism and efforts on behalf of the gospel. I was exposed to some of the greatest leadership and wisdom about the questions of social justice. I have been blessed by the wisdom and council of experts in the field: John Perkins, the founder of the Christian Community Development Association; Jim Wallis, the leader of Sojourners magazine and Call to Renewal; Brian McLaren of the Emergent Village; Gary Haugen, founder, president and CEO of International Justice Mission; just to name a few. While I am greatly indebted to these leaders, I still came away from these encounters feeling somewhat discouraged—there didn't seem to be a place where the questions I was asking for myself and on behalf of my church were being addressed. I was inspired by churches and individuals, but was left with little guidance as to how to apply what I was learning to ministry at Willow Creek. It seemed that no one could tell me how, in the context of my leadership, to implement the many new things I was learning.

I went to all of these events asking questions, and no one seemed to have the specific answers that I was looking for. I wanted to know the down and dirty pragmatics—the very basics of social justice, beyond academic articulation and systematic theology. I wanted to know how to define social justice. I wanted to understand the difference between social justice and biblical justice. I wanted to know at the core of my being what it means to live out social justice individually and corporately as the body of Christ.

To a degree every Christian and every church leader will come to the point where he or she personally grapples with an issue. By the grace and direction of God's prompting, it is the leader's responsibility to define what it means to fully embrace this problem in the context of their ministry. That has been my journey. This book is a compilation of the basic fundamentals that I have learned the past few years as I wrestled with these questions. My hope and desire is that all of the struggles our ministry has experienced might provide support and encouragement for others who are asking the same questions. This book is Social Justice 101. The basics. The fundamentals. These are what have been the core tenets of our journey, though they by far are not comprehensive.[1]

In the past Willow's evangelism ministry hosted conversations around the "big questions" of life. During the summer of 2005, we held a five-week series called "Biggies Unplugged." This series broke big issues down into small discussion groups. My group led one of these unplugged conversations. The basic outline for this book was developed during that event. Our conversations were certainly unplugged. We had the biggest table. On a given Sunday we had anywhere between fifteen and twenty people. We argued and wrestled and disagreed and prayed and began the spiritual process of asking some hard questions. I hope this book will provide a similar opportunity. Read with the desire to engage. This book is a "doing" book—calling the church into action. The evangelical church has strayed from its original roots. We must return to our twofold purpose of a contemplative tradition reflecting good theology and a church that put its beliefs into practice through action.

Social justice is complicated. People have strong ideas about it! Say "social justice" to one person, and he or she will think you are a saint, following in the footsteps of Mother Teresa. But someone else may throw a fit and declare that you are a liberal activist who has abandoned the true fundamentals of Scripture. There is a broad spectrum of history, beliefs and perspectives about social justice. This book is designed to explore the basics of social justice from a biblical perspective, rooted in Scripture and the core tenets of the Christian faith.

## How to Read This Book

*Social Justice Handbook* is divided into two main parts. Part one, "Foundations of Social Justice," is meant to be read chapter by chapter and provides a biblical and theological framework for justice, and addresses how individuals and the church can get involved. Chapters include information about the historical context of the evangelical church and its involvement in social justice. The movement from apathy to advocacy is one that should be pursued by all Christ followers. Part one addresses different types of advocacy and what involvement can look like for individuals and for the church.

Chapter one, "God's Heart for Justice," is a broad brushstroke of the theological foundation for social justice. What is biblical justice? What does the Old Testament have to say about it? How about the New?

Chapter two focuses on definitions and questions about social justice. What is social justice? In order to become an advocate of justice, we first need to understand some of the basic issues surrounding social justice. This chapter addresses whether or not there is a difference between social justice and charity or compassion. Some people think they are all the same thing. I would suggest that they are correlated, related and a part of the same family, but they are very different ideas and involve different actions. Most evangelical churches do a decent job at compassion, but in general they do a poor job of exercising justice.

Chapter three provides a history of Christian social justice in the Americas. Words and works are both vital modes of ministry. This chapter gives a brief summary of the history of how people who embraced one or the other came to be so opposed and differentiated. Few would disagree that the church of the future must find a balance between the two, living out holistic Christian ministry in a balance between works and words, actions and study of the Word.

Chapter four addresses the process people must embark on to allow their hearts to be opened and broken toward those who are most affected by injustice and oppression. God has called his people toward a radical transformation that involves not only the mind and heart, but the feet and the hands as well. In Jesus' inaugural address he called his followers to preach good news to the poor, proclaim freedom to the captives and proclaim the year of the Lord's favor. This chapter examines what it means for apathetic Christians to become individual and corporate agents of justice.

Chapter five focuses on the roles individuals, church, community and government can play in advocating social justice. Individuals, moved to respond to issues they have encountered, possess the energy and conviction that can be used to start a movement in their small groups, churches and communities. As individuals move from apathy to advocacy and invite others to join on the journey, social justice will be lived out and the kingdom of God will enter in!

Part two, "Social Justice Issues," is arranged alphabetically. It can be read front to back but is designed to be used more topically, as both a reflective tool and a reference guide. This part of the book wrestles with the nitty-gritty. Since social justice can be so nebulous and hard to define, it is important to understand the "core issues"—AIDS, the death penalty, education, the environment, health care, housing and poverty—of social justice. These topical entries are not comprehensive. They do, however, represent fundamental issues that are deeply seeded with pain, suffering, oppression and the lack of justice. These core issues, and many more, must be understood so that the church can respond with the strength and power of the Christian faith.

Many of the topics discussed are overwhelming. Do not be discouraged! My hope is that this book will serve as a resource and provoke questions that you might not have otherwise considered. It might even encourage you and others around you to take action, to step out in faith, preparing the soil with the hope that God will make it grow. The material includes descriptions of the topics, relevant statistics and other basic information, potential action steps, and resources for further study. In addition, the following features are found throughout the book.

*Profiles.* There are several people and ministry profiles that provide firsthand accounts of a ministry or person involved in social justice advocacy.[2] Learning about the advocacy efforts of others can be a great encouragement in our own pursuit of justice.

*Spiritual reflection exercise.* While this book is full of action items, it is important to take time to reflect on how God is moving in your own life. How is he calling you to personally respond? Spiritual reflection exercises encourage us to take the time and space to reflect about how God is personally leading us.

*Awareness exercise.* Much of the injustice that is perpetrated around the world stems from ignorance about the ways power, privilege and resources affect those who have limited opportunity and wealth. These exercises are a first step to raising awareness among individuals and the larger community about the stories of people groups who have experienced injustice in the United States and around the world.

*Take action.* This book provides practical first steps for getting involved and becoming an advocate of social justice. Many of the action items listed are small but important attempts to make a difference in the world. As each person progresses in the journey, I encourage strategic thinking about what action could and should be taken as the Christian community rises up in response to injustice around the world.

*For further study.* Each section includes references "For Further Study." Though some of the suggested readings come from a Christian perspective, the Christian community has not done enough scholarship in some topics or fields. Thus many of the readings are written by secular authors. I do not personally endorse the teachings in all of the recommended readings. I do, however, believe that the church should be informed and should engage with secular scholarship. My hope is that these readings will expand our understanding and help inform a Christian response to the issues being discussed.

Read this book to discern how God may be moving you to live a little different—or maybe even radically different! God clearly calls his children to be agents of justice:

> He has shown all you people what is good.
>> And what does the LORD require of you?
>> To act justly and to love mercy,
>> and to walk humbly with your God. (Mic 6:8)

# PART ONE

# Foundations of Justice

# 1

# God's Heart for Justice

*"There is no such thing as personal piety that does not affect society."*

BARBARA SKINNER,
WALNUT CREEK CCDA INSTITUTE
AT HILLSIDE COVENANT CHURCH

The greatest commandment in the Scriptures is: "Love the Lord your God with all of your heart and with all your soul and with all your mind" (Mt 22:37). Jesus continues with the second directive: "Love your neighbor as yourself" (Mt 22:39). For those who call themselves followers of Christ, these commandments may be excessively familiar; they may no longer seem revolutionary. Most Christians believe that the love and worship of God, acknowledging he is Lord, is the highest command for believers. From our love of God and his love for us, we are motivated and inspired to love those around us—even to the extent of loving our enemies. Jesus tells us "Love your enemies and pray for those who persecute you, that you may be children of your Father in heaven" (Mt 5:44-45).

In order to understand biblical justice, we must first understand love. Love is what motivates and compels. Love is complex, yet simple. Love is talked about too much—sometimes in the wrong context and in cheap ways—therefore its value is diminished and

its true power is not understood. At the same time the type of love that Christ teaches is talked about too little. Love that comes from Christ is the source of all good actions; it is the source of our true self-worth and identity before God:

> Dear friends, let us love one another, for love comes from God. Everyone who loves has been born of God and knows God. Whoever does not love does not know God, because God is love. This is how God showed his love among us: He sent his one and only Son into the world that we might live through him. This is love: not that we loved God, but that he loved us and sent his Son as an atoning sacrifice for our sins. Dear friends, since God so loved us, we also ought to love one another. No one has ever seen God; but if we love one another, God lives in us and his love is made complete in us. (1 Jn 4:7-12)

This type of love is manifest throughout the

world by those who have an intimate relationship with Christ. I see God's presence on earth through people who choose to sacrifice and give up privilege, power, money and even safety for the sake of someone else. For example, I have learned about this type of love from my friends Dick and Sibyl Towner. Sibyl is the director of Spiritual Mentoring at Willow Creek Community Church and Dick is the executive director of the Willow Creek Association Good Sense Stewardship Movement.

From the time Dick and Sibyl were married, they have welcomed people who are going through a hard time or just need a place to stay to be a part of their home—some young, some old, some divorced, some grieving, some joyous—people who needed community and a place to live. Over the years they have had over seventy people live in their home as a part of their family for extended periods of time. At some point in my life I hope I grow enough to practice Christian hospitality the way the Towners do!

When Sibyl meets with someone, she has the ability, in the first few moments together, to remind the person that not only she but also God loves the person more than he or she could imagine. As Christians learn to express this type of love, the love of Christ, there will be an increased desire to respond to people's needs in immediate circles of relationship and in the community beyond. The love of God is not dormant but is a progressively growing flame that burns powerfully and compels us into action when we submit to it.

How do we know what this love is and how to live it out? "This is how we know what love is: Jesus Christ laid down his life for

us. And we ought to lay down our lives for one another. If any one of you has material possessions and sees a brother or sister in need but has no pity on them, how can the love of God be in you?" (1 Jn 3:16-17). There is a direct correlation between our beliefs and actions in response to the needs of people.

First John goes so far as to say: when someone does not materially respond to the needs of people around them—they do not have the love of God. Christians must diligently seek to understand and experience the love that God has bestowed upon his followers. As that love is experienced and understood, Christ's followers will have a better sense how to put it into action in their immediate circles of influence and beyond. This book is an attempt to do just that: provide small steps at understanding the love that God has toward all people and his creation, small steps to learning how to live out the love of God toward others, small steps to a better world. In the pages ahead, please don't get lost in all of the opportunities and possibilities for action. Instead, continually be reminded that the true motivation for action comes from the love of Christ.

## Faith in Action

Consider the construction of many of the glorious churches throughout Europe. Over the centuries of building the cathedral of Notre Dame in Paris, hundreds of men (and even women) slaved for days, weeks, months and years. They died in the hope that their human effort would allow them a place in heaven. The Bible is clear about the source of salvation: "For it is by grace you have been saved, through faith—and this is not from yourselves, it is the gift of God—not by works, so that no one can boast. For we are God's handiwork, created in Christ Jesus to do good works, which God prepared in advance for us to do" (Eph 2:8-10). The source of salvation is the overly abundant grace of God. No one has done anything to deserve it. Salvation is a gift. No matter how much good someone does on earth, he or she will never be good enough to achieve rightness before God. Instead, all people are offered the gift of salvation. This is the grace of God.

### FOR FURTHER STUDY

*What's So Amazing About Grace?* by Philip Yancey

*The Discipline of Grace: God's Role and Our Role in the Pursuit of Holiness* by Jerry Bridges

Grace is not the end of the story! Grace shows itself in love and responsiveness to the needs of people. As Ephesians indicates, grace is expressed through "good works" in the lives of those who possess it. James goes so far as to say, "Faith without deeds is dead." We live our faith through what we do. James 2 says it this way:

> What good is it, my brothers and sisters, if people claim to have faith but have no deeds? Can such faith save them? Suppose a brother or sister is without clothes and daily food. If one of you says to them, "Go in peace; keep warm and well fed," but does nothing about their physical needs, what good is it? In the same way, faith by itself, if it is not accompanied by action, is dead. (Jas 2:14-17)

Faith in action—that is what justice is all about.

## Justice and Righteousness

***Old Testament justice.*** Justice is the manifestation of right action. Simply put, the basic concepts of *work* (or action) and *faith* (or righteousness) help lay the foundation for what God has to say about justice.[1] The Bible is full of God's concern for justice, from his holding Cain accountable for the murder of his brother (Genesis) to the justice of God expressed in his wrath toward Satan (Revelation). Clearly, God, in both the Old and New Testaments, declares his passion in regard to the rightness of our actions. He also cares about the conditions of our hearts.

Throughout the Scriptures justice and righteousness go hand in hand. Justice is right action—doing the right thing. Righteousness speaks to the condition of our hearts and is the attribute of being pure (or "right") before God. In order to better understand the relationship between these two words, it is helpful to look at how many times they are used together throughout the Scriptures.

In the Old Testament the Hebrew word often used for justice is *mišpāṭ*.[2] This Hebrew word occurs over four hundred times throughout the Old Testament—over sixty times in Psalms, thirty-six times in Deuteronomy. *Mišpāṭ*, or divine justice, refers to the execution of God's righteous standards. The Hebrew word for righteousness is *ṣedeq*, or *ṣĕdāqâ*, the quality or state of mind of being just, morally upright or without sin.[3]

These two ideas—God's justice and his righteousness—are inextricably linked throughout the Scriptures. Throughout history followers of God have wrestled with what it means to maintain both. In the Old Testament God expressed his frustration when the

Israelites were obedient but seemed to be missing the whole point (Is 58). In the New Testament Jesus criticized the Pharisees for focusing on outward actions while missing the inward transformation toward righteousness (Mt 23). It is helpful to study the degree to which these two words are used in parallel throughout the Old Testament. Consider the following verses:

> Righteousness [ṣedeq] and justice [mišpāṭ] are the foundation of your throne; love and faithfulness go before you. (Ps 89:14)

> Praise be to the LORD your God, who has delighted in you and placed you on his throne as king to rule for the LORD your God. Because of the love of your God for Israel and his desire to uphold them forever, he has made you king over them, to maintain justice [mišpāṭ] and righteousness [ṣĕdāqâ]. (2 Chron 9:8)

> The LORD loves righteousness [ṣĕdāqâ] and justice [mišpāṭ];
>      the earth is full of his unfailing love.
>      (Ps 33:5)

> This is what the LORD says:
> "Maintain justice [mišpāṭ]
>      and do what is right,
> for my salvation is close at hand
>      and my righteousness [ṣĕdāqâ] will
>           soon be revealed." (Is 56:1)

It is clear from these passages and many others that justice and righteousness go hand in hand. Righteousness represents the state of God's character—his goodness, his purity, his character. We inherit God's righteousness when we have faith and believe in him. Faith and belief in the gift of God's grace is what constitutes our righteousness.

Justice is the manifestation of God's righteous character in the world—the execution of God's righteousness. Justice is the expression of God's righteousness through right action. When justice completely exists on this earth, everything will be the way that God intended it to be. The righteous actions of Christ followers is the execution of faith. As believers practice good works, they become agents of justice.

***New Testament justice.*** In the New Testament the Greek work for righteousness, *dikaios*, appears over two hundred times. *Dikaios* has many meanings and connotations, including the observation of right laws, keeping the commandments of God, being virtuous, righteousness or justice. Sound familiar? In the New Testament, *dikaios* refers to both Old Testament ideas—justice and righteousness. The King James Version translates the word *dikaios* thirty-three times as being "just" and forty-one times as "righteous."[4] However, other English translations typically translate this word as "righteousness" and not "justice." For example, the New American Standard Bible only translates *dikaios* as "just" six times. In many Spanish translations *dikaios* is translated repeatedly as "justice" (and not "righteousness"). A lot has been lost in the translations of the Scriptures from their original languages to English. Consider the following verses where the word *dikaios* appears—use the idea of both justice and righteousness in your translation:

> Jesus replied, "Let it be so now; it is proper for us to do this to fulfill all right-

eousness [and justice: *dikaiosynē*]." Then John consented. (Mt 3:15)

Blessed are those who hunger and thirst for righteousness [and justice: *dikaiosynē*], for they will be filled. (Mt 5:6)

For in the gospel the righteousness [and justice: *dikaiosynē*] of God is revealed— a righteousness that is by faith from first to last, just as it is written: "The righteous [and just: *dikaios*] will live by faith." (Rom 1:17)

As it is written: "They have scattered abroad their gifts to the poor; their righteousness [and justice: *dikaiosynē*] endures forever." (2 Cor 9:9)

Of the two hundred times that *dikaios* is used in Scripture, most versions only use the translation *justice* once (Col 4:1).[5] (See "Slavery.")

Contemporary evangelicalism has emphasized personal righteousness and piety and has missed much of the intended meaning bursting through the Scriptures about justice. It is critical to understand that righteousness and justice are interconnected in both Testaments. In the Old Testament righteousness was obedience to the law of Moses. New Testament righteousness is received through faith in Christ. The demonstration of righteousness in our lives is *just* living—living out the justice of God. *Social Justice Handbook* is about pursuing a life of justice motivated by love for God and love for his people.

✝ *Spiritual reflection exercise.* Consider the implications of the relationship between justice and righteousness. How might this change your understanding of God? Go through the New Testament and look for references to "righteousness." (If you have access to a Greek New Testament, find verses that use the word *dikaios*.)[6] Translate "righteousness" (*dikaios* or *dikaiosynē*) as both righteousness and justice. How does your understanding of the verse change? How might this affect the way that you live out your faith? Reflect on and journal about your thoughts. Pray that God will reveal his truth to you in your studies.

## The Bible and Wealth

Almost every time I have been with John Perkins, I have heard him say that "justice is an economic issue."[7] Dr. Perkins's perspective is that the expression of justice is directly tied to money and resources. Justice is about the righteous and fair access to and distribution of resources. Injustice is often expressed through access or the lack thereof to financial resources and is discernable in both poverty and wealth.

In his book *Quiet Revolution* John Perkins says, "God meant for equality to be expressed in terms of economics."[8] God's economic system was first introduced in the Garden of Eden. He created man and woman and gave them the resources they needed to survive. They were told they could eat from every tree but the tree of life. They were to act as stewards of creation: "God blessed them and said to them, 'Be fruitful and increase in number; fill the earth and subdue it. Rule over the fish in the sea and the birds in the sky and over every living creature that moves on the ground'" (Gen 1:28). God created humans to steward creation and to model the way that God wanted things to be on earth.

The Old Testament is clear that if people were obedient to God, he would provide for their needs. In Deuteronomy, the Bible says: "There need be no poor people among you, for in the land the LORD your God is giving you to possess as your inheritance, he will richly bless you, if only you fully obey the LORD your God and are careful to follow all these commands I am giving you today" (Deut 15:4-5). The resources that God provides were made available to his people from the very beginning. Justice is expressed when God's resources are made available to all humans, which is what God intended. Biblical justice is the scriptural mandate to manifest the kingdom of God on earth by making God's blessings available to all.[9]

## God's Economy

> Keep falsehood and lies far from me;
> give me neither poverty nor riches,
> but give me only my daily bread.
> Otherwise, I may have too much and
> disown you
> and say, 'Who is the LORD?'
> Or I may become poor and steal,
> and so dishonor the name of my God.
> (Prov 30:8-9)

God's economy not only relates to his provision of fundamental needs but also to the way humans consume resources. The Bible is very clear that people should only take what they need. Consider when the manna fell from heaven. The Israelites were clearly instructed by God: "The people are to go out each day and gather enough for that day" (Ex 16:4). If they gathered more than they needed, the manna became full of maggots and

began to smell (Ex 16:20).

Certainly contemporary overconsumption would be tempered if modern-day indulgences turned into stinky bugs. The provision of manna in the desert was in sharp contrast to the conditions of oppression and need Israel experienced in Egypt: "The Israelites did as they were told; some gathered much, some little. And when they measured it by the omer, the one who gathered much did not have too much, and the one who gathered little did not have too little. Each one had gathered just as much as they needed" (Ex 16:17-18).

In God's economy, everyone has enough. There is no such thing as "too much" or "too little" because God provided each family with just what they needed.[10] God's justice is manifested by his provision for all people to have equal access to the resources he provides—be it manna or quail in the dessert, or the things people need to survive today (see "Consumerism" and "Poverty").

## The Problem of Evil

Pastor Mark Labberton aptly says:

> To live lives of faithful worship, to cultivate God's imagination for justice, to trust Jesus Christ to do a work of liberation and transformation means there will be times when our noses will be filled with the stench of human need and evil. But far more profoundly, we will also have glimpses of the glory of God that can set the captives free. That's God's imagination.[11]

Looking around the world today, anyone can see that resources are not distributed equally. Not all people have access to the fundamental things they need to survive. But Jesus told his followers not to worry, for God takes care of the birds of the air and the lilies of the field—how much more would he take care of those who follow him (Mt 6)? Has God not fulfilled his promises? Why is there so much disparity in the world today?

These questions may cause God's followers to despair. The world is clearly not the way that God intended it to be. He is all-powerful (omnipotent) but allows his creatures to choose whether or not to obey him. This choice is clearly seen throughout Scripture. Consider God's invitation to the Israelites in Deuteronomy 30: "This day I call the heavens and the earth as witnesses against you that I have set before you life and death, blessings and curses. Now choose life, so that you and your children may live and that you may love the LORD your God, listen to his voice, and hold fast to him" (Deut 30:19-20).

The first time humans chose to disobey God is recorded in Genesis 3: Adam and Eve ate fruit from the tree that was forbidden. The punishment for their disobedience was exclusion from the Garden of Eden and separation from God.

Some might ask how things came to be the way they are today? How can God be good and allow such devastation to be occurring around the world? Thousands die of hunger and preventable diseases every day. Little girls and boys are sold into slavery to be used as mere objects for sexual pleasure. People who are weak because they are disabled or developmentally challenged are abused and forced to do manual labor. These are only a few of the travesties in the world today. To understand

and pursue biblical justice, one must grapple with the reality of evil in the world.

The manifestation of evil is the antithesis of justice. N. T. Wright's book *Evil and the Justice of God* speaks directly to the theology behind this question. Throughout history thinkers have wrestled with why God chooses to not stop the evil in the world. While there are no easy answers to this question, God's promises assure his followers that one day all evil will be defeated and the injustices in this world will be brought to an end.

**FOR FURTHER STUDY**

*Evil and the Justice of God* by N. T. Wright
*He Is There and He Is Not Silent* by Francis Schaeffer

## The Goodness of God

Gary Haugen, founder and president of International Justice Mission, says:

> When falling into the well of doubt about why God permits injustice on the earth, I scrape my way out by standing first on the limits of my human knowledge. I grab on to the character of the compassionate Creator revealed on the cross. I step up to the mysterious foothold offered by the terrible gift of free will, and lunge up to the dusty ground onto the hope of eternity.[12]

The other huge theological question related to injustice is the character of God. How can a good God allow such horrible things to happen in the world? It is often distressing to know that God is perfectly powerful and present in all things but still allows them to happen. All believers must wrestle with this question, both personally and on behalf of those who suffer. Certainly some suffering is the result of disobedience, but not all. Why do bad things happen to good people?

This question is too big to tackle here—but the justice of God cannot be discussed adequately without making reference to his goodness. Scripture assures us that God cares deeply for those who are suffering and suffers with them. Pastor Jeff Reed of Hillside Covenant Church in Walnut Creek, California, observes, "Such is demonstrated in God's prophecy through Isaiah of the Suffering Servant who would one day come and vicariously bear suffering on behalf of his people [Is 52:13-15]. That these prophecies were fulfilled in the divine Messiah himself makes the point stunningly clear."[13] The Scriptures also declare that the Holy Spirit groans on behalf of the followers of Christ (Rom 8:26). And the psalmist said the promise was made that God's goodness would be revealed in the land of the living (Ps 27:13).

---

**FOR FURTHER STUDY**

*Disappointment with God* by Philip Yancey

*A Grace Disguised: How the Soul Grows Through Loss* by Gerald Sittser

---

## The Prosperity Gospel

Some Christians believe in the "prosperity gospel"—the idea that the more authentic our religious belief and faith, the more that God will bless us with material things. A Scriptural view of wealth precludes this possibility. God is not pleased when some people have too much and others have little. For example, the Israelites who horded manna in the desert were punished and did not please God. And Jesus said: "Do not store up for

yourselves treasures on earth, where moth and rust destroy, and where thieves break in and steal. But store up for yourselves treasures in heaven, where moth and rust do not destroy, and where thieves do not break in and steal" (Mt 6:19-20).

Over one billion people around the world live on less than $1 a day. In 2006, the median income for an individual in the United States was over $75 per day.[14] Is it possible that the citizens of developed countries are hoarding manna? Our understanding of kingdom economics should inform the way we accumulate wealth, invest assets and spend money—all issues very close to God's heart for justice.

## Shalom: The Peace of God

Martin Luther King Jr., a Baptist minister and civil rights activist, said, "True peace is not merely the absence of tension: it is the presence of justice."[15]

The biblical idea of peace (shalom) is the condition that exists when justice is fully expressed. In early antiquity the philosophers believed that peace and justice were two sides of the same coin. The early Greek philosopher Plato argued in the *Republic* that justice was "peace" or harmony. Justice was expressed when harmonious relationships existed between warring parts of the city. Martin Luther King Jr., expanded the idea of shalom even further when he said: "True peace is not merely the absence of tension; it is the presence of justice."[16] Peace is not merely the lack of physical conflict; it exists only when the justice of God is fully present.

Christian philosopher Nicholas Wolterstorff said:

The state of shalom is the state of flourishing in all dimensions of one's existence: in one's relation to God, in one's relation to one's fellow human beings, in one's relation to nature, and in one's relation to oneself. Evidently justice has something to do with the fact that God's love for each and every one of God's human creatures takes the form of God desiring the shalom of each and every one."[17]

As Wolterstorff describes, the Hebrew concept of shalom is much more than peace—it means wholeness, completeness, harmony—the total sense of well-being, what God initially intended before the Fall—for both individuals and for community. When shalom exists, it is expressed in blessings in every area of life—spiritual, social, economic and physical.[18] Shalom is unable to exist when God's people are limited by a natural or supernatural force in their ability to live as God desires for them. The limitation of shalom is *oppression.*

## Oppression: Theology of Power

The Almighty is beyond our reach and exalted in power;
   in his justice *[mišpāṭ]* and great righteousness *[ṣĕdāqâ]*, he does not oppress.
    (Job 37:23)

Oppression, the absence of justice, impedes shalom.[19] This is the use of power to subjugate an individual or group of people. Oppression is seen throughout the stories of the Bible: Cain's murder of Abel (Gen 4), the captivity and slavery of the Israelites in Egypt (Ex 1), Esther's sexual exploitation in the harem of King Xerxes (Esther 2), Tamar's rape

by her brother Amnon (2 Sam 13), to name a few. Oppression is the use of power or authority in an abusive way. Likewise, injustice is the violation of the rights of another in an oppressive way.

According to Gary Haugen, "Injustice occurs when power is misused to take from others what God has given them, namely their life, dignity, liberty or fruits of their love and labor."[20] Often the victims of injustice and oppression are women and children who are poor, widows, orphans, and foreigners (see "Children," "Immigration," "Sex Trafficking," "Slavery" and "Women"). The people in society who have less power than those around them are more vulnerable to oppression. Their safety often depends on the societal structures that are in place and whether or not laws or other measures exist to protect them.

God hates oppression: "This is what the Sovereign Lord says: You have gone far enough, princes of Israel! Give up your violence and oppression and do what is just and right. Stop dispossessing my people, declares the Sovereign Lord" (Ezek 45:9). Throughout the Old Testament there are severe consequences for those who oppressed others. In Genesis, Cain was sent into exile. Amnon, who had raped his sister, was killed by his brother Absalom. In Jeremiah, God declared that the city of Jerusalem must be punished because it was "filled with oppression" (Jer 6:6). Clearly, oppression will be punished.

Shalom, the peace of God, is in direct contrast to oppression. God hates oppression but loves justice. When all is in a state of justice, shalom exists. Shalom brings wholeness, completeness, safety, tranquility and restoration to creation—the way God intended things to be.

John Perkins says, "Not until we are all free will any of us be free."[21]

Sometimes oppression is overt and easily seen; other times it is covert and hidden. Oppression can have devastating effects on people. Thomas Hanks, the author of *God So Loved the Third World*, describes the effects of oppression: "It crushes, humiliates, animalizes, impoverishes, enslaves, and kills people created in the image of God."[22] Oppression not only affects the recipients of abuse but can devastate persons in power. "As the oppressors dehumanize others and violate their rights, they themselves also become dehumanized."[23] The entire community is affected when shalom is not present.

Rest assured that God hears the cries of the oppressed and desires to deliver them from bondage—from both the physical bondage of oppression and the spiritual bondage of sin. One of the most powerful accounts of God's heart for the oppressed is found in Exodus 3: God's encounter with Moses at the burning bush.

> The LORD said, "I have indeed seen the misery of my people in Egypt. I have heard them crying out because of their slave drivers, and I am concerned about their suffering. So I have come down to rescue them from the hand of the Egyptians and to bring them up out of that land into a good and spacious land, a land flowing with milk and honey— the home of the Canaanites, Hittites, Amorites, Perizzites, Hivites and Jebusites. And now the cry of the Israelites has reached me, and I have seen the way

the Egyptians are oppressing them. So now, go. I am sending you to Pharaoh to bring my people the Israelites out of Egypt." (Ex 3:7-10)

God cares about those who are vulnerable and weak. Lowell Noble, retired professor of sociology and anthropology, claims that the Old Testament theology of oppression has been largely ignored by evangelicals.[24] The people of God can no longer afford to ignore what God has to say about those who are oppressed. Instead, Christians are called to seek justice and to play a part in setting the oppressed free.

*Spiritual reflection exercise.* Take some time to look for stories of oppression in the Bible. What stories did you find? If you are having trouble, consider the book of Esther, Israel's exodus from Egypt (Ex 3–6), the story of Amnon and Tamar (2 Sam 13). What do these stories tell you about the things that are important to God? What happened to the people who were oppressed? What happened to the oppressor? Did justice occur in the story? Do you relate most to the victim or to the person in power? Reflect or journal about how God desires us to respond to those who are hurting and suffering. Ask God to speak to you and to give you a better understanding of his heart for justice.

## Sabbath and the Year of Jubilee

Throughout the first five books of the Bible, there are laws about the way the Hebrews were to relate to God and to one another. The most important laws are known as the Ten Commandments. The first five commandments direct how the people should relate to God. The second five address how God's people are to relate to one another. These laws defined justice for the people of Israel.

One of the commandments about living in community regards the sabbath: "Observe the Sabbath day by keeping it holy, as the LORD your God has commanded you" (Deut 5:12). The idea of a sabbath is relatively familiar: the people of God were to have a day of rest, a day dedicated to God, once a week. Christians often observe the sabbath on Sundays. God established three different types of sabbaths for the people of Israel in order to teach them how to relate to one another.[25] These sabbaths are important to the study of biblical justice because they were the foundational laws that affected the poor.

*The weekly sabbath.* The last day of the week the sabbath was to be observed as a day without work. This was to remind people of God's creation, when he rested on the seventh day. At the time these laws were given, Israel was an agricultural society. Taking a day off from farming the land could have significant consequences if the people did not believe that God would provide for and take care of them.

*The sabbath year.* The people would work for six years and then would rest during the entire seventh year. This sabbath is described in Leviticus: "When you enter the land I am going to give you, the land itself must observe a sabbath to the LORD. For six years sow your fields, and for six years prune your vineyards and gather their crops. But in the seventh year the land is to have a year of sabbath rest, a sabbath to the LORD" (Lev 25:2-4). There were several aspects to the observance of the sab-

bath year: (1) there was no work for the entire year and the people were to live off of the produce of the land; (2) all debts were forgiven; (3) those who were in slavery were set free; (4) and the law of the Lord was read to the people of Israel so they would be reminded that he was their provider and the land belonged to him. Again, the only way the people of Israel could obey the sabbath law was if they trusted that God would provide for their needs.

*The year of Jubilee.* After forty-nine years, a year was consecrated as a year of freedom, the year of the Lord's favor. Jubilee was the year following seven sabbath years. It was the year that proclaimed freedom for the captives, the restoration of land to its original owners, the forgiveness of debt. The Jubilee year was holy, set aside to honor God. The year of Jubilee celebrated holistic renewal for the entire community.

In ancient times, during the normal course of events, people who experienced hardship often went into great debt and some sold themselves into servitude to their family members or others, and some sold their land. In fifty year's time, these types of transactions would have led to a terrible disparity between the rich and the poor. But Jubilee rectified this problem. The debt of the people was to be completely wiped away. A relative state of equality was brought back to society. Israel was dependent on the land, which was not to be used as a possession to exploit but to be shared equitably.[26] These sabbath principles taught the people of Israel that the land and everything in it belonged to God. Jubilee "is God's comprehensive unilateral restructuring of the community's assets" and reminded the people "that they were an exodus people who must never return to a system of slavery" (Lev 25:42).[27] The people of Israel were freed from captivity and were called by God to extend to others around them the same kind of deliverance and compassion that he showed them.

There is debate by historians about whether or not Jubilee ever occurred. Most think it was never celebrated. It is easy to understand why, because it would have demanded complete dependence on God. It is hard to imagine what it would be like to wipe away every debt that exists in society and to start over with a fresh economic system.

Some suggest that God expected Israel to observe the sabbath years and the year of Jubilee for 490 years. During that time, they would have had seventy sabbath years—70 x 7. Does that sound familiar? Jesus tells us to forgive one another seventy times seven (Mt 18:22).[28] Although we are not certain of the dates, one person suggests that the king of Babylon captured Israel 490 years after the sabbath laws were given to Israel, and the people were taken into captivity for seventy years. Seventy sabbath years had been missed. Israel's time in captivity gave the Promised Land the rest it had been denied because the sabbath years were not observed. Since the people would not practice God's sabbath laws, he forced it on them. After the seventy years in captivity, God restored the people of Israel to their land and they were forgiven.[29]

In this context, what would the people of Israel have been thinking when Jesus began his ministry, centuries later, with the proclamation of Isaiah declaring the year of the Lord's favor?

The Spirit of the Lord is on me,
      because he has anointed me
      to proclaim good news to the poor.
He has sent me to proclaim freedom for
         the prisoners
      and recovery of sight for the blind,
to set the oppressed free,
      to proclaim the year of the Lord's
         favor. (Lk 4:18-19)

Jesus was declaring that his presence carried the same significance as the year of Jubilee—he came to earth to preach good news to the poor and to set the captives free.

The freedom that Jesus proclaimed was meant both literally and spiritually. He responded to the physical needs of those who were hurting and suffering, but also to the depravation of their souls by forgiving them of their sins. Consider Jesus' interaction with the paralyzed man. He first said, "Your sins are forgiven" and then continued by saying "Get up and walk" (Mt 9:1-8). Even when someone is not physically in captivity, he or she is captive to sin. Jesus came to bring both physical freedom to those who were sick, poor and in need—and spiritual freedom to all who might believe in him.

## Biblical Justice and the Gospel

Gary Haugen observes: "Seeking justice is the task of bringing truth and power to bear on behalf of those who are oppressed, and here the diverse gifts of the body are called out in glorious array."[30]

Jesus' declaration of Jubilee proclaimed freedom that would bring complete shalom—both righteousness and justice. This brings us back to where we began: what does it mean to wholeheartedly love God and our neigh-

bors? In order to do so, righteousness *and* justice must be pursued. Faith can no longer be
dichotomized. Christians must learn what it
means to care about people's souls as well as
their physical needs.

Comprehensive biblical justice is the scriptural mandate to manifest the kingdom of
God on earth by making God's blessing available to all humankind. The blessings of God
are both corporeal and spiritual. Matthew 5
mentions the poor in spirit and Matthew 25
addresses the poor in material goods. God's
expectation is that when biblical justice is
lived out, followers of Christ will respond to
those who are hungry, thirsty, naked or in
prison while also sharing the gospel with
those who are spiritually lost. The gospel
cannot be dichotomized into spiritual provision or material deliverance. Both are necessary components of the good news of salvation. Biblical justice is the manifestation of
the full gospel of Christ. The gospel explic-
itly proclaims the need to evangelize the lost
(Mt 28). Another, and sometimes neglected,
component of the gospel is the promise of
freedom and deliverance, as described by the
year of Jubilee, for the poor and oppressed
(Lk 4). Therefore, the proclamation of Christ,
without responding to the needs of those who
are poor and oppressed, is inadequate. When
both components—compassion and evangelism—are expressed, the kingdom of God is
manifested, biblical justice is exemplified,
and the good news of the gospel of Christ is
proclaimed.[31]

↕ *Spiritual reflection exercise.* Read Leviticus 25. What characteristics do you see described in the sabbath year and the year of
Jubilee? Read Luke 4:14-30? What in Jesus'
message is similar to the characteristics described in Leviticus? Do you think the sabbath laws are relevant to our faith today? If so,
how? Find where 70 x 7 is mentioned in
Scripture. What do you notice? Reflect and
journal about your study. Is there anyone you
need to extend forgiveness for a debt—either
material or otherwise? Do you believe that all
your possessions belong to God, and do you
trust God to provide for your life? Ask God to
increase your faith and dependence on him.

## Jesus and Justice

> Here is my servant whom I have
> chosen,
> the one I love, in whom I delight;
> I will put my Spirit on him,
> and he will proclaim justice to the
> nations. (Mt 12:18)

Jesus' entire life is an example of what it
means to live the gospel—living and requiring righteous behavior, expressing compassion and care, and embodying justice. Jesus
cared deeply for the souls of his followers. In
Matthew 5, Jesus expected righteousness
from his disciples and described a fulfillment
of the law that went beyond mere obedience,
and instead addressed the condition of their
souls. It is no longer enough to not kill; anger
is now unacceptable (Mt 5:22). The law says
that adultery is unrighteous; Jesus declared
that it is also unacceptable to have impure
thoughts (Mt 5:28). Jesus redefined righteousness by calling us to obey the law in both action and spirit. He commands, "Come, follow me" (Mt 4:19).

Jesus not only called his disciples to righteous perfection (Mt 5:48), he also expressed care and concern toward those who followed him and toward others he encountered along the way. At Lazarus's tomb, Jesus wept (Jn 11:35). In Jerusalem, he grieved when his people did not respond to his message (Lk 13:34-35). He expressed his love when he told Peter to care for and love his followers (Jn 21:15-17). When Jesus encountered the woman at the well and offered her living water, he called her to righteousness but also expressed compassion (Jn 4:1-26). These verses, and many others, reveal that Jesus compassionately cared for people.

In addition to Jesus' concern for his followers' souls, he also sought justice by responding to their physical needs and working to overturn the systems that caused their impoverished conditions. He healed the sick (Lk 5). He blessed the poor, the hungry, the sorrowful and those excluded from society (Lk 6). As a result of Jesus' ministry, the blind could see, the lame could walk, lepers were healed, the deaf could hear, the dead were raised, and the poor received the good news of the gospel (Lk 7:22).

The Pharisees, the religious leaders of Jesus' day, cared more about the legalistic observations of the law than responding to the needs of the poor and hurting. Jesus con-fronted them and revealed how their legalism hurt people who were suffering (Mt 12). Jesus' entire ministry challenged injustice and overturned the brokenness of the world. Ultimately, Christ was willing to endure suffering on the cross in order to demonstrate the justice of God in response to human sin (Rom 3:25-26).

**FOR FURTHER STUDY**

*Justice: A Biblical Perspective* by Carol J. Dempsey

*The Hole in Our Gospel: What Does God Expect of Us? The Answer That Changed My Life and Might Just Change the World* by Richard Stearns

*Spiritual reflection exercise.* Choose one of the four Gospels (Matthew, Mark, Luke or John). Read it through and look for passages that talk about Jesus' encounters with others. Where do you see him teaching or exemplifying righteousness? Where do you see him showing care or compassion for the hurting? What did Jesus have to say about the poor? Which verses address how his ministry was changing a system of oppression or injustice? Write your responses in a journal or notebook. Reflect about what you discover. Pray that God will reveal himself to you through the encounters you have read about Jesus.

# 2

# Social Justice

## Defining the Issue

*"My basic commitment as a Christian has not changed, nor has my view of the Gospel, but I have come to see in deeper ways the implications of my faith and the message I have been proclaiming. I can no longer proclaim the Cross and the Resurrection without proclaiming the whole message of the Kingdom, which is justice for all."*

Billy Graham, *Approaching Hoofbeats*

At the beginning of the twenty-first century the evangelical church is once again asking what it means to live out biblical justice. Social justice is so poorly understood! Sometimes, in a fervor to honor God and pursue biblical justice, the church causes more harm than good. Once a biblical foundation of justice is firmly grasped, other important questions must be addressed: How does social justice relate to biblical justice? What is the difference (if any) between compassion and justice? What is the source of justice? Is there more than one type of justice? What do power and authority have to do with justice? What are issues of injustice?

### FOR FURTHER STUDY

*Approaching Hoofbeats: The Four Horsemen of the Apocalypse* by Billy Graham

*Living Faith: How Faith Inspires Social Justice* by Curtiss Paul DeYoung

### Social Justice and Biblical Justice

Chuck Colson notes: "Biblical justice recognizes that both punishment and meeting social needs are essential to a just society" (see "Chuck Colson").[1]

Is there any difference between social justice and biblical justice? Social justice has to do with the way that material resources and social advantages are distributed and made accessible in society. Social justice is manifested when all people have equal access to resources and opportunities, such as health care, employment and education. For example, social justice is violated when children in city schools are given a substandard and underfunded education (see "Education—Domestic" and "Education—Global").

J. Philip Wogaman, a retired Methodist minister, helps Christians properly frame social justice: "Does *justice* . . . have to be preceded by the adjective *social?* Is there a difference between justice and social justice?" His response is very helpful: "Perhaps not. But since justice is so often taken at the narrower, more individualistic sense of giving people what they earn or deserve, the adjective *social* is a reminder that justice is about community."[2]

I have sometimes found conversations about social justice to be frustrating because it is hard to understand what is being talked about. There are so many different ideas about what *justice* means that many conversations may seem pointless. It may be helpful to first try to understand what the basic term *justice* means before attempting to define *social justice.* As mentioned in chapter one, justice is the expression of God's righteousness through right action. Jeremy Del Rio, organizational strategist and justice advocate, says, "Deep justice is about righting wrongs."[3]

Sometimes justice is described as the right use of power and injustice as the abuse of power. Social justice wrestles with questions about power systems within society and how they affect people. Sometimes severe harm is caused by unjust systems or because an individual injustice has taken place. If God commanded all people to be stewards of the earth, we can assume he desires all people to have access to the earth's resources. When access to those resources is unequally distributed or abused by those in power, social justice is impeded.

### FOR FURTHER STUDY

*Deep Justice in a Broken World: Helping Your Kids Serve Others and Right the Wrongs Around Them* by Chap Clark and Kara Powell

*I Am Not a Social Activist: Making Jesus the Agenda* by Ronald J. Sider

## Moving Beyond Compassion

One of the first questions people ask me about justice ministries is, What does all of that mean? I think that understanding and talking about compassion is a good place to start, because compassion, the way that we comfort those who have been hurt or harmed, is core to the Christ's gospel.

The great Catholic theologian Thomas Aquinas wrote: "I would rather feel compassion than know the meaning of it."[4] *Compassion* means to suffer with or to walk alongside someone by empathizing with their needs and experience. The church is clearly called to be compassionate to those around us. Christ was the greatest example of compassion as he took our pain and the consequences of our sin completely upon himself. We know that God showed us comfort and compassion "so that we can comfort those in any trouble with the comfort we ourselves receive from God" (2 Cor 1:4).

The contemporary church actively seeks to respond to people's immediate needs. There are compassion ministries (also called mercy ministries) for people suffering from the loss of a loved one, for those going through divorce and for people going through other personal crises. There are also compassion ministries that extend benevolence to those who are in need by distributing food and clothing, providing homeless shelters, and other acts of charity. These are all wonderful things! However, these ministries often are only responding to the consequences of injustice rather than working to fix the source of the problem.

The church must learn to move beyond acts of compassion and ask, Why are so many people homeless? Why are so many people getting divorced? Why are so many African Americans incarcerated? Compassion responds to the effects of these problems. Social justice seeks to address their systemic causes. When we work to solve the roots of these problems, a Band-Aid is no longer being put over the wound. Instead, the emphasis is on getting rid of the disease that caused the wound in the first place. When the disease is eradicated, social justice is being lived out.

A story about a group of people drowning in the river is often used to explain the difference between justice and compassion.[5] A man went to the river one day and noticed that someone was drowning in the middle of it. He quickly swam out to save the drowning person. He brought the person to safety and attempted to catch his breath. A short while later, the man noticed another person drowning in the river. He mustered up all of his strength and dove back into the river water to save the second drowning victim. The second person was brought safely to shore. By this time, the man was exhausted and had a hard time breathing. Several minutes later, as he looked up, to his dismay, he noticed a third person floating down the river, crying for help. Once again, feeling he didn't have a choice, he dove into the water to save the third person. However, the man was so tired from having saved the first two victims that he wasn't able to continue swimming and he drowned.

The man's response to the drowning people was one of compassion. His efforts were based on his love for them and his desire for them not to suffer. And his efforts made a huge difference to the first two people! The rescuer was certainly a compassionate man.

However, if the man had driven up the road along the bend in the river, he would have noticed someone at a factory who was throwing people into the river. The abusive man was the source of the problem. If the compassionate man had intervened at the factory, that would have been an act of justice.

My friend Dan Schmitz, a pastor in Oakland, California, puts it this way: "Compassion is about effects. Justice is about causes."[6] The church must learn to address systemic issues of injustice. If we learn how to solve the problem at the factory, no one else will be thrown into the river!

The current buzz around social justice concerns me. In the Christian subculture, people have a tendency to jump on the bandwagon without really understanding the cause. Churches that have been doing amazing works of compassion for the past several decades have declared they are committed to social justice, but instead of extending their works of compassion to fighting for institutional change, they have simply redubbed their *compassion ministry* a *justice ministry*. This is incredibly dangerous!

The twenty-first-century church might be doing a lot of good things to help those who are hurting, but will never be able to dig beneath the surface to tackle the root causes unless it understands the systemic issues deeply rooted in modern society. Systemic issues of injustice must be identified and fought against in order for Christians to be the agents of justice that God desires them to be.

Bono, the lead singer of the rock band U2, made a similar point at the 2006 National Prayer Breakfast: compassion (e.g., charity) is not enough:

Finally, it's not about charity after all, is it? It's about justice. Let me repeat that: It's not about charity, it's about justice. And that's too bad. Because you're good at charity. Americans, like the Irish, are good at it. We like to give, and we give a lot, even those who can't afford it. But justice is a higher standard. Africa makes a fool of our idea of justice; it makes a farce of our idea of equality. It mocks our pieties, it doubts our concern, it questions our commitment.[7]

## From Compassion to Justice

Charles Dickens famously quipped, "Charity begins at home and justice begins next door."[8] In some ways, it isn't so hard to be compassionate—bake lasagna for a family member who is sick, give a few dollars to the homeless man on the corner or visit someone who is lonely in a nursing home. These are all good acts that show care and compassion for those who are hurting! Justice, however, is harder, more costly and more painful, but has farther reaching effects. Justice means being willing to go next door and step out of your comfort zone. Justice demands that we step into the story and experience of others, that we learn

### Not-So-Deep Service

- Service makes us feel like a "great white savior" (or black or brown or some other skin color) who rescues the broken.

- Service often dehumanizes (even if only subtly) those who are labeled as the "receivers."

- Service is something we do *for* others.

- Service is an event.

- Service expects results immediately.

- The goal of service is to help others.

- Service focuses on what our own ministry can accomplish.

- Service is serving food at the local homeless shelter.

### Deep Justice

- Justice means God does the rescuing, but often he works through the united power of his great and diverse community to do it.

- Justice restores human dignity by creating an environment in which all involved "give" and "receive" in the spirit of reciprocal learning and mutual ministry.

- Justice is something we do *with* others.

- Justice is a lifestyle.

- Justice hopes for results some time soon but recognizes that systemic change takes time.

- The goal of justice is to remove obstacles so others can help themselves.

- Justice focuses on how we can work with other ministries and accomplish even more.

- Justice means asking *why* people are hungry and homeless in the first place— and then doing something about it.[9]

from them and walk alongside them in overcoming challenges and fixing external causes.

Kara Powell uses a helpful comparison of "not-so-deep service" and "truly deep justice." I would not say—by any means—that all compassionate serving is not so deep. But I do think we need to be careful that it doesn't become that way. It is sometimes easy to scratch the surface and because the surface is rough and may seem impenetrable to then feel like we are doing something significant. Powell's comparison can be a very helpful one at raising awareness.

Kevin Blue, author of *Practical Justice,* describes a threefold progression in response to injustice. First, we are called to provide direct relief when people are hurting—in other words, we should "give a man a fish." This is compassion ministry and responds to the immediate need. Second, we must fight injustice by teaching a person to fish or some other skills (job training, education, equipping). Distributing skills is a direct way to help people learn to be able to help themselves. Third, we learn to deal directly with the system—fixing the pond. If the fish are unhealthy or inedible, it probably means that the pond is polluted. Fixing the pond gets to the source of the problem, the root cause.

---

**FOR FURTHER STUDY**

*Practical Justice: Living Off-Center in a Self-Centered World* by Kevin Blue

*Faith Works: How to Live Your Beliefs and Ignite Positive Social Change* by Jim Wallis

---

## Philosophies of Justice

There are a few main philosophical perspectives about the source of justice. I will review two of them here.

***Divine command theory.*** Christians believe that justice is ultimately the manifestation of the righteousness of God. God is the source of justice. The laws and will of Yahweh, the God of Israel, defines what is right and what is wrong. His laws are expressed throughout the Old and New Testaments. God is the defining source of virtue, truth and justice. The source of justice is divine.

***Authoritative command theory.*** Many secularists believe that God is not the source of justice. The authoritative command theory suggests that justice is expressed in adherence to the rules and laws of society; injustice is disobedience to those public principles. The laws and principles of society are imposed by the public and the leaders of the community. Some philosophers espouse this view, claiming that the public establishes rules that define the parameters of justice. Thus justice is created by the command of an absolute sovereign power. The source of justice is not divine but human.

Christians believe that the source of justice is God. This is reassuring. Because the nature of God is unchanging, the nature of justice is unchanging. Christians believe that God's character is permanent, consistent and true:

> God is not a human, that he should lie,
>     not a human being, that he should
>     change his mind.
> Does he speak and then not act?
>     Does he promise and not fulfill?
>     (Num 23:19)

Nietzsche, who may be most known for the statement "God is dead," also claimed that "There is no eternal justice."[10] It is good to be reminded that the opposite is true. For the source of justice is God, and he is eternal and unswerving.

## Different Types of Justice

Many times when Christians talk about justice they are referring primarily to retributive justice. In addition to retributive justice, there are some other justice terms that contribute to the conversation: distributive justice, restorative justice, and redemptive justice.

*Retributive justice.* Retributive justice is what lies behind "eye for eye, tooth for tooth" (Ex 21:24). Retribution is the idea that someone should get what they deserve, especially that when someone does something wrong, they should be punished. This Old Testament concept suggests that reciprocity demands a response equal to but not greater than the wrong suffered, "life for life . . . wound for wound, stripe for stripe" (Ex 21:23, 25 KJV). Retributive justice responds to a lawbreaker with action that is justly imposed, morally correct and fully deserved. Military justice is often retributive.

Some have argued that the United States' use of the atomic bomb on Japan during World War II was an act of retributive justice. In 2007 Max Hastings, a popular historian, wrote a book called *Retribution: The Battle for Japan (1944-45)*. Hastings argued that the brutality of the Japanese and the bombing of Pearl Harbor demanded retributive justice and thus justified the use of atomic weapons (see "Asian American History" and "War"). The use of atomic weapons is highly debated among historians. Christians must ask the moral question of whether or not retributive justice is what God demands.

Retributive justice was common through-out the Old Testament. Jesus, however, redefined the Old Testament law:

> You have heard that it was said, "Love your neighbor and hate your enemy." But I tell you, love your enemies and pray for those who persecute you, that you may be children of your Father in heaven. He causes his sun to rise on the evil and the good, and sends rain on the righteous and the unrighteous. If you love those who love you, what reward will you get? Are not even the tax collectors doing that? And if you greet only your own people, what are you doing more than others? Do not even pagans do that? Be perfect, therefore, as your heavenly Father is perfect. (Mt 5:43-48)

Jesus calls us far beyond retributive justice and giving people what they deserve. Instead, Christians are told to forgive seventy times seven, to love their enemies, to bless those who persecute them (see "Sabbath" and "Year of Jubilee"). When we respond with grace and forgiveness, the grace that was extended through Jesus' death on the cross invites others to join the mysterious journey of faith.

**FOR FURTHER STUDY**

*Punishment vs. Reconciliation: Retributive Justice and Social Justice in Light of Social Ethics* by Patrick Kerans

*Early Christian Historiography: Narratives of Retributive Justice* by G. W. Trompf

*Distributive justice.* Distributive justice specifically addresses the allocation of resources such as wealth, power and reward. There are three relevant questions to distributive justice: (1) What are the resources being distributed (e.g., wealth, power, opportunity); (2) To whom are the resources being distributed (e.g., individuals, communities, cities, countries); and (3) By what means are they being divided within society (e.g., equally, divided by merit, according to status or some other delineation).[11]

Leviticus 25 and the year of Jubilee are examples of distributive justice in the Old Testament. There are also glimpses of distributive justice in the New Testament: "Anyone who has two shirts should share with the one who has none, and anyone who has food should do the same" (Lk 3:11), and "All believers were together and had everything in common" (Acts 2:44; see Acts 4:32). In the early 1990s the reallocation of resources in South Africa after the end of apartheid operated within the framework of distributive justice (see "Racism—Apartheid, South Africa"). Different philosophies of distributive justice are informative in understanding social justice.

---

**FOR FURTHER STUDY**

*Summa Theologica* by Thomas Aquinas

*A Short History of Distributive Justice* by Samuel Fleischacker

---

**Restorative justice.** Restorative justice uses problem-solving techniques that emphasize reconciliation and the rebuilding of relationships between victims and oppressors. Restorative justice is often applied in the criminal justice system. According to Prison Fellowship International, restorative justice is a "theory of justice that emphasizes repairing the harm caused or revealed by criminal behavior."[12] Howard Zehr, professor of sociology and restorative justice at Eastern Mennonite University, is the grandfather of the restorative justice

movement.[13] In restorative justice, the concerns and needs of the victim play a significant role in the process of reconciliation.

An example of restorative justice in the Scriptures is the story of Mephibosheth, a son of Jonathan and a descendent of Saul. Although David was the victim in this story, he was willing to practice restorative justice and be reconciled to the house of Saul. David said to Mephibosheth: "Don't be afraid, . . . for I will surely show you kindness for the sake of your father Jonathan. I will restore to you all the land that belonged to your grandfather Saul, and you will always eat at my table" (2 Sam 9:7). Saul had committed a grave injustice against David, the anointed king of Israel. Although David had been treated unjustly, he was willing to be reconciled to the family of his oppressor through his treatment of Mephibosheth.

---

**FOR FURTHER STUDY**

*The Little Book of Restorative Justice* by Howard Zehr

*Restorative Justice, Self-Interest, and Responsible Citizenship* by Lode Walgrave

---

*Awareness exercise.* There are some wonderful online resources with much information about the strengths and weaknesses of the restorative justice. Go to www.restorativejustice.org, a branch of Prison Fellowship International, and read some of the articles posted on their website.

**Redemptive justice.** Restorative justice is rooted in the biblical concept of redemption. Redemptive justice is very similar to restorative justice, but places less emphasis on the needs of the victim and instead focuses on the redemption of the oppressor.

## Chuck Colson

From 1969 to 1973, Charles (Chuck) Colson (b. 1931) was the chief counsel for President Richard Nixon and was one of the "Watergate Seven" arrested and sent to prison. In prison, he had a conversion experience and became a follower of Christ. Once released, he started the organization Prison Fellowship, whose primary mission is to "mobilize and assist the Christian community in its ministry to prisoners, ex-prisoners, victims, and their families; and in the advancement of restorative justice."[14]

Colson is one of the best-known proponents of restorative justice, a notion being practiced all over the United States throughout the prison system.

Restorative justice holds that crime is committed not against the state but against a victim and against God. In restorative justice, nonviolent criminals stay out of jail, remain in the community where they committed their crime, and work to support their families and pay restitution to the victim. Ideally, the criminal seeks reconciliation with the victim, too.[15]

Restorative justice promotes the idea of bringing together the perpetrator of a crime and the victim. Theologian N. T. Wright explains: "[Restorative justice] has about it both the mark of the cross (looking evil in the face and letting its full force be felt) and the hope of a world in which all is known and all is put to rights."[16]

### FOR FURTHER STUDY

*Charles Colson: A Story of Power, Corruption, and Redemption* by John Perry

*Justice That Restores* by Chuck Colson

One of the ways that Christians are called to respond when people violate principles of justice and hurt those around them is by practicing redemptive justice. Redemptive justice, like restorative justice, tries to find balance between forgiveness (e.g., wiping out debt) and consequence (e.g., the deserved response for the wrong that was committed). This satisfies both justice and peace and makes room for the work of reparation.[17] It does not demand complete repayment or retaliation for a wrong done, nor does it offer complete forgiveness of debt so that right consequences are abdicated.

The story of Saul is an example of redemptive justice in the New Testament. Saul was present at the stoning of Stephen and was one of the leaders of the persecution of the early church (Acts 7:58; 8:1-3). Scripture says that Saul began to "destroy the church." Saul's actions were horrific and unjust. One day, on the road to Damascus, Saul had an encounter with the risen Christ, who spoke these words: "Saul, Saul, why do you persecute me?" "Who are you, Lord?" Saul asked. "I am Jesus, whom you are persecuting" was the response (Acts 9:4-5). After his encounter on the road, the Christian leaders of the early church were wary of this man who had been one of their chief persecutors. The Lord paved the way through Ananias, and eventually the others slowly welcomed Saul into their community (Acts 9:13-15). The story of Saul's conversion and subsequent purpose as a minister of the gospel who preached all over the Roman empire is an example of redemptive justice.

*Awareness exercise.* By yourself or with a group of friends, watch the movie *The Shawshank Redemption* (1994). What themes of justice do you see in the movie: retributive, distributive, restorative or redemptive? Is there more than one theme present? Consider, or discuss with your friends, which aspects of these theories do you think are biblical? Why or why not?

## Justice, Laws and Society

To some degree, we can't understand the types of justice without further exploring the role of people in the creation and execution of laws in society. As the authoritative command theory of justice implies, in society the public often play a role in determining what is just or unjust. This raises the following questions: What is the role of the church in government and society? Where do laws come from? What makes moral or good laws and what makes unjust ones? These questions are beyond the scope of this book, but they are wonderful topics to be explored.

---

**FOR FURTHER STUDY**

*A Theory of Justice* by John Rawls

*Church, State and Public Justice: Five Views* edited by P. C. Kemeny

---

## Power and Authority

We can't talk about justice without talking about power and authority. Injustice can be defined as the abuse of authority. Gary Haugen says: "Justice is the right exercise of power—God is the ultimate power and authority in the universe, so justice occurs when power and authority is exercised in conformity with his standards."[18] When power and authority are exercised outside of the will of God, an injustice has occurred.

Identifying when injustice occurs is pretty simple. Consider two three-year-old children playing in the sandbox; one is bigger than the other (size is a legitimate source of power). The bigger toddler grabs the toy that the smaller child is playing with and makes her cry. An injustice has occurred—it might be a little one, but the action of the larger child was still unjust.

Consider a larger scenario where more drastic injustice occurred. For ten years, from 1935 to 1945, Adolf Hitler led the German army, which was called the Wehrmacht. The total number of soldiers who served in the German army during that period is believed to be close to eighteen million. The power that Hitler controlled as the commander of those troops was extraordinary. Many of the officials under his leadership in the army were tried for the massacres of civilians, rapes, executions of POWs, summary executions of foreign army officers, the rounding up of Jews and others to be sent to concentration camps, and ultimately the extermination and execution of over six million Jews.[19] The Jewish Holocaust, or *Shoah* (Hebrew), is one of the greatest injustices of the twentieth century.

Power can be distributed in a variety of ways. Size can determine power. Political and societal structures can determine power and denote authority. Gary Haugen identifies several sources of power distribution: political, economic, social, moral, religious, cultural, familial, coercive and intellectual.[20] Power is sometimes innate, sometimes achieved, sometimes inherited, and other times grasped or stolen. The source of earthly power, to some degree, is insignificant; how power is used is profound.

It is good to be reminded that God is the source of all power and authority. Before Jesus gave the Great Commission to make disciples of all nations, he made a tremendous statement: "All authority in heaven and on earth has been given to me" (Mt 28:18). A glimpse of his authority and power is seen in 1 Corinthians: "Then the end will come, when he hands over the kingdom to God the Father after he has destroyed all dominion, authority and power. For he must reign until he has put all his enemies under his feet" (1 Cor 15:24-25). When all other authority is fully submitted to the will of God the Father, earth will be in a state of shalom, just as it is in heaven.

Kevin Blue makes the claim that "All God's people are called to deal with power."[21] In order to engage successfully in battles that are not against flesh and blood, which are talked about in Ephesians, there must be a power in us that is greater than the powers that are being fought against. There are many different ways to engage the power structures of this world. The different types of engagement depend on one's call and gifts and on God's purposes for individuals and communities to help live out his purposes.

One way we can change systems is by being reformers. Blue says, "Reformers occupy a key position within a power structure and wield power in ways that bless many people and move forward God's purposes in the world."[22] Another way to handle the powers of the world is to isolate ourselves. This is seen historically in the tradition of the Pilgrims and Puritans.[23] Some groups separate from the world to preserve their culture, language and identity rather than being consumed by the dominant culture. Other groups feel threatened by the powers at work in the world and isolate themselves so the world cannot penetrate their communities. Regardless of how we choose to engage with the powers and authorities on this earth, it is clear that Christians are biblically called to struggle against them and to be equipped in battle with the armor of God: "Be strong in the Lord and in his mighty power" (Eph 6:10).

**FOR FURTHER STUDY**

*The Social Justice Agenda: Justice, Ecology, Power, and the Church* by Donald Dorr

*Love, Power, and Justice: Ontological Analysis and Ethical Applications* by Paul Tillich

## Justice and a Theology of Society

Lowell Noble's book *The Kingdom of God Versus the Cosmos* is a hidden treasure for anyone wrestling with the theology and social implications of justice. Noble calls the church to develop a theology of society that transforms it from a place of social evil to a more centered place of biblical (social) justice.[24] His progression is as follows:

| Social Evil | Social Justice |
| --- | --- |
| Satan | God/Jesus Christ |
| Principalities and Powers | Holy Spirit |
| Cosmos | Kingdom of God |
| Ethnocentrism | Justice |
| Oppression | Shalom |
| Damaged Individuals | Liberated Individuals[25] |

Noble juxtaposes oppression and shalom. The fallen world has not yet been fully released from the oppression of the evil one (Satan), but when Christ returns, complete shalom (peace) will be experienced and social justice realized because all things will be under the authority of the Father.

The Scriptures talk about the principalities and powers. Ephesians 6:12 says, "For our struggle is not against flesh and blood, but against the rulers, against the authorities, against the powers of this dark world and against the spiritual forces of evil in the heavenly realms." The Holy Spirit equips believers to respond and be strong in battles.

For Noble, the cosmos is the entire creation under the rule and authority of the kingdom of God. Ethnocentrism, Noble claims, is the antithesis of justice. Ethnocentrism is the belief that our own views, cultures and perspectives are superior to that of others. Justice, for Noble, is the idea that all people, groups, races and ethnicities are equally equipped with access to God and the ability to pursue righteousness.

In an unjust society individuals are damaged and broken. The unrighteousness of sin manifests itself in personal failure and in social oppression. In a just society, on the other hand, individuals are liberated and live in freedom. Righteousness in the kingdom of God reveals itself in personal salvation, social justice and freedom.

Noble's parallelism is easy to understand and sheds light on the battle between good and evil (Eph 5:12). A weakness, however, is that it is overly dualistic. The power of Satan is certainly not on par with the power of God. In addition, Noble places a strong emphasis on ethnocentrism as the greatest abuse of power experienced around the world. While significant and one of the leading contributors toward an unjust world, ethnocentrism is not the sole injustice (see "Poverty," "Racism" and "Women").

*Spiritual reflection exercise.* Several of Lowell Noble's workshops from the Christian Community Development Association (CCDA) are available online at <www.urbanministry .org/lowell-noble-0>. Download one of the talks and listen to Lowell Noble's teaching. Look up the Scripture passages that Nobel references. Do you agree with his interpretations? What other verses can you find in Scripture to either affirm his point or discredit it? Share your reflections with a friend or mentor. Pray that God would reveal his truth to you about the topic that is being addressed.

## Issues of Injustice

Many multifaceted and complex issues contribute to the injustice that exists around the world. Issues like health care, fair housing and living-wage jobs can contribute to social injustice. We must never forget that the issues are so important because of the people they affect. When injustice occurs, people's lives are damaged and destroyed. God is jealous for justice to be achieved in the world, and he cares deeply for those who are affected by the abuse of power and unjust systems.

Issues of justice are addressed throughout this book because we must be able to identify, understand and work through these complex and painful problems in order to work toward systemic solutions. We are compelled to delve into the muck and the mire because people's lives are affected. As 1 Corinthians 12 says, when one part of the body suffers, the whole body suffers. All believers suffer alongside those who are harmed and hurt by injustice. We struggle to understand issues of social justice because Christ's love drives us to care for our neighbors.

*Awareness exercise.* Spend fifteen minutes a day for at least four weeks reading the local, national or world news. Use an international source such as BBC News (news.bbc.co.uk) or *The Guardian* (www.guardian.co.uk), which will provide a more holistic perspective of U.S. foreign policy than American sources. Consider the events that you are learning about around the world. See if this makes any difference in your views about justice and poverty.[26]

## Direct and Indirect Injustice

One day I was having coffee and discussing social justice with my friend Mark who formerly worked for International Justice Mission (IJM) (see "Sex Trafficking"). We were talking about concept of justice and more specifically about the perspective that IJM takes in defining injustice. IJM speaks of injustice as an "abuse of power;" a person

with more power *directly* exerting power over a person with less power. IJM's understanding of justice is very poignant and very focused. Their work has a fourfold purpose: (1) victim relief, (2) perpetrator accountability, (3) victim aftercare, and (4) structural change.[27] IJM does amazing ministry around the world working through public justice systems to rescue victims of abuse and oppression.

As Mark and I were talking about definitions of justice, I started to recognize some of the restrictions in IJM's choice of language. They focus on only "direct injustice." Their work is critical, vital and certainly effective toward ending *direct* perpetrator violence. However, because their scope is so focused, there are aspects of justice that are not included in their descriptions or actions. In addition to *direct* injustice, there are many forms of *indirect* injustice—the indirect abuse of power to oppress others, which I believe is prevalent in the United States.

Consider the city school system in Chicago, Illinois (see "Education—Domestic" and "Education—Global"). The Chicago Public School (CPS) system does not directly violate the rights of any of the students under its care. However, students who attend schools in Chicago certainly do not have the same access to quality education as their counterparts in the suburbs.[28] Though CPS does not intentionally abuse students, I believe its students experience injustice. They are participating in a system that is not fair. This type of injustice can be terribly damaging and needs to be addressed just as much as the direct injustices. Indirect injustices must not be overlooked. Jus-

tice advocates seek ways to increase awareness and respond to all types of injustice,
direct or indirect.

**FOR FURTHER STUDY**

*Good News About Injustice* by Gary Haugen

*What If You Got Involved? Taking a Stand Against Social Injustice* by Graham Gordon

# 3

# A History of Christian
# Social Justice in the Americas

*"Misunderstanding of the present is the inevitable
consequence of ignorance of the past."*

Marc Bloch, *The Historian's Craft*

The history of Christians involved in social justice provides wisdom and insight about how things got to be the way they are today. U.S. history gives context to both the Christian historical tradition of responsibility on behalf of the poor and the journey of many of the people groups who remain in poverty today. It is easy to judge and misunderstand the poor. Some believe that the domestic poor are greedy. Others don't understand why the domestic poor don't just take advantage of the capitalistic system and the free market to "work their way out of poverty" (see "Capitalism"). History reveals why those assumptions are inaccurate and gives us perspective as solutions to injustice are explored today.

A few major themes present themselves in the history of Christian compassion and social justice involvement in the United States. On one hand, the founding settlers had a deeply rooted faith that informed their practice of Christian hospitality, so the burdens of individuals were shared by the surrounding community. Compassion was embodied in the local church and the community of believing Christians, which was the primary place where benevolence was expressed. The other theme, however, is a less positive one. At various periods throughout the history of the United States, Christians have sat on the sidelines and neglected to protect the vulnerable. Historically in the history of the Americas, white Europeans have often been the oppressor. Many of those Europeans were Christians.

## Colonization of the Americas

From the time of Christopher Columbus, the colonization of the Americas began with the invasion of foreign conquerors. Powerful European nations raced to see who could conquer and maintain the most land in the New World. The people groups already living in the Americas were decimated and their cultures were destroyed.

The sixteenth century was filled with the

oppression of the native people already living in the Americas. For example, in 1520 the Spanish adventurer and conquistador Hernán Cortés overthrew the Aztec empire and claimed Mexico for Spain. At the time of the conquest it is believed that the capital city of the Aztec empire, Tenochtitlan, was one of the largest and most progressive in the world. In the battle for Tenochtitlan, Cortés surrounded the city and cut off the Aztecs' food and water supply. Famine, dysentery and small pox reduced the forces of the Aztec people. After three months of siege, Tenochtitlan fell and more than forty thousand decomposed bodies littered the destroyed city of the fallen empire.[1]

The annihilation of the American aboriginal people groups is an example of the type of oppression mentioned in the Old Testament. We cannot ignore the many ways that the first European settlers took advantage of people groups and used power and authority for selfish gain. The light skinned people who traveled to the Americas from Europe became captors and barbarians. They brutalized the people who had preexisted on the American continent. The story of the Aztecs is only one of many that litter the sixteenth century.

It is helpful to look at the trajectory of native people groups who were on the receiving end of the oppression. Many of these groups are nearly extinct (see "Human Rights"). Other groups continue to exist on the lower margins of society. Have these people groups ever experienced justice?

## Early Christian Missions to the Americas

The movement of Christian missionaries across the American continents cannot be ig-

nored. Many of the European explorers were Christians and they brought along with them Spanish, French and English missionaries. Missionary work was a thriving business. There were several incentives for the establishment of the missions, not the least of which was the belief that the native people of the Americas were heathens in need of conversion.

In California, the Franciscan missionary system seized control of Native American land and the indigenous population. The goal was not only conversion but also the eradication of native culture and adaptation to the European way of life. The missions also helped secure the Spanish foothold in the New World. The Spaniards believed that converted Indians would help defend the Spanish lands and pay taxes.[2] The mission system was another way of controlling the indigenous people groups and keeping them subject to the powers of the European settlement system.[3]

---

**FOR FURTHER STUDY**

*American Indians and Christian Missions: Studies in Cultural Conflict* by Henry Warner Bowden

*The Missions of California: A Legacy of Genocide* edited by Rupert Costo and Jeannette Henry Costo

---

***Awareness exercise.*** Choose an American people group who preexisted European colonization. Purchase a couple of books about their history. Read their history. What role did Christians play in it? Did injustice occur in their story? Did justice? Consider the different types of justice addressed in chapter two: retributive, distributive, restorative, redemptive. How might these concepts be applied to their story?

## American Indians

U.S. history is not devoid of the destruction of American indigenous people groups. The majority of American settlers were Protestant Christians who had come to the New World for new opportunities and religious freedom. In fact, many of them had the distinct goal of converting the Native Americans and defeating the Spanish Catholics.[4]

Europeans immigrants nearly obliterated the population and cultures of the Native Americans for a number of reasons: diseases brought from Europe, violence and the annihilation of people groups, displacement from their land, warfare and enslavement.[5] Many Native American stories could be told.

Throughout the nineteenth century, the U.S. government's laws and policies continued to deny the Indians their rights and property. In 1830, the "Indian Removal Act" led to the deportation of seventeen thousand Cherokee Indians. The Cherokee nation was forced to march for thousands of miles from Georgia to an Indian reservation in Oklahoma, which is known as the "Trail of Tears." Many people died along the way; some estimates are as high as four thousand.[6]

As settlers moved further west, overhunting and the needless killing of the buffalo limited the Native Americans' food supply. Many conflicts, later known as the Indian Wars, broke out between the United States government and the American Indians. A number of treaties were issued by the United States and then subsequently broken when more land was desired. Battles broke out. Some, such as the Battle of Little Bighorn (1876), were won by the Native Americans. In others, though, Native American men, women and children were brutally murdered, which led to the decline of the Indian nations.

### FOR FURTHER STUDY

While I was on vacation this past year, I picked up Dee Brown's *Bury My Heart at Wounded Knee*, which had been on my shelf for quite sometime. The book broke my heart. This glimpse of the history of the people groups who lived in the United States prior to the European settlement gave me a new perspective. I read about the Long Walk of the Navajos (1860) and the massacre of the Sioux men, women and children at Wounded Knee (1890) in South Dakota. The colonization by white Europeans has taken a terrible toll on the indigenous people who lived on the land prior to the establishment of the United States. I encourage you to become familiar with the history of Native Americans, their customs, their traditions, culture and history. Consider using a resource like the American Indian website (www.americanindians.com) to help inform your study.

*Awareness exercise.* Watch the HBO made-for-TV movie *Bury My Heart at Wounded Knee* (2007). After watching the movie, look up events that were referenced in an historical encyclopedia or other reference material. Some questions to consider: What did you learn about the Indians' experience? Who is Chief Sitting Bull, and why was he important to the Lakota tribe? Who was Senator Henry Dawes, and how did his politics affect the future of Native Americans? What role did Christianity play in the history of the American Indians? The movie may be purchased at Amazon.com or rented from Blockbuster or several other video stores.

*Awareness exercise.* Awareness is the first step toward action. Consider taking a group or going by yourself to visit one of the locations of the National Museum of the American Indian: New York City; Suitland, Maryland; and the National Mall in Washington, D.C. For more information see their website at www.nmai.si.edu. How would the biblical idea of Jubilee apply to the context of the Native American story?

## American Indians in the Twenty-first Century

The challenges that Native American tribes and nations experience in the twenty-first century are numerous. They include "political sovereignty, economic development, constitutional reform, cultural and language maintenance and promotion, land and water rights,

---

### Ely Samuel Parker (Donehogawa)

Ely Samuel Parker (1828-1895), also known as Donehogawa or "keeper of the western door," was an Iroquois of the Seneca tribe. Educated at a Baptist school in New York by white teachers, Parker was acquainted with both Indian and white culture. He worked at a law firm in New York, and when he attempted to take the bar exam, he was rejected.[7] Parker served in leadership positions in both the Indian community and for the United States government. In 1851 he was appointed as the Grand Sachem, or leader of the Six Nations.[8] In 1857 he became a captain in the New York state militia. In 1863, after being rebuffed for wanting to serve in the United States Army, he was appointed by General Ulysses S. Grant as part of his military staff. Parker served alongside Grant for the remainder of the Civil War and wrote the final draft of the Confederate surrender at Appomattox.[9] In 1869 Parker became the first Native American to serve as the commissioner of Indian affairs.

Parker was one of the first Native Americans to serve in the United States government. He was a Christian who desired to serve his country and continually experienced limited opportunities because of his ancestry. Although Parker declared his commitment to the Christian faith, having professed that he "knelt at the cross of my Savior," he still was not accepted as a part of the Christian church.[10] He was not deterred and continued to try to make a difference on behalf of his people. His story is one that highlights the difficulties that he and other American Indians faced, even when trying to accommodate the dominant culture. He eventually resigned from his position in Indian Affairs and went into private business. He lost his financial security in the Panic of 1873 and spent the last several years of his life in poverty.[11]

**FOR FURTHER STUDY**

*The Life of General Ely S. Parker* by Arthur Caswell Parker

*Warrior in Two Camps: Ely S. Parker, Union General and Seneca Chief* by William H. Armstrong

religious freedom, health and social welfare, and education."[12] In 2000, U.S. Census data showed that 4.1 million people living in the United States reported their race as being at least partly Native American or Native Alas-kan.[13] The Native American community is among those most affected by drugs, alcohol abuse, domestic violence and crime.

According to the United States Department of Justice, the rate of violent crimes in

## Wiconi International

Richard Twiss, a Lakota Indian, had fond memories of powwows and extended family gatherings growing up on the Rosebud Lakota/Sioux reservation in South Dakota. Hoping to save her children from the alcoholism and violence on the reservation, Richard's mother moved the family to Oregon, where he spent his teenage years. After graduating from high school, Richard moved back to Rosebud and became a part of the American Indian Movement (AIM), where he felt more connected to his Indian culture and heritage.

In 1972, with six hundred other Native American people, Richard was a part of an armed takeover of the Bureau of Indian Affairs Office Building in Washington, D.C. After his experience in D.C., Richard ended up back in Washington State and was arrested for drug possession and a DUI. In the hopes that he could avoid the mandatory rehabilitation program that was a part of his sentencing, Richard moved to Hawaii. There, two men told Richard the story of Christ, and one night, while alone on the beach and desperate, he invited Jesus to be a part of his life.

Years later, while attempting to live out his faith in Christ, Richard was serving on staff with the International Bible Society with his wife and four boys on the Coeur d'Alene Reservation in Idaho. After Richard's position was eliminated for budgetary reasons, the Twiss family was in crisis and at a significant turning point. Stepping out in faith, Richard and Katherine moved their family back to Vancouver, Washington, and founded Wiconi International in 1997. *Wiconi* means "life" in the Lakota/Sioux language. The ministry was founded with the vision to invite people to follow the ways of Jesus by "affirming, respecting and embracing God-given cultural realities of Native/Indigenous people, not rejecting and demonizing them" but bringing them hope and life.[14]

↞ *Take action.* Consider spending a week or longer serving with an organization like Wiconi International that would allow you to spend time on a Native American Indian Reservation or in the Native American community. Prepare your heart so that you enter into your experience ready to serve and learn, not to fix the problems that you might witness and encounter. For a list of ministries to Native American Mission Agencies visit www.missionfinder.org.

the Native American population is the worst of any racial group and more than twice the rate for the nation.[15] In 1999, 55 percent of victims of violence in the Native American population reported that the offender was under the influence of drugs, alcohol or both.[16] In 2000, Mothers Against Drunk Driving (MADD) reported 44 percent of Native Americans who were convicted of driving under the influence (DUI) were identified as alcohol abusers or dependents.[17] In 2008, the United States government reported that Native American substance abuse levels are higher than for any other demographic group.[18] Those are just some of the staggering statistics affecting the Native American population in the United States today.

**FOR FURTHER STUDY**

*Native Americans in the 20th Century* by James Olson and Raymond Wilson

*Native Americans and the Christian Right: The Gendered Politics of Unlikely Alliances* by Andrea Smith

## Seventeenth-Century Colonial America

Europeans came to the Americas for a variety reasons: financial gain, overpopulation and religious freedom. The Pilgrims (Plymouth Colony in Massachusetts) and the Puritans (Massachusetts Bay Colony) were seeking religious freedom.

The Pilgrims separated from the Church of England because they believed it was corrupt. The life of a separatist in England was not easy, so they left their homeland in search of religious freedom. In the New World, they responded to their neighbors' needs because of their religious beliefs and because it was necessary for survival. As a result, "the need to offer personal help and hospitality became a frequent subject of sermons, which in colonial days were 'powerful in shaping cultural values, meanings, and a sense of corporate purpose.'"[19]

The seventeenth century is a period in U.S. history when compassion was an intimate part of society; it was expected and practiced as a part of everyday life. It was especially expressed in response to the devastating effects of illness and the hard settler lifestyle. According to Marvin Olasky, the author of *The Tragedy of American Compassion:*

> The model of early American generosity toward those in greatest need stressed personal aid in times of disease. Pilgrim leader William Bradford, describing how sickness shrank his small band of settlers following their landing at Plymouth in 1620, . . . wrote that they did 'all this willingly and cheerfully, without any grudging in the least, showing their true love unto their friends & brethren.'"[20]

Not only was compassion a part of everyday life for the settlers, but religious fervor and Christian commitments were integrated into the framework of society as well.

As the colonies developed, their relationship to the indigenous people and the local tribes was troublesome. Some of the settlements had positive relationships with the Indians, but others were very violent. A number of factors contributed to how those relationships played out. Many of the settlers feared the Indians because their customs and practices were so different from their own.

Although Virginia settlers are believed to have been more secular than their New England counterparts, many were committed to serving God. Religiously zealous colonists had the specific goal of "pulling the Indians from the pit of hell," however few natives wanted to be converted.[21] Most of the settlers viewed the Indians as untamable savages. The Indians viewed the settlers as barbarians.

Unfortunately, in many cases compassion was only expressed within the immediate settlement communities and did not extend to Native Americans. In the seventeenth century there was little tolerance of view-

## William Wilberforce

Although this chapter is focused on American Christian history, it is helpful to consider similar movements in other parts of the world. The antislavery movement in England was a precursor to the abolitionist movement in the United States. Much attention has been drawn to William Wilberforce because of the 2007 Hollywood movie *Amazing Grace.*

Wilberforce (1759-1833) was a British politician and philanthropist whose actions were deeply motivated by his faith in Christ. His evangelical faith informed his desire to bring about social reform and the end of the slave trade. He worked tirelessly as a member of Parliament and alongside the Prime Minister William Pitt. Wilberforce's antislave work in partnership with others led to the Slavery Abolition Act (1833), which abolished slavery in most of the British empire. He also worked on behalf of the poor and the oppressed around the world, and was committed to the introduction of Christianity in India, the freedom of the colony of Sierra Leone, the foundation of the Christian Mission Society, and the Society for the Prevention of Cruelty to Animals. He is buried in Westminster Abbey.

**FOR FURTHER STUDY**

*William Wilberforce: A Hero for Humanity* by Kevin Belmonte

*The Roots of Endurance: Invincible Perseverance in the Lives of John Newton, Charles Simeon, and William Wilberforce* by John Piper

*Awareness exercise.* Host a movie party and watch *Amazing Grace.* The movie tells the inspiring story of Wilberforce and his passion and perseverance to end the slave trade in the late eighteenth century. Several friends, including John Newton, a reformed slave-ship captain who penned the beloved hymn "Amazing Grace," urged Wilberforce to see the cause through. After viewing the movie, discuss the history of slavery and its effects. This is a way to not only learn from the history but also to understand the effect of slavery on today's Western society. Slavery still exists, and this is a great way to raise awareness about the problem (see "Slavery"). Resources and study questions for the movies are available at the Amazing Grace website, www.amazinggracemovie.com.

points, ideas or differences outside of the dominant culture.

Roger Williams, an English theologian and committed Christian, was kicked out of Massachusetts for what the Plymouth Colony viewed as liberal religious beliefs. Williams was also known for his tolerance and care toward the Indians.[22] In 1636, Williams founded Rhode Island.

In the colony of Virginia, Indians weren't the only people excluded from society. In 1660, the colony forbid ship captains from importing Quakers; Puritan clergy were banished; and Jews were kept out entirely for two generations.[23]

Georgia was another colony that was established on strict principles of virtue and morality. The 1732 charter of Georgia read in part:

> And whereas we think it highly becoming our crown and royal dignity, to protect all our loving subjects, be they ever so distant from us; to extend our fatherly compassion even to the meanest and most unfortunate of our people, and to relieve the wants of our above mentioned poor subjects.

Because religious freedom was practiced in Georgia, it did not have one primary faith. The colony was established as a refuge for English poor people who were willing to work hard. It also served as a buffer to the Spanish settlements in Florida. The colony's original charter forbade slavery, alcohol and other forms of immorality of the day. The original colony failed, and a reconstituted Georgia lifted many restrictions, allowed slavery, and the colony became successful. It is difficult to un-

derstand the development of the economy and societal conditions of the early colonies apart from the African slave trade.

## African Slave Trade

I had lunch with an African American pastor friend in Oakland, California. We were talking about how the white church can play a part in advocating for social justice, and how pastors can make the church aware of the brokenness within our church communities. My friend said we must first understand the genocide of two American people groups before we can begin to take measures to fight against racism and systemic injustice. I am ashamed to admit I could only think of the genocide of American Indians. I had no idea which other people group he was referring to.

As he continued to talk, it became clear he was also talking about the history of the African American people. Many groups and people of color have experienced oppression in the history of the United States, but blacks alone were forced to come to this country.

The history of other people groups of color in the United States is largely influenced by the experience of African Americans who were brought to the Americas as a part of the slave trade. The history of African Americans is not esteemed to the degree that it should be. The December 31, 2007, *New York Times* article "Forgotten Step Toward Freedom" calls attention to the fact that while we pay great attention to many aspects of U.S. history, we were neglecting the two hundredth anniversary of the end of the legal slave trade (January 1, 2008).[24]

According to historian Lerone Bennet Jr., the African slave trade to the Americas is the greatest migration in the history of the world. During the four hundred years of the slave trade (1444-1844), an estimated forty million people were taken out of Africa. Some twenty million slaves were brought to the New World. Millions died on the journey across the Atlantic ocean, while being taken into captivity on farms and plantations once they arrived.[25] These are astounding numbers. It is difficult for us to understand the horrors surrounding the slave trade.

> The slave trade was not a statistic, however astronomical. The slave trade was people living, lying, stealing, murdering, dying. The slave trade was a black man who stepped out of his house for a breath of fresh air and ended up, ten months later, in Georgia with bruises on his back and a brand on his chest. The slave trade was a black mother suffocating her newborn baby because she didn't want him to grow up a slave. The slave trade was a "kind" captain forcing his suicide-minded passengers to eat by breaking their teeth, though, as he said, he was "naturally compassionate." The slave trade was a bishop sitting on an ivory chair on a wharf in the Congo and extending his fat hand in wholesale baptism of slaves who were rowed beneath him, going in chains to the slave ships. The slave trade was a greedy king raiding his own villages to get slaves to buy brandy. The slave trade was a pious captain holding prayer services twice a day on his slave ship and writing later the famous hymn, "How Sweet the Name of Jesus Sounds."[26]

Can twenty-first-century Americans understand the devastating effects of slavery? Today, most African Americans are the descendents of this horrible history. Their great-grandparents were stripped of every possession, separated from their loved ones, treated worse than animals, forced to conduct backbreaking labor, beaten when not submissive and killed as if their lives were without meaning.

The institution of slavery was legal in the United States until the Emancipation Proclamation (1863) that was issued by Abraham Lincoln, but the emancipation could not be enforced until the end of the Civil War (1865).[27] It would be another hundred years before African Americans would have the same legal rights as whites (see "Civil Rights Movement," "Racism," "Slavery"). Society in the twenty-first century is still deeply affected by this history. Understanding this sad history is critical to rooting out systemic injustice in the framework of Western society.

***Awareness exercise.*** Gather some friends and watch the PBS documentary *Traces of Trade: A Story from the Deep North* (2008). The filmmaker Katrina Browne is a descendent of the DeWolfs of Briston, Rhone Island, the "single largest slave-trading family in U.S. history."[28] The film follows Browne and her relatives on their personal journey of understanding their past, the foundations of white privilege and the devastating consequences of their wealth as a result of slavery. Go to www.pbs.org/pov/pov2008/tracesofthetrade/ for more information about the film.

←◄ ***Take action.*** Gather a group of people or partner with neighboring churches to celebrate Juneteenth (also known as Emancipation Day). Although the effective date of the Emancipation Proclamation was January 1, 1863, it had very little effect on most slaves. On June 19, 1865, Union general Gordon Granger took two thousand troops to Galveston Island, Texas, to take possession of the state and to emancipate the slaves. The celebration of Juneteenth commemorates that emancipation and the freedom of all slaves. Juneteenth Celebrations often consist of BBQs, picnics, potlucks, parades, cookouts, music and other festivities. Juneteenth is now an annual holiday in twenty-six states. For more information visit www.juneteenth .com.

## The Great Awakening

Religion was a critical part of eighteenth-century American society. Some estimate that close to 80 percent of the population of the United States attended churches.[29] The Great Awakening took place in the American colonies in the 1730s and 1740s, which was a revival in the Christian faith. This movement affected Congregationalists, Presbyterians, Baptists and Methodists, and expressed itself in a holistic view of the gospel expressed in the pursuit of personal righteousness and the expression of faith in the acts of compassion and justice.

Largely inspired by Jonathan Edwards, a Congregationalist from Massachusetts, the movement emphasized the power of immediate and profound personal religious experience, expressed in personal piety and a high standard of individual and personal morality.[30]

Most American Christians in the eighteenth century believed that faith in Christ was manifested in a response to the poor. Personal righteousness was expressed in loving one's neighbor. In 1725 American preacher Benjamin Colman said, "Acts of Compassion and Mercy to our poor and needy Brethren [are] esteemed by the Lord of the Sabbath to be Holiness to himself."[31] Throughout the United States, programs were developed to respond to the needs of orphans, widows and other destitute people.

The church viewed caring for the poor as its responsibility. For example, in 1797 the "Society for the Relief of Poor Widows with Small Children" was founded in New York. The society focused on providing for the physical needs of poor widows and offered them gifts in kind, such as food, coal and clothing, not cash. During its first winter, the society helped "98 widows with 223 children; by 1800, 152 widows, with 420 children under the age of 12, were listed on its books."[32] The society assisted women in finding work so the women would be able to provide for their families. The society only accepted clients who "would rather eat their own bread, hardly earned, than that of others with idleness."[33] These programs were largely successful because they helped those who were struggling to get their feet underneath them rather than providing handouts that would continue to keep people living in poverty.

## The Second Great Awakening

The Second Great Awakening (nineteenth century) took place during the first several decades of the nineteenth century. The movement extended beyond personal renewal in salvation to concern for suffering people. The Second Great Awakening significantly affected abolition, prison reform, women's suffrage and the temperance movement.

Most nineteenth-century compassion initiatives were religiously based, and social reform was rooted in Christian theology. Communities had strong religious ideals and moral codes, and most people believed compassion was the responsibility of the community, not the government. The Second Great Awakening produced increased social activism based on Christian education. In 1816, movements like the American Bible Society were founded with the express purpose of translating, publishing and distributing the gospel message to as many people as possible. Social activism was largely encouraged by the Methodists, Baptists and Presbyterians, who formed organizations to promote temper-

### John Wesley

Methodism was one of the first widely successful evangelical movements in England. Methodist founder John Wesley (1703-1791), an Anglican minister, led the movement to focus on such social justice reforms as the abolition movement and modifications within the prison systems. Wesley's work began in England, where he was a part of the Holy Club at Oxford University. After spending some time serving as a parish priest in Savannah, Georgia, he returned to London, where he finished his ministry. Wesley gave most of his possessions and earnings to the poor. It is believed that he earned at least £20,000 for his writings (and that was in the eighteenth century)! He lived simply. He died famous, but poor. Wesley quipped, "Put yourself in the place of every poor man and deal with him as you would God deal with you."

Wesley's theology is the basis of Methodism, the Holiness Movement, Pentecostalism and parts of the charismatic movement.[34] John's younger brother Charles was also a leader in the Methodist movement and is known for his hymn writing, which includes "And Can It Be That I Should Gain?" "Christ the Lord Is Risen Today," "Hark! The Herald Angels Sing," and "Come Thou Long-Expected Jesus."

#### FOR FURTHER STUDY

*John Wesley's Life and Ethics* by Ronald H. Stone

*Social Justice Through the Eyes of Wesley: John Wesley's Theological Challenge to Slavery* by Irv Brendlinger

ance, abolition and prison reform.

The Second Great Awakening not only promoted social reform but also expansion of the church. In 1801, one revival meeting in Kentucky drew more than twenty thousand people who were overwhelmed by contagious fervor, crying out loud in prayer and song, and exhorting others to get involved in the movement. The meetings lasted for a week, until provisions ran out. The Second Great Awakening is one of the reasons that the nineteenth century is identified as a "century of kindness."[35]

## Nineteenth-Century Compassion in America

Josiah Strong, a nineteenth-century Christian writer and clergyman, wrote, "Probably during no hundred years in the history of the world have there been saved so many thieves, gamblers, drunkards, and prostitutes as during the past quarter of a century."[36]

During the nineteenth century, compassion was characterized by a sense of mutual obligation for both the poor and the rich. The wealthy felt that it was their obligation to walk alongside the poor, to encourage and to share their resources with them. Overall, there was greater connection, exposure and direct encounters between the rich and the poor.[37] The common belief was that everyone was connected. When one person suffered, everyone suffered. Success of one was a success for everyone. This philosophy was rooted in similar Scriptural ideals: "If one part suffers, every part suffers with it; if one part is honored, every part rejoices with it" (1 Cor 12:26). Christians are called to be the body of Christ through mutual accountability and submission. Nineteenth-century Christians believed that they were their "brother's

keeper."[38] There was a sense of community and mutual responsibility.[39]

During the 1800s it was commonly believed that distributing aid to despondent people was not an effective way of responding to poverty. Those in need were expected to be involved; charity programs required the participation of the recipient.[40] Poor people were encouraged to demonstrate a willingness to change and if able to work their way out of poverty. Upward mobility was expected.[41] The poor were categorized into (1) those who were poor because of their own actions, and (2) those who had fallen into misfortune, through no fault of their own. Aid was more readily offered to those who were deemed deserving of it. Societies were created to help the poor who were the most "worthy" of help.[42] American activist and political thinker Charles Murray notes:

> Human needs were answered by other human beings, not by bureaucracies, and the response to those needs was not compartmentalized. People didn't used to be so foolish as to think that providing food would cure everything except hunger, nor so shallow as to think that physical hunger was more important than the other human hungers, nor so blind as to ignore the interaction between the way that one helps and the effects of that help on the human spirit and human behavior."[43]

The French philosopher Alexis de Tocqueville observed that American people displayed a general sense of compassion for one another. On the other hand, throughout nineteenth-century Europe: "[the] state almost exclusively undertakes to supply bread to the hungry, assistance and shelter to the sick, work to the idle, and to act as the sole reliever of all kinds of misery."[44] It wasn't until the Great Depression that care for the poor became the U.S. government's responsibility.

## United States Civil War

During the nineteenth century the United States expanded further west. In 1803 Thomas Jefferson purchased from France the land west of the Mississippi River, which covers close to a quarter of today's United States territory. Manifest destiny—the idea that the United States was not only justified but destined to expand from the Atlantic to the Pacific—was a common belief during that time. The Lewis and Clark expedition (1804-1806) was the first time Anglo Americans had traveled by land to

---

### Young Men's Christian Association (YMCA)

The YMCA is one of the most effective evangelical organizations of the nineteenth century. Founded in 1844 in London, England, the YMCA was birthed by George Williams and a group of Christian evangelicals to put into practice the principles that Jesus had taught. The YMCA's purpose was to give hope to men who were living on the streets in conditions of squalor. Its efforts extended to all men, women and children regardless of race, religion or nationality. This was unusual in nineteenth-century society. The YMCA's approach to ministry was holistic and included spiritual, intellectual and physical approaches to social development.

In 1851, the first YMCA chapters came to the United States. Two years later the first YMCA for African Americans was founded in Washington, D.C., by Anthony Bowen, a freed slave. The organization played a supportive role in the Civil War by providing nursing, shelter and other aid.

By 1900 there were 1,429 local YMCA centers in the United States, with approximately 250,000 members nationwide.[45] Throughout subsequent history the YMCA played a supportive role in responding to global crises. During WWII the YMCA helped prisoners of war and aided the Japanese who were in the internment camps (see "Asian American History"). Since its conception the YMCA has grown into a worldwide movement of more than 45 million members in 124 nations. Although the roots of the organization are markedly Christian, today the degree to which the Christian faith is expressed varies between different YMCA associations. The first winner of the Nobel Peace Prize, Henry Dunant, was a cofounder of the Geneva branch of the YMCA. He won the prize for his founding of the International Committee of the Red Cross (1863). For more information about the YMCA visit its website at www .ymca.net.

the Pacific and back.[46] Of course, the westward expansion had devastating effects on the Native Americans residing in the west

As new territories became part of the Union, slavery was a major economic and political issue (see "Human Rights" and "Slavery"). Even though slavery was at its height, many historians consider the nineteenth century as one of the most compassionate in the history of North America. In 1860, there were close to four million slaves in the United States.[47] The slave trade from Africa officially ended in 1808, because by this time it was largely recognized as a "crime against humanity."[48] Nonetheless, slavery continued within the borders of the United States and the population of slaves continued to grow up to the Civil War (1861-1865). The Underground Railroad was a way for slaves to escape the oppressive conditions in the South and to obtain relative freedom in the northern U.S. or Canada.

In the Dred Scott Decision (1857), the Supreme Court determined that slaves were property, and that slave owners could take their property wherever they wanted. This allowed slave owners to take slaves into free territories. The decision also determined that African Americans could not be citizens, which resulted in northern blacks losing some of the freedoms that they had previously exercised.[49] Tensions continued to rise between the northern free states and southern slave states. In 1854 the Kansas-Nebraska Act was passed, which allowed new territories to decide whether or not slavery would be allowed. This led to the "Bleeding Kansas" conflict, where guerilla violence led to the deaths of over fifty people. Tensions continued to mount through slave rebellions and abolition-

ist initiatives like John Brown's raid on Harpers Ferry. The Civil War began in 1861 with the attack on Fort Sumter in South Carolina. It continued through 1865, when Confederate General Robert E. Lee surrendered to the General Ulysses S. Grant at the Appomattox Courthouse (see "Ely Samuel Parker").

---

**FOR FURTHER STUDY**

*Upon the Altar of a Nation: A Moral History of the Civil War* by Harry Stout

*The Civil War as a Theological Crisis* by Mark Noll

---

## Abolitionist Movement

The U.S. abolitionist movement was chiefly influenced by the Christian benevolence movement, inspired by Christian evangelicals, of the nineteenth century. For example, William Lloyd Garrison was a fervent, if not fanatical, abolitionist who published the antislavery newspaper *The Liberator* (1831-1865), and led the protest of slavery in the United States. Frustrated with both the church and government, Garrison embraced a doctrine of Christian perfectionism, and based on the biblical notion of not participating in a corrupt society or supporting its unjust institutions, he joined abolition, women's rights and nonresistance movements. (Many abolitionists did not support the participation of women in the movement; see "Women" and "Women's Suffrage.") Garrison's beliefs became increasingly radical, and although he was a pacifist he supported the freedom of the slaves even through the use of violence. In 1865 with the freedom proclamation of the slaves, Garrison felt that his career as an abolitionist had ended.[50]

Many northern Christians did not participate in the antislavery movement. In fact, many southern slave-holders were Christians. Jefferson Davis, the president of the Confederate States of America, said slavery "was established by the decree of Almighty God . . . it was sanctioned in the Bible, in both Testaments, from Genesis to Revelation . . . it has existed in all ages, has been found among the people of the highest civilization, and in nations of the highest proficiency in the arts."[51] The Bible was used by many to not only defend slavery but to justify it. Among Christians, the Methodists, under the leadership of John Wesley, were one of the first groups to develop the small protest against slavery into a mass movement.

**FOR FURTHER STUDY**

*All on Fire: William Lloyd Garrison and the Abolition of Slavery* by Henry Mayer

*Against Slavery: An Abolitionist Reader* edited by Mason Lowance

## Sojourner Truth

Through her work as an evangelist, civil rights worker and abolitionist, Sojourner Truth (1797-1883) is a forerunner of Christian activism. Truth was born a slave in New York State under the name Isabella Baumfree. Sold from owner to owner, many of them cruel, she escaped at the age of thirty. Her journey led her to the home of a Quaker couple, Isaac and Maria Van Wagener, whose home she had seen in a vision she believed God gave her. The Van Wagener's purchased her from her owner and then set her free.[52]

After her initial conversion, Isabella felt led astray in her faith and asked that God would call her back to himself and give her a new name. Again she had a vision. Her name was to be Sojourner "because I was to travel up an' down the land, showin' people their sins, an' bein' a sign unto them," and Truth "because I was to declare the truth to the people."[53] She traveled all over the eastern seaboard attending prayer meetings, telling people about the gospel and speaking against the institution of slavery. Sojourner proclaimed, "I have borne thirteen children, and seen most all sold off to slavery, and when I cried out with my mother's grief, none but Jesus heard me! And ain't I a woman?"

In 1850 Sojourner Truth published her autobiography, which brought her both fame and torment. She lived under the threat of violence and was told at one point that a building she was going to speak in would be burned if she preached. After one angry mob assaulted her, she had to walk with a cane for the rest of her life.[54] Her life is a testimony of how trials and tribulations can be overcome to take a stand on behalf of the things that are close to the heart of God.

**FOR FURTHER STUDY**

*The Narrative of Sojourner Truth* by Sojourner Truth

*Sojourner Truth: A Life, A Symbol* by Nell Irvin Painter

## Women's Suffrage

The woman's suffrage movement was linked very closely to the anti-slavery and abolition movement. As history progressed, women would be involved in all of the major social reform movements in the United States, including the temperance movement, advocacy of prison reform and the settlement house movement, being led by women like Jane Addams, Lillian Wald and Emma Whittemore. All of those women lived during a time when women had a limited voice in society.

Prior to the twentieth century the role of women was largely defined by their family roles. Women were expected to marry and to have children, and their status was dependent on their husband's position and status in society. Women had limited rights in terms of property ownership, directing their children's lives and finding professional vocations. Women of color had even less rights and often had to work outside of the home in menial jobs, factories or less desirable professions.

In "Why Christians Should Support Slavery," a pamphlet advanced by southern church leaders, the subjugation of women was used as an example of how slaves were to be submissive. It stated: "Just as women are called to play a subordinate role, so slaves are stationed by God in their place."[55]

The church did not respond favorably to the women's suffrage movement. Not only did the suffrage movement espouse women's right to have a voice in politics but it also challenged the limitations that were placed on women within the church. Susan B. Anthony, Elizabeth Stanton, Matilda Joslyn Gage and Ida Husted Harper, leaders in the suffrage movement, wrote with vehemence about the church's treatment of women: "With fierce warnings and denunciations from the pulpit, and false interpretations of Scripture, women have been intimidated and misled, and their religious feelings have been played upon for their more complete subjugation."[56]

Women of all races joined the campaign for women's suffrage. In the United States, women did not get the right to vote until 1920. Many black men, including Frederick Douglass, supported both the abolition movement and the women's suffrage movement. However, some African American men abandoned the cause for women after the passing of the Fifteenth Amendment (1870), which gave black men the right to vote.[57]

---

**FOR FURTHER STUDY**

*We Are Your Sisters: Black Women in the Nineteenth Century* by Dorothy Sterling

*Frederick Douglass on Women's Rights* by Frederick Douglass and Philip Foner

---

## Reconstruction

The period after the Civil War is known as the Reconstruction Era (1866-1877). Life for American blacks significantly changed after the end of the war. Not only were they emancipated from slavery, but there were also opportunities for economic development because of government support. The Fourteenth Amendment (1868) provided former slaves with citizenship, and the Fifteenth Amendment (1870) granted black men the right to vote.[58]

There were more blacks in political positions of power during Reconstruction than at the end of the twentieth century. "Nor was this all. Blacks and whites were going to school together, riding on streetcars together and cohabiting, in and out of wedlock."[59] For the first time in the history of the United States, there was hope for blacks. Historian Lerone Bennett Jr. observes, "There had never been an age like this one before."[60]

The initial glory of the Reconstruction was only to last about a decade. One of the programs that was developed determined to give each emancipated slave forty acres and a mule.[61] Initially, this program distributed close to 400,000 acres to around 10,000 freed slaves. However, President Andrew Johnson later revoked the order and the land was returned to its original white owners.[62]

There were many challenges unique to postslavery black society. For example, on plantations, slaves had been forced to marry in order to "breed" or create more slaves. Thus many slaves had more than one spouse. Many slaves returned to their original husbands and wives from whom they had been separated. There were far more black women than men, which posed problems in terms of establishing a balanced society.[63] Land proved to be one of the greatest problems. Close to four million slaves were set free, but did not have a place to live or a way to earn a living. Chaos and riots ensued. Laws were developed to limit the opportunities and freedoms of the former slaves. These laws came to be known as "black codes," more commonly referred to as the Jim Crow Laws (see "Civil Rights Movement").

## The Ku Klux Klan

Groups like the Knights of the Ku Klux Klan (KKK) sprang up during the Reconstruction era, led by powerful men like the Confederate general Nathan Bedford Forrest, who was the first national leader of the KKK. The purpose of the Klan was to establish white supremacy after the Civil War. Lerone Bennett described the influence of the Klan this way:

> The plan: reduce blacks to political impotence. How? By the boldest and most ruthless political operation in American history. By stealth and murder, by economic intimidation and political assassinations, by the political use of terror, by the braining of the baby in its mother's arms, the slaying of the husband at his wife's feet, the raping of the wife before her husband's eyes. By fear.[64]

Through underground and overt initiatives, blacks' ability to rebuild their lives was limited after the war.

Throughout its history the Ku Klux Klan experienced several resurgences. One of its most prominent was in the 1960s, as the group terrorized blacks during the civil rights movement (see "Civil Rights Movement"). This history is important, for it identifies the roots of many sentiments surrounding African American people.

In the mid-1980s the Christian Identity Movement began, which is closely affiliated with KKK. This group espouses racialized theology of white superiority and teaches that Christianity offers salvation for Caucasians alone. The Christian Identity Movement teaches that nonwhites "have no soul, no standing in the Kingdom of God."[65]

FOR FURTHER STUDY

*White Terror: The Ku Klux Klan Conspiracy and Southern Reconstruction* by Allen W. Trelease

## The Social Gospel

Around the time of Reconstruction, a theologically liberal religious movement was sweeping through northern American Protestantism. The social gospel movement attempted to respond to problems of industrialization. Washington Gladden and Walter Rauschenbusch, leaders of the movement, feared that religion was no longer accessible to the working class.

In 1908 the Federal Council of the Churches of Christ in America adopted a social creed that identified the core tenants of this new philosophy, including the abolition of child labor, better working conditions for women, one day off during the week and the right of every worker to a living wage. Of course, none of these initiatives are bad! However, some social gospel proponents pursued these reforms to the abandonment of scriptural principles and a solid theological foundation. The Social Gospel claims that all people have a natural right to access fundamental resources. Many of the beliefs about the social gospel were later embodied in the governmental reforms of the New Deal legislation in the 1930s.

The social gospel separated those who adhered to its ideals and those who believed in a gospel of righteousness. The social gospel movement developed into liberal Christianity and is manifested today in many mainline churches. Some of those who adhered to the social gospel began to follow a more universalistic theology, which taught that because of the love of Christ all people are saved regardless of their beliefs or actions.[66]

The opposing view believed that it was more essential to focus on the teachings found in Scripture. Evangelicals continued to uphold orthodox Christian beliefs rooted in systematic theology and Scripture. The necessity of faith in Christ for salvation continues to be a core tenant of the evangelical faith. However, though twentieth-century evangelicals held strongly to traditional doctrine, they largely neglected to respond to the needs of the poor, as taught by the gospel of Christ.

*Awareness exercise.* Read the series of blogs from Paul Rauschenbusch (great-grandson of Walter Rauschenbusch) and Bill Hybels (pastor of Willow Creek Community Church) as they dialogue about salvation and sustenance—concern for the soul and transforming the material existence of the poor. Visit the Beliefnet website at blog.beliefnet.com/blogalogue/save-souls-or-feed-the-poor. Reflect on the dialogue. Where do you agree or disagree? Why? Share your thoughts with someone you know and get their perspective on the dialogue.

FOR FURTHER STUDY

*The Great Reversal: Reconciling Evangelicalism and Social Concern* by David Moberg

*Christianity and the Social Crisis in the 21st Century* by Walter Rauschenbusch

*Spiritual reflection exercise.* Interview a pastor that you know and ask how he or she would explain the gospel. Does the pastor believe that the gospel relates to personal righteousness? To social reform? Why or why not? Think about the pastor's responses and reflect on what you heard. As you read the Scriptures, what do you think the gospel says about this question? Is there value in what the social gospel taught about the poor? Is it possible that both personal righteousness and social reform are important? What does the Bible say about personal salvation? If you get stuck read John 14:5-7, Romans 10:9 and Ephesians 1:12-14. Reflect and ask God to speak to you in your study.

## Women and Benevolence

In the nineteenth century, women were the primary initiators and participants in the benevolence movement. Women couldn't vote, couldn't serve in political office, and couldn't own property (see "Women's Suffrage Movement"). And Caucasian women typically did not work outside the home, which gave them time to participate in other projects and activities.[69] This does not necessarily mean that

### Salvation Army

The Salvation Army is an example of a holistic and egalitarian organization that came out of the evangelical movement. Founded in London in 1878 by William and Catherine Booth, the expressed purpose of the Salvation Army is to bring salvation to the poor, the hungry and the homeless through education, poverty relief and the proclamation of the Word of God.

In 1880 Commissioner George Scott Raiton and Captain Emma Westbrook, with six women "soldiers," set out to start the Salvation Army in the New York area.[67] The Salvation Army is one of the first evangelical organizations to allow women to serve in all leadership capacities.

By 1900 the Army had 700 corps and outposts with 2,600 officers and employees and 20,000 volunteers. The Salvation Army placed about 4,800 persons per month with their employment agencies; they sponsored 141 social relief institutions, including 52 shelters for men and women, 8 labor bureaus, 14 rescue homes for fallen women, and 2 children's homes.[68] Today, the Salvation Army is stronger and more powerful than ever. Now in over 106 nations around the world, the Salvation Army continues to work where the need is greatest, guided by faith in God and love for all people. In 2007 the Salvation Army established an International Social Justice Commission and appointed Commissioner M. Christine MacMillan as its director.

#### FOR FURTHER STUDY

*In Darkest England and the Way Out* by William Booth

*The Life and Ministry of William Booth: Founder of the Salvation Army* by Roger Green

←* *Take action.* Consider volunteering with the Salvation Army. Ways to get involved include monetary contributions, volunteering, donating to thrift stores, auto donations and airline miles donations. Go to www.salvationarmyusa.org/usn/www_usn_2.nsf to find out how to volunteer in your area.

women of the eighteenth and nineteenth centuries were more compassionate than women today. Because their freedoms were so limited in other arenas, benevolent involvement was one of the few ways that women could meaningfully contribute to society during that time.

## Settlement Houses

After the Civil War the United States experienced a recession, and urban poverty became worse than it had ever been. Serious urban problems included drug abuse, alcoholism, homelessness, abandoned children (orphans), prostitution and gambling. For example, in New York City after the Civil War, there were 5,500 liquor houses and 647 prostitution houses.[70]

The increasing growth of the urban poor led to the development of "settlement houses" that provided charity on behalf of wealthy donors and offered food, shelter and education. According to Marvin Olasky:

> The settlement house movement, through its emphasis on the material over the spiritual and the political over the personal, became the inspiration of governmental social work programs of the 1930s and community action programs of the 1960s. Some historians have argued that "the real novelty" of the settlement house movement "lay in the buoyant spirit, the fresh outlook, and the new attitudes its leaders introduced into philanthropic work."[71]

The establishment of settlement houses was part of the progressive era reform. One of the most famous settlement houses was the Hull House (1889), started by Jane Addams in Chicago. Similarly, Lillian Wald founded the Henry Street Settlement (1893) in New York. At the turn of the nineteenth century the church and local community were still expected to rally around individuals who were down and out. But with the increasing numbers of poor, some people began to think that the social needs might eventually become too great for the local church. Hull House and most other settlement houses were independent from religious organizations and contributed to the secularization of charity work. This shift is important because it increasingly led to government involvement in the needs of the poor. The settlement house movement continued into the 1930s with Dorothy Day's Catholic Worker House movement with the development of hospitality houses.

## Turn-of-the-Century Compassion

After the "century of compassion" there were increasing campaigns for government support for the poor. Most of this support came in the form of public funds distributed to private institutions (most of which were Christian). Religious-based charities, such as orphanages, settlement houses and homeless shelters received public aid, which meant there was less funding available for private nonreligious organizations.[72]

The general public also started to voice concern with the methods of Christian social services. There was a sense that charity was "moralistic, paternalistic and controlling," and that the overall programs were not as effective as they could have been.[73] "Compassion fatigue" began to surface, and there was a sense that if the communities and private sector would or could not respond to the

### Emma Whittemore

Socialite Emma Whittemore's (1844-1931) friends and acquaintances were some of the wealthiest people in New York City. She was surrounded by money, jewels and servants, and filled her time attending social events, parties and balls. One day a friend invited her to go to a YMCA meeting to hear an evangelist. Unbeknownst to Emma, her husband, Sydney, had also been invited to the event. Independently, they were convicted by the preaching. Though both knew they wanted to live differently, the details of how that would occur were not yet clear.

Emma and her husband were encouraged to hear another preacher, Jerry MuAuley, an ex-convict and reformed drunkard who had opened a mission in one of the worst parts of the city. When they arrived at the meeting, they had disdain for the people who had gathered there. The environment was filled with cussing and fighting. Emma recalled the place smelled as if she were surrounded by "sin-bedraggled people," and Sydney made disparaging remarks about their company. Then, as Emma notes, something happened:

> As the meeting progressed, however, God got such possession of him and later of myself also that we were both held in painful silence as we were convicted of our useless lives. We no longer felt superior to the "poor creatures" . . . but actually hung our heads in shame.[74]

needs of the poor, the government should intervene.[75] This sentiment paved the way for the government reforms that began at the beginning of the twentieth century.

Evangelicals began to lose their influence and no longer led in benevolence work. As with the settlement house movement, the emphasis was no longer on spiritual poverty but on the physical and material poverty of the individual and the community.

Following the depression in the late 1800s, money was thrown into impoverished communities. And with the growing number of poor, there was less opportunity for giving personal attention, time and care. Immigration and increased urbanization meant that the problems of poverty were different than they had been. The gap between the rich and the poor began to increase, and there was no longer a direct connection between the wealthy and the underresourced.[76] Ambitious for the new century, communities focused on the progress that would come with the future and became unresponsive to the needs of the poor.[77]

### Child Welfare: The Beginning of Government Involvement

One example of the increased governmental involvement with the poor is The United States Children's Bureau (1912). The Children's Bu-

Both Sydney and Emma glimpsed first-hand the transforming power of Jesus in the worst segments of their society. At the meeting the Whittemores asked for prayer, and Emma described the scene of a group praying for them: "a drunk-ard, a thief and a tramp on my husband's side, and on my side one or two poor women."[78]

From that meeting, the Whittemores developed an ongoing relationship with the mission and could often be found sharing the gospel with the people there. Emma felt God breaking her heart for women who were living on the street—some trying to escape prostitution, others who were pregnant and not married. Homes were needed to care for these women, so in 1890, the first house called "Door of Hope" opened.

In the first four years, 325 women had been helped. Emma's first purpose was to share the love of Jesus with the women who were coming off the street. Her second goal was to teach these women how to evangelize others and to share the hope that they had found with others who were hurting. Emma and her husband became key leaders in the Salvation Army and partnered with other Christian care organizations around the world. Door of Hope was so successful that it became an international movement. By the end of Emma's life, there were 97 homes worldwide that were providing the true message of the gospel—salvation for the lost and care for the poor.[79]

**FOR FURTHER STUDY**

*Delia, the Bluebird of Mulberry Bend* by Emma Whittemore

reau was created to prevent child abuse, provide foster care and promote adoption. Prior to government intervention, the local communities, particularly the local church, would open their homes to offer the necessary resources and care to orphans or children in distress. In fact, the model for the government's welfare system as it was to relate to children came from Charles Loring Brace, a Christian actively involved in organizing programs to meet the needs of orphans and children in need of care.

## Maternity and Infancy Protection Act

Tapping into the efforts of Christians such as Brace, the U.S. government started to get more involved in responding to the needs of children and their mothers. In 1921 the first formal act of federal welfare, the Sheppard-Towner Act (or the Maternity and Infancy Protection Act), was extended to children. This government program offered assistance to both women and children who needed support. Feminist activists led the charge, and this effort contributed to the growing women's movement in the twentieth century.

The Sheppard-Towner Act was the only program offering federal support until Roosevelt's New Deal in the 1930s. The Act has a part in history because it not only represented increased government involvement but also validated the importance of responding to the needs of women and children. The United States could no longer claim that people's needs were being met by their neighbors, for citizens increasingly expected the state to intervene when help was needed.

The Sheppard-Towner Act was passed

## Charles Loring Brace

A graduate of Yale University, Charles Loring Brace (1826-1890) was a nineteenth-century clergyman and social reformer. In 1853 he founded the Children's Aid Society of New York, an organization designed to care for the city's street children. Brace's programs were the precursor for our contemporary foster care systems, and many of his practices are still in effect today. Brace, like many evangelicals who had gone before him, believed that spiritual and material poverty were inextricably linked. As a Christian, he believed that it was his role to provide opportunities for both spiritual and physical reform. He set up meetings in New York where the gospel was preached to children and their physical needs were also met.

Brace's convictions led him to develop a family-based model for caring for orphans, based on the belief that transformation and development is more likely to happen in Christian community through a loving family unit. On "orphan trains" Brace transported street urchins to families living on farms and in other nonurban communities.[80] The relationship between orphans and their new families would be symbiotic. Children needed homes, food and care, and farm families needed the help and sup-

port of additional labor.

While Brace's efforts on behalf of children were magnanimous, his beliefs were tainted by racist superiority. Though he frequently stated his opposition to racial inequality, he nevertheless represented whites as "noble" (particularly the English) and blacks as "low" or even "hideous."[81] Although his programs placed some nonwhite children, they largely focused on European children.

To give you an idea of the scope of Brace's influence, the Children's Aid Society placed close to one thousand children per year during the mid- to late 1850s, two thousand per year by the late 1860s, and close to four thousand per year by the late 1870s. The total between 1853 and 1893 was 91,536, of which 42 percent went to homes in New York State, and about the same number to seven Midwestern states (Illinois, Iowa, Missouri, Ohio, Indiana, Kansas and Michigan).[82]

### FOR FURTHER STUDY

*Orphan Trains: Story of Charles Loring Brace and the Children He Saved and Failed* by Stephen O'Connor

*The Dangerous Classes of New York and Twenty Years' Work Among Them* by Charles Loring Brace

shortly after the passing of the Nineteenth Amendment (1920), in which women received the right to vote. In light of the women's liberation movement this law was understood as a statement of the increased independence of women. Around the same time, Christian fundamentalism was gaining steam, which was in part opposed to these increased freedoms for women.

**FOR FURTHER STUDY**

*Women's Liberation and the Church: The New Demand for Freedom in the Life of the Christian Church* by J. Raitt

*The Sheppard-Towner Act in Relation to Public Health* by Anna Elizabeth Rude

## The Temperance Movement

The temperance movement (1920-1933) was clearly led by the Christian church. With good intentions, Christians wanted to shape the morality of society by encouraging right living through the absence of alcohol. The main supporters of the temperance movement were women, and it's easy to understand why. At the beginning of the twentieth century, women had significantly less rights than their husbands, and men who drank excessively often beat their wives. Thus women wanted to limit the amount of alcohol consumed by their husbands.

In 1873 the Women's Christian Temperance Union (WCTU) formed a nonsectarian group that began to crusade for the prohibition of alcohol. The Union advanced their cause by singing and praying in bars, and urging customers and store owners to stop selling and consuming alcohol. WCTU's interests also extended to other social reforms: labor, prostitution, public health, sanitation and peace. There was also a direct correlation be-

tween the temperance movement and the women suffragist movement. The temperance movement showed the vast influence of evangelicals in America. Unfortunately, its implementation was a devastating mess.

By the time of Prohibition, World War I had ended and women had received the right to vote through the Nineteenth Amendment to the Constitution. Prohibition, during which the sale, manufacturing and transportation of alcohol for consumption was illegal, began in the United States in 1920. Lasting for just over a decade, Prohibition was widely unpopular and had the opposite effect of what was intended. The prohibition against alcohol led to more prevalent drinking and increased verbal and physical abuse, unemployment, poverty and destitution, rape and violence.[83]

While certainly a social justice movement, prohibition attempted to get at the root causes of poverty, abuse, mistreatment of women and other social ills. It was ineffective not because of its intentions but because its imposition was not desired by those who were required to submit to its laws. Tim Stafford, author of *Shaking the System,* writes, "Prohibition was the high-water mark for Christian influence in America, and as a result of its dramatic failure, many white evangelicals lost hope. Added to it were the discouraging fundamentalist-modernist controversy and the *Scopes* monkey trial. Most withdrew from the public square."[84]

**FOR FURTHER STUDY**

*Women's World/Women's Empire: The Women's Christian Temperance Union in International Perspective (1880-1930)* by Ian Tyrrell

*Disruptive Religion: The Force of Faith in Social-Movement Activism* by Christian Smith

## The Scopes Trial

Another critical piece of history that influenced society's perception of evangelicals took place in the courthouse of Dayton, Tennessee—the Scopes Monkey Trial (1925). Though this trial may seem to have nothing to do with social justice, I believe it was a critical turning point in the American church and its voice in the public square. Prior to this trial Christians were an integral part of the dominant culture and even shaped many social expectations of the day. After the trial Christian influence diminished and Christians were taken less seriously. Many began to view Christianity as an antiquated religion having much less relevance than in prior decades. The church's ability to influence public opinion had been lost and its voice against injustice was muted.

The legal case surrounding the Monkey Trial is perhaps one of the most famous in American history. In an attempt to challenge the recently passed anti-evolution statute, teacher John Scopes went to trial for teaching about evolution in a public school. The Tennessee statute made it unlawful for anyone to teach "any theory that denies the story of Divine Creation of man as taught in the Bible."[85] History books describe the trial as a circus; lemonade was sold in stands and chimpanzees did cartwheels on the courthouse lawn. The trial began as a publicity stunt to try to call attention to Dayton, a small town suffering from economic hardship. Fundamentalist Christians, who championed traditionalist values and did not want evolution taught in schools, were defended by the testimony of statesman William Jennings Bryan. The progressives were represented by the American

Civil Liberties Union (ACLU), which had formed in 1920 as an advocacy group to protect the rights bestowed by the United States Constitution.

Scopes lost the trial, and it remained illegal to teach evolutionary theory in Tennessee's public school. Although the prosecution won the case, William Jennings Bryan's testimony was not well received: "Bryan came across to many as old, tired and foolish. In the end he disappointed even his supporters by admitting that some biblical events should not be taken literally."[86] The trial reinforced nationwide concerns about conservative Christians, namely, that they were irrational obscurants. The Scopes trial had devastating effects on public opinion toward Christians and it marked the end of centuries of influence that Christians had on social reform in the United States.

**FOR FURTHER STUDY**

*Summer for the Gods: The Scopes Trial and America's Continuing Debate Over Science and Religion* by Edward Larson

*Darwin on Trial* by Phillip Johnson

## The Fundamentalist Movement

During the first decades of the twentieth century, fundamentalism grew in the evangelical church. Fundamentalism's goal was to preserve and uphold what they felt to be orthodox, evangelical beliefs. Church historian Joel Carpenter says fundamentalism "combined a biblicist, generally Calvinist orthodoxy, an evangelical spirit, an emphasis on the higher Christian (Holy Spirit directed) life and a millenarian eschatology."[87] Tensions between fundamentalists and broader society mounted in the first half of the century.

Following the Scopes trial, fundamentalists lost much of their public support. As U.S. culture became more secular, fundamentalists withdrew from the public square, built their own schools and media outlets, and faced off with the "modernists" (theological liberals) in the church. There was a strong negative response to the social gospel among fundamentalists. They increasingly emphasized preaching and teaching the Word, and sending out missionaries to spread the evangelical message. By the 1950s, preachers and evangelists such as Charles Fuller represented fundamentalism well and the movement grew.[88]

## Fundamentalist-Modernist Controversy

Modernists attempted to reconcile and reinterpret the Christian doctrine in a way that aligned with scientific discovery and standards.[89] In the 1940s the growing modernist movement provoked fundamentalists to respond strongly to the idea that traditional belief systems were inadequate. Modernists insisted that Christianity should follow the lead of modern culture. Christianity must adapt to modern culture.[90]

The interplay between fundamentalists and modernists shaped the way the church engaged with society's problems. The core pursuit of fundamentalists was the evangelization of the lost. Though they reached out to the poor, the focus was less on the alleviation of suffering than the proclamation of truth. Modernists also were not overtly focused on compassion and justice. They were more interested in ensuring that faith followed the trends of modern society and scientific discovery.

## Social Darwinism

Charles Darwin's work on evolution not only influenced the conversation about creation, it also contributed to society's understanding of race. At the turn of the twentieth century, a growing number of people in the United States adopted social Darwinism.[91] Social Darwinists equate the economic struggle of humans with the struggle for survival among animals: "Society is constantly excreting its unhealthy, imbecile, slow, vacillating, faithless members to leave room for the deserving."[92] Any race that was not Aryan or Caucasian was undeserving and inferior.

Early in the twentieth century, U.S. doctors launched a eugenics movement that they believed would rid the country of those who were considered "feebleminded" or unfit. By 1940, over forty thousand people classified as insane or unintelligent were involuntarily sterilized. From the mid-1940s through 1963, an additional twenty-two thousand were neutered. Involuntary sterilization was legal in many states, and this took place primarily in public mental institutions, which housed the poor and racial minorities in disproportionately higher numbers. The eugenics movement was largely motivated by social Darwinism. Some have argued that Hitler modeled his eugenics program in Germany after the practices that were being readily employed in the United States (see "Human Rights).[93]

### FOR FURTHER STUDY

*Preaching Eugenics: Religious Leaders and the American Eugenics Movement* by Christine Rosen

*War Against the Weak: Eugenics and America's Campaign to Create a Master Race* by Edwin Black

## The Great Depression

The Great Depression (1928-1939) was the most significant turning point in the church's responsibility to care for the poor. In the late 1920s the world experienced an economic downturn that was manifested in the Wall Street stock market crash of October 29, 1929. By the end of the following month, market investors lost close to $100 billion in assets. The period became known as the "Great Stock Market Crash."[94] The crash on Wall Street marked the end of the "roaring twenties" and the commencement of the Great Depression. In the first year of the Depression, over twenty thousand people in the United States took their own lives, a record high at that time.[95] In rural areas, crop prices fell as much as 60 percent.[96] The depression had devastating effects on poverty in the United States and around the world.[97]

In the United States the Great Depression marked a time of unprecedented material need for a significant percentage of the population. Private welfare could not keep up with the growing demands, which flamed the demand for governmental charity. In the first few years of the depression, over four hundred private welfare agencies closed their doors.[98] Private charity became increasingly irrelevant, and other means were pursued to address the problem of the poor politically and through large-scale social change. Unemployment was so extreme that one in three people were out of work.[99] Most people did not think that it was acceptable to receive aid or to take help from someone else. The prevailing sentiment was that it's better to be dead than to take relief.[100] The Roosevelt administration developed the Federal Emergency Relief Administration (FERA) in 1932 with the purpose of providing unemployment relief. The establishment of FERA was the first of many relief operations under Roosevelt's New Deal.

As the government became more involved in providing care for people's needs, there was less need for private religious involvement. After the Depression, there were three subtle changes in the fabric of social reform: emphasis on collective action (as opposed to action by individuals), decreased emphasis on personal responsibility (no longer necessary to have personal relationships to provide relief), and an increasing professionalism of care through social work initiatives.[101] From the 1930s onward, Christian influence steadily diminished in the public square.[102]

## Welfare in the United States

In the mid-twentieth century the church played less of a role responding to injustice. The Scopes Trial and the Great Depression contributed to this decline of influence. Thinking had shifted to believing social welfare should be offered by the state.

Yet another shift occurred in social justice thinking: it no longer seemed to matter whether the poor participated in their ascension out of poverty. Society now believed that welfare should be distributed without reservation to all whether or not a person contributed to his or her own upward mobility. Robert Ellis Thompson of the University of Pennsylvania typifies the new consensus about government welfare:

> Every dollar it [the state] spends on the relief of the poor, is an admission that they have the right to be supported at

the public expense, whether their need be due to idleness and improvidence, or to a blameless failure to succeed in life. . . . State relief of the poor cannot but be indiscriminate and degrading. The state, at its best, has a wooden uniformity in its operations. . . . It must treat all on the basis of equality, without much regard to merit, motives, or equity.[103]

## The New Deal

The New Deal (1933-1939) was launched by President Franklin Roosevelt and his administration in response to the need for social and economic reconstruction after the Great Depression. The plan, which was strongly resisted by conservatives, did not prevent recession until the beginning of the World War II. It is impossible to say whether New Deal programs would have been effective, because the advent of the war brought industrial expansion, improved employment opportunities and agricultural prosperity.

The New Deal included initiatives like the Federal Emergency Relief Administration (FERA), which helped combat unemployment. FERA birthed the Civil Works Administration (CWA), which invested $400 million as a short-term solution to try to get people work.[104] Other New Deal programs included the Social Security Act, which provided resources to retirees and the unemployed, and the Aid to Families with Dependent Children (AFDC) programs, which provided assistance to families with low or no income.

Shortly after the New Deal initiatives World War II (1939-1945) began, bolstering the American economy. In the wake of the war the Russell Sage Foundation, which re-searched programs for the "improvement of social and living conditions," proposed increased government involvement in the professions of medicine, law and social work to develop a comprehensive public policy in regard to the welfare system.[105] Even though the domestic economy was improving, people increasingly relied on government programs.

During the 1950s, the AFDC lists grew by 110,000 families (17 percent). During the 1960s the increase was 107 percent (by 800,000 families)—three-quarters of which came between 1965 and 1968, a time of general prosperity and decreasing unemployment.[106] This increased utilization seemed to indicate that public programs established to respond to the material needs of the poor were creating incentives to stay on welfare, not to progress out of it.

## The Great Society

The next wave of social reform came in the 1960s under President Lyndon Johnson. The president declared a "war on poverty" and described his vision of a "Great Society" in his 1965 State of the Union Address. Programs that came out of the Great Society include food stamp legislation, Medicare and Medicaid (see "Health Care—Domestic," "Health Care—Global"). The Great Society was also committed to protecting African American rights and to providing legal protection for those who were deprived of voting rights by state regulations.

The U.S. Department of Housing and Urban Development (HUD), which coordinates federal housing projects, is also a part of this initiative. There was much hope that the

Great Society legislation might end American domestic poverty. In the mid-1960s, there was still a stigma to being on welfare. People expected that the underresourced would be motivated to work toward personal economic progress.[107] But little emphasis was placed on the cause or contributing factors of poverty. Government support was provided without categorization.

## The Civil Rights Movement

The civil rights movement (1955-1968) was one of the most significant social reform movements in the history of the United States. African Americans, a few generations removed from slavery, had very limited rights and expressions of freedom in the mid-twentieth century. The enforcement of Jim Crow laws and other societal restrictions manifested themselves in abuses of black Americans, including substandard education, restricted admittance to public places designated as "whites only" and roadblocks to voting in public elections.

Extreme racist ideologies present in the South and other parts of the United States maintained a culture of fear, coercing African Americans to "keep their place" and not overstep bounds as they went about their daily life. Parameters were enforced in many different areas to deprive blacks of privileges. African Americans, for example, were forced

### Martin Luther King Jr.

Martin Luther King Jr.'s (1929-1968) childhood was spent as a part of Ebenezer Baptist Church, in Atlanta, Georgia, where his grandfather began his tenure as preacher and pastor. King grew up attending segregated schools and pursued his education all the way through to his doctorate, which he received in 1955 from Boston University. In 1954 King's first call was to Montgomery, Alabama, as the pastor of Dexter Avenue Baptist Church. Although actively involved in organizations for the betterment of African Americans, Martin Luther King Jr. did not aspire to be at the helm of the civil rights movement. In the first few years of the movement he was a reluctant leader. Despite his reticence, King became one of the most significant leaders of a justice movement in the history of the world.

King's involvement in the Montgomery Bus Boycott (1955) marked his foray into abuse, imprisonment and family stress that would characterize the rest of his life as he worked toward freedom and justice on behalf of the marginalized. Martin Luther King's work and service was motivated by his faith in Jesus. His skilled and powerful rhetoric was expressed in his many sermons and speeches. King was awarded the Nobel Peace Prize in 1964 for his contribution to and leadership of the civil rights movement in the United States. During the decade before his death, King traveled over six million miles, spoke over twenty-five hundred times, and wrote five books and numerous articles.[111] One of King's most famous speeches, "I Have a Dream," was delivered on August 28, 1963, at the Linto take seats on the back of the bus while whites sat in the front. Blacks and whites were segregated in schools, hospitals and restaurants. These degradations were justified by the slogan "separate but equal." However, the experiences and opportunities for African Americans and other people of color were far from equal.

One of the most powerful experiences that I have ever had was my first civil rights pilgrimage through the South on a trip called "Sankofa." *Sankofa* is an African word that means "looking back in order to move forward." The Evangelical Covenant Church had been leading these four-day trips for many years, and I had the privilege of travel-

ing on a bus with more than forty other people of various races to witness firsthand the history of the civil rights movement. We started in Atlanta and traveled through bits and pieces of Martin Luther King Jr.'s life. From there we progressed to Birmingham, Alabama, and saw firsthand 16th Street Baptist Church, where four little girls were killed in a bomb that exploded while they were getting dressed for Sunday school. The white evangelical churches in the area were silent about the bombing. Indeed, John Perkins observes that "the civil rights movement probably marks a low point in evangelical involvement in the black community and possibly the lowest level of evangelical

coln Memorial in Washington, D.C., to over 250,000 civil rights advocates.

King's legacy has been esteemed by both Christians and secularists, who acknowledge the significant impact his life had on the well-being of all people in the United States. It is important to not forget that his inspiration came from his deeply rooted faith in Christ and his belief that Christians are called to love as Jesus loved. King's life was cut short when he was assassinated at the Lorraine Motel in Memphis, Tennessee, on April 4, 1968.

On the day before he was assassinated, King declared these words:

> I just want to do God's will. And he's allowed me to go up to the mountain. And I've looked over. And I've seen the Promised Land. I may not get there with you. But I want you to

know tonight, that we, as a people, will get to the promised land![112]

*Awareness exercise.* If you are able, visit the Martin Luther King Memorial in Washington, D.C. The dedication of the memorial is scheduled tentatively for 2010. You can take a virtual tour of the memorial and learn about King and his legacy at www.mlkmemorial.org. What principles did King espouse in his preaching? What was the foundation of his faith and belief? What did King teach about reconciliation and justice?

**FOR FURTHER STUDY**

*A Testament of Hope: The Essential Writings and Speeches of Martin Luther King Jr.* by Martin Luther King Jr. and James M. Washington

*Bearing the Cross: Martin Luther King, Jr., and the Southern Christian Leadership Conference* by David Garrow

conscience in this country."[108]

Throughout the civil rights movement, there was a significant lack of participation by white Christians.[109] This trip broke my heart. I think I cried through the entire thing. Some might think things were not that bad during this era. But ask people who lived through it, before their generation passes away. I pray that God would open his followers' eyes to see what has happened, to see the past and the present through his perspective.

Shortly after my first journey, I was hired at Willow Creek and helped lead similar trips that were called "the Justice Journey." We expanded the length of our travels and included Selma, Alabama, and the Voting Rights Museum, where Bloody Sunday occurred as blacks were attempting to peacefully march from Selma to Montgomery. The effect of the march eventually led to the 1965 passing of the Voting Rights Act. For the rest of my life I will remember one of the women from our partner church, Salem Baptist, singing in Brown Chapel:

Oh-o freedom
Oh-o freedom
Oh freedom over me,

And before I be a slave
I'll be buried in my grave.
And go home to my Lord and be free.[110]

We visited Montgomery where King served as the pastor of Dexter Avenue Baptist Church and where Rosa Parks sat in the front of a bus. We walked on the very patio where Martin Luther King Jr. lost his life at the Lorraine Hotel in Memphis, Tennessee. If you haven't had the opportunity to visit these places, pack your bags if you are able and take some people with you. Regardless of the color of your skin, the pilgrimage will change your life.

*Awareness exercise.* Invite some friends to watch the video *4 Little Girls* (1997), directed by Spike Lee. Reflect on what was happening in Birmingham during the time of the bombing. What must life have been like for people living in the community? For blacks? For whites? What role do you seeing the Christian church playing in the story? The African American church? The white church? Journal about what you have seen and learned.

*Spiritual reflection exercise.* Have you ever witnessed someone being put down or beat up? Maybe it was a mild form of oppression or maybe it was overt. Remember back to that moment. What were you thinking and feeling? Were you a perpetrator or the recipient? What might the recipient have been thinking or feeling? Ask God to meet you in your memory. Journal about your experience and the role that you played. Repent of ways that you might not have honored God in your response.

*Awareness exercise.* Invite people who were involved in the civil rights movement to bring their story to your church. Listen to their perspective of history and how they see race relations today. Ask them questions about their experiences and invite God to speak to you through what you hear.

*Awareness exercise.* Visit a museum about the history of the civil rights movement. They present difficult stories, but it is history that we must not forget. The Birmingham Civil Rights Institute is my favorite (see www.bcri.org). It is well done, clearly articulated and tells the story in a powerful and compelling way. The National Civil Rights Museum in Memphis is also quite good and is located at the hotel in which Dr. King was assassinated (see www.civilrightsmuseum .org). The National Underground Railroad Freedom Center in Cincinnati, Ohio, is committed to presenting information that will inspire people to act to pursue justice and freedom for all people (see www.freedom center.org).

***Awareness exercise.*** Gather a group of friends to watch the movie *Rosewood* (1997), which is about the effects of extreme racism on an African American town in Florida in 1923. After watching the movie, discuss the things that you learned. How were blacks portrayed in the movie? Whites? What was thought-provoking? What resonated with you? Do you see any similarities today in the way that different races relate to one another?

---

**FOR FURTHER STUDY**

*The Beloved Community: How Faith Shapes Social Justice, from the Civil Rights Movement to Today* by Charles Marsh

*Rhetoric, Religion, and the Civil Rights Movement (1954-1965)* by Davis Houck and David Dixon

---

## Women's Liberation Movement

Following the success of the suffrage movement, another major shift in the role of women in the United States occurred during World War II. While men were away at war, women were needed to work in factories and businesses. After the war women were expected to return to homemaking as their primary profession. But many women remained in the workforce in "pink colored" jobs, such as nursing, teaching and working as secretaries.

From 1961 through 1963 the President's Commission on the Status of Women, chaired by Eleanor Roosevelt, researched legislation and services to help women progress in the United States. As a result, in 1963 President John F. Kennedy signed the Equal Pay Act, which allowed women to participate in jury duty, to own property and businesses, and to legally control their earnings.[113] These reforms and others like them culminated in the feminist movement of the 1960s and 1970s. This movement included campaigns related to domestic violence, equal pay, sexual harassment, sexual violence and reproductive rights. Though some of the feminist reforms were legitimate, the movement is viewed as extreme by conservative Christians. One woman observed:

> The Women's Liberation Movement is possibly the most misunderstood of all the current issues facing the Christian today. And it's no wonder. Most of what the average person hears about the movement is either extremely radical or downright ridiculous. The news media has capitalized on the shock value of bra-burnings and female sewer-diggers so long that most people have decided the issue is not worth serious consideration.[114]

Many Bible-based churches ignored the message of the women's rights movement altogether. Instead of sorting through the extremes to see if there was truth buried behind the media messages, they threw the baby out with the bathwater. In many evangelical churches today, any mention of the women's movement immediately shuts down the conversation.

Now that we are almost a half a century removed from the movement, I hope we might be able to look more objectively at some of the concerns raised by women of that time, including equal opportunity, equal pay and respect as contributing members of society.

**FOR FURTHER STUDY**

*The World Split Open: How the Modern Women's Movement Changed America* by Ruth Rosen

## Asian American History

Asian Americans have been called by some the "model minority." Chinese Americans, Korean Americans, Japanese Americans, Indian Americans and other Asian American groups have been largely successful in terms of their economic status, education and low crime rates. Nevertheless, Asian Americans have faced oppression.

One of the first things I noticed in moving from Chicago to California is the large number of Chinese Americans who have lived in the United States for generations. The Chinese began immigrating to the United States at the beginning of the nineteenth century, largely to work as laborers, many on the transcontinental railroad.[115] Western society feared and disdained the Chinese, and referred to them as the "yellow peril."[116] The Chinese were considered an inferior race, and in 1882 Congress passed the "Chinese Exclusion Act" to prevent the immigration of the Chinese. The Exclusion Act was the only law to ever prohibit immigration based on race. Today about 1 percent of the American population is of Chinese descent. In the twenty-first century, Chinese immigration to the United States is only surpassed by Mexicans.[117]

During World War II, Americans of Japanese descent experienced a complete degradation of their homes, work and lifestyles as a result of the United States being at war with Japan. The entire Japanese American population, more than 110,000 people, were incarcerated at facilities called "War Relocation Camps."[118] Many were successful produce farmers who were resented by their white counterparts. In 1942 one white farmer declared to the *Saturday Evening Post:*

> We're charged with wanting to get rid of the Japs for selfish reasons. We do. It's a question of whether the white man lives on the Pacific Coast or the brown men. . . . If all the Japs were removed tomorrow, we would never miss them in two weeks, because the white farmers can take over and produce everything the Jap grows. And we do not want them back when the war ends, either.[119]

Many families forced into the camps lost their land, property and their livelihood. Everything was taken away. Wealthy Japanese Americans were forced to live in makeshift housing units that were cramped and rustic. According to the *New York Times*, the value of the Japanese Americans' lost property was between $2.5 and $6.2 billion.[120] In 1988, President Ronald Reagan apologized for the government's actions and declared they were based on "race prejudice, war hysteria, and a failure of political leadership."[121]

Many other stories could be told about the experience of Asian Americans in the United States. In 2006 the population of Asian Americans in the United States was around

13.1 million Americans, just over 4 percent of the total U.S. population.[122] Although the percentage is relatively small, we have much to learn from the experiences of Asian Americans. As the church seeks racial reconciliation and social justice, the presence and participation of Asian Americans is a must.

**FOR FURTHER STUDY**

*Invitation to Lead: Guidance for Emerging Asian American Leaders* by Paul Tokunaga

*Faithful Generations: Race and New Asian American Churches* by Russell Jeung and Robert Bellah

## Hispanic American History

The Hispanic American population is the fastest growing minority group in the United States. In 2008, one out of five people under the age of thirty-five in the United States was Hispanic.[123] Approximately 15 percent of the United States population is Hispanic.[124] Hispanic Americans consist of many subgroups, including Mexican Americans, Cuban Americans, Columbian Americans, Dominican Americans and other groups from Spanish speaking countries. Hispanics have lived in territory that is now the United States since the sixteenth century and the founding of St. Augustine, Florida, by the Spanish.[125] Hispanics lived in the regions of Texas, Arizona, New Mexico, California and other southwestern states prior to their absorption into the United States. Most of those territories became a part of the Union after physical conflict and war.

One of the greatest challenges facing Hispanic Americans is English fluency. In California, language is less of a problem because the state is rapidly becoming bilingual. In other parts of the country, however, the inability to speak English severely limits a person's ability to succeed. Many of the challenges that face African Americans, as they relate to race, also affect Hispanic Americans. Poverty, incarceration and employment are all greater for Hispanics than for all other Americans, other than African Americans.

←⚹ *Take action.* Partner with an organization like Esperanza (Hope) International that works with the Hispanic community to help free children and their families from poverty. This group generates income, provides education and health services, and restores self-worth and dignity to those who have lost hope. Esperanza International is committed to following Christ and living out the gospel through relationships, partnerships and systemic change (see www.esperanza.org).

←⚹ *Take action.* Offer a language-exchange program through your church where both Spanish and English are taught and used conversationally. This is a great way to develop relationships crossculturally while also honing language skills. If there are people in your community with experience as educators or in English as a Second Language (ESL), tap into their wisdom about best practices.

**FOR FURTHER STUDY**

*On the Move: A History of the Hispanic Church in the United States* by Moises Sandoval

*Mañana: Christian Theology from a Hispanic Perspective* by Justo Gonzales

*The Hispanic Challenge: Opportunities Confronting the Church* by Manuel Ortiz

## Modern Perceptions on Poverty Reform

During the twentieth century the care provided to the poor by private organizations was limited in comparison to previous centuries. The church's influence was scarce and its response to many of the country's domestic crises was diminished. The evangelical church was largely silent during reform movements like the civil rights movement (see "Civil Rights Movement," and "Poverty"). The responsibility of caring for the poor had fallen mostly on the government's shoulders through welfare reform and other public policy initiatives. By the late twentieth century, however, there was an increasing perception that the government welfare system was becoming excessively bureaucratic and inefficient. The Social Security system, which originated under the New Deal initiatives, faced severe public criticism. Large segments of the church lost faith in the government's ability to adequately provide the fundamental needs for the poor in society.

In the twenty-first century, under political leaders like President George W. Bush, there has been an increased emphasis on government support of faith-based initiatives. Bush, among others, has argued for a more work-based system of welfare provision. The void in effective programs and the continual problem of domestic poverty has opened the doors to the possibility of private involvement once again. Rockefeller Foundation president Judith Rodin remarks, "In the 20th century, foundations operated more as aid institutions. . . . In the 21st century, foundations are looking to take on big thorny problems, find partners who are willing to work on those prob-lems with them, and often now the partners are in the private sector."[126] Churches and Christian institutions represent a significant portion of that private sector.

In the first decade of the twenty-first century, participation of religious organizations has increased, largely due to the White House Office of Faith-Based and Community Initiatives (OFBCI) that was launched in January 2001. "Compassionate conservatism" was one of President George W. Bush's key domestic policies at the turn of the millennium. Faith-based initiatives was a return to nineteenth-century compassion, when the government could partner with private faith-based groups to help meet the needs of the impoverished in the community. Critics of faith-based initiatives include Americans United for Separation of Church and State and the American Civil Liberties Union (ACLU), who claim that governmental monies are used to fund religion. In 2005 more than $2.2 billion was awarded in competitive social service grants to faith-based organizations.[127] There is much debate about whether or not these initiatives will be effective in the years to come.

Future solutions will need to holistically address the material and emotional needs of the poor and underresourced. The church and faith-based communities will play a vital role. And it's not a one-way street; the Christian community needs to learn from those who do not have material wealth. The faith-based movement will face significant limitations if the church is not able to cooperate with the government to advocate for societal reform. The private sector cannot successfully address poverty without the government's involvement in issues such as living wage, affordable daycare, health care for children, and workplace and government policies that prioritize the family.

## Christianity in the Public Square

The church's role in the public square has been debated for centuries. Should the politics and ruling body of a nation be inherently Christian? Can morality be legislated by the government? It is possible for the church to maintain its commitment to morality and purity in Christ while meeting the material needs of the "least of these"?

It's obvious that the challenges of the twenty-first century demand church involvement with the physical needs of so many people in the United States and around the world. The body of Christ must be mobilized to enter into heart-transforming relationships with all people. We cannot sit idly by while oppression and injustice continues in the world around us.

---

### Sojourners: Christians for Justice and Peace

Jim Wallis's book *Faith Works: Lessons from the Life of an Activist Preacher* was one of my first introductions to how the gospel can be practiced among the poor. Wallis, a former student at Trinity Evangelical Divinity School in Deerfield, Illinois, founded Sojourners in 1971 with the mission to "articulate the biblical call to social justice, inspiring hope and building a movement to transform individuals, communities, the church, and the world."[128] The movement includes a monthly *Sojourners* magazine, summer Pentecost events for churches and Christian leaders to learn in community, rallies on the Mall in Washington, D.C., and a constant call to government officials for the end of poverty, the establishment of a moral budget, and other governmental reforms.

In 1995, Sojourners founded Call to Renewal, a network of churches and other groups committed to a faith-based response to end poverty and advocate for social justice. The organization has supporters from a broad spectrum of the Christian community and includes evangelicals, Catholics, Pentecostals and mainline Protestants who have united around the common cause of engaging in faith, politics and culture. Wallis has played a significant role in encouraging politicians to talk about their faith in the public square. In 2007 he organized a conversation about faith and politics with the Democratic candidates for the 2008 presidential election. Soledad O'Brien hosted the conversation that aired on CNN.[129] Wallis's work in Washington has mobilized Christians across a broad spectrum of political beliefs to raise up the biblical values of compassion and justice.

**FOR FURTHER STUDY**

*Faith Works: Lessons from the Life of an Activist Preacher* by Jim Wallis

*The Great Awakening: Reviving Faith and Politics in a Post-Religious Right America* by Jim Wallis

FOR FURTHER STUDY

*Religion in the Public Square: The Place of Religious Convictions in Political Debate* by Nicholas Wolterstorff and Robert Audi

*The Contested Public Square: The Crisis of Christianity and Politics* by Greg Forster

## Twenty-First-Century Justice Movements

*Jeffrey Sachs and* The End of Poverty. At the start of the twenty-first century, one of the books that has provoked great dialogue in secular and religious communities about the current global economic situation is *The End of Poverty: Economic Possibilities for Our Time* by Jeffrey Sachs. Sachs serves as the director of the Earth Institute at Columbia University and is a leading global economist and profes-

sor. In both 2004 and 2005 *Time* magazine named Sachs one of the top one hundred most influential leaders in the world. In 2007 a *Vanity Fair* article said:

> [Jeffrey Sachs] has done more than anyone else to move the issue of global poverty into the mainstream—to force the developed world to consider his utopian thesis: with enough focus, enough determination, and, especially, enough money, extreme poverty can finally be eradicated.[130]

Jeffrey Sachs is a dreamer, but one with solid credentials. He attended Harvard for his undergraduate and doctoral work and became a professor there after his studies.

Sachs proposed that the wealthy of the

### Bono and DATA

In the first decade of the twenty-first century the general public has shown renewed interest in global poverty. Some of the attention might be attributed to celebrities and rock stars, one of whom has caused quite a few ripples. For decades Bono, the lead singer and lyricist for the rock group U2, has increased global awareness about poverty, justice and AIDS. In 2002 he, Bobby Shriver and other activists started DATA (Debt, AIDS, Trade, Africa), an organization that calls on the governments of the world's wealthiest nations to keep their existing commitments to Africa and adopt new trade and aid policies that will help

Africans put themselves on the path to long-term prosperity and stability. Bono's message has also influenced churches.

Bono played an important role in exposing Bill and Lynne Hybels to the magnitude of the AIDS crisis in Africa. In 2006 Hybels interviewed Bono as a guest for the Leadership Summit at Willow Creek Community Church, and thousands of pastors and church leaders around the world heard the message of the effects of extreme poverty and AIDS. That same year Bono was the keynote speaker at the National Prayer Breakfast in Washington, D.C., calling churches

world, particularly developed nations, should increase their foreign aid to extreme poverty to one percent of their GDP. He argues that one percent of the wealth of the world would end extreme poverty by the year 2015. His work started a global movement "to make poverty history." Sachs says, "The basic truth is that for less than a percent of the income of the rich world nobody has to die of poverty on the planet. That's really a powerful truth."[131]

However, not all are as idealistic as Sachs. In a response to his ideas, William Easterly, formerly an economist at the World Bank and now a professor at New York University, wrote *The White Man's Burden: Why the West's Efforts to Aid the Rest Have Done So Much Ill and So Little Good*, which presents

counterarguments to Sachs's plan. He argues that the right way to fight against global poverty is to not have a plan. Those who plan, according to Easterly, raise expectations but are not accountable to seeing them be fulfilled. He recommends "searchers" who seek things that work and then implement them. (See "Poverty—Biblical Perspectives," "Poverty—Causes" and "Poverty—Cycles.")

---

**FOR FURTHER STUDY**

*The End of Poverty: Economic Possibilities for Our Time* by Jeffrey Sachs

*The White Man's Burden: Why the West's Efforts to Aid the Rest Have Done So Much Ill and So Little Good* by William Easterly

---

and individual Christians to partner with others around the world to alleviate global poverty. Bono has supported Jeffrey Sach's economic proposal through DATA and the ONE Campaign. During his speech at the prayer breakfast he affirmed Christians and churches for being involved:

> When churches started demonstrating on debt, governments listened—and acted. When churches starting organizing, petitioning, and even—that most unholy of acts today, God forbid, lobbying . . . on AIDS and global health, governments listened—and acted. I'm here today in

all humility to say: you changed minds; you changed policy; you changed the world.[132]

***Awareness exercise.*** Read through the DATA website (www.data.org) to learn more about debt relief, HIV/AIDS in Africa, trade, development assistance, the DATA Report and the G8 Group of global leaders who have committed their countries to participate in the fight against global poverty.

**FOR FURTHER STUDY**

*On the Move* by Bono

*Bono* by Michka Assayas

## The United Nations Millennium Development Goals (MDGs)

The United Nations has a history of working for peace and development on behalf of the world. In 2000 the UN adopted the United Nations Millennium Declaration, and along with 188 other nations the United States agreed to affirm the declaration.[133] This declaration manifested itself in eight Millennium Development Goals, which range from the goal of cutting extreme poverty in half, immobilizing the spread of HIV/AIDS and providing universal education by the year 2015. The MDGs were established to provide a blueprint for all of the world's countries and contributing developmental institutions to unite around a common goal and purpose. The eight Millennium Development Goals are as follows:

1. Eradicate Extreme Poverty and Hunger

   *Target:* Halve, between 1990 and 2015, the proportion of people whose income is less than $1 a day.

   *Target:* Halve, between 1990 and 2015, the proportion of people who suffer from hunger.

2. Achieve Universal Primary Education

   *Target:* Ensure that by 2015 children everywhere, boys and girls alike, will be able to complete a full course of primary schooling.

3. Promote Gender Equality and Empower Women

   *Target:* Eliminate gender disparity in primary and secondary education preferably by 2005 and in all levels of education no later than 2015.

4. Reduce Child Mortality

   *Target:* Between 1990 and 2015 reduce by two-thirds the under five mortality rate.

5. Improve Maternal Health

   *Target:* Reduce by three quarters, between 1990 and 2015, the maternal mortality ratio.

6. Combat HIV/AIDS, Malaria and Other Diseases

   *Target:* By 2015, to have halted and begun to reverse the spread of HIV/AIDS.

   *Target:* Have halted by 2015 and begun to reverse the incidence of malaria and other major diseases.

7. Ensure Environmental Sustainability

   *Target:* Integrate the principles of sustainable development into country policies and programs and reverse the loss of environmental resources.

   *Target:* Halve by 2015 the proportion of population without sustainable access to safe drinking water and basic sanitation.

8. Develop a Global Partnership for Development

   *Target:* Address the special needs of the least developed countries, landlocked countries, and small island developing states.

   *Target:* Develop an open, rule-based, predictable, non-discriminatory trading and financial system.

To find out more about the UN Millennium Development Goals visit www.un.org/millenniumgoals/.

## 2007 UN Millennium Development Goals Progress Report

Most of the UN Millennium Development Goals were set to be accomplished by the year 2015. The year 2007 marked the half-way point for the accomplishment of these goals. Below is a summary of progress during the first portion of that fifteen-year period.

1. Eradicate Extreme Poverty and Hunger

   In 1990 about a third of the worldwide population lived on less than $1 a day. By 2004 this percentage had decreased to around 19 percent of the world's population living on less than $1 a day.

   Between 1990 and 2004 the share of national consumption by the poorest fifth of the population in developing regions decreased from 4.6 to 3.9 per cent (in countries where consumption figures were unavailable, data on income were used). If trends continue the 2015 goal will be missed by around 30 million children.

2. Achieve Universal Primary Education

   In 2005, enrollment data shows about 72 million children of primary school age were not in school; 57 percent of them were girls.

3. Promote Gender Equality and Empower Women

   The participation of global women in political representation is increasing slowly. In 1990 only 13 percent of par-

liamentarians were women. By January 2007 this number increased to 17 percent worldwide.

4. Reduce Child Mortality

   In 2005 the estimated number of deaths of children before their fifth birthday from preventable causes was 10.1 million children.

5. Improve Maternal Health

   As of 2007 half a million women continue to die every year during pregnancy or childbirth, almost all of them in sub-Saharan Africa and Asia.

6. Combat HIV/AIDS, Malaria and Other Diseases

   The number of people globally dying from AIDS increased from 2.2 million in 2001 to 2.9 million in 2006.

   In 2005 the number of new cases of tuberculosis has been rising slightly worldwide due to population growth. In 2005 an estimated 8.8 million new tuberculosis cases were reported.

7. Ensure Environmental Sustainability

   The decrease of forests worldwide was 3 percent between 1990 and 2005, a decrease of 0.2 percent a year.

   By 2006 a total of about 20 million square kilometers of land and sea were under protection around the globe.

   By 2007 only 22 per cent of the

world's fisheries were sustainable, compared to 40 percent in 1975.

In order to hit the MDG goal for access to water and sanitation, 1.6 billion people would need to be affected. Current trends suggest that this goal will be missed by approximately 600 million people.

8. Develop a Global Partnership for Development

In 2001, members of the World Trade Organization (WTO) decided to complete by 2004 trade negotiations that would improve opportunities for de-

veloping countries. By 2007 no agreement had been adopted.

Since 2003 aid to the least developed countries (LDCs) was essentially stalled.

The only donors to reach or exceed the United Nations target of 0.7 percent of gross national income for development aid were Denmark, Luxembourg, the Netherlands, Norway and Sweden.

(Statistics from "The Millennium Development Goals Report 2007," United Nations.)

Jeffrey Sachs was one of the key thinkers behind the development of the United Nations Millennium Development Goals. From 2002 to 2006 Sachs was director of the UN Millennium Project and special advisor to United Nations Secretary-General Kofi Annan. He also served as the president and co-founder of Millennium Promise Alliance, a nonprofit organization that functions as the action arm working to carry out MDGs to reduce extreme poverty, disease and hunger by the year 2015. Many other partner organizations like the ONE Campaign believe that the solution to extreme poverty rests in the increase of international government funding of developing nations to one percent. Dozens of organizations around the world were formed to help implement these goals on the local, regional and national levels.

←ⱪ *Take action.* Observe October 17 as the

World Day to End Poverty (see www.oct17. org/en). Host a special awareness event or attend one of the international events already established. Research organizations that are involved (e.g., Stand Up & Take Action or the Millennium Campaign).

## ONE Campaign

When I first learned of the ONE Campaign, I was confused about what it was all about. I even went to a few events where people talked about it, white wrist bands were passed out, people signed a declaration—and I was still confused. The ONE Campaign calls people around the world to "help make poverty history." ONE is a loose confederation of individuals and organizations committed to the eradication of poverty by calling on world governments to increase the amount of aid distributed to poor nations around the world.

ONE is a campaign of over 2.4 million

## Micah Challenge

One of the most significant Christian movements working in collaboration with the ONE Campaign and the UN Millennium goals is Micah Challenge. According to its website, Micah Challenge International is a global Christian initiative working to eradicate extreme poverty worldwide. In partnership with the World Evangelical Alliance (WEA), the Micah Challenge campaign aims to deepen Christian engagement with impoverished and marginalized communities, and to influence leaders of rich and poor nations to fulfill their promise to achieve the Millennium Development Goals.

Micah Challenge has communities in thirty-two countries that are working toward raising awareness about the MDGs and mobilizing the Christian community to get involved. The organization seeks to deepen Christian engagement and to encourage the church to live out the prophetical call in Micah 6:8 "to act justly and to love mercy / and to walk humbly with your God." For more information about Micah Challenge in the United States visit www.micahchallenge.us.

↤ *Take action.* Sign the Micah Call at www.micahchallenge.org.

## The Micah Call

This is a moment in history of unique potential,
when the stated intentions of world leaders
echo something of the mind of the Biblical prophets
and the teachings of Jesus concerning the poor, and
when we have the means to dramatically reduce poverty.

We commit ourselves, as followers of Jesus,
to work together for the holistic transformation of our communities,
to pursue justice, be passionate about kindness
and to walk humbly with God.

We call on international and national decision-makers
of both rich and poor nations, to fulfill their public promise
to achieve the Millennium Development Goals
and so halve absolute global poverty by 2015.

We call on Christians everywhere to be agents of hope
for and with the poor, and to work with others
to hold our national and global leaders accountable
in securing a more just and merciful world.

people, and growing, from all fifty states and over one hundred of America's most well-known and respected nonprofit, advocacy and humanitarian organizations. ONE raises public awareness about global poverty, hunger, disease and efforts to fight such problem's in the world's poorest countries. ONE believes that allocating more of the U.S. budget toward providing basic needs like health, education, clean water and food would transform the futures of an entire generation in the world's poorest countries. The United States is not alone in this venture. The United Kingdom has a similar initiative called Make Poverty History, and ONE has counterparts all around the world advocating for the end of poverty. ONE is also linked to the international effort to achieve the Millennium Development Goals by 2015.

←« *Take action.* Sign the ONE Declaration (see www.one.org). Attend a ONE Campaign event. Wear a ONE wrist band. Join ONE on Facebook or MySpace. Sign up as a ONE Volunteer.

## 2005 G8 Summit

Every year leaders from eight of the world's richest and most powerful countries—Canada, France, Germany, Italy, Japan, Russia, the United Kingdom and the United States—gather at the G8 Summit. The first summit was held in Rambouillet, France, in 1975. Summits have been held every year since, hosted by the country that holds the rotating year-long G8 Presidency.

In 2005 the G8 Summit met in Perthshire, Scotland, to discuss the major social, political and economic conditions that contribute to poverty. This summit was unique because there was a wave of global support and advocacy building up to the event. Ten Live8 concerts were held around the world with some of the world's most famous celebrities, rock stars, musicians and artists contributing their talents in support of the global movement to make poverty history and to pressure world leaders to drop the debt of the world's poorest nations, increase and improve aid, and negotiate fair trade rules in the interest of poorer countries. It is estimated that over three billion people around the world attended the concerts, tuned in on the radio or logged in on the Internet to show their support. More than half a million Americans signed a letter to President Bush asking him to support the campaign to make poverty history.[134]

At the 2005 G8 Summit the leaders focused on two primary topics: relief to Africa and tackling the global climate change. The relief for Africa discussion attempted to move the eight countries closer to the accomplishment of the United Nation's Millennium Development Goals. Some of the highlights of their agreement include a commitment to double international aid by 2010 (which would result in an extra $50 billion worldwide and $25 billion for Africa); writing off the debt of eighteen of the world's poorest countries, most of which are in Africa (worth over $40 billion in 2005); writing off Nigeria's debt of $17 billion (the biggest single debt any Third World country has ever had); access to universal treatment for HIV/AIDS as much as possible by 2010; funding for malaria to save the lives of over 600,000 children every year; full funding to eradicate polio worldwide; provide peacekeeping troops for places in Africa like Darfur; and to make free and compulsory education and health care available to all children by the year 2015.[135] These ambitious goals had significant support from the public around the world.

## Learning from History

Today Christians must decide what role individuals, the church and faith-based organizations should play in responding to domestic and worldwide social needs. Government attempts to eradicate domestic poverty have failed. In fact, the income gap is growing between the rich and the poor (see "Poverty"). The failure of government programs could be due to (1) poor oversight and administration or (2) unwillingness to invest the necessary resources to successfully carry out programs. Christians need to wrestle with these issues to best determine how to make a difference in the years ahead.

History can help us to understand the significance of past spiritual social movements. Indeed, Jim Wallis notes that "history teaches us that the most effective social movements are also spiritual ones, which change people's thinking and attitudes by appealing to moral and religious values."[136] Charles Loring Brace,

William Lloyd Garrison and Emma Whittemore are wonderful examples of past Christ followers who fought institutional injustice in pursuit of the biblical ideal of shalom. Gary Haugen says:

> Historians have long recognized that the great achievements in humanitarian reform and social justice in the West during the nineteenth century—the abolition of slavery, prison reform, the establishment of hospitals and schools for the poor, women's rights, opposition to forced prostitution, the fight against child labor—were largely built on the faithful zeal of evangelical Christians.[137]

When Christians of the twenty-first century are obedient to the gospel and follow in the footsteps of their faithful predecessors, the challenges of global poverty, slavery, racial injustice and other forms of oppression will be overcome by the power of Christ.

---

**FOR FURTHER STUDY**

*Toward an Evangelical Public Policy: Political Strategies for the Health of the Nation* edited by Ronald J. Sider and Diane Knippers

*Shaking the System* by Tim Stafford

---

# 4

# Moving from
# Apathy to Advocacy

*"The pathway out of a nearly comatose state of boredom,
ineffectiveness and triviality lies in the struggle for justice."*

GARY A. HAUGEN, *JUST COURAGE*

Having worked in many churches and Christian communities, I have seen numerous well-intentioned Christ followers living simple lifestyles apathetic to many of the world's travesties around them. We are well-meaning and profess to love Jesus. We care about our neighbors—those we encounter on rare occasions. We give money to the church and to the poor, but often we don't know any poor people by name. I think there are many reasons for this. Perhaps we are too consumed with full schedules—TV shows, committee meetings, soccer games and taekwondo practice—or are overwhelmed because the surrounding problems seem too big to tackle. Have we become apathetic to the things that break the heart of God because of the many things that have gotten in the way? Life, it seems, keeps us from living on behalf of the gospel.

I wish moving from apathy to advocacy could be outlined in a four-step process. But the fight against injustice is specific to the time, space, region and context to which God has called each individual and community. To become an advocate for justice we must begin the spiritual process of discerning how God is calling us to get involved. Not only does each person have a unique call on his or her life but each church, ministry and community is also called to witness to the kingdom of God locally, regionally, nationally and around the world.

Some of us are called to battle against human trafficking in Southeast Asia. Others are called to support better educational programs in their local school district. Some are called to pass legislation regarding health care for the poor. Still others are called to work with disabled orphans across the globe. The beauty of the kingdom of God is that each person has a significant part to play in the body (1 Cor 12:12-31). When each part (person) of the body of Christ functions properly, Jesus' promise is fulfilled: "Very truly I tell you, all who have faith in me will do the works I have been doing, and they will do even greater things than these" (Jn 14:12).

Though social justice cannot be simplified to a step-by-step program, I have identified nine components to be consistently helpful in the movement from apathy to advocacy: prayer, awareness, lament, repentance, partnership and community, sacrifice, advocacy, evangelism, and celebration. Sometimes these elements happen in a linear progression, sometimes they happen simultaneously, and at other times they are cyclical. In any case, they are part of the ongoing process of personal transformation and spiritual growth toward Christlikeness. The Holy Spirit does the work, but in the process we must be willing to submit in humility and obedience.

While individual practice is emphasized here, each of these principles can be practiced in community. Chapter five will focus more deeply on what it might mean for Christ followers to join hands in unity in the quest for justice.

Although there is no logical progression from one component to another, some naturally follow others. For example, we can't be advocates without having some degree of awareness. Nonetheless, awareness is an ongoing process. I often find myself getting discouraged when I vacillate and feel like reverting to passivity or apathy. Until the coming of Christ, believers will struggle with grief and repentance and apathy. But the grace of God also provides glimpses of his kingdom as we taste celebration and community.

## Apathy

One dictionary definition of *apathy* is the "absence or suppression of passion, emotion, or excitement or a lack of interest or concern." Apathy leads to passivity and passivity is a great sin. I don't mean to be critical, but I believe that individuals and churches have become apathetic to the painful reality of injustices that exist around them. My assessment comes from the small numbers of people that are engaged in holistic justice work on behalf of the gospel. I am greatly encouraged, though, that the numbers seem to be growing! Nonetheless, until the entire community of believers takes up the cause of the poor and the oppressed, I think that we are guilty of apathy. According to Gary Haugen, "the pathway out of a nearly comatose state of boredom, ineffectiveness and triviality lies in the struggle for justice."[1]

Sometimes when I am traveling, I try to take time to intentionally "see" the people around me. I wonder about the stories of the men and women who join me on an elevator. I watch a young mother cross the street while holding the hand of her toddler and wonder if all of their needs are being met at home. I observe the migrant workers on the street corner waiting for work to help fill their day and put food on their family's table. It has become increasingly difficult to connect with the people we cross paths with on a daily basis. Our culture propels people into an all-consuming lifestyle that leaves little room to care for those who are not in our immediate sphere of influence. The apathy that is present isn't intentional, it is a byproduct of full agendas and busy lives.

Our frenetic lives isolate us from community. One of the primary reasons for our lack of interest in justice issues is that we are completely unaware of those who are hurting. It has become less and less obvious when a neighbor is in need. Another reason for our apathy is the enormity of the injustice that exists in the world today. Television documents daily the devastating effects of poverty, global hunger, AIDS, crime and other abuses. The result: "we do nothing is because we have lost any hope of making a difference."[2] Christians must trust that God's mercy and grace are enough to sustain them while addressing injustice.

✝ *Spiritual reflection exercise.* Apathy can mean "emotionless, without feelings, unexcited, complacency, indifferent, to ignore, disinterested, anesthetized by popular culture, a postmodern intellectual narcosis, too lazy, too busy, self-indulgent, a subconscious blocking of distressing information, and less ethically excusable than ignorance."[3] The apostle Paul says, "Hope does not put us to shame, because God's love has been poured out into our hearts through the Holy Spirit, who has been given to us" (Rom 5:5). Ask God to reveal to you if there are any places in your life where you are being apathetic. Ask God to give you more of his love for the people around you who are hurting. Spend intentional time with God seeking to know more about his heart for those people.

## Power of Prayer

N. T. Wright's book *Surprised by Hope* gives insight into how we should live in the light of the gospel:

> The mission of the church is nothing more or less than the outworking, in the power of the Spirit, of Jesus' bodily resurrection. It is the anticipation of the time when God will fill the earth with his glory, transform the old heavens and earth into the new, and raise his children from the dead to populate and rule

over the redeemed world he has made. . . . The split between saving souls and doing good in the world is not a product of the Bible or the gospel, but of the cultural captivity of both.[4]

We must be willing to shed the cultural captivity that Wright describes and be shaped by Christ's Spirit as transforming agents in the world. Prayer launches the movement from apathy to advocacy. Prayer is one of the best tools to combat injustice in the world. Jesus taught his disciples to pray, "Your kingdom come, your will be done, on earth as it is in heaven" (Mt 6:10). Sometimes it takes more courage and fortitude to submit oneself in prayer than to take any other action.

We must not be afraid to forgo movement until we have prayed and God has given clear direction. Personally, I am guilty of not praying enough. I am an initiator; I put together plans and ideas and then rally people to get them done. Sometimes the plans I make are for naught because I haven't first fallen on my knees in submission before God. Prayer allows me to know God better, which in turn helps me to better know myself. I believe it is through prayer that God gives clarity about the actions that he has called his people to take.

Prayer not only aligns our will with the will of God, it also reminds us of the source of our passions, desires and hopes. If our pursuit is biblical justice, the way God intended life to be, then prayer is the most powerful way to enter into that reality. Satan loves nothing more than deterring the mission to preach the gospel and to care for those who are hurting. Prayer provides security in our battles against the evil one.

✝ *Spiritual reflection exercise.* Pray regularly that God will open your eyes to the injustice occurring around you. Use the following prayer (or write your own) to provoke your reflection and encourage you to listen as you spend time alone with God.

> God of compassion & justice, give us eyes to see your beauty in a fresh way this week. Give us eyes to see it and hearts to appreciate it. And then give us eyes to see where that beauty is being threatened. Give us the will and the wisdom to protect it. Give us the courage to fight for it. And bond us all more

deeply into a community of faith so that together we can be your body, your flesh and blood at work in this world. Thank you for this privilege. Amen.[5]

↩ *Take action.* Host a prayer event for a small group of friends, your church or your community. Ask God to make you aware of the most pressing needs in your community and how you and your group can get involved to make a difference.

**FOR FURTHER STUDY**

*Daring to Draw Near* by John White

*Prayer: Finding the Heart's True Home* by Richard Foster

## Concerts of Prayer, Greater New York

The Concerts of Prayer in Greater New York were inspired by Jonathan Edwards who coined the term "concerts of prayer" during the First Great Awakening. Two centuries later Mac Pier, an InterVarsity Christian Fellowship staff worker in New York City, was inspired by colleague Rick Richardson, who had gathered a thousand people in Chicago's Moody Church in 1987, to continue the movement by gathering New York Christians to "seek the peace and prosperity of the city. . . . Pray to the LORD for it" (Jer 29:7). The first prayer gathering was held in 1988 with more than seventy churches in attendance.

Throughout the 1990s Christian leaders and pastors continued to be a part of the movement and met at least yearly to

pray for the city, the region, the nation and the world. By the turn of the millennium, the murder rate in New York City had dropped 70 percent, and New York became the safest city of more than a million people in the United States.[6] The ministry was incorporated in 1997 as The Concerts of Prayer Greater New York (www.copgny.org) and continues to promote unity and community transformation through prayer.

**FOR FURTHER STUDY**

*The Power of a City at Prayer: What Happens When Churches Unite for Renewal* by Mac Pier and Katie Sweeting

*Spiritual Leadership in the Global City* by Mac Pier

## Awareness (Truth)

God is the god of truth. The prophet Isaiah confirms this:

> Justice is driven back,
>     and righteousness stands at a distance;
> truth has stumbled in the streets,
>     honesty cannot enter.
> Truth is nowhere to be found,
>     and whoever shuns evil becomes
>         a prey.
> The Lord looked and was displeased
>     that there was no justice. (Is 59:14-15)

Awareness is the process of coming to terms with God's truth. God is the light shining in the midst of darkness; he's the God of revelation and goodness. There is nothing in him that is dishonest, corrupt or deceitful. Psalm 139 addresses some of God's attributes and describes his relationship to darkness:

> If I say, "Surely the darkness will hide me
>     and the light become night around
>         me,"
> even the darkness will not be dark to
>     you;
>     the night will shine like the day,
>     for darkness is as light to you.
> (Ps 139:11-12)

One of the ways that God graciously moves people out of apathy and closer to advocacy is by opening their eyes to what is happening in the world. God is light in the midst of darkness! Many of the great social reform movements began when people were exposed to a truth that had otherwise been ignored.[7]

Consider how truth affected John Newton, the slave ship owner who wrote the hymn *Amazing Grace* after being convicted of the pain and agony that he caused. In describing the American abolition movement Tim Stafford says:

> So what launched American antislavery? Truth. A penetrating truth broke through American lethargy, first with a few people here and there, eventually with large numbers. The truth was simple: slavery is sin. Today the revelation that slavery is sin seems obvious, on a level with murder is sin. But at the time, it revolutionized the discussion.[8]

The contemporary church must ask God where we need to see the light. We need him to help us to not be apathetic but to see, to help us not to be immobilized but to move forward in cautious action for the sake of the gospel. As we become more aware of the truth and what is close to the heart of God, we will become move alive, motivated and loving followers of Jesus.

Awareness is part of the education process; it breaks down physical and spiritual barriers. Some of the most powerful awareness experiences are simple relationship-building opportunities between communities. These experiences bring the community of Christ together across racial, gender and socioeconomic barriers. People are given the opportunity to share their stories, experiences and perspectives. Misperceptions are corrected as the body of Christ worships together in community. This is never an easy process, but through the presence of the Holy Spirit it can be incredibly healing!

Awareness can also be a disheartening. Minority groups are usually stereotyped by the dominant culture, being evaluated by a set of standards that are unrealistic. In *The Next Evangelicalism: Freeing the Church from Western Cultural Captivity*, Soong-Chan Rah says:

> White evangelicals marginalize the African American Christian community by embracing only the stories of white Christianity and continuing to fail to acknowledge the contributions of significant black Christian leaders. The Western, white captivity of the church allows for the telling of one story, the story of the celebrating white community, while ignoring the stories of other communities of suffering.[9]

Regardless of our skin color, part of the awareness process is coming to grips with the way that our cultural group has responded to other people groups. For whites, awareness means admitting and understanding the significant benefits of being the dominant group. The history of whites in the United States has been rife with the oppression and subjugation of people of color. Nonwhites too must go through a process of awareness. Minority groups are often unwilling to see things from others' perspectives. Acknowledging where disparity has been expressed within society is a critical component of awareness. Sometimes awareness means gaining deeper understanding of history. Other times awareness means owning up to the ways we have responded to injustice sinfully rather than with love and fortitude.

People can spend eternity stuck in the process of becoming aware. It is tempting to be theoretically involved, seeking to know more, philosophizing and waiting to figure things out before beginning down the road of action and advocacy. We must be willing to pursue awareness without being immobilized by the process.

↩❧ **Take action.** A great way to invite your friends, family and community on the journey to awareness is by starting a blog, an online forum similar to a diary or journal. Start a blog to inform your community how God is teaching you about compassion and justice. If you need help getting started, visit the blog "Compassion in Politics: Christian Social Justice, Non-Profits, and Life Theology" (compassioninpolitics.wordpress.com). There are a number of free blog sites available on the Internet (e.g., www.blogger.com).

↩❧ **Take action.** Consider a long-distance run or biking event to raise awareness for a cause. In 2008, six students from North Park University set out on an eleven-week bike trip from San Francisco to Boston to raise money for two international projects, while discussing issues of compassion, mercy and justice with Covenant churches along the way. Traveling fifty to seventy miles each day, these students raised awareness about social justice and the things that are close to the heart of God.[10]

## Lament (Love)

Mother Teresa wisely said, "Following Jesus is simple, but not easy. Love until it hurts, and then love more."[11] As we seek to raise awareness in our communities, we must do so with humility and brokenness. The only way to become sensitive to injustice is to allow our hearts to be broken by the things that break the heart of God. This may seem unrealistic—for how can our limited spirits grasp the magnitude of the things that God cares about? We must rest in the promise that God will sustain us as we seek to become more like him (1 Cor 10:13).

Most of us have a strong aversion to grief. We will do almost anything rather than entering into what John of the Cross called the "dark night of the soul." Yet this is a profoundly significant part of our journey. The process of grief—allowing our hearts to be broken on behalf of those who are suffering and hurting—is really the process of love. We are to love as Christ does, so much so that we carry the pain and agony of our brothers and sisters who are hurting.

We are told that Christ first showed us compassion so that we might show compassion toward others:

> Praise be to the God and Father of our Lord Jesus Christ, the Father of compassion and the God of all comfort, who comforts us in all our troubles, so that we can comfort those in any trouble with the comfort we ourselves receive from God. (2 Cor 1:3-4)

This is not "feel good" love. Instead, this type of love takes on the very nature of God and is willing to *suffer with* others who are hurting. In order to allow our hearts to be broken, we must be willing to build intimate relationships with the entire community of God, regardless of how different our backgrounds and personal stories. There is a deep void within us when we only hear part of the story. Because of their suffering, the theology and practice of Christian communities of color are deeply rooted in compassion. As we discover and listen to marginalized voices, we will be transformed to more closely reflect the nature of Christ Jesus, the suffering Servant.

The lament that we experience for the downtrodden is motivated by love. Even Mother Teresa, the Saint of the Gutters, experienced this type of grief on behalf of others.[12] If not given over to God, our lamentation can easily lead to despair or hopelessness. Despair can short-circuit and derail people right back to apathy. Mother Teresa is a wonderful example of one who, in the midst of deep lament, did not abandon her faith or ministry. Rather, she allowed God to break her heart for the poorest of the poor, and through her God did amazing work.

---

**FOR FURTHER STUDY**

*Mother Teresa: Come Be My Light* by Mother Teresa and Brian Kolodiejchuk

*Dark Night of the Soul* by John of the Cross

---

⚑ *Spiritual reflection exercise.* Read a story or watch a movie about someone or a group of people who have experienced injustice. Even better, listen to the story of someone you know who has been oppressed. As you learn about the experience, ask God to give you a heart of love and compassion toward that individual or group. Reflect on God's heart toward those who suffer. Ask God to give a greater capacity to love the way that he loves.

## Repentance

The Gospel of John tells us, "In those days John the Baptist came, preaching in the wilderness of Judea and saying, 'Repent, for the kingdom of heaven has come near' " (Mt 3:1-2). Repentance occurs when we acknowledge the truth of our condition and frailty before God. We must come to a place of accepting the ways we have contributed, whether consciously or not, to the oppression of others. Sometimes we must repent for the sin of omission or the lack of willingness to get involved. Sometimes we must repent for arrogance or overconfidence in thinking we know how to solve the problem. Some communities must repent for attitudes, mindsets and cultures that do not glorify to God. Other communities must repent for anger, frustration and giving up. Whether we are the oppressor or the oppressed, we contribute to the problem. Repentance and taking responsibility are absolutely necessary for healing and shalom. Repentance is necessary in order for justice to prevail.

Some of us struggle with the idea that we have contributed toward injustice. Many whites are reticent to admit their skin color provides benefits, privileges and opportunities. Regarding the unjust experiences of people of color, I have heard whites say, "Why don't they just get over it?" Such statements reflect ignorance and lack of understanding. It is easy for whites to push the experiences of minorities under the carpet.

As Christians who are a part of dominant culture, whites need to appreciate how they have benefited from the sins of their ancestors, whether directly or indirectly. Biblically, people are called to repent not only of their own sins but of the sins of their predecessors as well (e.g., Lev 26:40; Neh 9:2; Is 65:7). This process seems repulsive to many white believers. Is it pride? One of my greatest concerns in breaking down barriers within the Christian community is the white defensiveness during conversations about race, poverty and gender.

Not only do whites need to repent of passive participation in an oppressive system, they also need to repent of ways they have closed their eyes and ignored the pain and suffering of brothers and sisters. When we are standing before God in heaven, I don't think that the Lord will be pleased with "But God, I didn't know" or "I didn't see." My prayer is that God will gently and graciously open all of our eyes, and we will ask him to forgive us for the lack of love and even hatred entangled around our hearts. We need to ask God to transform us and make us completely whole by his grace.

But I don't believe repentance is only for the dominant culture. Many people of color, women, the poor and others who have experienced injustice have responded in anger, which is not honoring to God. As Eleanor Roosevelt said, "When will our consciences grow so tender that we will act to prevent human misery rather than avenge it?"[13] Certainly righteous anger is a part of the equation, but too often people have taken things into their own hands rather than allowing God to be our avenger. We often use our anger as an excuse to not love our brothers and sisters in Christ who are misled, even allowing it to play a role in our oppression.

Many people of color need to repent of their anger. When oppression occurs, righteous anger is a completely legitimate response. However, there is a fine line between righteous anger and hatred. Communities of color must ask whether their attitude toward whites is one of love and forgiveness. I don't think this means

## Journey Toward
## Racial Righteousness

I have been a part of numerous racial reconciliation conversations—intentional opportunities for people of different races to sit around a table or a meal, to share their stories and personal experiences, and to seek healing for past hurts and wrongs. Some of these conversations have gone remarkably well. Some have been filled with anger. Some end well; others end without much resolution. I believe God calls all believers to have these kinds of discussions, to listen to and learn from one another. Nonetheless, I always get a pit in my stomach before entering into this type of dialogue. These discussions are never easy.

In January 2006 I attended a special luncheon as a part of a denominational conference whose theme was "Journey to Racial Righteousness."[14] While I was eager to connect with friends, I was not looking forward to having another "reconciliation" conversation. I hesitantly sat down at a table and introduced myself to others who were present. Across the table was a middle-aged Caucasian man. To my right was Wilson Herrera, a leader of Hispanic Ministries for the Evangelical Covenant Church.

As our lunch conversation continued under the direction of group facilitators, we began to share stories with one another about our past experiences with race. After a few minutes the Caucasian gentleman told us about picking on and teasing a Hispanic boy he went to grammar school with. He called him names and made fun of him because he was the only student in the class who wasn't white. As the man continued with his story, tears slowly started to stream down his cheeks. From across the table, Wilson Herrera looked at the man and said, "Do you want to ask forgiveness to me on behalf of that Hispanic child?" The man, continuing to be deeply moved by emotion said, "I am so sorry for what I have done. I am so very sorry." Wilson put his arms around the man and said, "You are forgiven."

The entire table entered into that moment. We cried together and tasted a small piece of the love of Christ, the mercy of his forgiveness and the power of his reconciliation. The community of Christ needs to be reconciled to one another. In order for that healing to take place, we must be willing to sit down at the table. For more information about Journey to Racial Righteousness programs offered by the Evangelical Covenant Church visit www.covchurch.org/cmj/ministry/rr/the-invitation-to-racial-righteousness.

ignoring oppression or not standing up to it. Nonetheless, repentance is terribly important for communities that have been oppressed. Resentment can easily seep into relationships and corporate attitudes. Unrepentance can easily lead individuals and communities away from the direction God would take them.

In *The Wounded Heart* Christian psychologist Dan Allender writes about repentance and adult survivors of sexual abuse. When I first read the book I was angered that he calls victims to repentance (not for contributing to the abuse that occurred but for their response to it). But as I reflected, I was reminded that we have all sinned and fallen short of the glory of God (Rom 3:23), and that apart from Christ, our response to injustice will not naturally be full of love and grace.[15]

We are all human. Though we want to respond to bad situations in ways that are glorifying to God, we all blow it sometimes. Communities get caught up in passion and energy, and often pursue directions that lead to selfish gain and disobedience. Seeking forgiveness for actions, thoughts and ideas—small or large—where the ways of God are not being pursued opens the door for healing, redemption and ultimately the peace of God (shalom).

### FOR FURTHER STUDY

*Repentance in Christian Theology* edited by Mark Boda and Gordon Smith

*The Walk of Repentance: A 24 Week Guide to Personal Transformation* by Steve Gallagher

 

✢ *Spiritual reflection exercise.* The prophet Amos declared:

Seek the Lord and live,

or he will sweep through the house of
    Joseph like a fire;
it will devour them,
    and Bethel will have no one to quench it.
There are those who turn justice into
    bitterness
and cast righteousness to the ground.
(Amos 5:6-7)

Did the section on repentance provoke you or stir any emotions within you? Reflect on your beliefs about forgiveness and repentance. Do you believe that confession is a necessary component in your relationship with God? Find a quiet and comfortable place—in your home or out in nature—and be still before God. Ask him to meet with you. Ask him to shed light on any ways where you have participated in causing or inflicting injustice.

Some things to consider: What actions do you need to repent of? Ask God to shed light on a time when you may have been the recipient of injustice. Was your response glorifying to God? Were there ways that you responded that were dishonoring to him? Repent. Ask for forgiveness for the ways your actions, thoughts and beliefs did not honor Christ. Ask for wisdom about how your future behaviors could be more honoring to God. What steps do you need to take to allow God to transform you and change your heart? Ask that God would have his way with you, forgiving you and continuing to transform you more into his image.

### Partnerships and Community

In your majesty ride forth victoriously
    in the cause of truth, humility and
       justice;

let your right hand achieve awesome
deeds. (Ps 45:4)

As a new wave of interest in social justice
sweeps through the evangelical church, the
people who have for decades advocated social
change must not be ignored. Often our new-
found passion and excitement for justice
bursts forth with new ideas and strategies for
change that ignore the experts in the field
who have humbly been toiling the soil for
years and years. And sometime new initiatives unintentionally reinforce oppressive systems. The church should get to know and
understand those who have been faithfully
serving long before *justice* became a Christian
buzzword! We must manifest a posture of humility for true partnership and relationships
to grow and develop.

Partnership is an essential component of
successful ministry. The church should build
sustainable partnerships with others—churches, nonprofits, change-seeking organizations—taking a supportive role. That is,
Christians should support initiatives that have
already been established, developed and are
working toward effective change.

I learned a lot about partnership in my
ministry experiences at Willow Creek. It is
easy for big churches, or churches with influence, to unwittingly trample on smaller
grassroots organizations that are working to
bring about effective change from the bottom
up. We must not bulldoze anyone in our justice efforts!

Sometimes the size and resources of a large
church can be burdensome for smaller organizations. It is rare to see a large church humble
itself and give voice to the very people it is trying to help. I don't think that most churches

are intentionally paternalistic, but this is a trap
that churches readily fall into. Paternalism occurs when an organization, group or individual acts like the parent of another individual or
group. The paternalistic organization assumes
it knows what is best for the recipients and
therefore imposes its will on them. Their good
intentions often produce devastating results.

The roots of paternalism come from a false
theology, often the "theology of empire." A
theology of empire assumes that people with
the most capital, resources and determination
will be successful. Empire theology is filled
with rulers and despots. Because of their
power, affluence and influence, the nations of
the Northern Hemisphere often fall into this
type of thinking. We must understand how
developed countries embrace and use the theology of empire.

This shouldn't surprise us. Even Jesus' disciples exhibited empire thinking. Along with
many other Jews, they thought the Messiah
would use power to overthrow all the rulers
of the day. We see glimpses of this when the
disciples asked Jesus who would be first in the
kingdom of heaven. In response, Jesus said,
"Truly I tell you, unless you change and become like little children, you will never enter
the kingdom of heaven" (Mt 18:3).

Theology based on the kingdom of God is
the opposite of empire theology. Chap Clark
and Kara Powell describe the kingdom:

> What do we mean by the kingdom of
> God? We mean that which is under the
> rule of God, our King. The kingdom is
> not a geographical place but rather the
> order of perfect love, righteousness,
> justice, and peace that offers hope to
> our broken world. As others are touched

by the kingdom, they are transformed by the King's love and power.[16]

The theology that God has called Christians to practice is not based on empire but on his kingdom, which reorients our way of thinking.

The kingdom turns the wisdom of the world upside down: the first will be last and the last first (Mt 19:30); those who lose their lives for the sake of the gospel will gain life (Mt 10:39); Jesus' followers are called to be like little children (Mt 18:3) and to imitate him who "did not come to be served, but to serve, and to give his life as a ransom for many" (Mt 20:28).

Reconciliation occurs when Christ's followers humbly partner with individuals, groups and organizations who are advocates of justice. The kingdom theology of repentance and love shapes the relationships of people standing together against injustice in the context of biblical community.

**FOR FURTHER STUDY**

*Exclusion and Embrace: A Theological Exploration of Identity, Otherness, and Reconciliation* by Miroslav Volf

*Dynamic Diversity: Bridging Class, Age, Race and Gender in the Church* by Bruce Milne

## Word and Deed Network

The Word and Deed Network (WDN) of Evangelicals for Social Action (ESA) is a ministry that is committed to "connecting churches to make a difference."[17] Its name is based on Paul's instruction in Colossians 3:17: "And whatever you do, whether in word or deed, do it all in the name of the Lord Jesus, giving thanks to God the Father through him." For the network, this includes evangelism, the restoration of communities and working toward social transformation. Partnership includes five main types of networking opportunities: (1) geographically based, (2) denominationally based, (3) urban-suburban partnerships, (4) global partnerships, and (5) organizational partnerships. The Word and Deed Network has online resources and tools to help equip ministries (www .worddeednetwork.org).

Al Tizon, the director of the Word and Deed Network, is the former lead pastor at Berkeley Covenant Church and has served all over the world doing work in community development, ministry with street children, and church leadership on behalf of those living in poverty or oppression. Tizon is committed to encouraging and developing healthy partnerships that will better equip the local church and the body of Christ to be advocates of evangelism, compassion and justice.

**FOR FURTHER STUDY**

*Linking Arms, Linking Lives* by Al Tizon, Ron Sider, John Perkins and Wayne Gordon

*Transformation After Lausanne: Radical Evangelical Mission in Global-Local Perspective* by Al Tizon

## Sacrifice

When the community of God seeks shalom, sacrifice is a necessary component. Perhaps we need to sacrifice our expectations or the belief that things should be a certain way. Perhaps it is money, material resources, power or privilege. God sometimes calls his people to sacrifice righteous anger in pursuit of unity and reconciliation. When you are called to practice justice, there will be some sacrifice along the way. Do not be surprised when the road is hard to travel. Jesus said to his disciples, "Whoever wants to be my disciple must deny themselves and take up their cross and follow me" (Mt 16:24). The road to justice requires great sacrifice, but also offers great rewards.

**FOR FURTHER STUDY**

*The Cost of Commitment* by John White

*Can You Drink the Cup?* by Henri Nouwen

## Advocacy

In the New Testament, Jesus promised when he left he would send a helper to his followers: "The Advocate, the Holy Spirit, whom the Father will send in my name, will teach you all things and will remind you of everything I have said to you" (Jn 14:26). Christians are also told that Jesus is their advocate with the Father in heaven (1 Jn 2:1). An advocate is someone who supports or defends someone else. Just as Jesus and the Holy Spirit are our advocates, we are called to advocate for one another on earth.

The Scriptures are clear about our call to stand up for the poor and the oppressed. Christians are to express our faith by being intercessors and advocates for the least in society. Advocates are change agents who work on behalf of others who might not have a voice or the power to change their unfortunate circumstances. Advocates are people who help secure justice for those who are experiencing injustice. Advocacy can take several different forms: spiritual advocacy, social advocacy, legal advocacy and political advocacy.

*1. Spiritual advocacy.* Spiritual advocacy parallels the role that the Holy Spirit plays as an intercessor between Christians and the Trinity.

> The Spirit helps us in our weakness. We do not know what we ought to pray for, but the Spirit himself intercedes for us through wordless groans. And he who searches our hearts knows the mind of the Spirit, because the Spirit intercedes for God's people in accordance with the will of God. (Rom 8:26-27)

Similarly, people can be intercessors and spiritual advocates on behalf of each another. This type of advocacy should not be minimized. Spiritual advocacy believes that the struggles of justice are not just against flesh and blood, but are "against the rulers, against the authorities, against the powers of this dark world and against the spiritual forces of evil in the heavenly realms" (Eph 6:12). Spiritual advocates pray for people who are in distress, suffering and experiencing oppression. Spiritual advocacy can be expressed through prayer, worship and other spiritual disciplines.

*Spiritual reflection exercise.* In Genesis 18, Abraham plays the role of spiritual advo-

## Prison Entrepreneurship Program

Catherine Rohr, a guest speaker at the 2008 Leadership Summit at Willow Creek, caused quite a stir. Her story is one of great sacrifice and also great reward. A graduate of Haas School of Business at the University of California, Berkeley, Catherine was very successful working in venture capital and private equity. But her life changed when she encountered the men incarcerated in the Texas prison system. She explains:

When I went on that first prison tour . . . I really thought that I was going to see these wild caged animals. When I arrived to prison and saw human beings who were just as much in need of grace as I am, I was humbled, more than ashamed, and really saw the ugliness in my own heart.[18]

Catherine discovered that upon release former inmates had great difficulty finding work because they had few transferable skills. Moved by the Spirit and her experience, Catherine says "I starting asking God to show me how I could combine my new heart for injustice with my business skills and my network."[19] Catherine decided to sacrifice her corporate job, stable paycheck and her home to make a difference. As a follower of Jesus, she was willing to sacrifice it all. She and her husband cashed in their 401(k)s, paid the necessary penalties and moved to Texas. On their first night in their new home, they were robbed of everything they had brought with them. A church community took a love offering and helped the Rohrs get back on their feet to restart their life.[20]

Once back on their feet, the Rohrs invested their life savings in a nonprofit start-up to serve incarcerated men. In May 2004 Catherine started Prison Entrepreneurship Program (PEP) to equip incarcerated men wth skills of business and entrepreneurship.[21] As of July 1, 2008, 370 men have graduated from the PEP program with a recidivism rate of less than five percent. Within a month of release, more than 97 percent of PEP graduates are employed. Utilizing over one thousand executive volunteers and more than four hundred volunteers with MBA degrees, PEP is on target to reaching their 2012 goal of one thousand graduates per year and more than five hundred graduate entrepreneurs.[22]

cate on behalf of the people in Sodom. Abraham says to God: "Will you sweep away the righteous with the wicked? What if there are fifty righteous people in the city? Will you really sweep it away and not spare the place for the sake of the fifty righteous people in it?" (Gen 18:23-24). God responds and declares his willingness to spare the city for fifty righteous. Abraham continues to advocate and God hears his cry on behalf of the righteous, saying even "For the sake of ten, I will not destroy it" (v. 32).

Identify people group who you know are not receiving justice. Step into the role of spiritual advocate on behalf of these people. Start by praying for them every day for a week. Ask God to send his Spirit on them and to minister to their hearts. Ask God to intercede on their behalf and to alleviate their pain and suffering. Pray that he would reveal himself in the situation and give you wisdom if he is calling you to take action in another way.

**2. Social advocacy.** Social advocacy can be the most difficult because it means being willing to stand up to people in our immediate social sphere of influence—friends, family, peers, and colleagues—when derogatory or racist comments are made about others. Social advocacy raises awareness about ignorance and misperceptions and stands in the gap on behalf of those in society who are often overlooked or underrepresented.

↤ *Take action.* Have you ever been in a situation in your work place, your family or even at church when someone has said something that dishonors another person or group of people? Make a commitment to God to be a voice, an advocate, for those who would be hurt by harsh words. Prepare yourself with possible responses when such a situation arises.[23]

**3. Legal advocacy.** Legal advocacy is one of the ways that Christians can stand in the gap on behalf of those whose rights have been violated. Legal advocacy is when someone represents children or adults within the legal system. The National Organization for Vic-

tim Assistance (NOVA), the Court Appointed Advocates for Children and other organizations provide legal advocacy for children, victims of sexual assault, and others who have experienced injustices. There are also advocacy organizations that work to rehabilitate criminals and offending parties.

↤ *Take action.* Many programs take volunteers as advocates for abused children. Court Appointed Special Advocates for Children (CASA) is a good example. CASA is a network of over 59,000 volunteers that speak on behalf of abused and neglected children in court (see www.nationalcasa.org). Become a volunteer with CASA or a similar organization that practices legal advocacy.

**4. Political advocacy.** Through political advocacy we work to right unjust aspects of our governmental structure through the political system. Many social problems are deeply rooted in the structure of government. People can advocate for systemic change by voting, visiting or writing government representatives on both the state and federal level, and publicly addressing issues that we believe are close to the heart of God. Many Christian organizations, including Bread for the World (www.bread.org) and Call to Renewal (www.calltorenewal.org), use political advocacy as their primary mechanism of working toward social justice.

↤ *Take action.* Political advocacy can be as simple as writing a letter or sending an e-mail to your state representative or senator. Many justice organizations provide sample letters or e-mails to use as a template. Often handwritten letters, phone calls and personal visits have the most impact, but no action is too small to get started. Contact your congressional representative and use your voice as a political advocate.

## Advocates for Christ

The most important advocacy is sharing the gospel of Christ. The gospel is shared by the study, reflection and proclamation of the Scriptures, and by the way that the followers of Christ live the gospel in action. Francis of Assisi aptly said, "Preach the Gospel, if necessary use words."[24] Regardless of the type of advocacy pursued, God has called all of his followers to be change agents and witnesses to the kingdom of God. Restlessly seek after his kingdom by being advocates on behalf of the poor and the oppressed for the sake of the gospel of Christ.

---

### Law ElderLaw

I was first introduced to Rick Law through a writing project for *Prism* magazine, the magazine for Evangelicals for Social Action. Rick, a Christian attorney in Aurora, Illinois, started a firm, Law ElderLaw, to provide legal assistance to those struggling with disability or special needs. People with disabilities might be young and physically challenged or elderly suffering with dementia. Rick is passionate about his work and faith.

Law ElderLaw specifically focuses on responding to the needs of families who have a loved one with a disability. There are exorbitant costs, intense emotional stresses and other unknown factors that significantly affect families who are providing long-term care for a disabled loved one. Rick has committed his life to giving legal counsel to the elderly, many of whom are widows, in need of care. About his work and ministry Rick says:

> I aspire to believe and to act in a consistent way with the "way of Christ." . . . The bottom line for me is that I must lead and act authentically and consistently with the Golden Rule, to demonstrate both faith and action, and to:
>
> 1. Love God; and
> 2. Act in love to benefit others

It's not really a "religious thing" after all. Our law practice is focused on the issues of life, death (whether quick or lingering), disability, health care, caregiver support, estate planning, veterans benefits for the over 65, Medicaid, and healthy spouse survival issues. My work as the lead attorney of Law ElderLaw, LLP is a calling to practice law as "faith at work." This combination of faith and action improves lives on both sides of all of our relationships.[25]

Many resources and materials are available at the Law ElderLaw website www.lawelderlaw.com.

**FOR FURTHER STUDY**

*Just Courage: God's Great Expedition for the Restless Christian* by Gary Haugen

*Hope Lives: A Journey of Restoration* by Amber Van Schooneveld and Wess Stafford

## Evangelism

Jesus said, "A new command I give you: Love one another. As I have loved you, so you must love one another. By this everyone will know that you are my disciples, if you love one another" (Jn 13:34-35). Engaging in social justice is the greatest evangelistic opportunity the church has in the twenty-first century. The world will see the love of Christ expressed through the actions of his followers who diligently seek justice. Many people who do not have a relationship with God are willing to serve alongside the church when the church is offering compassionate care and pursuing justice. Scripture says that the world will know the Christ's followers by the love they express. Cornel West, scholar, pastor and civil rights advocate says, "Justice is what love looks like in public."[26]

The church cannot afford to idly sit by and allow injustice to occur. Rather, the people of God must rise up and stamp out the injustice that exists all the while pursuing the shalom of God, which is expressed in Christ's perfect love. Then the world will see the Word made flesh, the living Christ, manifested in love and justice and perfect shalom.

**FOR FURTHER STUDY**

*Reimagining Evangelism* by Rick Richardson

*A Credible Witness: Reflections on Power, Evangelism and Race* by Brenda Salter McNeil

## Celebration

There are times when God allows us to experience brief moments of his kingdom being manifested on the earth. These are cause for great celebration and joy. You cannot overlook the spiritual discipline of celebration. Jesus said, "When you give a banquet, invite the poor, the crippled, the lame, the blind, and you will be blessed. Although they cannot repay you, you will be repaid at the resurrection of the righteous" (Lk 14:13-14). Rejoice in the assurance that one day every tear will be wiped from the eyes of those who are hurting. There will be no more death, mourning, crying or pain—for the old order of things will have passed away (Rev 21:4) and the kingdom of God will be here.

Celebrating is just as important as prayer, awareness, lament, repentance, partnership, advocacy and evangelism. Celebration is worship—acknowledging the character and nature of God—that he is good! He is all-knowing, all-powerful, ever-present and our Deliverer. Celebration does not always come at the end of the journey but should be experienced as little victories and successes occur along the way. We experience great tension when we witness grief and suffering. However, followers of Christ may celebrate in the fact that this is not the way that God intends the world to be. One day Christ will return in all of his power and glory to make things right and his shalom will return to earth once again.

**FOR FURTHER STUDY**

*Celebration of Discipline: The Path to Spiritual Growth* by Richard Foster

*Joy* by Calvin Miller

✝ *Spiritual reflection exercise.* A candle and some type of notebook are necessary for this exercise. When something occurs that encourages you along your journey toward justice, set aside time to thank God for the victory. Write in your notebook the date and what you experienced. Keep track of big and small victories. When you write in your notebook, light your victory candle and say a prayer of thanksgiving for the way that the Lord is working in your life. Periodically light the candle and review what you have written in your notebook. Celebrate the victories that God has given you.

When you are discouraged, ask for God to reveal himself to you and to encourage you in your pursuit of justice.[27]

> He will not quarrel or cry out;
> 　no one will hear his voice in the
> 　　streets.
> A bruised reed he will not break,
> 　and a smoldering wick he will not
> 　　snuff out,
> till he leads justice to victory.
> 　In his name the nations will put
> 　　their hope. (Mt 12:19-21)

# 5

# Solutions to Injustice

*On the issue of who's primarily responsible for addressing poverty, two-thirds of Americans (64 percent) consider it to be the government's responsibility. Nearly one out of five people (18 percent) say it's the primary responsibility of each individual citizen to address poverty. Much smaller numbers of people say it's the duty of churches (4 percent), nonprofit organizations (4 percent), or businesses (3 percent) to take the lead on dealing with poverty.*

DAVID KINNAMAN, "DO WE GIVE A RIP ABOUT THE POOR?"

Various methodologies are offered to solve systemic injustice and to provoke effective change. For example, providing food or teaching people how to farm and cultivate land will certainly help mitigate hunger. But what will stop others from stealing the food once it has been harvested? Nonprofits are doing good humanitarian work around the world; however, material change is not enough. Change must go deeper. It must happen on a spiritual level. Lasting and effective change comes when the soul is transformed and true community is pursued. When powerful people are transformed they no longer threaten, steal and oppress their neighbors.

What does holistic and genuine change look like? Some people believe that change happens as a result of personal involvement (e.g., compassion movements of previous centuries in the United States). Others believe that government intervention is the most successful solution to the problem of injustice. Some believe that corporate compassion should be left to professional counselors, social workers, lawyers and others who have chosen to vocationally engage injustice. Still others believe it is the responsibility of private nongovernmental organizations (NGOs) and nonprofits to respond to poverty, homelessness, lack of housing and limited access to health care.

While all of these engage injustice and advocate for justice, they leave out the most important factor—the presence and participation of individual Christians and the larger contribution of the church. When Christians respond to who we are called to be, bearing witness to the kingdom of God and the return of our Savior, the world will be changed.

## FOR FURTHER STUDY

*unChristian* by David Kinnaman and Gabe Lyons

*Everything Must Change: Jesus, Global Crises, and a Revolution of Hope* by Brian McLaren

## Personal Involvement

Throughout the history of the United States, compassionate and kind individuals have shared their resources with those who are poor and suffering. For centuries, in the history of compassion in the United States, it was believed that it is the role of individuals within the community to care for their neighbor and others around them. People knew one another, knew about each other's needs, and helped care for each other. As society evolved, there has been less personal connection between members of a community. Increased separation and a lack of mutual responsibility have increased the gap between people who live in close proximity.

Individualism is running rampant in America today. And individuals' needs, wants and desires are the bottom line. Personal comfort is the goal. Sacrifice is a foreign concept. Isolation is commonplace; we no longer connect with people in our immediate community.

Members of agrarian societies recognize their dependence on others. But in the urbanized United States, such interdependence is neither obvious nor pursued. As other solutions to injustice are considered—including the government and NGOs—we must remember the significant role that individuals have played and continue to play. Regarding this, Marvin Olasky observes that some people

> argue that the free market itself solves all problems of poverty. The more conventional approach stresses government intervention to restructure economic relations. But neither kind emphasizes the crucial role of truly compassionate individuals and groups in the long fight against poverty.

Neither goes beyond smug rejection or neglect of pre-twentieth-century moral understandings.[1]

Though solutions shouldn't stop at the individual level, we cannot discredit the influence that individuals have at bringing about meaningful change.

Small actions by a single person or a group of people can lead to great change. Over time a small brook eventually carves a deep channel in the bedrock.[2] Individuals can make a significant difference. Patience, persistence and faith are the necessary components to keep people in the game as they work to overturn wrongs and to bring about justice. Faithful individuals also need community support and encouragement along the way. While God calls each of us to individually work on behalf of justice, he does not call us to labor alone. Rather, his greatest purpose is that people would unite around the common vision of his gospel, working together in unity.[3] Individual acts of faithfulness are all the more powerful and effective when they occur in community. On the journey, pray that God would bring like-minded people to walk alongside you and to help carry the burdens that advocates of justice face.

←* ***Take action.*** Take a couple of people to meet with civic leaders in your community. Tell the leaders that you are interested in learning about the immediate needs of those who live around you. Set the stage so that they are not expecting you to jump in and fix any of the problems. The core idea is to "underpromise and overdeliver"—but listen to what the leaders have to say. After the meeting, as a group pray and discuss if God might be calling you to get involved.

## Breakthrough Urban Ministries

Chicago's Breakthrough Urban Ministries has an inspiring story (see www.breakthroughministries.com). In 1992 Arloa Sutter and members of the First Evangelical Free Church on the northside of Chicago began to respond to homeless people in the community. Arloa, prompted by the desire to make a difference, started a ministry through the simple act of sharing a pot of coffee and holding conversations with people in the community.

Arloa says that urban ministry can be overwhelming because of the ever-present need. Thus, it is necessary to be "led by the Spirit and not driven by the need."[4] From her years of working with the homeless, Arloa has learned the value of recognizing that everyone needs the Savior. Every person, whether homeless or not, must come to grips with their own brokenness and the fact that we are all on the same boat—all of us are needy, don't have it all together and are in need of the Savior.

Following the lead of the Holy Spirit, Breakthrough Urban Ministries has continued to develop and prosper. It provides services for the homeless community through basic need services that focus on food and emergency shelter for men, women, and youth. By 2008 it had fifty-three staff members, over one thousand volunteers and a budget of $8.5 million.

←* *Take action.* Consider starting a ministry to the homeless through your church. Meet with some of the homeless in the community and find out about their immediate needs and how your church can offer support and encouragement. Contact leaders at organizations like Breakthrough Urban Ministries to learn how to get started and about best practices. Perhaps you can begin your efforts by providing coffee and a meal once a week. Invite the homeless to join you at your church or meet them in a park or at some other location (see "Homelessness" and "Poverty").

←* *Take action.* In *Deep Justice in a Broken World* Chap Clark and Kara Powell suggest: "Next Christmas, buy some gifts for kids in an under-resourced neighborhood, but instead of delivering the gifts yourselves, set up a temporary store with dramatic discounts so parents in the community can come and purchase gifts for their kids. That way the parents have picked out and bought gifts for their own kids."[5]

## Church Involvement

Rick Rusaw and Eric Swanson ask, "If your church left town, would anybody notice?" I hope to goodness the answer is yes! The church has so much power and potential. It's a gathering place for broken and hurting people who acknowledge their desperate need for God. Yes, it is messy. Things aren't always (if ever) organized as well as they could be—sometimes the sound on Sunday morning is a little loud, the driveway could be paved more smoothly, the coffee might be watery. But the church has the ability to make a difference in the lives of people in their community. Indeed, Rusaw and Swanson observe, "Externally focused churches are internally strong, but they are oriented externally. . . . Because they engage their communities with the good works and good news of Jesus Christ, their communities are better places in which to live."[6]

The church is one of the most untapped resources in the world. When the church has a vision for change, the people of God rise up with passion and energy and conviction. The love of Christ should be bursting through the walls of the church so that every neighborhood is transformed by Christ's followers. This type of change shoots a burning arrow into the heart of injustice. The larger community of believers, the church, must get involved at every level of society as servants who are willing to take a stand against injustice.

A critical component of community organizing is that every member of the community is heard. As churches become impassioned, they must not ignore the voices of indigenous leaders within the community. Rather, they should be at the head of the charge, paving the way, calling the shots and helping to shape the direction of how the church can support and uplift those in need. The church has such great potential. Pray that by the Holy Spirit the potential of the people of God will be unleashed as agents of justice.

**FOR FURTHER STUDY**

*The Externally Focused Church* by Rick Rusaw and Eric Swanson

*High Impact African-American Churches* by George Barna and Harry R. Jackson Jr.

## Government Involvement

In 2006 I had the privilege of dialoging with Jim Wallis and some of his team from Call to Renewal. I was leading conversations about social justice at Willow Creek Community Church and took my team to meet with Jim to seek insights on how we could best pursue justice in our ministry. As our conversation commenced, I felt like most of Jim's suggestions for action were in the realm of politics. I told him that I couldn't present a plan for social justice to the elders that was purely political. I will never forget his response: "Then you need to redefine politics."

Tim Stafford, author of *Shaking the System*, writes about the significant role that government plays in shaping social reform: "Then comes politics. In America every reform movement will be drawn toward it because we are a people who instinctively trust our democracy and bring our causes to it. Even movements to reduce the scope of government work through the government."[7] Regardless of people's perspective about the role and size of government, it is a force to be reckoned with when it comes to the pursuit of justice and equality. Jimmy Carter quipped: "The sad duty of politics is to establish justice in a sinful world."[8] Government involvement in alleviating poverty and oppression can take many forms, including foreign aid, debt relief and trade agreements.

Several studies have asked evangelical Christians whether they would support the allocation of government resources to fight poverty and other world issues. In a DATA study, a poll revealed that nine out of ten evangelicals would vote for the inclusion of the United States' initiative to work with other countries to help the poorest people in the world overcome AIDS and global poverty. Evangelicals, however, were less willing to help an AIDS orphan in Africa out of their own resources.[9] When it comes to the HIV/AIDS crisis, evangelicals support governmental intervention but are less likely to give sacrificially from their own means.

### FOR FURTHER STUDY

*Jesus for President: Politics for Ordinary Radicals* by Shane Claiborne

*Red Letter Christians: A Citizen's Guide to Faith and Politics* by Tony Campolo

**Foreign Aid.** The United States government's foreign aid initiatives have been largely influenced by many antipoverty groups around the world, including the ONE Campaign, the UN Millennium Goals and other global poverty initiatives that call for the world's global community to increase governmental support through foreign aid to poor nations. Regarding foreign aid, Jeffrey Sachs writes:

> I'm not saying the only way for the rich and the poor to live together is if the rich cut their living standards by half, give up their cars, understand modern life is a false contrivance and a false consciousness that is destroying the planet. . . . I don't believe that stuff anyway, but that's not the kind of battle that this is about. We're just talking about one percent of our income in the world for the need to avert potential calamity.[10]

Antipoverty groups are calling for world governments to donate 1 percent of their GDPs to fight extreme poverty around the world. One of the great criticisms of the allocation of government funding to fight international poverty is the small percentage of dollars that actually reaches the poorest people in need. Economists argue about the effectiveness of funding poor nations through increased governmental support. Several of the books recommended, such as *Ending Global Poverty* by Jeffrey Sachs and *The Bottom Billion* by Paul Collier, discuss in great detail the economic possibilities and pitfalls of foreign aid initiatives.

In 2008 the United States only devoted about half of one percent of the government's entire budget to poverty-focused development assistance.[11] According to CARE, the amount is 0.39 percent.[12] Figuring out what part of the United States budget goes toward poverty reduction is difficult. For example, a large portion of U.S. foreign assistance goes toward developing strategic diplomatic partnerships around the world, including relationships with Egypt, Jordan, Pakistan, and Israel.[13] It could be argued that these monies are not poverty-focused development assistance.

To give you a better idea of some of the ways that the United States government invests tax dollars, in 2006, $499 billion was spent on the military.

> In sharp contrast, it spent $22.7 billion directly on foreign aid. Measured in dollars, the sum of $22.7 billion makes the US the biggest foreign-aid donor in the world. Considered as a percentage of the countries GNP, America's foreign-aid budget (at only 0.17 percent) is almost negligible. Points of comparison—Britain and France gave away 0.52 and 0.47

respectively. The goal established by the U.N. is for every developed country to contribute at least 0.7 percent of its G.N.P. to foreign aid.[14]

The United States agreed to work toward the goal of one percent by 2015, but thus far it is falling short of its promise.

←※ *Take action.* Depending on where you are in your vocational career, consider working in a field that would allow you to advocate for effective change from within the government. Consider a career within the State Department (see www.state.gov). Or consider a career in economic development—one possibility is the Economic Development Administration of the U.S. Department of Commerce (see www.eda.gov).

If a career shift is not right for you, consider completing a certificate program or degree to equip you to contribute to justice conversations on the government level. Virginia Tech's Urban Affairs and Planning Program offers a graduate certificate in economic development (see www.nvc.vt.edu). Penn State offers two online programs in community and economic development on the graduate level (see www.worldcampus.psu.edu).

*Debt Relief.* Another initiative responding to global poverty is the movement toward debt relief for poor nations. According to Dale Hanson Bourke, "Debt relief is the partial or total forgiveness of debt or the slowing or stopping of debt growth, owed by individuals, corporations, or nations."[15] Debt relief is conditioned on requirements that countries limit government spending, private basic services or change international and domestic trade and investment rules. Much of these

countries' debt is from bad-faith lending, which includes pushing loans on developing nations because banks had too much money and needed it to be dispersed, money lent to corrupt governments for political purposes, and lending conditions that ensured profit returns to the creditors.[16]

According to the United Nations, many developing countries are spending more financial resources on debt service than on social services. For example, between 1970 and 2002, Africa received approximately $540 billion in loans and paid back $550 billion in principle and interest. Nonetheless, the remaining debt for Africa today is over $295 billion.[17] According to *The aWAKE Project:* "Every day countries in sub-Saharan Africa spend thirty million dollars repaying debts to the world's richest countries and international institutions. Some of these loans were given to governments that are now long gone and some were given by rich countries in ways that served their own self-interest."[18]

In the past few decades movements for debt relief largely have been successful. The Jubilee Network, under the "Jubilee 2000" initiative, made debt relief popular in the 1990s and continues to advocate domestically and abroad. As a result of such efforts, the Heavily Indebted Poor Countries (HIPC) initiative was launched by the World Bank and the International Monetary Fund to provide systematic debt relief for the world's poorest countries.[19] Some of the success stories of debt relief include Uganda, where money was taken from debt relief and used toward universal primary education (the rate of enrollment has more than doubled to 94 percent). Monies were also used to provide

## Jubilee USA Network

Jubilee was founded as a collaboration of faith groups attempting to live out the call for debt relief in Leviticus 25:10: "Proclaim liberty throughout the land to all its inhabitants. It shall be a jubilee for you." In the past Jubilee has organized one day of the year for a mass call-in to Congress urging support. In 2007 Jubilee USA Lobby Day took place on October 17, the same day as Global White Band Day: An International Day of Action to Eradicate Poverty. See www.jubileeusa.org for the most recent information about Jubilee USA Network campaigns.

clean water through drilling wells and to fight AIDS. Debt relief to Mozambique was used to vaccinate half a million children against disease (tetanus, whooping cough, diphtheria) and for education. In Cameroon the money saved from debt relief was used to develop a national plan to fight AIDS through prevention, education, testing and mother-to-child transmission abatement.[20]

*Awareness exercise.* Order the twenty-minute DVD "Stand Up Take Action: End Global Poverty and Unjust Debt" for $10 from Jubilee USA. The DVD has footage of interviews with leaders from the organization and highlights the 2007 Jubilee delegation to Kenya and Zambia, the Cancel Debt Fast campaign, and the Picture New Leadership Campaign. Help raise awareness in your local community by showing the film and discussing the Jubilee campaign and ways to advocate on behalf of economic justice around the world. To order the video go to www.jubileeusa.org

←⊷ *Take action.* Join organizations like Jubilee USA Network in their advocacy work to relieve debt. Visit the Jubilee USA website (see www.jubileeusa.org) to find out when their next call-in day to Congress is scheduled. Invite your friends, family, coworkers and others to join in this advocacy campaign.

### FOR FURTHER STUDY

*The Debt Threat: How Debt Is Destroying the Developing World* by Noreena Hertz

*Who Owes Who? 50 Questions about World Debt* by Damien Millet and Eric Toussaint

*Trade Agreements and Fair Trade.* Another tool that world governments can use to impact the world's poor are economic sanctions (see "Capitalism"). Sanctions are a way for countries to exercise their power by imposing penalties on imports or exports through tariffs, restrictions on trade, duties or quotas. To give an idea of the economic disparity between different country's contribution to international trade, Africa makes up 12 percent of the world's population, but it is only responsible for about 2 percent of world trade. DATA reports, "If Africa could regain just an additional one percent share of global trade, it would earn seventy billion dollars more in exports each year—more than three times what the region currently receives in international assistance."[21] According to the United

Nations, close to $700 billion is denied to poor countries every year because of unfair trade routes.

Part of the challenge with trade agreements is that wealthy countries work diligently to protect their market by imposing import duties, quotas and subsidizing agricultural sectors, often stopping smaller developing countries from competing internationally. In 2000 the United States signed the Africa Growth and Opportunity Act (AGOA) to offer incentives for African countries to continue their efforts to build up their economies and build free markets.[22] The AGOA allows thirty-seven qualifying African countries to export certain products to the United States duty free, and by 2002 this had already created 250,000 jobs and approximately 500 million dollars in new investments around Africa.[23]

According to Dale Hanson Bourke, fair trade is a growing movement that "promotes equitable standards for labor and helps preserve the environment, especially on products exported from developing countries in the developing world."[24] The fair trade market in Europe has progressed more rapidly than in the United States. TransFair USA is one of twenty international labeling organizations that certifies products as fair trade and is the third-party certifier of fair trade products in the United States (see www.trans fairusa.org). Labeling agencies research, study and evaluate what products and marketplaces meet international standards for the fair treatment of workers and payment of fair market value for their wares. Informed consumers can use their buying power to help promote fair trade practices (see "Capitalism" and

"Consumerism").

*Awareness exercise.* Numerous articles have been written about trade practices and what makes them fair. Take some time to research what constitutes good trade practices. Look up articles on the Web. Take notes about what you have learned. Consider Fair Trade Ireland as a resource (see www.fairtrade.ie).

## Professional Industry

Morley Glicken aptly observes:

> I can tell you honestly that there is no romance in being poor. There is nothing honorable, intriguing, or inspiring about poverty. It immediately makes you a nonperson. . . . There are millions of poor people in America. I think they feel the same way I do about being poor; It's a hateful experience.[25]

In the late nineteenth century there was an increased movement away from personal involvement with the poor in the United States. This eventually gave way to professionals who were educated, trained and compensated to respond to the needs of the underresourced. The social work profession was born at the turn of the twentieth century with the goal of creating a place where people of all different faiths and perspectives could come with their needs for support and practical help. Marvin Olasky says that the profession of social work was meant to be a "'sympathetic consideration' of all attitudes and beliefs in order to be of 'service to humanity.'"[26]

Because of its secularization, social work contrasted with the church's compassion toward needs while encouraging moral reform and Christlikeness. In 1931 Reinhold Niebuhr criticized professional social work by saying that faith was a necessary component of responding to the ills of society and personal consequence.[27] Olasky says the rise of social work is one of the major factors in the decrease of volunteerism: "Professionals began to dominate the realm of compassion, volunteers began to depart."[28] Social work contributed toward the secularization of compassion. Christians no longer felt responsible to respond to their needy neighbors, because people who were paid and resourced would respond.

Although social work is in large part a secular field, many Christians have chosen to pursue it as a way of extending compassion and care to people in need. There are networks of Christian social workers, such as the North American Association of Christian Social Workers (NAACS) (see www.nacsw.org/2008/2008-index.shtml) who strive to provide encouragement, support and networking opportunities for Christians in the field of social work. Thus social work has provided a professional outlet for Christians to answer the call of Scripture to help those living in poverty.

The professionalization of compassion also

---

### Trade as One

In 2004 Nathan George, moved by God, took a 40 percent pay cut from his job and began working only three days a week in order to create space for theological reflection and study, hoping to find a "faith that made sense." He had grown up a missionary kid and a Christ follower, but somehow had missed the New Testament message of "good news to the poor." He worked for over twenty years in business and traveled around the world as an adult, but had missed the connection between the gospel, business and good news to the poor. Through his reading, study and engagement with the poor, he was moved to start a fair trade organization that would not impose help on the poor in the developing world, but would instead provide accessibility for their products to be purchased in the Western world. Having seen the model

work powerfully through churches in the United Kingdom, George wondered if it could work in America, so he took his ideas to thought leaders and practitioners in the U.S. church.

Nathan was told consistently that for theological and cultural reasons the evangelical church would not grasp his vision. Overwhelmingly, his advisers said the idea would never work. Nonetheless, he felt compelled to take a risk. In July 2006 George left his job and moved his family from the United Kingdom to the San Francisco Bay Area and began Trade as One shortly thereafter (see tradeasone.com). The basic idea of Trade as One is that people in America would have the opportunity to use their buying power to help bring jobs to the poorest of the poor in the developing world. George believes that business done right can be profitable, prophetic and a sus-

affected the financial resources that previously were distributed through the church community. Secularization increased the overall financial resources poured into alleviating poverty, creating the poverty industry. Some argue that few of the resources actually trickle down to the people who are most in need of assistance. According to the political thinker and activist Charles Murray:

> In practical terms, we don't (cure poverty) because much of the $190 billion (that it would take to end poverty in the US) is not "for persons of limited income" at all,

but for the poverty industry—bureaucrats, caseworkers, service providers, and a grab-bag of vendors in the private sector who plan, implement, and evaluate social programs on government contracts.[29]

---

**FOR FURTHER STUDY**

*Social Work in the 21st Century: An Introduction to Social Welfare, Social Issues, and the Profession* by Morley Glicken

*Christianity and Social Work: Readings on the Integration of Christian Faith and Social Work Practice* by T. Laine Scales and Beryl Hugen

---

tainable path out of poverty. He says, "We partner closely with faith communities because we believe that faith is a powerful and under-utilized motivator for ethical purchasing in America. By choosing to substitute ethically traded goods for conventional ones, people have daily opportunities to put their values and faith into action. Our spending, not just our giving, becomes a discipleship issue."[30]

In their first year of business, Trade as One sold over $150,000 worth of products, including consumables (e.g., coffee, tea, rice, sugar) and crafts (e.g., jewelry, fashion accessories and housewares). All of the products are made by the poor, those with HIV/AIDS or women taken from human trafficking and commercial sex work. The products are made in accordance with the principles of fair trade (i.e., no child labor, providing living wages, gender equality and environmental stewardship). "Something excit-

ing is happening in the American church right now. I believe we are seeing more evangelicals embrace a fuller understanding of the Kingdom of God as they include acts of compassion with proclamation," George says as he reflects on what has happened in the last twelve months. In their second year, Trade as One was on course to quadruple its first year's revenues.

←* ***Take action.*** Buy fair trade products like coffee, tea, chocolate and snacks for personal use or in your church. Partner with organizations like Equal Exchange (see www.equalexchange.coop) and Pura Vida (see www.puravidacoffee.com) for fair trade products. For Christmas, housewarmings, birthday parties and other events buy gifts through organizations like Trade as One (see tradeasone.com) and "Change Lives With Everything You Buy."

## Private Non-Government Organizations (NGOs)

For many people the debate is not whether to respond to global poverty but how much should fall to the government and to private nongovernment organizations (NGOs). It is helpful to distinguish between secular and Christian nonprofit organizations. There are many amazing nonprofits that are doing great work around the world, but they are doing it independent of a faith-based focus.

Christians should be willing to partner with non-faith-based organizations, but we cannot neglect the gospel and our commission to carry the good news of Christ by making disciples of all nations (Mt 28:19-20). Many of the organizations that are detailed in the appendix are nongovernmental organizations. Groups of believers around the world are partnering to respond to people suffering from lack of economic resources, health crises, slavery, prostitution and other societal ills. The body of Christ must partner with these organizations to work on behalf of social justice for the least of these around the world.

### Christian Community Development Association (CCDA)

A subset of NGOs is community development organizations. Holistic community development does not only consider one problem that a group of people might be experiencing, but instead considers all of the needs of the community, such as access to nutritious food sources, adequate housing, living-wage jobs and access to health care. The Christian Community Development Association (CCDA) was founded by John Perkins and is "an association of like-minded churches, ministries, families, schools, businesses, and individuals. These individuals work together to mobilize spiritual and physical resources in and for communities through the church in a community determined, redemptive way."[32]

The Christian Community Development Association seeks to bring together a network of Christians who will work collectively to combat the conditions facing today's poor. It is the belief of the CCDA that the most creative and long-term solutions to problems of the poor come from grassroots and church-based efforts. The principles CCDA adopts include meeting felt needs, holistic care (evangelism and social action), relocation (living among the poor), reconciliation (people to God and neighbor to neighbor), redistribution (empowering the poor), leadership development and church based care. CCDA includes over 3,000 individuals and more than 500 organizations from community-based groups to some of the largest relief and development organizations in the world.[33]

Communities around the country have been transformed as a result of CCDA. One example is Lawndale, a neighborhood community in Chicago, Illinois. In the fall of 1975 Wayne Gordon began

## A Movement of Advocacy within the Church

Many of the justice issues in this book have been around since the beginning of time. Yet I believe that there is hope. Hope for those who are living in extreme poverty, hope for those who have been marginalized because of their race or culture, hope for women to be set free to use their gifts all around the world, hope for every person who has been a victim of violence or oppression that we can be healed, hope that all lost people will one day have the choice about whether they will follow Christ and experience eternal life, hope that the corporate church will rise up to be advocates of God's justice on behalf of the poor and the oppressed around the world.

The problems of poverty and injustice are some of the greatest challenges to ever face humanity. The response to these injustices should be a combination of government programs, faith-based compassion initiatives and personal involvement, and the church should be leading the way. As the church walks alongside secular nonprofits and other organizations, it will have the opportunity to wit-

teaching and coaching at Farragut High School on Chicago's Westside. At that time he and his wife moved into an apartment in the Lawndale. Lawndale was considered the nation's fifteenth poorest neighborhood.[33] Gordon started leading a Bible study for male athletes in his home. Three years later, in March of 1978, Lawndale Community Church held its first service with barely more than a dozen people present. During that service Wayne Gordon was declared pastor and since then has been known as "Coach" Gordon. A couple of months later this small church took its first formal act of outreach. The purpose was to listen to the community about the needs of the neighborhood. They started to make a list of the neighborhood's needs: health care, education, jobs, housing, recreation, combating violence, drugs and so forth. A vision was born to build a gym and health center. It is an amazing story to follow: God planted dreams in the hearts of these individuals and those dreams have come true.

Since the birth of the church and its partner, community development corporation, Lawndale has been transformed. The Lawndale Christian Health Center opened in 1984 and by 2004 was seeing over seventy-five thousand patients a year.[34] The church also planted ministries that respond to needs of housing, do job training, help men transitioning out of prison back into the community and create opportunities to keep kids off the streets. I wish that I had the time to detail the amazing work of God through his church in Lawndale. As John Perkins says, "Biblical social action has its roots in lives changed by Jesus Christ."[35]

**FOR FURTHER STUDY**

*Real Hope in Chicago* by Wayne Gordon

*Restoring At-Risk Communities: Doing It Together and Doing It Right* by John M. Perkins

ness to the love of Christ. Christians need to respond with hands-on compassion and organizational change to bring about an end to oppressive systems and to promote individual responsibility. The powerful and privileged should not impose their ideas on the poor and the oppressed, but instead should partner with the downcast to find workable solutions to the problems they face. God has chosen to work through the broken vessels of his followers to bring about the change that he desires. Gary Haugen asks, "How does God seek justice? By some great mystery and enormous privilege, he has chosen to use his people, empowered by his Spirit, to complete this task. He simply does not have another plan."[36]

I truly believe that Christians desire to make a difference in the world and to care for those who are hurting. One of the greatest challenges for twenty-first century believers is isolation. Isolation from the poor and from victims of gross injustice. Thus they often lack awareness of specific problems. Once their eyes are opened by the grace of God, people are often overwhelmed and immobilized because of the magnitude of brokenness that exists in the world. But faith gives the greatest advantage! The Bible assures Christ's victory over the forces of evil in the world. The apostle Paul tells us, "His intent was that now, through the church, the manifold wisdom of God should be made known to the rulers and authorities in the heavenly realms, according to his eternal purpose that he accomplished in Christ Jesus our Lord" (Eph 3:10-11). Believers are called and commissioned to witness to the kingdom of God and to be advocates and agents of justice through the guidance and power of the Holy Spirit.

The world has over six billion people. Approximately one-third of the world's population, close to two billion people, claim to be followers of Christ.[37] These people believe in the teachings of Jesus—the evangelization of the lost and caring for the needs of the poor and suffering. Think about what an unstoppable force the church of Christ can be!

We must be willing to remedy and alleviate the great brokenness of our world until all is fully redeemed by our coming Lord and Savior. We see brokenness not only in our own failure to be reconciled to God but also in the frailty of the human condition around us with famine, disease, war, violence and poverty. As we wait for Jesus' coming, we celebrate the brief glimpses of him we see around us. We are reminded of him by the beauty of creation, the smile of a child, the kiss of an octogenarian. While we wait for his coming we are called to love one another, to willingly sacrifice and give up our power and privilege to be a servant to the body of Christ and the world. We are to teach our children to walk in the ways of God's justice and to be advocates on behalf of the poor and the oppressed. We are called to worship the Lord our God with all of our hearts, souls, mind and strength. We rest assured that one day his kingdom will be fully manifested on earth. His righteousness and justice will prevail.

# PART TWO

# Social Justice Issues

Part two is broken into topics that constitute different social justice issues. This list is by no means comprehensive, rather it serves as an introduction to the basic injustices that occur in the United States and around the world. Many of these issues are interrelated and overlap. Much of the world's inequality has to do with poverty, race and gender.

## Poverty

We can't talk about social justice without having some understanding of poverty. A library could be filled with the books written about poverty; Scripture speaks more about the poor than almost any other issue. The magnitude of problems and challenges that surround the issues of resources and access to wealth and opportunity are overwhelming.

Many people, especially those living in the United States, are blind to the true amount of abject poverty in the world today. The United States is the richest country in the world and reaps the benefits of the majority of the world's resources. Pictures of the Third World are readily available, but most people do not have daily encounters with those who are hungry, thirsty, naked and without a place to lay their heads at night. There is extreme poverty all over the globe, including America. Cities are full of broken systems that allow the poor to continue to survive, only to be thrown back into the continual cycle of despair. Agents of social justice must not only be educated and aware of issues of poverty, we must be equipped to stand up and fight against it. Scripture is full of instruction and encouragement about the right way to respond to the needs of the poor.

## Race

The coils of racism in America have yet to be unraveled. There is a significant difference of opinion between whites and people of color about whether or not racism is still a problem today and to what degree. Michael Emerson and Christian Smith wrote in *Divided by Faith* that two-thirds of whites believe the conditions for blacks in the United States are improving, whereas only one-third of African Americans believe it.[1] God cares deeply about these issues!

Scripture calls Christians to love one another. Love does not discriminate because of skin color. There is no caveat to the command to love your neighbor. There is no postscript at the end of the Bible that says we are safe and secure and should live comfortably in our monocultural, isolated and segregated worlds. If there is any issue that the church in America needs to overcome, this is at the very top of the list. With the 2008 election of Barack Obama as the first African American president, some might think that race is no longer an issue domestically. The election of a black man to the most powerful position in the United States is certainly something to be celebrated and denotes racial progress. Nonetheless, whites continue to benefit from privileges that result from their racial identity. Americans must not be ignorant of how these privileges and opportunities have been obtained. Many people groups, races and classes have been oppressed in the history of the United States and today. Biblical justice demands that the wounds of injustice be healed and that Christ-centered reconciliation be pursued at all costs.

## Gender

For some, gender is the most controversial issue of all. Throughout history, women have been systemically oppressed around the world. Need convincing? Consider some of the statistics of female genital mutilation, forced prostitution, the sex trade, rape abuse, and assault—both in developed countries and in the Third World. This is not a feminist rampage, but a deep and painful reality that women are viewed as less then men. Regardless of your theological perspective about women in leadership in the church, no Christian would rightly endorse the types of injustices that are perpetrated toward women around the world. So many social-justice issues reflect these facts. The truth is that twenty-first-century women face gender challenges even in the United States.

## ABORTION

In 1964 birth control pills became readily available for the first time. Women could choose to have sex without the consequence of pregnancy.[2] For many in the women's liberation movement, this victory gave women greater choice over their bodies and the consequences of their actions. Many Christian leaders and churches, though, believed that birth control promoted promiscuity and moved away from God's command that his people be pure and holy and to abstain from sexual immorality. The increased sexual promiscuity of the 1960s soon led to one of the greatest rifts between the church and society.

Abortion is the *intentional ending* of an unborn fetus' life prior to the child being carried to term. The right for a woman to choose whether or not to carry her child to term is one of the main features of the feminist movement that caused distance from the church. The landmark decision of *Roe v. Wade* in 1973 made abortion permissible for any reason a woman chooses, up until the point where the fetus, or unborn child, is considered viable.[3] (Viability means the fetus has developed to the extent that it is capable of living outside the uterus.) This decision was one of the most controversial in the history of the United States Supreme Court. For the church and those who believe in the embryo's inherent right to life, the decision was a devastating loss.

One of the main moral questions around the issue of abortion is whether or not the human embryo (or developing fetus) has an inherent right to life. This question is often addressed using the language about "human dignity," emphasizing the truth that the unborn are made in the image of the Creator and God's desire for human life to be valued and protected. It is good for Christians to lovingly raise awareness about God's heart for the unborn while actively working to decrease to occurrence of abortions.

The Bible clearly teaches that life is valuable and that it is good (Gen 1). Several passages in Scripture teach that God is the creator of humankind:

> This is what the LORD says—
> your Redeemer, who formed you in
> the womb:
> I am the LORD,
> who has made all things. (Is 44:24)

The legalization of abortion is a law that does not acknowledge the dignity and rights of the human embryo or unborn child. For believers, this is in direct opposition to what we believe God teaches about the unborn child:

> For you created my inmost being;
> you knit me together in my mother's
> womb.
> I praise you because I am fearfully and
> wonderfully made;
> your works are wonderful, I know
> that full well. (Ps 139:13-14).

Even in some Christian circles the question of abortion is hotly debated. Some radical Christians went so far as to harass abortion advocates, assassinate abortion doctors and bomb abortion clinics in an attempt to prove their point. In the mid-1990s there was "over $13 million in damage caused by violent anti-abortion groups since 1982 in over 150 attacks, bombings, and shootings."[4] Such misled advocacy is greatly disturbing and not in alignment with how God calls believers to respond. In addition, such extremism only harms the voice of Christians in the debate. Instead, advocacy should occur by raising awareness about the issue and by expressing Christian love, even toward those who might be causing great harm.

In 2008 40 percent of all pregnancies in the United States ended in an abortion. Nonetheless, the overall number of abortions has been in decline. According to the *Time* article "Why Have Abortion Rates Fallen?" crisis pregnancy centers have played an important role in decreasing the number of abortions.[5] According to the Guttmacher Institute's 2005 survey, over the preceding five years, the abortion rate in the United States fell by 9 percent.[6] About the decline, *Time* writer Nancy Gibbs says:

> That would seem to be evidence that the quiet campaign for women's hearts and minds, conducted in thousands of crisis pregnancy centers around the country, on billboards, phone banks and websites, is having an effect, while the combination of tighter access, waiting periods and parental notification laws invite—or force—women to think twice about terminating a pregnancy."[7]

This information should be a great encouragement for Christians to make themselves available for care and support to pregnant mothers through Christian crisis pregnancy centers.

←* *Take action.* Many Christian organizations exist that help raise awareness about abortion in the public square. Consider volunteering with one of these ministries by answering phones, serving as a counselor or hosting events on their behalf. There is also an increased movement to join bipartisan public-policy organizations like the Common Ground Network for Life and Choice (Washington, D.C.) where both pro-life and pro-choice people work together to minimize the number of abortions by pursuing alternatives such as adoption. Care Net is a Christian crisis pregnancy center based in Illinois that shares the love of Christ in word and deed and encourages women to make positive and healthy choices that are motivated by Christ's love. Care Net also has an affiliation of pregnancy centers across North America in which Christians can volunteer, organize fundraisers, work on the website, provide administrative assistance, serve as peer counselors, coordinate clothing and diaper drives, distribute promotional items and brochures, and other types of service (see www.care-net.org).

**FOR FURTHER STUDY**

*Abortion: A Christian Understanding and Response* by James K. Hoffmeier

*Why Pro-Life? Caring for the Unborn and Their Mothers* by Randy Alcorn

*See also* "Assisted Reproductive Technologies," "Bioethics" and "Women."

## AIDS

AIDS manifests itself in symptoms and infections that result in damage to the immune system, making infected individuals susceptible to other infections and tumors. A person may be infected with HIV for many years before developing AIDS, which is considered to be the last stage of the illness resulting from the HIV virus.[8] Of the forty million people in the world living with HIV/AIDS, the vast majority of them (68 percent) live in sub-Saharan Africa.[9]

Infectious diseases continue to blight the lives of the poor across the world. AIDS (Acquired Immune Deficiency Syndrome) is one of the deadliest killers of all time. AIDS is the first epidemic of a new disease since the 1400s and is the fourth leading cause of death around the world.[10] HIV (Human Immunodeficiency Virus) is the precursor to AIDS. An estimated forty million people are living with HIV/AIDS.[11] HIV/AIDS kills more than three million people—the equivalent to the entire population of the city of Chicago—each year.[12] Every day, seven thousand people become infected and nearly six thousand die.[13] The number of people dying of AIDS is equal to twenty 747 jets crashing daily.[14] The spread of AIDS has now become pandemic. Former Secretary of State Colin Powell says, "AIDS is the greatest weapon of mass destruction on earth."[15]

← *Take action.* Educate yourself and others about the effects of HIV/AIDS around the world. Attend a conference to become more aware about the disease and explore how you or your church can get involved. For example, Saddleback Church in Lake Forrest, California, has offered Global Summits on AIDS and the Church in which they bring in experts, including pastors, church leaders, health care specialists, politicians and business leaders, to collaborate about how to best respond to the AIDS crisis. Visit their HIV/AIDS Caring Community website at www.hivandthechurch.com/en-US/Home.htm.

← *Take action.* To commemorate the millions of lives affected by AIDS, observe World AIDS Day on December 1 through prayer, reflection and action through a Christian organization working in opposition to HIV/AIDS. See www.worldvision.org/worldaidsday for ideas.

**FOR FURTHER STUDY**

*Dangerous Surrender* by Kay Warren

## AIDS—AFRICA

The AIDS pandemic is a growing world crisis that affects every continent. Africa is among the worst affected. In 2008 in sub-Saharan Africa alone there were over twenty-five million adults and children living with HIV.[16] In 2002 Dr. Volney Gay, chair of the religious studies department at Vanderbilt University, hosted a conference called "AIDS and Africa: Science and Religion," from which *The aWAKE Project* was born. *The aWAKE Project* is a book that compiles the work of scientists, pastors and other Christian voices in a commitment to "work toward awareness, knowledge, and engagement" in an united effort against the AIDS crisis in Africa. The following is an excerpt from Johanna McGeary, a senior correspondent for *Time* magazine and an author featured in *The aWAKE Project:*

> Imagine your life this way. You get up in the morning and breakfast with your three kids. One is already doomed to die in infancy. Your husband works 200 miles away, comes home twice a year, and sleeps around in between. You risk your life in every act of sexual intercourse. You go to work past a house where a teenager lives alone tending young siblings without any source of in-

come. At another house, the wife was branded a whore when she asked her husband to use a condom, beaten silly and thrown into the streets. Over there lies a man desperately sick without access to a doctor or clinic or medicine or food or blankets or even a kind word. At work you eat with colleagues, and every third one is already fatally ill. You whisper about a friend who admitted she had the plague and whose neighbors stoned her to death. Your leisure is occupied by the funerals you attend every Saturday. You go to bed fearing adults your age will not live into their 40s. You and your neighbors and your political and popular leaders act as if nothing is happening. Across the southern quadrant of Africa, this nightmare is real."[17]

Rock star and AIDS activist Bono observes, "History will judge us on how we respond to the AIDS emergency in Africa . . . whether we stood around with watering cans and watched while a whole continent bursts into flames . . . or not."[18]

←* *Take action.* Get involved and start an HIV/AIDS ministry within your church. Sad-

## AIDS Bracelet Project

Dale Hanson Bourke, author of *The Skeptic's Guide to the Global AIDS Crisis*, recounts her first encounters with AIDS:

Like many people, I had become a skeptic about HIV/AIDS. . . . But unlike most people, I had the opportunity to travel to Africa and Asia. There I was confronted with the irrefutable evidence that I—and many people like me—was missing something. In Africa I saw roadside stands with wooden coffins being sold as quickly as they could be made. In Asia I visited a home for sick and orphaned children whose mothers were prostitutes who had died of AIDS. In one country, I met a wrinkled and stooped-over woman who, barely able to walk, had to care for ten children, including an infant. Through a translator, she explained that these were her grandchildren, the survivors of her own sons and daughters, all of whom had died of AIDS. "Pray for me that I will live long enough to raise these children," she implored, her eyes filled with tears. It didn't take long for these encounters to motivate me to action. But what could I do? It seemed like there was an immense gap between what I knew and what it would take to really help someone."[22]

In 2005 I had the opportunity to spend some time with Dale, when I led the organization of a Compassion Expo for "Breathe," a women's conference at Willow Creek Community Church. One of the projects that we worked on for the

dleback Community Church provides some wonderful resources and tools regarding HIV/AIDS, including *What Your Church Can Do*, a DVD and toolkit that provides information about how to start an HIV/AIDS ministry (see www.saddlebackresources.com)

---

**FOR FURTHER STUDY**

*The aWAKE Project: United Against the African AIDS Crisis* by W Publishing

*The Skeptic's Guide to the Global AIDS Crisis* by Dale Hanson Bourke

*An African Awakening: My Journey Into AIDS Activism* by Valerie Bell

---

## AIDS—ORPHANS

One of the greatest tragedies surrounding the spread of AIDS is the destruction of the family unit in Africa. In Africa alone there are twelve million AIDS orphans.[19] UNICEF claims that the number of HIV/AIDS orphans worldwide is over fifteen million, similar to the total population of children in Germany and the United Kingdom.[20] There are different philosophies about how to respond to the children who have lost parents and extended family to HIV/AIDS. Many organizations financially support orphanages that house these children. Others believe that orphanages iso-

---

Expo was a video called *Changing the World One Woman at a Time*, which Lynne Hybels hosted.[23] We brought Dale to Willow Creek for the video shoot and spent time together talking about her experiences. Upon returning from Africa Dale not only wrote *The Skeptic's Guide to the Global AIDS Crisis* and more recently and *The Skeptics Guide to Global Poverty*, but she also started an organization called the AIDS Orphan Bracelet Project, which offers for a suggested $20 donation a simple red, yellow and green bracelet that is made by AIDS orphans in Africa or the women who support them. The bracelets help to raise awareness about AIDS and are a tangible expression of concern. Red represents the devastation that has been caused by AIDS. Yellow represents hope. And green is for the abundance that Americans have the opportunity to share. The donation is used for the following: antiretroviral treatments for an infected child for six weeks, training AIDS orphans in marketable skills, legally defending the rights of a orphan or widow to keep their home, providing food supplements to a family, supporting an additional child for three months, providing materials about AIDS education to an entire youth group, or paying school fees for an AIDS orphan for three months.

←̶ *Take action.* Partner with the AIDS Orphan Bracelet Project (see www.aidsbracelets.org). Because the project is completely funded through the support of a foundation, all of the monies raised go directly to Opportunity International, World Vision, Compassion International and the Chikumbuso Widows and Orphans Project.

late children from the larger community and are not good models of how to respond to the crisis. Whatever the response might be, Christians are called by God to meet the needs of orphans around the world. James 1:27 says, "Religion that God our Father accepts as pure and faultless is this: to look after orphans and widows in their distress and to keep oneself from being polluted by the world."

Kofi Annan, former Secretary General of the United Nations, says, "The global HIV/AIDS epidemic is an unprecedented crisis that requires an unprecedented response. In particular, it requires solidarity—between the healthy and the sick, between the rich and the poor, and above all, between richer and poorer nations. We have 30 million orphans already. How many more do we have to get to wake up?"[21]

←* *Take action.* Participate in a two-week trip to Africa with Village Care or another relief organization to reach out to orphans and widows distressed because of the HIV/AIDS endemic. Volunteers work under African leadership to help communities implement practices that keep children and families safe, health, happy and contributing to their communities. Find out more by contacting the Village Care volunteer coordinator at info@villagecare.com.

## AIDS—POVERTY

AIDS and poverty are related because people who are poor and malnourished often also have poor health.[24] A comprehensive and holistic response is needed to win the battle against AIDS. According to the United Na-

tions, killer diseases like AIDS have erased a generation of development gains. However, the UN claims to have made significant progress at stopping HIV in its tracks in countries like Brazil, Senegal, Thailand and Uganda. The estimated cost to stop the AIDS epidemic in the world is about $7 to 8 billion annually. It is interesting to note that Africa pays almost twice that (an estimated $15 billion) in their annual debt service.[25] (See also "Solutions to Injustice.") There are many underlying circumstances that contribute to AIDS and its continued spread, including extreme poverty and "promiscuity, starvation, civil unrest, limited access to health care, meager education systems, drug use, and reemerging infectious diseases. Stronger societies, economies, and democracies will facilitate an improved response to HIV/AIDS."[26]

←* *Take action.* Meet with a member of Congress or congressional staff to advocate on behalf of global HIV/AIDS relief. Lobbying is one of the most powerful tools for affecting U.S. policy. Many nonprofits provide helpful tools for advocacy. Genocide Intervention Network has a wonderful advocacy guide available at www.genocideintervention.net/files/Advocacy How-to Guide_2.pdf.

*See also "Poverty."*

## AIDS—PREVENTION

Antiretroviral drugs have been available in the United States for the past couple of decades and are able to prolong the lives of those who are HIV positive and to significantly decrease the symptoms of the disease.[27] By and large, these drugs have not been available in the developing world because of their cost and the need for medical supervision when they are administered. Global concern about the exorbitant cost of AIDS drugs has helped focus international attention on the epidemic.

One senator noted, "This year, more than a half a million babies in the developing world will contract from their mothers the virus that causes AIDS, despite the fact that drugs and therapies exist that could virtually eliminate mother-to-child transmission of the killer disease."[28]

In addition, one of the UN Millennium Development Goals is to help combat HIV/AIDS, malaria and other diseases. Because of these efforts, drugs are now available in some developing countries for more affordable prices, which will allow treatment to occur.

←※ ***Take action.*** Wear red. (RED)'s primary objective is to engage the private sector in raising awareness and funds for the Global Fund to help fight AIDS in Africa. Companies whose products have the (RED) mark contribute a significant percentage of the sales or portion of the profits from that product to the Global Fund to finance AIDS programs in Africa, with an emphasis on the health of women and children. Current partners are American Express (U.K. only), Apple, Converse, Gap, Giorgio Armani and Motorola. Visit www.joinred.com for more information.

*See also* "Malaria."

## AIDS—SOCIAL IMPACT

The effects of AIDS are so widespread they are easily witnessed in the cities, suburbs and remote villages all over the continent of Africa. One traveler observed that the schools where he visited had classrooms without teachers because their lives had been taken by the disease. Another visitor said, "A pastor explained that he performs funerals three at a time. If he did each one individually he would spend every day burying the dead, with no time left to serve the living in his congregation."[29] Just imagine: classrooms without teachers, children without parents, parents without children, houses without families, churches without clergy. The people who are most needed to help raise Africa out of economic privation are being destroyed by the devastating disease. Christian sociologist Tony Campolo observes, "The social impact of AIDS is horrendous."[30]

***Awareness exercise.*** Allow your heart to be broken over the men, women and children around the world who have lost loved ones to HIV/AIDS. Take a few minutes to reflect on the online experience that is offered by World Vision at www.worldvisionexperience.org. Even better, take a group of friends or colleagues through the World Vision AIDS exhibit, "Step Into Africa," when it is available in your area. This interactive exhibit transports you to the heart of Africa and offers a glimpse of AIDS through a stirring audio tour with captivating photography. After experiencing the World Vision "Step Into Africa" exhibit, consider mobilizing your church to host the World Vision AIDS exhibit in your own community.

## AIDS—TRANSMISSION

AIDS is transmitted through the exchange of body fluids. There are several reasons the disease has spread so rapidly. The HIV virus can be a hidden disease; although they are infectious, people might not know they have the virus for as many as ten years because they have no symptoms. And access to testing is limited in many parts of the world. In addition, because there is a stigmatism to the disease, many infected people hide their illness and thereby spread it to others. HIV/AIDS can be transmitted to children through childbirth, which has also continued to spread the disease. In many parts of the world, women are forced to marry at a young age, when they are more prone to infection. People who have had multiple sexual partners or who have slept with prostitutes are more likely to be infected with HIV. Because of poverty, men in the developing world are often forced to work away from home and they frequent prostitutes, which further spreads the disease.[31] People with diseases like malaria and tuberculosis are more susceptible to contracting HIV/AIDS. Malnourishment also increases the possibility of infection and prevents the ability to fight against the disease. (See also "Hunger.") Thus in underresourced countries and developing nations, the spread of the disease is more prevalent.

←※ *Take action.* Neviraprine is an antiretroviral drug that, in a single dose at birth, reduces the mother-to-child transmission rate by 50 percent. Neviraprine is very affordable by Western standards (only $0.85 per dose), but it is not readily available and is underutilized in Christian hospitals, clinics and community testing centers, largely because of cost.[32] *The aWAKE Project* has a "Skip a Lunch & Save a Bunch" program to help combat HIV/AIDS. Schedule a time when you, your friends and community skip a lunch together. Take the money that you

would have spent on one day's lunch and use it to buy doses of Nevirapine for use by Christian clinics in sub-Saharan Africa. During your gathering, educate people about HIV/AIDS and pray for those who are being affected by the pandemic and for those involved in Christian ministry to prevent it. For more information see World Vision's Hope Initiative at www.worldvision.org/content.nsf/getinvolved/hope-home.

*See also* "Malaria."

## AIDS—WOMEN

Women are among those who are most affected by AIDS. "Globally, approximately 50 percent of all HIV-Positive people are female; in sub-Saharan Africa it averages nearly 60 percent."[33] A widely believed myth that has had a significant effect on women is that AIDS is curable if an infected person has sex with a virgin. Many sexual and power issues make poor women more vulnerable to the disease: rape, abuse in the home, an infected husband's refusal to use protection, trading sex for food.[34]

←※ *Take action.* Get your grandmothers involved! In 2006, through a program called "GoGo Grandmothers," American grandmothers provided each of 155 poor Malawian grandmothers funds for a 120-pound bag of commercial fertilizer. *Gogo* is a common African term for "grandmother." The Gogo Grandmothers meet both in the village and urban areas on a monthly basis to socialize, share needs, give and receive help. The African grandmothers enjoy monthly times of fellowship, reading the Word of God, praying, singing and dancing. Visit www.gogograndmothers.com for more information.

*See also* "Women."

## ASSISTED REPRODUCTIVE TECHNOLOGIES

Many couples dream of one day starting a family and having children of their own. For those couples who struggle with infertility—one out of every six in the United States—starting a family can be filled with many harsh realities and can place them in the center of a heated moral debate. Infertility is understood as difficulty in conceiving a child within a year. While some infertile couples choose adoption, a growing number choose to use complex assisted reproductive technologies (ARTs) to have biological children. In 2001, 40,687 children were born after ARTs attempts, up from 20,021 in 1996. The process of choosing adoption or ARTs can be emotionally grueling and painful.[35]

Several justice issues are raised with the invention of new technologies. One of the most obvious in ART cases is how God desires embryos to be treated. (See also "Abortion.") Viable embryos are human life forms and should be treated as such. What effect should this have on ARTs and other fertility technologies? Another justice concern surrounding fertility is in vitro fertilization (IVF).

In IVF, eggs are surgically retrieved from a woman's ovaries. It is often a painful procedure. Emotions run high as a result of the fertility drugs that are regularly injected into the woman before her eggs are surgically removed.

Once the eggs have been extracted, they are fertilized outside of the woman's body in the laboratory. Any eggs that have been successfully fertilized (embryos) are left to grow, and the two or three best are transferred into the woman's womb. Any remaining embryos may be frozen for future use or are discarded."[36]

When IVF is pursued, some physicians implant a limited number of embryos in the woman's uterus, but others may place four or more. When several embryos are successfully implanted, problems arise related to multiple births. In order to increase the likelihood of carrying one fetus to term, women are often advised to choose the most viable fetus and selectively abort those that are considered least viable.[37] Many parents pursue IVF without knowing that these types of moral decisions could be waiting for them. In the United States there are very few laws limiting the application and use of reproductive technologies.[38] In addition, when multiple embryos were fertilized and not implanted, what should be done with them? Christian embryo adoption programs, like Snowflake (see www.snowflakes.org), provide an option for embryos that might otherwise be discarded.

←⚓ ***Take action.*** Invite a Christian bioethicist or physician to your church to teach about the moral choices surrounding reproductive technologies. If you don't know where to start, consult an organization like The Center for Bioethics and Human Dignity (www.cbhd.org) for suggestions.

**FOR FURTHER STUDY**

*The Elusive Embryo* by Gay Becker

*New Ways of Making Babies: The Case of Egg Donation* by Cynthia B. Cohen

*See also* "Bioethics," "Human Rights" and "Women."

## BIOETHICS

Bioethics is directly relevant to justice because it concerns the morality of decisions related to technology, biological advancement and the application of scientific knowledge to the human race. Moral issues surrounding bioethics include questions about assisted reproductive technologies, physician-assisted suicide or euthanasia, cloning and stem-cell research.

Stem cell research is a highly debated bioethics topic. Stem cells have the ability to renew themselves and differentiate into specialized types of cells. Embryonic stems cells can be found in the umbilical chord of fetuses and also in embryos of humans during their early stages of development. When stem cells are harvested from human embryos (early stages of human life), the embryos are destroyed. Because many people believe human embryos should have the inherent right to life, stem cell research is often criticized. Obviously, this is a justice issue because it examines what is right and wrong, what should and shouldn't be allowed and, for Christians, what is best from a biblical perspective.

There is a direct correlation between bioethics and race; often the people groups most affected by immoral research or ethical violations are minority groups or people of color.

*Awareness exercise.* The Nuremburg Code,

established after World War II, was one of the first significant international statements on bioethics. The code was established to place regulations and ethical guidelines around the use of humans as experimental subjects. Read the Nuremburg Code and discuss it with someone you know. What does the code communicate about human life? What limitations and guidelines are placed around the pursuit of scientific knowledge? How do you think the Christian faith should inform this conversation? The Code may be found on the National Institutes of Health website at ohsr.od.nih.gov/guidelines/nuremberg.html.[39]

*Awareness exercise.* One of the most influential Christian think tanks that wrestles with questions of bioethics is the Wilberforce Forum, which was founded by Chuck Colson. Using the talents of leading Christian thinkers and writers, the Forum seeks to help Christians think and live Christianly not only in church and family circles but also in the public square. Visit www.wilberforce.org for more information.

↤ *Take Action.* Trinity International University in Deerfield, Illinois, has one of the first bioethics programs offered by an evangelical institution. Partnering with Trinity Evangelical Divinity School, the university offers a Masters of Arts in Bioethics that equips pastors, health care professionals, lawyers, scientists, educators and nonprofit workers to address issues of bioethics from a Christian perspective. Consider pursuing a degree in this field or attending their annual summer conference offered by the Center for Bioethics and Human Dignity (www.cbhd.org).

**FOR FURTHER STUDY**

*The Foundation of Christian Bioethics* by
H. Tristram Engelhardt Jr.

*Bioethics: A Primer for Christians* by Gilbert
Meilaender

*See also* "Abortion," "Assisted Reproductive
Technologies," "Cloning," "Euthanasia,"
"Family," "Human Rights" and "Stem Cell
Research."

## CAPITAL PUNISHMENT

Capital punishment and the death penalty are
very controversial topics, for Christians and
non-Christians alike. At the beginning of the
twentieth century several states in the United
States outlawed the death penalty (except for
treason), but this reform was short-lived because of World War I and other major events.
There was another decline in the number of
cases of domestic capital punishment during
the mid-twentieth century, with 1,289 executions in the 1940s, 715 in the 1950s, and
only 191 from 1960 to 1976. In the United
States, death sentences have steadily declined
from 300 in 1998 to 143 in 2003.[40]

The Bible has much to help inform this
discussion, although many of the intricacies
found in the Scriptures are beyond the scope
of this discussion. On one hand the Scriptures
promote the idea of a life for a life; for example, "If there is serious injury, you are to
take life for life, eye for eye, tooth for tooth,
hand for hand, foot for foot, burn for burn,
wound for wound, bruise for bruise" (Ex
21:23-25). In the Old Testament a number of
crimes called for the death penalty—murder
(Ex 21:12), desecration of the sabbath (Ex
31:14), adultery (Deut 22:22), and sacrificing

to another God (Ex 22:20), to name a few. In
the New Testament Paul says that the wages
of sin is death (Rom 6:23). According to that
text, any offense that causes separation between people and God warrants death. On
the other hand, when some leaders demanded
that an adulterous woman be stoned, Jesus responded, "Let any one of you who is without
sin be the first to throw a stone" (Jn 8:7). Jesus' actions toward the woman caught in
adultery clearly communicates that the response of those in positions of power and
judgment should not be one of condemnation
but one of love and grace.

Some have argued that the death penalty
should be outlawed because it is not equitably
applied across race and class. Jim Wallis says,
"The death penalty is clearly biased against
the poor who cannot afford adequate legal
representation and is outrageously disproportionate along racial lines."[41] However, the
data presented by the Death Penalty Information Center does not seem completely con-
gruent with Wallis's statement. Statistics show
that the race of those executed since 1976 has
been 624 (57 percent) white, 373 (34 percent)
black and 76 (7 percent) Hispanic and 24 (2
percent) other.[42] However, according to the
Department of Justice, the total number of
people on death row was higher for blacks
than whites almost consistently through the
early 1970s.[43]

One of the problems with the death penalty is that some on death row are innocent.
Since the discovery of DNA technology,
many inmates have been released who were
falsely convicted. Since 1973 at least 123
death row inmates have been released after
evidence proved their innocence.[44] In 2003

the governor of Illinois granted clemency to all remaining 167 death row inmates because of the flawed processes that led to their sentencing. In one case in North Carolina, Jonathon Hoffman was sent to death row for a murder committed in 1995. Close to ten years later, his conviction was overturned because there was no physical evidence that linked him to the crime. It was later revealed that his prosecutors made undisclosed deals with their witnesses. Hoffman is black. The victim was white. Hoffman was convicted by an all-white jury. The prosecutors were not charged with misconduct or wrongdoing.[45]

On the global front, in April 1999, the United Nations Human Rights Commission passed a resolution supporting a "worldwide moratorium on executions" for countries that have not abolished the death penalty to end its use. Ten countries, including the United States, voted against the resolution. An additional resolution was passed on November 15, 2007, by the General Assembly of the United Nations, again calling for a global moratorium on executions with a "view to eventually abolish the death penalty entirely."[46] This resolution for a global moratorium and abolition of the death penalty was reaffirmed on December 18, 2008, when over one hundred countries voted in favor of the resolution. According to Amnesty International whereas the Americas are almost free of executions, "Since 2003, only the United States of America continues to execute on a regular basis."[47]

Christians must wrestle through what Scripture teaches about truth and justice. The death penalty is a critical justice issue that necessitates the involvement of loving Christians in the conversation and debate. When considering this difficult issue, my hope is that believers will model the response of Christ toward the woman caught in adultery, a sin punishable by death, with love, kindness and forgiveness.

*Awareness exercise.* Familiarize yourself with the Death Penalty Information Center (www.deathpenaltyinfo.org), a resource center dedicated to "serving the media and the public with analysis and information on issues concerning capital punishment." The DPIC provides national and state statistics, resources, book lists, articles, reports, and other information to help familiarize you with issues surrounding the death penalty in the United States.

←* *Take action.* Consider organizing a peaceful walk or other event to raise awareness about the death penalty and to encourage people to take a stand against it. Since 2003, one day each year is set aside as "World Day Against the Death Penalty." On October 10, 2008, groups from all around the world hosted events such as jazz concerts, film screenings, symposiums, workshops, press conferences and petitions to work toward the abolition of the death penalty. Look up future dates for this event and join the World Coalition Against the Death Penalty (www.worldcoalition.org) to take action and end global executions.

←* *Take action.* Watch the movie *The Exonerated,* and help raise funds for Pennsylvania Alternatives for the Death Penalty (PADP). Visit www.pa-abolitionists.org/?q=content/exonerated-dvd. Another movie based on true-life events is *Dead Man Walking,* which shows some of the painful realities of the death penalty.

**FOR FURTHER STUDY**

*Religion and the Death Penalty: A Call for Reckoning* edited by Eric Owens, John Carlson and Eric Elshtain

*Dead Man Walking: An Eyewitness Account of the Death Penalty in the United States* by Helen Prejean

*The Executed God: The Way of the Cross in Lockdown America* by Mark Lewis Taylor

## CAPITALISM

Random House Dictionary defines *capitalism* as an economic system in which investment in and ownership of the means of production, distribution, and exchange of wealth is made and maintained chiefly by private individuals or corporations.[48] In a capitalistic society, everything is owned either by individuals or corporations. A person who has access to resources (or capital) can invest them in the economic system, which will produce more wealth. People who lack access to capital (the poor) are limited in their ability to advance out of their current economic conditions. This is true domestically and abroad. As my grandfather used to say, "It takes money to be able to make money."

Access to capital is critical to the conditions of the poor. Hernando De Soto, a Peruvian economist, contends that the poor are kept in the cycle of poverty because they do not own the land they live on. According to some statistics, the poor occupy at least $9.3 trillion in real estate.[49] Microenterprise has been successful at helping lift the poor out of poverty because of the capital it brings into their individual economic situation (*see* "Microfinance").

In many ways capitalism is good. One of the main benefits is that people who have opportunities, a strong work ethic and resources can navigate successfully within the society. A fundamental assumption of capitalism is, according to Adam Smith, that the pursuit of personal gain is a natural human tendency and should be given free reign within society.[50] This contradicts Christian belief that selfish ambition and the pursuit of material possessions are not attributes of faithful believers. Luke 12:15 says, "Watch out! Be on your guard against all kinds of greed; life does not consist in an abundance of possessions." Nonetheless, the principles of capitalism suggest that the more individuals pursue self-gain and personal development, the greater the good that occurs within society for the whole. Yet, President John F. Kennedy noted, "If a free society cannot help the many who are poor, it cannot save the few who are rich."[51]

Economists have been writing about the fundamentals of supply and demand in society for centuries. James Doti, who received advanced degrees in economics from the University of Chicago, currently serves as the president of Chapman University in Orange, California. He says: "Not only do I believe that self-interest benefits society, but I also contend that it is the only efficient way goods can be produced and distributed in a modern economic system."[52] According to Doti, compassionate acts do not represent the "actual production of the charitable good" but are rather a "voluntary redistribution of income," and still require that charitable individuals purchase food for the hungry from the capitalistic system.

There are many challenges to living in a

capitalistic society. One difficulty is that individuals or communities who do not have a trade, skill or product to sell are excluded from participation in the economic system. Some believe that capitalism helps contribute to extreme poverty and destitution around the world. David Hilfiker is a Christian physician who worked for years as a rural doctor in Minnesota and then founded Joseph's House, an eleven-bed home and community for formerly homeless men with AIDS in Washington, D.C. He is the author of several books, including *Not All of Us Are Saints* (1994) and *Urban Injustice: How Ghettos Happen* (2002). In 2007, Hilfiker taught about the limits of capitalism in a lecture that he gave at the Servant Leadership School: "Capitalism is inherently incapable of dealing with the extraordinary problems of externalization of costs onto society and inequality."[53] Hilfiker writes about the limits of capitalism and the necessity for societies to ensure that all people have access to job training, education, health care and childcare. In order to find possible solutions to the extreme poverty that exists around the world, it's necessary to understand the fundamentals of the capitalistic economic system.

**FOR FURTHER STUDY**

*The Best Things in Life: A Contemporary Socrates Looks at Power, Pleasure, Truth and the Good Life* by Peter Kreeft

*The Victory of Reason: How Christianity Led to Freedom, Capitalism, and Western Success* by Rodney Stark

*See also* "Consumerism," "Microfinance" and "Poverty."

# CHILDREN

Children are among those the most affected by poverty and global injustice. Children have the least resources to be able to provide self-care when natural disasters, disease, hunger or other natural causes threaten them. They are the least able to protect themselves when they face abuse or other types of oppression. When the church considers ways to get involved in social justice, children should be a priority. Jesus said, "Let the little children come to me, and do not hinder them, for the kingdom of heaven belongs to such as these" (Mt 19:14).

← ☀ ***Take action.*** Samaritan's Purse is an international relief organization started by Bob Pierce, who said, "Let my heart be broken with the things that break the heart of God."[54] Currently under the leadership of Franklin Graham, the ministry is committed to "meet the emergency needs in crisis areas through existing evangelical mission agencies and national churches." Operation Christmas Child is one of their programs that offers encouragement and support to children around the world. Host an "Operation Christmas Child" campaign at your church, school or office, and provide people with the opportunity to pack boxes full of toys, school supplies, hygiene items, candy along with a donation of $7 or more to help cover shipping costs, and a personal note with a picture of you or your family. When you include your name and address, sometimes children are able to write back. Go to www.operationchristmaschild.org for details.

**FOR FURTHER STUDY**

*Understanding God's Heart for Children: Toward a Biblical Framework* edited by Douglass McConnell, Jennifer Orona and Paul Stockley

*Child Poverty: Love, Justice and Social Responsibility* by Pamela Couture

*See also* "Family."

## Wess Stafford and Compassion International

Wess Stafford, president of Compassion International, is a devoted follower of Christ who has committed his life to responding to the needs of children around the world. Stafford grew up as a missionary kid in Ivory Coast, Africa. He says that he learned everything he needed to know about leading a multinational organization from the poor while growing up in an African village. Stafford views the children of the world as in desperate need of God's love and an untapped resource of great potential. He has been used in powerful ways to provide the world's young people with the basic necessities of life while being exposed to the love of Christ.

Compassion International "exists as a Christian child advocacy ministry that releases children from spiritual, economic, social and physical poverty, and enables them to become responsible, fulfilled Christian adults."[55] The ministry offers many programs, including child sponsorship, leadership development, church partnerships and other holistic ways to respond and support children living in poverty around the world. In 2008 Compassion had sponsors for over one million children in twenty-five countries around the world. "Change the world—one child at a time" by visiting Compassion International's website at www.compassion.com.

### FOR FURTHER STUDY

*Too Small to Ignore: Why the Least of These Matter Most* by Wess Stafford

*← ⚞ Take action.* Consider personally sponsoring a child through Compassion International. Arrange to host a "Compassion Sunday" at your church, which will give people the opportunity to sponsor children through Compassion. It is possible to sponsor children in the same geographic area so that your church could take a trip to visit your children in their home community. Visit www.compassion.com to sponsor a child, order a planning folder for Compassion Sunday or for other information.

*← ⚞ Take action.* Another way to support Compassion International is to become a Compassion Advocate. Justin McRoberts, a singer songwriter and talented musician, decided to use his gifts to make a difference by becoming an advocate through Compassion International. At concerts and shows, Justin features children who can be sponsored through Compassion.

While Justin was on staff with Young Life, he was introduced to the two principles that would prominently shape his life and work. The first is the Young Life mantra: "Earning the right to be heard," which proposes that, as urgent as the Christian message is, it must always be communicated from a platform of patience, compassion and empathy. The second principle was Young Life's focus on reaching "the furthest out kid." It is from the combination of these two principles, that Justin concludes, "If the Church is serious about its role, we must earn the right to be heard by caring for the poor and the oppressed."[56] Isaiah 58:10 says:

> If you spend yourself in behalf of
>     the hungry
> and satisfy the needs of the
>     oppressed,
> then your light will rise in the
>     darkness,

and your night will become like the noonday.

←＊ *Take action.* Consider having Justin McRoberts give a concert at your church or your school. He shares the story of Christ and his call upon all Christians to respond to the needs of the least of these around the world. Visit Justin's website to be introduced to his music and ministry at www.justinmcroberts.com.

## CHILD SOLDIERS

"Child Soldiers: Global Report 2008," published by the Coalition to Stop the Use of Child Soldiers, begins, "Child soldiers. Two simple words. But they describe a world of atrocities committed against children and sometimes by children. Committed in many different countries and often hidden from the public eye."

According to UNICEF, a child soldier is a boy or girl "under 18 years of age, who is part of any kind of regular or irregular armed force or armed group in any capacity, including, but not limited to: cooks, porters, messengers, and anyone accompanying such groups other than family members."[57] In 2008 the United Nations reported that there are over three hundred thousand child soldiers fighting in thirty countries. Over ten thousand children fought in the Sierra Leone ten-year civil war. An additional half million children are in paramilitary groups around the world.[58] The problem of child soldiers has become more prevalent in the public eye because of exposure in the popular media such

as the Hollywood movie *Blood Diamond* (2006) and Starbucks's endorsement and distribution of the memoirs of a child soldier, *A Long Way Gone* by Ishmael Beah. Now twenty-six years old, Beah tells the story of being a child traumatized by the horrors of war. At the age of thirteen, Beah was picked up by a government army in Sierra Leone and taught to commit terrible acts as child soldier. Removed from the fighting by UNICEF at the age of sixteen, he sought healing and wrestled with what it meant to be restored as a human. Beah's story tells of the horrors children experience when they are traumatized, drugged and equipped with weapons of war.[59]

*Awareness exercise.* The United Nations has designed a lesson plan on child soldiers that presents an overview of where, how, why and in what conditions children are used as child soldiers. One resource they recommend is the documentary *What's Going On? Child Soldiers in Sierra Leone.*[60] Watch the documentary by yourself, with some friends or as a school project. Brainstorm what you can do to continue to raise awareness about children who are exploited on behalf of war efforts and political conflicts around the world. For an overview of the program, visit the UN website at www.un .org/works/goingon/soldiers/lessonplan_ soldiers.html.

←* *Take action.* As a part of their Gifts for Peace initiative the World Organization of the Scout Movement is committed to working on behalf of children soldiers around the world. Consider working with a Boy Scout troop in your area to determine a project that could help tackle this issue. The Scouts recommend the following approach: Learn about the issue and how to empathize with the experience of child soldiers. Learn to recognize difficulties that they might face as they try to integrate back into society. Ponder how scouting can help. Use the following process as you consider a project: (1) identify the problem, (2) develop awareness and empathy, (3) take action and (4) measure the change.[61] Consider how your project could support the Coalition to Stop the Use of Child Soldiers (www.child-soldiers.org) or some other similar organization.

**FOR FURTHER STUDY**

*Child Soldiers: Global Report 2008* (www .childsoldiersglobalreport.org)

*A Long Way Gone: Memoirs of a Boy Soldier* by Ishmael Beah

## CLASS SYSTEMS

Many societies, even in the twenty-first century, are still defined by class systems. When the distribution and access to resources, wealth and power is limited to a small group of people, there is a differentiation of class. All who do not fit into that elitist group are left to pick up the crumbs that fall from the table of extreme wealth and resources. *Class* can be defined as the hierarchical distinctions between individuals and groups in a community or culture. Most of the time, class is based on wealth and resources, but sometimes other considerations are involved.

The relationship between economics and class has been heatedly debated over the centuries. Karl Marx coined the term *bourgeoisie* to identify members of the upper merchant class whose social status came from education or employment rather than having been born as aristocrats or nobility. Relationships between classes has been wrought with tension throughout history. The ruling class, those with power and money, have often been held accountable by the working and lower classes for the way their power is exercised within society.

The caste system of India is an example of the systemic institutionalism of class. The Indian caste system is based on birth and heredity. It is particularly rigid and there is no upward or downward mobility within the system. The "untouchables" are people considered to be at the lowest ebb of society. In 2003 "India's Untouchables Face Violence, Discrimination," a *National Geographic News* article, described the conditions of the untouchables during the twenty-first century. Some of the atrocities against the "untouchables" or Dalits is highlighted by the titles of news articles: "Dalit Boy Beaten to Death for Plucking Flowers," "Dalit Tortured by Cops for Three Days," "7 Dalits Burnt Alive in Caste Clash," "Dalit Woman Gang-

Raped and Paraded Naked."[62]

In the early twentieth century, Mohandas Gandhi spent his life working to free the Indian people from the caste system through nonviolence. In the 1930s Gandhi fasted in prison as one of his many protests to the treatment of the untouchables in India. Martin Luther King Jr. modeled some of his peaceful protests during the civil rights movements after Gandhi. Gandhi said, "To say that a single human being, because of his birth, becomes an untouchable, unapproachable, or invisible, is to deny God."[63]

The condition, even in the twenty-first century, of India's Dalits is a major human rights concern. During the mid-twentieth century, the Indian constitution outlawed discrimination based on caste.[64] In most major cities the situation has gotten better, but the system is still in effect in many rural areas.

Christians must be aware of the way that class privilege is exercised in the twenty-first century. Although today nobility and aristocracy is less obvious, there is a clear and growing difference between the rich and the poor. Western nations play a critical role in the global economy and world order. The actions, methods and decisions of the privileged have significant influence on an individual, domestic and global scale. Christians must be careful to not isolate themselves from others based on class differences: "All the believers were together and had everything in common. They sold property and possessions to give to anyone who had need" (Acts 2:44-45).

←* *Take action.* Start an intentional dialogue and Bible study with participants across different social classes. Consider inviting some homeless people from your community to participate. Seek to learn from one another as you study the Word of God. Ask God to speak to you through your conversations.

---

**FOR FURTHER STUDY**

*Christianity and the Class Struggle* by Harold Brown

*Class Matters: Cross-Class Alliance Building for Middle-Class Activists* by Betsy Leondar-Wright

---

## CLONING

Cloning has been in the public eye since the 1996 cloning of the sheep named Dolly, the first mammal cloned with DNA taken from an adult cell.[65] Dolly represents a scientific breakthrough in technology, and many predict that the cloning of humans will not be far behind. As of 2003, Great Britain law allows for therapeutic cloning—"the duplication of human embryos for research aimed at developing new stem cell treatments."[66] British law does not allow for the cloning of humans.

In the United States most members of Congress are opposed to reproductive cloning, which is generally defined as "the use of cloning technology, also called somatic cell nuclear transfer (SCNT), for initiating a pregnancy."[67] On the other hand, therapeutic cloning, the use of SCNT for purposes of research, is highly controversial. In 2005 U.S. Senator Sam Brownback introduced a total cloning ban in the United States Senate (S. 658) that would make it a crime to clone or attempt to clone a human being. Since the introduction of S. 658, no further action has occurred within Congress on this legislation.[68] Several other pieces of legislation have been proposed or introduced in both the House and the Senate regarding the legality of cloning and restrictions around its use.

At the outset, many individuals are repulsed by the idea of raising a child who is genetically identical to themselves or their spouse. Leon Kass, chairman of the President's Council on Bioethics, calls this the "wisdom of repugnance."[69] There are tremendous implications for social relationships once a child has been cloned for reproductive purposes. Similarly, it is important to understand the possible psychological harm and social concern that would be a direct consequence of reproductive cloning. If the door to human cloning is opened, it is highly probable that this technique will be exploited and used toward devastating ends.[70]

There are also moral questions at stake, such as the experimentation on (potential) human subjects, the right of an individual to have a unique identity, and the right to ignorance about a person's future.[71] These moral questions raise the concern that the legalization allowing reproductive cloning would violate human rights. Leon Kass specifies three objections to the moral permissibility of cloning:

> Cloning threatens confusion of identity and individuality, even in small-scale cloning; cloning represents a giant step (though not the first one) toward transforming procreation into manufacture, that is, toward the increasing depersonalization of the process of generation and, increasingly, toward the "production" of human children as artifacts, products of human will and design (what others have called the problem of

"commodification" of new life); and cloning—like other forms of eugenic engineering of the next generation—represents a form of despotism of the cloners over the cloned, and thus (even in benevolent cases) represents a blatant violation of the inner meaning of parent-child relations, of what it means to have a child, of what it means to say "yes" to our own demise and "replacement."[72]

There are several legitimate arguments against the legalization of human cloning. If reproductive cloning were to be legally acceptable, Kass argues, it would degrade the nature of the parent-child relationship. In addition, reproductive cloning demeans the process of natural reproduction by reducing potential offspring to the mere manipulation of genetic material. Obviously, there is great potential for the abuse of this technology. A slippery-slope argument can be employed as well: if reproductive cloning were legally permissible in some situations (even those that are altruistically motivated), what restrictions could be adequately enforced to ensure that the technology is not misused?

Christians should be an active part of this discussion, dialogue and debate. We must ask what role humans play in the "creation" of human life. As technologies continue to develop, the capabilities of science will allow increased liberty and expression in the manipulation of the human body. Already it is possible to identify and select embryos that are the "most viable" for implantation in a woman's uterus. It is possible to select gender and other genetic characteristics. When will these decisions cross the line of moral acceptability? Isaiah 42:5 says:

> This is what God the LORD says—
> he who created the heavens and
>     stretched them out,
>   who spread out the earth with all
>     that springs from it,
> who gives breath to its people,
>   and life to those who walk on it.

Christians must decide whether technologies should be used liberally or whether restrictions are necessary to help protect those who might not be able to protect themselves (e.g., the embryo and a being that has yet to be cloned).

*See also* "Assisted Reproductive Technologies," "Bioethics" and "Stem Cell Research."

## CONSUMERISM

One of the marks of a capitalistic society is consumerism, which is based on the idea that material possessions and consumption bring happiness. Twenty percent of the population in developed nations consume 86 percent of the world's goods.[73] The United States population is approximately 4 percent of the world's population, yet it consumes 22 percent of the world's energy.[74] The United States gross domestic product (GDP) makes up 27 percent of the global economy. The combined GDP of the developing world makes up only 3.9 percent.[75] It has become clear that developed nations overconsume, and the poor in developing nations pay the price with their lowered standards of living and increasing environmental damage. It is estimated that

### New Monasticism

Today, some Christians are attracted to following Christ through simpler lifestyles in the context of community. Several of these communities identified twelve attributes that help them encourage others and discern the work of God in their midst. These traits, which can be read about in *School(s) for Conversion: 12 Marks of a New Monasticism*, include relocating to abandoned places, sharing economic resources with fellow community members and the needy, hospitality to the stranger, and humble submission to Christ's body, the church.

←← *Take action.* Learn more about the new monastic movement and the trend toward simpler living. Schedule a three-day visit to stay in a new monastic community in order to learn about their theology and way of life. Arrangements can be made at www.newmonasticism.org. For an interactive map of the United States and a listing of new monastic communities, visit www.communityofcommunities.info.

#### FOR FURTHER STUDY

*The New Monasticism: What It Has to Say to Today's Church* by Jonathan Wilson-Hartgrove

*School(s) for Conversion: 12 Marks of a New Monasticism* edited by Rutba House

*The New Friars: The Emerging Movement Serving the World's Poor* by Scott Bessenecker

## The Simple Way

Shane Claiborne has had a vast array of ministry exposure, including an internship at Willow Creek Community Church in the wealthy suburbs of Chicago and serving alongside Mother Teresa for ten weeks in Calcutta, India. While living in Philadelphia, it came to his attention that homeless people were living in an abandoned church building. Soon after, Shane discovered that the church owners were going to kick the homeless out, so Shane moved in. This was the beginning of the Simple Way—a faith community in the heart of Philadelphia that has helped to birth and connect radical faith communities around the world. Many of the communities are part of the new monasticism movement, which produced the book *School(s) for Conversion.*

These monastic communities seek to follow Jesus, to rediscover the spirit of the early church and to incarnate the kingdom of God—which stands in stark contrast to the world of militarism and materialism. At the Simple Way, days are spent feeding hungry folks, doing collaborative arts with children, running a community store, hanging out with neighbors and reclaiming trash-strewn lots by planting gardens. Shane observes, "The early Christians used to write that when they did not have enough food for the hungry people at their door, the entire community would fast until everyone could share a meal together. What an incredible economy of love."[76] Shane and the Simple Way do much work to expose the fundamental structures that create poverty and to imagine alternatives to them. Visit www.thesimpleway.org for more information.

### FOR FURTHER STUDY

*The Irresistible Revolution: Living as an Ordinary Radical* by Shane Claiborne

*See also* "Consumerism" and "Poverty."

---

four to six hectares of land is needed to maintain the consumption level of the average person from an industrialized country, but in 1990 only 1.7 hectares of ecologically productive land was available for each person.[77]

***Awareness exercise.*** Shane Claiborne, founder of the Simple Way, and Tony Campolo, Christian leader and social justice advocate, created a video resource called *Simply Enough*, which offers alternatives to consumerism through the pursuit of a more simple lifestyle. Watch *Simply Enough* with some friends or a small group. Talk through the discussion questions that are provided. Are there ways that God is calling you to live differently? This resource may be found at the Alternatives for Simple Living website (www.simpleliving.org). Alternatives for Simple Living was founded in the 1970s and is a nonprofit organization that works with Protestant and Catholic churches to "provide materials on responsible living, social justice, and peace."[78] They have other great resources to help your journey toward simplicity. Another DVD that could be used for the same purpose is the PBS documentary *Affluenza,* which addresses the high social and environmental costs of overconsumption and materialism. A teacher's guide and other resources are available on PBS's website at www.pbs.org/kcts/affluenza.

←« *Take action.* Consider your patterns of consumption in your household. What could you give up for a while to limit your consumption? Choose a specific amount of time—one week, one month, three months—and intentionally limit your consumption. Consider this as a way of fasting, in which you can redirect your time and energy spent on things that will not satisfy the soul. Send the money that you save in this effort to an organization that helps the developing world. For help finding a ministry, see the list of organizations in the "Organizations" appendix.

←« *Take action.* Pick a holiday season to fast from buying presents and instead spend time refocusing your spiritual life. Use the money that you save to respond to the needs of the poor. Consider visiting the elderly at a retirement center; spend time with those who might not have family. Consider partnering with an organization like Advent Conspiracy (www.adventconspiracy.org), a movement attempting to "restore the scandal of Christmas by worshiping Jesus through compassion, not consumption."

**FOR FURTHER STUDY**

*Consuming Jesus: Beyond Race and Class Divisions in a Consumer Church* by Paul Louis Metzger

*The Overspent American: Why We Want What We Don't Need* by Juliet Schor

*Christ and Consumerism: A Critical Analysis of the Spirit of the Age* edited by Craig Bartholomew and Thorsten Moritz

*See also* "Capitalism," "Family" and "Global Economy."

## DISASTER RELIEF

Disaster relief consists of emergency response efforts on behalf of communities that are affected by crises such as floods, earthquakes, tornadoes, disease, draught, fire, famine, power outages and acts of terror. Many times the response to these types of occurrences is best left to professionals. There is, however, a critical role the church can play in providing financial support, through gifts-in-kind initiatives and, when appropriate, by equipping and sending volunteers.

Typically, there are five stages of operation in responding to a disaster. The first and most immediate stage is life saving. This occurs immediately after the disaster strikes and typically winds down within the first ninety-six hours. The vast majority (approximately 95 percent) of the first responders are local.

The second stage gets the most attention and requires the support of volunteers from outside of the community: emergency relief for the living. Emergency relief includes the basic necessities of getting life back in order—clean water, adequate shelter and food—and typically takes one to three months, depending on the access to the community. The responders usually work through government

# Willow Creek Community Church

While on staff at Willow Creek I had the privilege of working with and assisting in the church's disaster response efforts. Prompted by the overwhelming response of people in the congregation, Willow decided to develop a disaster response team that would be ready when disasters occurred. In response to Hurricane Katrina, Willow Creek mobilized over one thousand volunteers and raised approximately $880,000 which was used to provide direct assistance and immediate support to churches in the Gulf Coast region; to send support teams to Waveland, Mississippi; and to provide materials and supplies for the relief site in the Gulf Coast. Accounts from participants who volunteered in the Gulf Coast in response to Hurricane Katrina can be read on Willow Creek's blog site at wccc.blogs.com/hurricane/2005/09/index.html.

Inspired by her experience, one of the team leaders Willow sent to Waveland, Mississippi, wrote this paraphrase of Matthew 25:35-40:

I was hungry and you fed me
biscuits, sausage and sweet tea.
I was thirsty and you listened to my
story and cared for my heart.
I was a stranger and you invited me
into your church's clothing tent
with hugs and love.
I needed clothes and you showered
me with shirts, shoes, sheets and
underwear.
I was sick and you prayed for me.

I was in the prison of poverty after
losing all my possessions and you
declared dignity on me.
In turn, I was hungry to help
others outside my suburban
world and you let me in.
I was thirsty for a fresh meaning of
thankfulness and you showered
me with an attitude of gratitude.
You clothed me with love and
warmth.
I was sick from the worldly race
and an insane pace, and you
poured the healing balm of
contentment and simplicity over
me.
I was a stranger and you welcomed
me into your washed-away
Waveland world with open
arms.
I was in the prison of perfection
and performance, and you
showed me what really matters
in this life.
And I tell you the truth, whatever
you did for the least of my
people you did for me.

Jan Sullivan[80]

You can read more about some of Willow's efforts in response to disasters such as the tsunami in Southeast Asia (December 2004), Hurricane Katrina (August 2005), Tropical Storm Noel (October 2007) and the Myanmar Cyclone (May 2008) at www.willowcreek.org/disasterresponse.

and nongovernmental agencies like the Red Cross, World Relief, World Vision and Samaritans Purse.

The third stage is community stabilization. This occurs when people are moved from temporary structures to more permanent ones. The provision of adequate long-term shelter is typically the main component of this stage.

The fourth component is economic revitalization. Many communities affected by disasters have lost at least some of their infrastructure and potential for livelihood. Once food, clothing and shelter are reestablished, economic revitalization can take an extensive period of time, even years, depending on the magnitude of the disaster.

The final stage in disaster response is the rebuilding of infrastructure, such as roads, schools and other community organizations and services.[79]

The greatest need in disaster response is long-term after-care. Two, three or even four years after the crisis occurs, will the volunteers and servants still be there? There is little glamor in the work and service, but the residue of community trauma and devastation continue to exist.

Christians and church leaders must not be captivated by the immediate need after disasters strike. Instead, a commitment should be made to persist in providing long-term sustainable support. I returned to Waveland, Mississippi, several times after Katrina struck in 2005. During my last trip in 2007, I noticed that much hadn't changed two years after the storm. However, there were fewer churches and volunteers present to help clean up the mess.

←* *Take action.* Consider starting a disaster response group at your church. Be sure that you are working in partnership with the church's leadership. (1) Determine what type of strategy your church will have for its involvement in disaster response. (2) Develop an implementation plan for use once disaster strikes. (3) Meet immediately (in person or on the phone) after a disaster occurs to determine your church's course of action (if any). Then assign specific guidelines for all the roles played in your response. (4) Once a plan of action has been agreed upon, implement your response. During and after your service, evaluate (and ask outside observers and participants to contribute to the evaluation process) what went well and where your ministry was effective, as well as areas where you could improve in the future.

---

**FOR FURTHER STUDY**

*Soul Storm: Finding God Amidst Disaster* by Bruce Lee Smith

*Group's Emergency Response Handbook for Disaster Relief* by the Salvation Army

---

## DOMESTIC ABUSE AND VIOLENCE

One of the major justice issues affecting women in the United States is the abuse of power through sexual or domestic violence. One in three women in the United States and around the world will have been sexually abused in their lifetime.[81] Regina Shands Stoltzfus says:

Violence against women needs to be named, and violence against people of color needs to be named. In order to name them, we need to learn to recognize them. For too long, these stories have been untold. Women's struggles must be put into a framework that includes the struggle of women of color, and antiracism work must include the voices of women.[82]

Violence is an unjust or unwanted exertion of force or power, which is manifest many ways, including physical, sexual and emotional behaviors. It is most often perpetrated toward women and children.

Domestic violence is the systematic domination and oppression of one group or person over another in such a way that the oppressor has made it clear that the other is not safe.[83] More often than not, men are the perpetrators, because they are physically more powerful than women. Thirty percent of Americans say they know a woman who has been physically abused by her boyfriend or husband in the past year.[84] In 2001 more than half a million American women were victims of nonfatal violence committed by an intimate partner.[85] The church cannot be involved in justice and ignore the presence of violence against women and children, both in the United States and abroad.

We can no longer afford to be silent about the issues of sexual abuse and domestic violence. Although these topics are highly sensitive, the church must learn how to address them clearly and without compromise. God takes up the cause of the oppressed and does not turn a deaf ear to their cries.

You, Lord, hear the desire of the
   afflicted;
  you encourage them, and you listen
   to their cry,

defending the fatherless and the
   oppressed,
  so that mere earthly morals
  will never again strike terror.
(Ps 10:17-18)

The church must not be guilty of sitting on the sidelines and not standing up on behalf of men, women and children who are being victimized by violence and abuse.

Sometimes the church not only neglects to intervene to prevent domestic violence, but contributes to the problem.[86] Some Christian communities encourage women to stay in broken relationships in order to win their abusers to Christ through their submission. A person's theological view about women can contribute to this dynamic. Complementarians believe that it is the woman's role to submit to her husband. And many believe that women should submit to men in general. Some conservatives use their complementarian beliefs to justify abuse and violence. The view that women are "less than" and do not have an equal voice in marriage relationships contributes to their oppression in that context.

←※ *Take action.* Sponsor a class on anger management that includes training in conflict management and communications skills within relationships. You may be able to find someone within your congregation who has skills in this area or contact your local community organizations to find someone who could facilitate the class. One program that might be helpful is "What's Good About Anger?" offered by Christian Counselor Lynette Hoy. Resources can be found at www.whats goodaboutanger.com.

←⚞ *Take action.* Ensure that your church is a place where victims of domestic violence, sexual assault, stalking and dating violence can come for help and healing. Display materials that include local and state hotlines for these problems. And provide ways for members of the congregation to learn as much as they can about domestic violence, sexual assault, stalking and dating violence. Include information in monthly newsletters, on bulletin boards and in marriage preparation classes. Sponsor educational seminars for your congregation on violence against women.[87] For more information visit the Violence Against Women website at www.womenshealth.gov/violence.

←⚞ *Take action.* Consider volunteering at a women's shelter in your community. Often women who are isolated from their family for the sake of protection are lonely and in need of trusting people who might offer support and encouragement. Shelters need volunteers, financial support and gifts-in-kind that can be used by women and families in residence.

The best way to find a shelter in your community is to go to Google and type in "Christian Domestic Violence Shelter." For example, the Family Renewal Shelter (www.domesticviolencehelp.com) is a Christian domestic-violence shelter based in Tacoma, Washington, that offers many services, including case management, legal referrals, emergency advocacy and transportation, onsite warehouse for the storage of possessions, transitional housing and a national domestic violence hotline to help connect women to programs in their own communities.

**FOR FURTHER READING**

*The Abuse of Power: A Theological Problem* by James Poling

*The Wounded Heart: Hope for Adult Victims of Childhood Sexual Abuse* by Dan Allender

*Women Submit! Christians and Domestic Violence* by Jocelyn E. Anderson

*No Place for Abuse* by Catherine Clark Kroeger and Nancy Nason-Clark

*Refuge from Abuse* by Catherine Clark Kroeger and Nancy Nason-Clark

*See also* "Family" and "Women."

## DRUGS AND ADDICTION

Despairing people often turn to remedies that might alleviate their pain and suffering. The percentage of homeless people who struggle with drugs and other addictions is very high. According to a 1996 survey the percentage of homeless people struggling with drug or alcohol abuse or mental illness was over 60 percent.[88] Cycles of poverty keep people from feeling there is hope. But there are also stories of people who have, by the grace of God, been able to come out of that lifestyle.

←⚞ *Take action.* Celebrate Recovery is a Christian twelve-step program founded in Lake Forest, California, at Saddleback Church. The program is now available at 3,500 churches and at treatment centers around the country. The goal of the program is to "celebrate God's healing power" by using Scripture and biblical principles to encourage people to live healthy lives, free of addition and full of hope. Consider attending a Celebrate Recovery seminar, which are offered all over the United States, or starting a small group at your church. Visit www

# The Story of Ms. Pearl

Ms. Pearl was one of thirteen siblings who grew up on the Southside of Chicago. When Pearl was fifteen years old she was in custody of the state because her life was in such disarray. During that time Pearl's mother told her that her name, Pearl, came from Jesus, "Do you know what a pearl is?" she asked. When Pearl shook her head, her mother told her that she was precious. She said that a pearl is a rare thing and that her daughter was one of a kind. Pearl laughed and couldn't believe her mother's words.

At sixteen, Pearl found herself pregnant and alone. She dropped out of school and her life spiraled downward. She lived on and off the streets. Addicted to drugs and alcohol, she traded her body to satisfy her addictions. She had another child and her life seemed hopeless as she tried to balance raising her family alone while satisfying her need for drugs. She tried to end her life twice, but was unsuccessful. God had bigger things in mind. Through tears, Ms. Pearl talks about that time in her life, "I found myself in the shower, scrubbing my body, literally looking to be clean. I didn't know what it meant that you could be clean on the inside."

One day Pearl went to a church group where a man began to tell her about the forgiveness that she could experience through Jesus Christ. She looked at the man and said, "You are a liar!" She couldn't imagine a God that would forgive her, a God who would reach down to her with his loving hands of compassion. It took seventeen years of God reaching out to Pearl before she came to know him. He was reaching toward her, and one day she understood and accepted Christ as her Savior. She came to understand that God saved her and loved her enough that Jesus died for her sins and gave her the free gift of love and salvation. Pearl experienced compassion from God.

After Pearl met Jesus, her daughter introduced her to a fourteen-year-old friend who couldn't go back to school because she had a baby. Each of the girls brought another girl until Ms. Pearl was taking care of the children of a dozen high school girls. With faith leading Ms. Pearl, one thing led to another. Now Pearl is the executive director of Roseland Good News Daycare. Ms. Pearl talks about the girls she works with: "If God can bring me out, I believe he can bring anybody out." Pearl feels that the girls can relate to her because she has been where they are. She offers them hope in the midst of their situations. All of the girls who bring their kids to Roseland are required to go to a weekly Bible study to learn about Jesus. Ms. Pearl says proudly, "Look around you, I teach about Jesus." Anyone who visits Roseland wouldn't doubt that is where the power to change has come from. Ms. Pearl can't tell her story without weeping in remembrance of the compassion she has experienced from Christ. She lives out her conviction and has made a profound impact in the Roseland Community.

When Roseland started, there were five drug houses on the block. Over the years, through prayer and persistence, one by one the drug houses closed. Ms. Pearl started her daycare with a few high school moms; now the ministry blesses hundreds of families. She talks about her work with a gleam of celebration in her eye, "We have had thirty-one high school graduates, and all of them know Jesus as their Lord and Savior. We have had sixteen special-education graduates, and all of them know Jesus as their Lord and Savior; eleven college graduates, and all of them know Jesus as their Lord and Savior. That is the fulfillment. It is greater than money. It is greater than a house on the seashore . . . to know within yourself that they are going to be sitting with you in heaven one day." She talks about the hope that can be found in Christ. Her life is living proof that there is hope. Ms. Pearl says, "If God can bring me out of seventeen years of addiction, he can do anything."[89]

*Awareness exercise.* Ms. Pearl's story can be heard in detail on the video *Changing the World One Woman at a Time* (available at www.willowcreek.com). Watch her story (and the others on the DVD) with a group and discuss. How might God be calling you to respond?

---

.celebraterecovery.com to find out more.

←❋ *Take action.* Consider serving as a volunteer at a Christian treatment center for recovery from addictions. For more information about treatment centers that offer Celebrate Recovery's philosophy and programs, visit Sober Living By the Sea (www.sober living.com). Pacific Hills Treatment Centers, Inc., (www.pachills.com) is another Christian-based recovery program for alcohol and drug rehabilitation.

←❋ *Take action.* Start an education program about the use of drugs and alcohol in your church, school or other context. Follow the model of an organization like Hope UK (www.hopeuk.org), a Christian charity committed to enabling young people to make drug-free choices. Hope UK is based on the principles of Scripture and teaches youth how to care for themselves and others. Volunteers may serve as church representatives, prayer partners, educators or in some other capacity.

**FOR FURTHER STUDY**

*Managing the Madness: From Addiction to Devotions* by Revel Dawson

*Life's Healing Choices: Freedom from Your Hurt's, Hang-Ups, and Habits* by John Baker

See also "Family," "Homelessness," "Poverty" and "Race."

## EDUCATION—DOMESTIC

Education may be the single most influential factor contributing to the success of our future. Statistics show that education is a foundational stepping stone to helping people progress out of poverty. Regarding this, Sanford Cloud Jr. says:

> Education is the cornerstone to the success of each individual in our society. From the time a child is born, the education process begins in our homes. This is formalized through schooling and the results are quantified through grades, test scores, and eventually a job or career. Eventually, the degree to which one performs in school often sets one's life path: where one lives, works, plays, and raises one's own children. Having access to quality education should therefore be a fundamental right for all residents of this country.[90]

Throughout the history of education in the United States, there have been questions about the access to equal education. This was especially a challenge for low-income students of color. Prior to the civil rights movements, educational programs and schools were completely segregated, with most of a community's resources (financial and otherwise) allocated to white schools and programs. Since the announcement of the historic decision *Brown v. Board of Education*, May 17, 1954, Americans have operated with the understanding that "separate educational facilities are inherently unequal."[91]

Even in the twenty-first century, there are significant differences in the public school systems of the United States. Children in underresourced areas are the most affected by these disparities. Most of these are children of color. In 2002, Sanford Cloud Jr. said, "The federal government knows the academic arena is unequal, and yet they continue to insti-

tute policies which proliferate disparities versus a plan to expose and stop the essence of the problem: bias, bigotry and racism."[92]

In the late 1990s, African American and Latino high school graduates had skills in reading and mathematics that were equivalent to that of white eighth graders. Approximately one in ten whites, one in thirty Latinos and one in one hundred African Americans could easily solve an elementary algebra problem.[93]

Between October 2004 and October 2005, the drop-out rates for students in the United States school systems were 7.3 percent for blacks, 5.0 percent for Hispanics and 2.8 percent for whites.[94]

In 2006 the percentage of sixteen to twenty-four-year-olds who were not enrolled in high school and who lack a high school credential (such as the GED) was 5.8 percent for white students, 10.7 percent for black students and 22.1 percent for Hispanic students.[95]

African Americans are only half as likely as white students to earn a bachelor's degree by age twenty-nine, and Latinos are one-third as likely as whites to earn a college degree.[96]

***No Child Left Behind.*** One of the most significant attempts to address problems in education by the U.S. government has been the No Child Left Behind (NCLB) program. Many sociologists believe that No Child Left Behind may in fact lessen the poverty gap. No Child Left Behind, enacted in 2001, is a federal program designed to improve the performance of primary and secondary schools while also providing more flexibility for parents to choose which school their child will attend. The success and implementation of

# Confrontation with Chicago Public Schools

My brother moved in with us when he was 16 years old. He's a really smart kid, but had some trouble in the traditional school system. When he moved in with us, he should have been in the middle of his sophomore year of high school. However, he had enough high school credits to skip a year and enter the Chicago Public School (CPS) system as a junior. We had the task of registering him in our local Chicago public high school. I would have thought that a young man with off-the-chart test scores, who had already skipped a year because of his academic progress, would have been a shoo-in for one of the magnet schools in the city of Chicago.

Magnet schools are public schools that first came into being in the 1960s and 1970s as a way to further implement the legislation of *Brown v. Board of Education*. The schools were established to attract students from other school districts based on their academic excellence and special emphases. They were designed to help desegregation occur more naturally. Today, magnet schools receive additional funding to enable them to spend more money on teachers, students, and special programs. As we explored our options, we discovered that the magnet schools accept almost all of their students directly out of competitive middle school programs. The percentage of students that they allow to transfer in from other schools, even if they are kids moving into the area from out-of-

state, is negligible at best. In addition, we discovered that magnet schools do not allow transfers mid-year. That would not have been a problem except for the fact that they also do not accept any Senior transfers. In other words, a young man in my brother's situation didn't have a chance. His only option was to apply to a selective enrollment high school within CPS that would allow him some of the benefits of gifted and academic classes.

After much trepidation, we enrolled him in a high school that was not too far away from our home. Within a few weeks, we knew that the situation was not going to work out. He came home with class work that was remedial at best. The resources that were provided were out of date. His texts books were falling apart. He didn't feel challenged and was frustrated by the limiting restrictions on students in his school because of all of the gang violence and other social pressures. After a few months, he dropped out and completed his GED. By the following fall, he had been accepted in community college and shortly thereafter transferred to a four-year college. It was incredibly disappointing to experience first hand the limitations of the Chicago Public School system.

While all of this was happening, I was working in one of the more affluent suburbs of Chicago and talking to other families who had their children enrolled in public school. The amenities offered to suburban students far outweighed the exposure and experiences in CPS. Recently, in an address made about the extreme deficit that the public school system is facing, Arne Duncan, Chief Executive Officer of Chicago Public Schools, stated that CPS currently spends approximately $10,500 per pupil, per year. Some surrounding school districts spend close to $20,000. Having spoken with many of my friends and colleagues in the Chicago suburbs, it is very easy to see the discrepancy in the education that is being provided for students. What an atrocity that city kids are not being given the same opportunities to grow, develop, and learn because of the limits in our education system.

The growing divide between equal education of students both in magnet schools and in different school districts is an injustice that needs to be addressed. Historically, education funding in the State of Illinois has been based on property tax. This means that students who have wealthy parents and live in expensive districts will receive a cream-of-the-crop education while children who come from poverty and underresourced families will suffer by not being provided with acceptable education.[97]

NCLB is hotly debated. The primary concern is that it could reduce effective instruction because achievement goals may be lowered by individual states and students may be overly directed to study for the standardized tests. Another critique of NCLB is that it provides little support for underfunded schools, which will not help students meet the NCLB benchmarks.

←※ *Take action.* Find out what types of tutoring programs are offered in your community. Volunteer to develop relationships with some of the children in the program. As you get involved, develop relationships with the school's administrators. Ask questions and advocate for changes that will improve the educational programs. Consider joining the board of your school district to be in a position of influence and help make just decisions.

←※ *Take action.* Contact a local school in your community. Find out which students need school supplies and if the school has a mechanism for distributing the supplies. Ask the school how you can help support their efforts. In August, host a "Back to School" drive that provides backpacks filled with school supplies (e.g., paper, pens, markers) to help children be well equipped. If the school is willing, you could include an age-appropriate Bible. Children from your church's Sunday school program could write notes of encouragement to be included in the backpacks.

←※ *Take action.* Consider partnering with a Christian nonprofit that is focused on education reform in an underresourced community. If a nonprofit like that does not exist in your community, ask God if he might be leading you to start one! (Read *Starting a Nonprofit at*

*Your Church* by Joy Skjegstad.) There are numerous foundations that provide grants to Christian organizations and ministries committed to bringing quality education to underserved communities. Research these foundations and apply for a grant on behalf of the organization (with the support of their leadership) with whom you are serving. Consider using a philanthropic management tool such as the one provided by Bank of America at www.bankofamerica.com/philanthropic/ grantmaking.action. Many of the grants listed are available for Christian ministries.

**FOR FURTHER STUDY**

*Challenging Racism in Higher Education: Promoting Justice* by Mark Chesler, Amanda Lewis and James Crowfoot

*Handbook of Social Justice in Education* edited by William Ayres, Therese Quinn and David Stovall

*Standards-Based Reform and the Poverty Gap: Lessons for "No Child Left Behind"* by Adam Gamoran

## EDUCATION—GLOBAL

According to the World Bank more than 100 million primary-school-age children are too poor to go to school. Compassion International states that number as closer to 121 million. In 2008 it was estimated that of these children, 55 percent were girls. And these are optimistic numbers.[98] One statistic showed that less than 1 percent of what the world spent every year on weapons was needed to put every child into school by the year 2000. It didn't happen.[99]

Around the world, illiteracy is a huge problem. Nearly a billion people (approximately one out of six people in the world) cannot read or write their own name.[100] Two-thirds of the world's illiterates are women, and 80 percent of its refugees are women and children.[101] According to Bread for the World, about one-fifth of the world's adult population—771 million adults—do not have basic literacy skills.[102]

Education is one of the primary ways out of poverty and destitution. Education provides opportunities for growth and exposure to opportunities. The United Nations has declared that education is essential in the fight against global poverty. Julius Nyerere, former president of Tanzania, observes, "Education is not a way to escape poverty. It is a way of fighting it."[103] Developing nations will not be able to sustain themselves in the larger global community without significant efforts toward the education of their people. According to the 2001 International Workshop on Education and Poverty Eradication, the integration of school programs within the economic activities of the community encourage individuals and "empower them by heightening their awareness of their rights and responsibilities, their abilities, and enhance their self-confidence to enable them to improve their lives."[104] Christians may partner with government and nonprofit organizations that are working around the globe on behalf of education for the poor to improve literacy, critical-thinking skills and other fundamental aspects of learning and development.

←* ***Take action.*** Lead a campaign for education working with an organization like World Vision. For $50, World Vision is able to send a poor child to school for a year. See how many children you and your community can sponsor. Visit www.worldvision.org/content .nsf/learn/ways-we-help-education#need.

## Teachers Without Borders

Teachers Without Borders is an organization working to support global education initiatives. Teachers Without Borders is a nondenominational educational service organization that provides educational aid for constructive social change in the global information age. They connect teachers to resources, technical skills and each other. Teachers Without Borders offers teaching and learning centers, certificate of mastery, youth programs, programs for disability access, and students without borders. For more information visit www .teacherswithoutborders.org.

←**❋** *Take action.* Contact your local elementary school to see if a class (or grade) could host a read-a-thon to raise funds on behalf of an international school. (This could also be done with a Sunday school class.) Set a time for the read-a-thon. Ask students to solicit pledges from friends, family and neighbors for every book that they read in a given period of time. The read-a-thon could take place over a few weeks, a month or longer. Be sure the parameters are set ahead of time. Sponsors could choose to donate a set amount (e.g., $5, $10, $20, etc.) or to donate per book read (e.g., $0.50/book, $1/book, $5/book, etc.). This is a great way to encourage young people to read while also making a difference by supporting international education in a developing community. If your church does not have a relationship with an international school, work with a nonprofit such as Compassion International or World Vision to identify a community where your gift could be used to support the education of the poor.

←**❋** *Take action.* Compassion International has expanded their child sponsorship to include a leadership development program by providing access to higher education and leadership training for young Christian men and women in the developing world. Compassion's Leadership Development Program (LDP) identifies young people who "have shown potential to become Christian leaders who can, in turn, influence their own families, churches, communities, and nations." In 2008, sponsorship of an LDP student was $300 per month and provided for the cost of undergraduate tuition, books, school-related expenses, room and board, transportation, one-on-one mentoring with a Christian professional, and Christian leadership training. Visit www.compassion.com/contribution/le adershipdevelopmenthtm?MoreInfo=1.

### FOR FURTHER STUDY

*Learning in the Global Era: International Perspectives on Globalization and Education* by Marcelo Suarez

*Education in a Global Society: A Comparative Perspective* by Kas Mazurek, Margret Winzer and Czeslaw Majorek.

*And the Children Shall Lead: An NGO Journey Into Peace Education* edited by Bill Lowry, Allen Harder and Vachel Miller

*See also* "Children," "Education—Domestic" and "Women."

## ENVIRONMENTAL JUSTICE

Environmental justice refers to the way that society and the environment interact and place an inequitable burden on groups such as racial minorities, women, and residents in developing nations. In our postmodern age there is a growing understanding that those living in poverty and developing countries are most significantly affected by global warming and climate change, pollution, and the degradation of the environment. God desires for his followers to care for his creation! John Stott says:

> Christian people should surely have been in the vanguard of the movement for environmental responsibility, because of our doctrines of creation and stewardship. Did God make the world? Does he sustain it? Has he committed its resources to our care? His personal concern for his own creation should be sufficient to inspire us to be equally concerned.[105]

*Global warming and climate change.* The world's climate affects everything—the ability for vegetation to be able to grow; the amount of water in estuaries, bays, rivers, seas and oceans; whether or not animals and other creatures are able to thrive; the spread of disease around the world; the environment in which humans live and exist. Global warming has already begun to have negative effects on the earth's environment. Environmental experts and some of the world's leading scientists agree that if this phenomena goes unchecked, the effects will be devastating—particularly for the world's poor.

According to the Evangelical Environmental Network, because of global warming the land's ability to produce agriculturally will be significantly impaired and an additional 40 to 170 million poor people could be at risk of hunger and malnutrition in this century. Worldwide, more than 100 million people will be adversely impacted by coastal flooding. By 2050, 20 to 30 percent of the world's creatures could be on the road to extinction, "making global warming the largest threat to biodiversity."[106] These are just some of the anticipated effects of global warming. Reality is, no one knows for sure exactly what is going to happen. However, trends clearly indicate that the results of global warming are not good and that the poorest of the poor are the most adversely affected.

*Pollution.* In addition to global warming, consider pollution. Those who have subsistence lifestyles depend on the land for food. Food produced on land that was (or is) a dumping ground or is irrigated by water contaminated by fertilizers is dangerous to eat. There is a direct correlation between the environment and global food supply. Environmental concerns such as deforestation, overcrowding or natural disasters have the greatest effect on the poor. Air pollution is a major problem to underresourced people, even leading to death. Indoor air pollution resulting from the use of solid fuels (by poorer segments of society) is also a major killer. Indoor air pollution claims the lives of 1.5 million people each year (4,000 deaths per day), more than half of them under the age of five. This number exceeds the total deaths from malaria, and rivals the number of deaths from tuberculosis.[107]

There is growing concern among Christians about the way that we are living out God's commandment in Genesis 1 to steward God's creation. The more we are aware of our ecological footprint, our impact on the environment, the better able we are to steward God's creation.

*Awareness exercise.* Be aware of your global footprint. Search online to learn about the impact that you are having on the environment. Global Footprint Network (www .footprintnetwork.org) has a great online quiz that will allow you to see how your activities affect the earth's resources.

←❋ *Take action.* Launched in 2006, the Evangelical Climate Change Initiative (ECI), alongside more than 250 evangelical leaders, launched a "Call to Action on Climate Change" to mobilize Christians to help solve the problem of global warming. The statement makes four primary claims: (1) human-induced climate change is real; (2) the consequences of climate change will be significant, and will hit the poor the hardest; (3) Christian moral convictions demand our response to the climate change problem; and (4) The need to act now is urgent. Government, businesses, churches and individuals all have a role to play in addressing climate change. Go to the ECI website (christiansandclimate.org). Read the detailed statement. If you are in agreement, make a declaration to join in this effort by signing the initiative.

←❋ *Take action.* Celebrate Earth Day on April 22! You don't have to be an environmental extremist to believe that God has revealed himself to us through his creation. Earth day is a way to partner with others to show that you care about the earth. Visit www.earthday.net for ideas about how to get involved.

←❋ *Take action.* Consider becoming an intern for six-weeks in Jaguar Creek, Belize, at Target Earth. Target Earth (www.targetearth .org) is committed to serving the earth and the poor in Jesus' name. It is a national movement of Christians (individuals, churches, college fellowships and Christian ministries) devoted to God's call to be faithful stewards of everything that he has created.

←❋ *Take action.* Ask your pastor if he or she would be willing to dedicate a Sunday service to education about global warming, the environment and creation care. Encourage your pastor to preach a sermon about the issue. Creation Care for Pastors (www.creationcare forpastors.com) distributes a helpful reference book that summarizes some of the core issues and provides Scripture passages for how God calls the church to love his creation. As a part of your creation Sunday, you can distribute reusable shopping bags with your church logo to members of the congregation.[108]

←❋ *Take action.* Go green! Become more energy efficient as an individual, in your home, your church community and your work. There are tons of ways to practice good stewardship of the environment. For example: change your light bulbs with LED energy-saving bulbs or compact fluorescent lights; drive a car that gets good gas mileage and is energy efficient; walk or bike whenever you can; moderate the heating or cooling in your home; use energy-efficient appliances;

don't leave your water running; recycle; use reusable products instead of disposables; buy things with minimum packaging; shop from local farmers and growers; unplug electronics not in use; use less paper; and convert toilets and shower heads so that they use less water. Research, study, read a book, look at a website as there are many other things that you can do!

←▪ *Take action.* Work with officials on your school board to have your community schools go green. Earth Day Network has partnered with the U.S. Green Building Council and the Clinton Foundation for every K-12 school in the United States to become green within this generation. This initiative, called GREEN ReModel (www.earthday.net/greenremodel) is committed to converting schools by tightening the building envelope; installing high-performance heating, cooling and ventilation systems; installing on-site renewable energy; installing high efficiency lighting and increasing natural lighting; and other sustainable solutions that will mitigate climate change and lower the impact of schools on the environment.

**FOR FURTHER STUDY**

*Green Revolution* by Ben Lowe

*Serve God, Save the Planet* by J. Matthew Sleeth

*Saving God's Green Earth* by Tri Robinson with Jason Chatraw

*See also* "Education," "Malaria," "Poverty" and "Tuberculosis."

✽ *Spiritual reflection exercise.* During seminary, I had the opportunity to take a "Wilderness and Faith" course that took a few stu-

dents into the wilderness of the Boundary Waters Canoe Area (BWCA) in northern Minnesota. We spent a week studying theology of creation and wilderness and then took a five-day trek through the lakes of the Boundary Waters. That course shaped my understanding of the way that God speaks to us through his creation. In *Spiritual Pathways* Gary Thomas mentions that for many people creation is a pathway to experience God. In the Boundary Waters I found that to be true. Being in the wilderness helped me to get a glimpse of the magnitude of God's creative powers. Verses like Isaiah 40:28 took on new meaning, "The LORD is the everlasting God, / the Creator of the ends of the earth." My experience reminded me of how God is manifest in creation.

If you can, take your Bible and do this exercise outside, in the middle of God's creation. Even better, enter into the wilderness for a day or more. Read Genesis 1:26-30.

> God spoke: "Let us make human
>     beings in our image, make them
>     reflecting our nature
> So they can be responsible for the
>     fish in the sea,
> the birds in the air, the cattle,
>     And, yes, Earth itself,
> and every animal that moves on the
>     face of Earth."
>     God created human beings;
> he created them godlike,
>     Reflecting God's nature.
> He created them male and female.
>     God blessed them:
> "Prosper! Reproduce! Fill Earth! Take
>     charge!
>     Be responsible for fish in the sea and

birds in the air,
for every living thing that moves on
the face of Earth."
Then God said, "I've given you
every sort of seed-bearing plant on
Earth
And every kind of fruit-bearing
tree,
given them to you for food.
To all animals and all birds,
everything that moves and breathes,
I give whatever grows out of the
ground for food."
And there it was. (Gen 1:26-30 *The
Message*)

What does this passage have to say about God's creation? What other passages can you find about God's creation? What are they saying to you? What passages can you find that talk about wilderness? How has God spoken to the Old Testament prophets, Jesus and other biblical characters during their times in the wilderness? Ask God to reveal himself to you through his Word.

---

**FOR FURTHER STUDY**

*Christian Environmental Ethics: A Case Method Approach* by James Martin-Schramm and Robert Stivers

*Our Father's World* by Edward R. Brown

---

## EUTHANASIA AND PHYSICIAN-ASSISTED SUICIDE

The questions that surround assisted death are becoming more prevalent in contemporary society. At the turn of the twenty-first century the state of Oregon and several countries permit different forms of assisted death, including Belgium, the Netherlands, Colombia

and Australia. Obviously, the morality of suicide, euthanasia and physician involvement is broadly questioned. The assisted-death movement is often broken into two categories: physician-assisted suicide (PAS) and euthanasia. Physician-assisted suicide is defined as a self-inflicted death that occurs when information, prescriptions or suicide aides have been provided by a physician or health care professional.[109] *Euthanasia* literally means "easy death," but is understood to mean the direct taking of a terminally ill or dying person's life by another person for compassionate reasons.[110] Active euthanasia is understood to be taking some purposeful action to end a life, whereas passive euthanasia refers to the withholding or refusal of treatment to sustain life.[111]

There are numerous arguments for and against the assisted-death movement. One side of the issue claims that assisted death is compassionate and morally justified.[112] The opposing side holds that "sanctity of life" is the highest good and thus PAS and euthanasia are not morally permissible.

After looking closely at both the call for compassion and the proponents of the sanctity of life view, it becomes clear that PAS and euthanasia are not based on simple altruistic motives. There is abundant evidence that assisted death is the first step down the slippery slope to the killing of the unsuspecting, the incompetent and the uninformed.[113] Sanctity of life is inherent and should be respected by all. The assisted-death movement is a direct affront to the belief that humans have the natural and intrinsic right to life.

The right-to-die movement is one of the most active organizations in the assisted-death movement in the United States. Founded by Derek Humphrey it claims that euthanasia is motivated primarily out of compassion and is justified as an exercise of individual freedom guaranteed in the constitution.[114] This view is based on a fundamental principle of autonomy. According to the right-to-die movement, the principle of autonomy is violated if an individual is not allowed to exercise his or her free will.

The argument for autonomy makes its claim based in part on the foundation of liberty spelled out in the U.S. Constitution and in the cultural context of liberal democracy. This, however, is a gross misuse of the liberties guaranteed by the Constitution. The foundation of freedom in the United States is based largely on the works of libertarians and political philosophers such as John Locke. Locke argued that an individual's freedom was unlimited as long as it did not impose on the freedom of another individual.[115] Thus, even if an act is immoral, one is free to commit an act as long as it does not deny or limit the freedom of another individual.[116] This applies directly to the assisted-death movement. Supporters of PAS and euthanasia are not seeking the right to commit suicide but attempting to obtain legal and moral validity for the death of a second party. The issue here is not whether suicide is moral, but whether it is ethical for another individual to be involved. Thus justification based on autonomy is invalid. Physician-assisted suicide and euthanasia are not purely autonomous acts. They involve the presence and participation of not only a second party but also cannot be considered in isolation of family, friends and the community of the person involved.

The claim on compassion cannot be monopolized by the assisted-death movement. The evangelical Christian perspective fully advocates for compassionate care of the dying. In fact, the assisted-death movement uses compassion as a shield to cover the real issues at stake. When an individual is suffering, how might an invitation to assist in his or her death be experienced? For example, in the Netherlands a gentleman opted for PAS because his wife threatened to put him in a nursing home if he did not consent.[117] This is not compassion but coercion. Oregon's Death with Dignity Act's 2005 Annual Report reveals that inadequate pain control was the second-to-last concern out of eight reasons for seeking assisted death.[118] Thus compassion for the pain and suffering of the dying is not a significant motivational factor for seeking assisted death. Ultimately, it is more compassionate to care for the dying than to leave them feeling isolated, abandoned and without reason for holding onto the last stages of life.

Christian ethicist Paul Ramsey taught that a physician should never abandon care.[119] Human life has inherent value, thus individuals facing death should receive care and experience the company and love of others. Christians believe life is sacred and should be valued, not discarded. True compassion is manifest when an individual is given the freedom to die while experiencing the presence and support of loved ones.

*Awareness exercise.* Host a bioethics seminar at your church. Invite a physician, ethicist or nurse practitioner to speak to your congregation about the dying process and possible decisions that may need to be made when a medical crisis occurs. Ask your guest to educate your group about choices surrounding surrogates, DNRs (Do Not Resuscitate) and other ethical decisions surrounding the dying process. If you need assistance identifying someone to teach on these issues from a Christian perspective, contact the Center for Bioethics and Human Dignity at info@cbhd.org.

↩ ✳ *Take action.* Consider taking a course in clinical pastoral education and volunteering in a hospital as a chaplain. One of the primary responsibilities of hospital chaplains is to support individuals and family members as they go through the dying process. The Association for Clinical Pastoral Education (www .acpe.edu) has resources available for education and placement of chaplains.

↩ ✳ *Take action.* Start a grief support group for those who are suffering through the loss of a loved one. God desires the community of faith to come alongside those grieving the loss of a loved one. Two books that provide perspective about grief and the dying process are *How We Die: Reflections on Life's Final Chapter* by Sherwin Nuland and *On Death and Dying* by Elisabeth Kübler-Ross. A book written from personal experience and the Christian perspective is *Hope for the Brokenhearted: God's Voice of Comfort in the Midst of Grief and Loss* by John Luke Terveen.

---

**FOR FURTHER STUDY**

*Suicide: A Christian Response: Crucial Considerations for Choosing Life* edited by Timothy Demy and Gary Stewart

*Ethics for a Brave New World* by John Feinberg and Paul Feinberg

---

*See also* "Bioethics" and "Death Penalty."

# FAMILY

Some Christian leaders, such as Jim Wallis, have argued that the breakdown of the family is the cause of poverty.[120] The past several hundred years certainly has seen a movement away from the family. Before the nineteenth century, the family, along with the church and neighbors, was the answer to most of societies problems.[121] Community, it seems, has disintegrated since then.

Today, people are living much more scattered and across vastly larger geographical areas. Technology allows someone to live in San Francisco and work in Chicago. I know of several families who split their time between cities. One wife works in Texas, her husband in Florida. They meet on the weekends. Good thing their kids are grown. What about the families that have young children? What does it mean for a toddler to only see one parent a few times a month? Doesn't this in effect create a single-parent household? These are some of the challenges facing the family in the twenty-first century.

Statistics show that the two-parent family has decreased rapidly over the past several decades. In 2006, 67 percent of children from birth to age 17 lived with two married parents, down from 77 percent in 1980. That same year, one out of four children (23 percent) lived only with their mothers, 5 percent of all children lived only with their fathers, and 5 percent lived with neither. These statistics are even more horrifying when looked at through the lens of race. In 2006, 76 percent of white, non-Hispanic; 66 percent of Hispanic; and 35 percent of black children lived with two married parents.[122] Jim Wallis says, "Stagnant wages, the loss of health care and other job benefits, the rising cost of housing, and the demands of multiple jobs for low-income workers are all an assault on family time and values."[123]

Justice demands that we look at domestic poverty holistically. There is a correlation between the destruction of the family and the percentage of families needing financial support and welfare. Jobs and housing affect parents ability to be able to provide good childcare for their children. Young children often run around unsupervised or without quality developmental opportunities. The lack of money affects the emotional stability of the family system. The church can help struggling families rise up out of poverty and into more stable environments. The church of the twenty-first century must place a growing emphasis on vibrant marriages and strong family life.

One challenge Christians face is the role that the government and public policy should play in protecting and supporting families. Some Christians believe that laws should define and protect marriage; that is, Christian values should be expressed in the policy and legislation of the United States government. Other believers think the government should have no role in defining family, marriage and morality. The following action items provide exposure to organizations that espouse both beliefs about the role of public policy and the government.

*Awareness exercise.* Look up some of the public policy organizations in Washington, D.C., to see how they engage the government in regard to family values. Consider the Family Research Council (www.frc.org)—founded in 1983 "as an organization dedicated to the promotion of marriage and family

and the sanctity of human life in national policy." Discover how Family Research Council believes the church can influence public policy. Visit their legislative action arm at www.fraction.org. Another organization of interest is the Howard Center for Family, Religion and Society (www.profam.org) located in Rockford, Illinois. Look up the National Council on Family Relations (www.ncfr.org). How does it define family? What is their mission and strategy as it relates to public policy and shaping the political conversation about family values? How do these organizations inform your understanding of the role that Christians should play in public policy about family values?

← *Take action.* Start a family night in your community in which you open your home once a week, provide a meal (potlucks are great!) and space for families to fellowship in community. Do you know your neighbors well enough to invite them to such a gathering? During the summer or for a holiday, host a family event open house so you can introduce yourself to the families in your immediate area. Read *The Connecting Church* by Randy Frazee for more ideas about community-building experiences.

← *Take action.* Consider serving in a youth mentoring program where you will have the opportunity to share your faith, encourage good choices and mentor young men and women who may not have a stable family life. Christian organizations like Young Life provide great opportunities to reach out to kids with the love of Christ through club meetings, camps, tutoring programs and Bible

## Focus on the Family

Founded by Dr. James Dobson, Focus on the Family (www.focusonthefamily.com) is committed to helping families thrive. With an emphasis on evangelism and Scripture, Focus on the Family has educational programs and tools to help support families by emphasizing marriages, healthy child rearing, the sanctity of human life and the importance of social responsibility. The mission of Focus on the Family is to "cooperate with the Holy Spirit in sharing the Gospel of Christ with as many people as possible by nurturing and defending the God-ordained institution of the family and promoting biblical truths worldwide." Focus on the Family is a complementarian organization that provides support to families from a conservative perspective. The lobbying arm of Focus on the Family is Focus on the Family Action (www.citizen link.org/focusaction).

studies. These types of activities are a great way to support kids who may have limited parental support and resources. Visit www .younglife.org to find out how to get involved in a mentoring program.

**FOR FURTHER STUDY**

*Family Ministry* by Diana Garland

*The Family: A Christian Perspective on the Contemporary Home* by Jack Balswick and Judith Balswick

*See also* "Children" and "Poverty."

## FEMALE GENITAL MUTILATION

Female genital mutilation (FGM), or genital cutting, refers to "all procedures involving partial or total removal of the external female genitalia or other injury to the female genital organs whether for cultural, religious, or other non-therapeutic reasons."[124] Amnesty International estimates that 135 million women and girls worldwide have undergone genital mutilation.[125] In Africa about three million girls are at risk for FGM each year. The procedure has no health benefits and can cause severe bleeding, problems urinating, potential childbirth complications and newborn deaths. Most procedures take place before a woman is fifteen years old.

Female genital mutilation occurs significantly in Africa and is based on a mixture of cultural, religious and societal expectations. Some anthropologists have argued for the continuation of this practice, saying it is justifiable as a cultural tradition.[126] FGM is recognized internationally as a violation of the human rights of women and girls.[127] FGM is one of the few issues that evangelicals, regardless of their view of women, rally behind.

**FOR FURTHER STUDY**

*Female Genital Mutilation: Legal, Cultural, and Medical Issues* by Rosemarie Skaine

*The Female Circumcision Controversy: An Anthropological Perspective* by Ellen Gruenbaum

↤ *Take action.* Partner with an organization like Forward (www.forwarduk.org.uk), based in the United Kingdom, and join the campaign to end female genital mutilation. Become a sponsor of Forward, help promote awareness about FGM and discriminatory practices based on gender, and write to your local congressmen about FGM and its effect on women and young girls.

*See also* "Women."

## GENOCIDE

Genocide is the intentional mass extermination of a people group. In 1948 the Convention on the Prevention and Punishment of the Crime of Genocide defined "genocide" as:

> Any of the following acts committed with the intent to destroy, in whole or in part, a national, ethnic, racial or religious group, as such: killing members of the group; causing serious bodily or mental harm to members of the group; deliberately inflicting on the group conditions of life calculated to bring about its physical destruction in whole or in part; imposing measures intended to prevent birth within the group . . . forcibly transferring children of the group to another group.[128]

The General Assembly of the United Nations adopted this convention, which went into effect January 1951. Historical examples of genocide include (1) the massive destruction of over one million Armenians by the Ottoman Empire toward the end of the nineteenth century, (2) the systematic annihilation over six million Jews by the Nazis during World War II, (3) the Killing Fields of Cambodia under the leadership of Pol Pot and the

Khmer Rouge, where close to two million Cambodians were tortured and murdered. In Bosnia, between 1992 and 1995, over two hundred thousand Muslims were confined to concentration camps, starved, tortured and killed. Also in the mid-1990s, the Rwandan genocide saw close to one million people exterminated with no intervention by the West. Conflicts continue to rage in Sudan well into the twenty-first century.

The church cannot sit by idly while these atrocities continue to occur. Rather Christians must be informed about evil happenings around the world. We must get involved, lift our voices and work actively to end the extreme pain and suffering that is caused by genocide and other atrocities against the human race.

←« *Take action.* Partner with the Enough (www.enoughproject.org)—the project to end genocide and crimes against humanity. Working against genocide and mass atrocities, Enough is striving to stop these horrors where they are already occurring and to prevent them from happening in the future through "3Ps": peace, protection and punishment. Get involved by joining the campaign, signing petitions, lobbying your senators and representatives, spreading the word in your communities, supporting partner organizations that are working for change, and hosting community events.

←« *Take action.* Join a network like Genocide Intervention Network (www.genocide intervention.net), a community of concerned citizens fighting to stop genocide through education, advocacy and action. Sign up for their e-mail updates so you can keep informed about international events and the effectiveness of efforts against genocide.

**FOR FURTHER STUDY**

*Led by Faith: Rising from the Ashes of the Rwandan Genocide* by Immaculée Ilibagiza

*Blood and Soil: A World History of Genocide and Extermination from Sparta to Darfur* by Ben Kiernan

## GENOCIDE—DARFUR, SUDAN

Genocide is an injustice of the present as well as the past. Darfur is a region of western Sudan. Since February of 2003, Darfur has been filled with military conflict that is largely based on ethnicity. The Sudanese military is at war with a variety of rebel groups, including the Sudan Liberation Movement and the Justice and Equality Movement. The U.S. government has determined the Sudanese military has engaged in genocide.[129]

According to the United Nations, an estimated 400,000 people have died of violence or disease in Sudan. Other estimates suggest that close to 100,000 people have died every month as a result of the government attacks. Information has been suppressed because of strict governmental control, the imprisonment of news people, and the tampering with and covering up of mass graves. The Sudanese government has strongly objected to intervention by the international community. On August 31, 2006, the UN Security Council approved a resolution calling for peacekeeping forces to supplement the African Union Mission that was serving in Sudan.[130] In response, the Sudanese government protested by launching a major military initiative in the region.

←*₩ **Take action.** Divest from Sudan; take back American dollars funding foreign companies doing business in Sudan. In 2006, the University of California was the first public university to divest from Sudan. Be sure that your own investments through mutual funds or other financial resources are not being used to support corrupt foreign governments. You can use the screening tool that is available from the Sudan Divestment Task Force at www.sudandivestment.org.

←*₩ **Take action.** Contact your elected officials to do more to end the genocide in Darfur. You can evaluate how your members of Congress have been involved in the conflict through www.darfurscores.org, which is committed to calling Congress to stop genocide.

←*₩ **Take action.** Write a letter to your local newspaper to help raise awareness about the conflict in Darfur. Visit www.genocideintervention.net if you need tools to help you get started.

←*₩ **Take action.** Join Darfur Christian Action (www.darfurchristianaction.org) in partnership with the Enough Project and the Church Communication Network (CCN). Visit their website to sign the petition for intervention in Darfur. Start a Bible study using their Christian companion to *Not on Our Watch*. Participate in events and use your voice to help end the genocide in Darfur.

**FOR FURTHER STUDY**

*Not on Our Watch: The Mission to End Genocide in Darfur and Beyond* by Don Cheadle and Jon Prendergast

*The Not on Our Watch Christian Companion* by Bill Mefford and Greg Leffel

*See also* "Human Rights."

## GENOCIDE—RWANDA

Race has played a huge role in the development of Rwanda as a nation. The people of the country were categorized into two major groups: Tutsi and Hutu. Before World War I, both Germany and Belgium ruled the Rwandan people. Belgian colonists identified the Tutsi as "anyone with a long nose." The Hutu's were the racial majority in the country, and the Tutsi's were not only considered a minority race but also foreigners. In 1994, during the Rwandan Civil War, Hutu extremists attempted to completely exterminate the Tutsi people. Close to one million men, women and children were brutally murdered.[131] King Kigeli V Ndahindurwa said, "Rwanda: The most preventable genocide of our time."[132] It woke the world to the fact that mass exterminations were still occurring in the late twentieth century.

Western nations received global criticism for their lack of involvement in the Rwandan conflict. An international commission was established that condemned the United Nations Security Council for refusing to intervene.[133] In the aftermath, it was discovered that a Rwandan informant sent a fax to the United Nations force commander detailing the plan to eliminate the Tutsi people from the highest positions in the government and the president's court. When the fax was received, it was treated as routine correspondence by the peacekeeping headquarters of the United Nations in New York City. No information was leaked to the press. No concern or alarm bells were raised. The Rwandan president, Habyarimana, was shot down by missiles as his plane was landing following a peace meeting with regional leaders. Fol-

lowing the president's assassination, everything that was detailed in the fax came true and hundreds of thousands of people were killed.[134] After its occurrence, the world recommitted to preventing such atrocities in the future.

---

**FOR FURTHER STUDY**

*Justice on the Grass: Three Rwandan Journalists, Their Trial and War Crimes, and a Nation's Quest for Redemption* by Dina Temple-Raston

---

←* ***Take action.*** Research the genocide in Rwanda. You may want to use resources like the PBS *Frontline* program "The Triumph of Evil."[135] Gather a group of friends to watch the movie *Hotel Rwanda* (2004) and talk about what you learned from your studies. Use this time to educate people about the truth of the Tutsi massacre.

## GLOBAL ECONOMY

There are obvious disparities in the global distribution of wealth. The Gross Domestic Product (GDP) of the poorest forty-eight countries in the world is *less* than the combined wealth of the world's three richest individuals.[136] The gap between the rich and the poor is growing wider. In 1820 the financial distance between the richest and the poorest countries was about 3 to 1. By 1992 that number had grown to 72 to 1, showing a sharply increasing trend.[137] More than 80 percent of the world's population lives in countries where income differentials are widening.[138] The United States has the widest gap between the resourced and the underresourced of any industrialized nation.[139]

One of the greatest problems with the growing gap between the rich and the poor is that those who are wealthy are isolated from those who are living in poverty. Wealthy suburbs, gated communities, freeways and other mechanisms keep those with access to financial resources from directly encountering those without.

When I was a kid, I watched the Patrick Swayze movie *City of Joy* (1992). I was moved to tears to see the conditions of the poor and the leper communities in India. I was captivated by the American doctor who had lost so much and found joy in a place full of poverty and material destitution. That movie was a life-shaping experience for me.

In one scene the wealthy ruler of the community was petitioned to give one of the main characters use of a rickshaw so that he could make a living. The ruler was obese and surrounded by opulence. All around him there were hurting, hungry, suffering and dying people. The movie revealed the accumulated wealth of the ruling class and how a portion of it would have been enough to alleviate so much pain. I asked my mom why the ruler would not share his money with the common people. I couldn't understand the cruelty that I witnessed in that movie. Now that I am older, I am not sure that those who are rich are purposefully cruel. I think that much of the time people are ignorant of the ways our consumption affects others around the world.

In an effort to call attention to the growing gap between the rich and the poor, Stephen Colbert on *Comedy Central* has a "platinum report" in which he pokes fun at the crazy things available for purchase in the twenty-first century: convertibles that use SCUBA technology and can run underwater,

dinosaur bones and a $100 cup of coffee harvested from Indonesian jungle cat feces.

The vast majority of people have no idea how much the way they live, consume and spend affects the poor and the hurting. On the other hand, once people are made aware of the huge needs, they have a tendency to become overwhelmed (and even immobilized) because they don't know what to do about it!

Spiritual reflection exercise. Read James 2:1-10.

My brothers and sisters, believers in our glorious Lord Jesus Christ must not show favoritism. Suppose someone comes into your meeting wearing a gold ring and fine clothes, and a poor person in filthy old clothes also comes in. If you show special attention to the one wearing fine clothes and say, "Here's a good seat for you," but say to the one who is poor, "You stand there" or "Sit on the floor by my feet," have you not discriminated among yourselves and become judges with evil thoughts? Listen, my dear brothers and sisters: Has not God chosen those who are poor in the eyes of the world to be rich in faith and to inherit the kingdom he promised those who love him? But you have dishonored the poor. Is it not the rich who are exploiting you? Are they not the ones who are dragging you into court? Are they not the ones who are blaspheming the noble name of him to whom you belong? If you really keep the royal law found in Scripture, "Love your neighbor as yourself," you are doing right. But if you show favoritism, you sin and are convicted by the law as lawbreakers. For whoever keeps the whole law and yet stumbles at just one point is guilty of breaking all of it.

How has this passage spoken to you? Has there ever been a time when you have shown favoritism based on the way that someone was dressed? For some other reason? What does James say about the poor in this passage? About the rich? From this passage, what does it mean to "do right"? Reflect on these words. Do you know anyone who is poor? Take some time and lift him or her up to the Lord. Ask God what you might have to learn from that person. Pray that God might give you the opportunity to have a direct encounter with someone who is poor.

*Awareness exercise.* Seek opportunities to develop relationships with people of different economic statuses. This may be by traveling to a neighboring town or community or even traveling internationally. Consider traveling

## Red Del Camino for Integral Mission in Latin America and Caribbean

The Red del Camino (RdC) is a movement that began in the mid-1990s as a small group of diverse churches in Latin America and the Caribbean. They are committed to living more fully as followers of Jesus by practicing radical kingdom compassion and justice (shalom) in their communities.

These churches connected as friends first and accompanied each other in what they collectively understood as God's mission—the total restoration of all things in Christ, which signals to the world that his kingdom is indeed among us. RdC churches are characterized by their powerful presence in their communities and their commitment to seeking kingdom alternatives in a world where unjust systems and powers have damaged, destroyed and debilitated every area of life. In small but compelling ways RdC churches are actively bringing the kind of real hope, love and faith that Jesus brought to people. The network is joined by pro-church organizations that identify with church-based participation in God's mission. As RdC continues to gain momentum, the dream is to encourage, serve and accompany increasing numbers of churches that are passionately living out God's integral mission.

Any individual or group wanting to work toward justice and compassionate change with faith communities who have a proven track record can join the initiatives of RdC networks through Del Camino Connection (DCC). Visit their websites to learn more at www.delcamino connection.org/en and www.lareddel camino.net/en.[140]

**FOR FURTHER STUDY**

*The Upside-Down Kingdom* by Don Kraybill

with a ministry or organization that has an established relationship with a local church in the area you will be visiting. If you aren't sure where to begin, contact the Red Del Camino Network in Latin America at www.del caminoconnection.org/en.

**FOR FURTHER STUDY**

*God So Loved the Third World* by Hank Thomas

*Neither Poverty Nor Riches: A Biblical Theology of Possessions* by Craig Blomberg

*See also* "Capitalism," "Consumerism," "Globalization" and "Poverty."

## GLOBALIZATION

Globalization is the movement toward greater interdependence and integration around the world. Globalization is an economic phenomena and may be understood as the increased flow of capital, people, commodities, ideas and cultures across national boarders. Globalization also refers to the decentralization and fragmentation of production process of goods and the establishment of global institutions to regulate and control trade and markets.[141] Countries around the world are becoming increasingly dependent on one another.

Though there are other factors, globalization is largely the result of economics. Globalization has significant effects on the job market in the United States as many jobs are outsourced to countries where people work for less and where there is less overhead. Globalization also makes it easier for powerful multinational corporations to exploit the poor. Colonization is another negative consequence; developed countries are able to exert force over less strong nations because the global economy is interconnected.[142] In addi-

tion, cultures are pressured toward homogenization and lose their unique identities in order to be able survive in the global market.

The United Nations Millennium Declaration says: "We believe that the central challenge we face today is to ensure that globalization becomes a positive force for all the world's people. For while globalization offers great opportunities, at present its benefits are very unevenly shared, while its costs are unevenly distributed."[143]

**FOR FURTHER STUDY**

*Rethinking Globalization: Teaching for Justice in an Unjust World* by Bill Bigelow and Bob Peterson

*Making Globalization Work* by Joseph E. Stiglitz

*Christianity, Social Change, and Globalization in the Americas* by Manuel Vasquez, Anna Lisa Peterson and Phillip J. Williams

Intentionally and unwittingly, Westerners, who have most of the resources and power, are imposing their culture and worldview on the rest of the world. Christians should be advocates for and partners with their brothers and sisters in developing nations. Christ followers must discover what the developing world can teach about community, interdependent relationships and the ways that God may be worshiped. Believers are obligated to practice Christian hospitality and to take a posture of mutual submission in relationship to the global body of Christ.

**FOR FURTHER STUDY**

*God's Global Mosaic: What We Can Learn from Christians Around the World* by Paul-Gordon Chandler

*Cross-Cultural Connections* by Duane Elmer

*See also* "Capitalism," "Consumerism" and "Poverty."

## HEALTH CARE—DOMESTIC

Following the ceremonial signing of the Medicare-Medicaid Act in July 1965, President Lyndon Johnson declared:

> No longer will older Americans be denied the healing miracle of modern medicine. No longer will illness crush and destroy the savings that they have so carefully put away over a lifetime so that they might enjoy dignity in their later years. No longer will young families see their own incomes, and their own hopes, eaten away simply because they are carrying out their deep moral obligations to their parents, and to their uncles and their aunts. And no longer will this nation refuse the hand of justice to those who have given a lifetime of service and wisdom and labor to the progress of this progressive country.[144]

The Medicare-Medicaid Act was part of a sweeping set of domestic programs intended to eliminate poverty and racial injustice in the United States by legislating spending for and reform of education, health care, urban issues, and transportation. Many of those reforms have since been eliminated, but the medical-aid programs are among the few that prevail. Medicare ensures that people aged sixty-five and older have access to affordable medical services, while Medicaid serves low-income parents of children under age twenty, children, seniors and people with disabilities.[145]

When Johnson declared his vision for the Great Society, few people imagined that the elderly would need access to long-term care to the extent that is commonplace today. Thanks to improved medical technology and services, Americans now live considerably longer than they did four decades ago. According to the Centers for Disease Control and Prevention and the National Center for Health Statistics, the average U.S. life expectancy in the 1960s was 67 years for men and 73 years for women; today those ages have risen to 75 and 80 respectively.[146] Medicare programs were not designed with this increase in mind. Given that the fastest growing segment of the population today is among people over 85, it is not surprising that the long-term care crisis facing the health care system has become alarming.[147]

Medicare was developed as an acute-care model in which more benefits are extended to more curable illnesses or maladies. For conditions that are incurable, such as dementia, Medicare services are not readily available. Today, almost half of Americans over eighty suffer from some type of dementia; about 80 percent of those sixty-five and older have one chronic condition, and two-thirds have two or more.[148] The health care ailments of these individuals are not considered treatable by the acute care provided by Medicare.

According to a study at the Population Studies Center of the Institute for Social Research, University of Michigan, Medicare contains sizable gaps; most notably it fails to cover extended hospital stays or most long-term care. By 2020, over 80 percent of all health care expenditures in the United States will be spent on people with chronic conditions; direct health care for chronic conditions will exceed $1 trillion in expenditures.[149] This means a lack of care for people who need extended hospital stays or long-term care. The result is an increasing number of elderly Americans who are living below the poverty level or are an extreme burden on their families.

In today's Medicare system, people requiring long-term but not acute care are responsible for covering their own health care costs—until the point that they are officially impoverished. Medicaid eligibility does not commence until people meet state poverty levels, which for a single person (usually a widow) means approximately $2,000 in countable assets, with a $30 per month personal needs allowance.[150] The elderly are increasingly concerned—and with good reason—that their limited Social Security benefits and pension will fall short of covering the costs of their long-term care needs not met by Medicare.

And Medicare is itself in danger. The May 25, 2005, edition of PBS's *NewsHour with Jim Lehrer* addressed "The Graying of America." Speaking about the health care crisis, *NewsHour* guest Courtney Coile, associate professor of economics at Wellesley College, said:

> The costs for Medicare are projected to rise even more quickly than those for Social Security. [Thanks to demographic changes], rapidly increasing healthcare costs, and a new prescription drug benefit that we've just added to Medicare . . . the Medicare Trust Fund is due to go bankrupt two decades sooner than the Social Security Trust Fund, and the increases in Medicare spending over the next 75 years are projected to be five times greater than those in Social Security.[151]

One of the main predicaments facing our society today is the growing number of elderly widows who lack financial stability. Because our current health care system favors those in need of acute care, many elderly women are obliged to spend their family retirement money in order to meet their partner's long-term care needs. If their husband's illness is not eligible for Medicare, Medicaid kicks in, but only when most of the couple's investments and other securities are severely diminished, leaving women with limited resources to sustain their own life—and health care—once their husbands have passed away.

Rick Law, a Christian attorney in Aurora, Illinois, founded Law ElderLaw (www.lawelderlaw.com) in order to provide support to the elderly who might be in danger of sinking under the weight of long-term care needs. According to Law, "Long-term care in this country is a woman's problem and is unfair to women."[152] In most cases, men become the weaker sex as they age. Statistics show that, on average, men decline more rapidly and die more quickly than do women. However, women often sacrifice their own care to respond to the needs of their male counterparts in their later years of life, ending up paying a high price both in dollars and in health. "I suspect that if this were more of a man's issue," said Law, "we'd see some more just action taking place."[153]

The poverty rate of U.S. women has been increasing over the past few years. In 2005, 2.1 million women were living in poverty in the United States—that's nearly 400,000 more than in 2004.[154] A woman's chances of living in poverty increase with age. Women are almost twice as likely as men to live in poverty in their senior years. According to the U.S. Census Bureau, women of color are the most affected. Among women over sixty-five, 30.2 percent of African American women and close to 25.3 percent of Hispanic women live in poverty, compared to 11.1 percent of white women.[155]

Consider this commonplace story of a hardworking family doing their best to provide for their children and close relatives, and preparing for retirement. The husband worked many decades in a factory; he and his wife lived frugally while raising their three children. Now of retirement age, they live on two Social Security checks and a modest pension, with an annual income of approximately $35,000. Their home is paid for, and they anticipate no financial hardships during their last years of life because of their modest savings and retirement benefits. Then the wrecking ball of dementia hits. At the entry level, long-term care costs for the afflicted man range from $2,000 to $8,000 or more per month.[156]

Living on less than $3,000 a month, this couple has severely limited discretionary income with which to pay additional health care costs. The husband declines and his health care costs drain their resources while his wife faithfully supports him, doing her best to attend to his growing needs. Medicaid pays for only a portion of his health care costs; the remainder comes out of their personal savings and fixed income. After several years and thousands of dollars spent on his care, he passes away. After his death his widow loses both his pension and one Social Security check, and is abruptly obliged to live exclusively on a single Social Security check. This is all the more serious since almost all of her

excess assets were spent on her husband's long-term care costs.

Studies have shown that this scenario is common among the elderly in the United States today. Because of gaps in Medicare coverage, there is a genuine risk that the beneficiary will incur substantial expenditures, perhaps of a magnitude sufficient to eliminate the savings of a couple and to jeopardize the financial well-being of the surviving spouse.

What's more, government policy seems to be moving in the wrong direction in terms of allocating resources toward long-term care costs of the elderly. The Deficit Reduction Act of 2005 was an attempt to bring mandatory government spending under control. In the House of Representatives, 217 Republicans voted in favor of the bill while 215 Democrats voted against it. In the Senate the bill was so divided that Vice President Dick Cheney cast the deciding vote in favor of the bill. The goal of the bill was to cut approximately $40 billion of long-term care coverage from Medicaid. The Deficit Reduction Act was signed by President Bush on February 8, 2006, effectively breaking Lyndon Johnson's promise of affordable health care costs for the elderly.[157]

The White House declared that the Deficit Reduction Act is an important step forward in bringing mandatory government spending under control, because entitlement programs like Medicare, Medicaid and Social Security account for some of the biggest areas of government spending. The Office of the Press Secretary issued the following statement: "By 2030, spending for Medicare, Medicaid, and Social Security alone will be almost 60 percent of the entire Federal budget. The annual growth of entitlement programs needs to be slowed to affordable levels, but these programs do not need to be cut."[158] The White House has assured the public that while the Deficit Reduction Act restrains the budget toward vital programs like Medicaid and Medicare, Americans can still rely on these programs for their continued care.

One of the implications of the Deficit Reduction Act, along with the Medicare Act of 2003, is that wealthier seniors pay higher premiums for their Medicare coverage. In the long run, the stability of the Medicare and Medicaid programs are in jeopardy unless significant structural reform takes place. As the baby boomer generation begins to retire, the strain on these systems will inevitably increase. In response to these changes, Dr. Bob Edgar, general secretary of the National Council of Churches, issued the following statement: "The Congress has now passed a budget that is based on the assumption that the poor are expendable. . . . But history will record that at a time of great need, when the citizens of this nation were struggling with the ill effects of war and natural disaster, this government turned its back on the poor."[159]

One of the government-proposed solutions to the crisis is increased engagement by faith-based groups funded by Charitable Choice, the program that allows faith-based groups providing social services to receive federal funding without secularizing their identity. Throughout the Scriptures we see God's call to his people to respond to the needs of the poor and the oppressed, including the elderly. "Stand up in the presence of the aged, show respect for the elderly and revere your God. I am the LORD" (Lev 19:32).

What is the role of the church in understanding and responding to the health care crisis facing the elderly in America today? How can we as the hands and feet of Christ "give proper recognition to those widows who are really in need" (1 Tim 5:3)?[160]

←⚖ *Take action.* Develop ministries to serve as care partners. As the body of Christ, we must exercise compassion and advocate for justice as we attempt to respond to the physical and spiritual needs of the elderly, especially as they experience health challenges and the oppression of a complex and unsupportive health care system. Churches can begin by developing deacon boards, care teams and other groups who meet with and walk alongside elderly men, women, and their families who are in the midst of health care crises. Once immediate care needs are met, churches can launch health care advocacy programs to partner with healthcare-burdened men and women to be a voice for them in their hospital or care facilities, with their health care professionals, and with their insurance agents.

←⚖ *Take action.* Partner with and serve alongside state advocacy organizations. Most states have advocacy training organizations like Health Care for All in Massachusetts (hcfama.org). Advocates speak on behalf of the voiceless and help them navigate the nation's obscenely complicated health care system.

←⚖ *Take action.* Partner with lawyers and firms who specialize in elder law and help make these resources available to the underresourced.

Churches can call on attorneys in their congregation to research and compile a list of trustworthy law firms that deal in estate planning/asset protection and disability and Medicaid assistance. The National Academy of Elder Law Attorneys (naela.org) and Elder Law Answers (elderlawanswers.com) are national directories that provide an excellent place to start.

←# *Take action.* Engage in political advocacy. Individuals and groups can raise their political concerns to their congressmen on a local, state and national level through letter-writing campaigns, phone calls and personal visits. Organizations like the Alliance for Retired Americans (retiredamericans.org) can be a good resource for staying abreast of pending public policy decisions on both national and state levels. When you lobby, speak out against the "diagnosis lottery."

In our system, if you win the diagnosis lottery by having a heart problem that costs half a million dollars, Medicare will pay for your health care. But if you lose the diagnosis lottery by developing Alzheimer's, our healthcare system pays nothing until you are reduced to penury. Write to your legislators and ask them to address our fragmented, almost primitive healthcare system. There is no reason it should make a distinction between a person with a heart problem and a person with dementia, but it does. Contact information for your legislators can be found at senate.gov and congress.org.[161]

Certainly God cares about the plight of the widows and the oppressed and would have his followers engage in advocating on their behalf. We are a long way from the Great Society that President Johnson envisioned in 1965, and as Christians we are called to be aware of, work to reform and advocate for elder care.

---

**FOR FURTHER STUDY**

Sick: *The Untold Story of America's Health Care Crisis—and the People Who Pay the Price* by Jonathan Cohn

*The Future of Medicine: Megatrends in Health Care That Will Improve Your Quality of Life* by Stephen C. Schimpff

---

See also "Health Care—Domestic Children" and "Health Care—Global."

## HEALTH CARE—DOMESTIC CHILDREN

According to the Center for Disease Control and Prevention (CDC), the U.S. spends approximately $5,000 per person on public health per year for vaccinations, epidemic prevention and wellness.[162] This is in addition to health care that is provided through insurance or private funding. The percentage of children who have health insurance coverage for at least part of the year is one measure of the extent to which families can obtain preventive care or health care for a sick or injured child.

In 2005, the number of children in the U.S. who had no health insurance at any time was 8.1 million, or 11 percent of all children. The percentage of children of color who do not have health insurance is higher than that of white children. Hispanic children are less likely to have health insurance than white, non-Hispanic or black children. In 2005, 79 percent of Hispanic children were covered by health insurance, compared with 93 percent of white, non-Hispanic children and 88 percent of black children.[163] Approximately one third of children who have health care coverage are provided for by the government and other public programs. Jim Wallis observes:

> Jesus made healing a principal sign of his ministry and of the presence of the kingdom of God. From a biblical point of view, it is simply wrong when health becomes a commodity and accessibility depends upon wealth. Until something is done to make universal health care a reality in America, millions of families will remain poor.[164]

State Children's Health Insurance Programs (SCHIP) became available in 1997 and agreed to provide $24 billion of government funding over a ten-year period to help states expand health care coverage to over five million of the United State's uninsured children.[165] On October 3, 2007, President Bush vetoed the SCHIP bill, which caused outrage in the Christian community. Glenn R. Palmberg, former president of the Evangelical Covenant Church said of this decision:

> An earlier administration, some 20 years ago, tried to declare ketchup a vegetable in the children's school lunch program. It was seen as a cruel and cynical response to the plight of low-income children. I still hear that talked about as the legacy of that administration regarding poor children some 20 years later. I think this veto has the potential of being talked about 20 years from now as part of the legacy of this administration, and it is seen as a cruel and cynical response to the needs of poor children.[166]

There is great debate about solutions surrounding health care. Many argue that government should provide universal health care. Others believe strongly that the bulk of health care should be provided by the private sector. Regardless of where people stand on this issue, few would argue that children should not have access to the bare fundamentals of medical care such as vaccinations and emergency care.

←⚒ *Take action.* Access to adequate health care for underresourced children should be an issue that the church cares deeply about. Located in Chicago, Lawndale Christian Health Center is a Christian health care facility that provides primary care services to patients regardless of their ability to pay and is committed to ending health care disparities (www.lawndale.org). Find out if there are similar Christian health care facilities in your community or a city that could use your time, money and resources. Volunteer opportunities include providing community service, entry-level positions and administrative work.

**FOR FURTHER STUDY**

*The State Children's Health Insurance Program (SCHIP): Issues and Analysis* by Arthur Rose

See also "Children," "Health Care—Domestic" and "Health Care—Global."

## HEALTH CARE—GLOBAL

Access to adequate health care is an issue for children in the United States and even more so in other parts of the world. Around the world, there are 1.9 billion children in developing countries—one in seven (270 million) have no access to health services.[167] The total annual sum spent on health care in sub-

Saharan Africa is typically $20 per person or less. To put that into perspective, in the United States we spend about $6,000 per person each year on health care. In some areas of Africa, the annual budget for health care is only $1.90 per person.[168]

In the developing world, health care is a major issue for a number of reasons. Many villages and rural areas do not have people educated about hygiene and other health practices. There are few doctors or nurses. When basic information about hygiene and caretaking is known, it is not shared with others, often because there is no means for it to be dispersed. There are no clinics, hospitals or other care facilities available for many people. When diseases occur, they are not addressed and thus often become epidemics. There is little public support for these types of initiatives.

Most children in the developing world die in the first year because of dehydration, diarrhea and disease. Health care plays a significant role in infant mortality. In 2007, infant mortality rates in the United States were 6.37 deaths per 1,000 births. In Angola, Africa, infant mortality was over 184 deaths per 1,000 births. Other countries had the following infant mortality rates: Afghanistan (157), Nigeria (96), Sudan (92) Senegal (60), Bolivia (50), Papua New Guinea (48), Australia (4.57).[169] The disparity of access to health care becomes a major problem when a disease is introduced into a society. This has been the case with both AIDS and malaria.

←* *Take action.* Partner with an organization like Bright Hope to create Med Paks, which provide the most basic medical sup-

plies and brings the love of Christ to one person who is suffering. A Med Pak is a box filled with basic toiletries and hygiene items, including soap, antibiotic cream, toothpaste and toothbrush, lotion, talcum powder, cotton swabs, facial tissues, petroleum jelly, and a wash cloth. The items in the Med Pak can reduce the rate of infection, ease pain, prolong life and bring hope to those who need it. Med Paks also include Bibles, which are often used to teach reading in the schools as well as to teach God's Word in the churches. The cost of a Med Pak is about $30. Go to www.brighthope.org/group_resources/medpacks.php for more information.

**FOR FURTHER STUDY**

*Global Healthcare Issues and Policies* by Carol Holtz

*A Primer for Christian Healthcare Practice* by Schoeninger

*See also* "AIDS," "Health Care—Domestic," "Malaria" and "Tuberculosis."

## HOMELESSNESS

In 2002 the United States National Law Center on Homelessness and Poverty estimated that approximately three million men, women and children would be homeless for some part of that year.[170] On any given night in America, anywhere from seven hundred thousand to two million people are homeless, according to estimates by the same center.[171] The U.S. Conference of Mayors estimates that the homeless population is about 50 percent African American, 35 percent white, 12 percent Hispanic, 2 percent Native American and 1 percent Asian.[172]

In the late twentieth century, people used to believe that the homeless were mentally ill or suffered from psychological problems. Other common perceptions were that homeless people were not willing to work or were unable to hold down jobs. Neither of these perceptions are true. In 1996 a survey of the homeless reported that the average income of the homeless was $348 over the past thirty days prior to the survey; that equals about 51 percent of the 1996 federal poverty level of $680 per month for one person. Of those interviewed, 44 percent reported having worked for pay during the prior month.[173]

Reliable information about homelessness is necessary in order to be able to work toward positive change. Activists working to address the problem through policy changes need to provide reliable statistics about the homeless and recommend concrete policy alternatives and other solutions.[174]

←❋ *Take action.* Consider starting a Bridge of Hope ministry to help eradicate homelessness. The vision of Bridge of Hope is "to end and prevent homelessness for women and children across the United States by calling churches into action." Bridge of Hope uses mentoring groups to help empower homeless and at-risk mothers attain permanent housing, financial independence through employment and a community of relationships based on Christ's love. Learn how to start this kind of ministry and become an affiliate of Bridge of Hope at www.bridgeofhopeinc.org.

**FOR FURTHER STUDY**

*Beyond Homelessness: Christian Faith in a Culture of Displacement* by Steven Bouma-Prediger and Brian Walsh

*Making Room: Rediscovering Hospitality As a Christian Tradition* by Christine Pohl

## HOUSING

In the United States, homelessness and adequate housing is a problem for children and adults. In 1999, the Department of Housing and Urban Development issued a comprehensive report stating that over eleven million Americans have "worst case" housing needs in which most spend over half of their income on housing, often sharing space with other families or living in houses that are falling apart.[175]

Some may overlook whether people have adequate housing in the United States because they view U.S. living conditions in comparison to Third World countries. While the extreme poverty in the developing world is rarely found in the United States, we must be sure not to minimize the conditions of the urban and rural poor living in low-income housing areas. The book *There Are No Children Here* by Alex Kotlowitz describes the childhood years of two young boys growing up in the housing projects in Chicago. This book and others like it recount nightmares about the living conditions. Many U.S. children growing up in the heart of the city do not have access to proper education, nutritional diets, basic health care and safe housing.

←❋ *Take action.* One of the ministries of World Vision is called Storehouse (www .worldvision.org/content.nsf/learn/metro-chicago-programs-storehouse). Storehouses are warehouses that provide new and donated building materials and other supplies to lower-income families in Chicago and Fox Valley, Illinois. These ministries use volunteer support and donations to help provide building supplies at discounted prices to the poor.

## Walking by the Homeless

One day I was traveling downtown for a meeting that I had with a mentor in the city of San Francisco. I had taken the train into town and was walking a few blocks through the financial district on my way to the meeting. It is not uncommon, during those walks, for me to encounter the homeless lying or sitting on the streets and asking for money or trying to sell street newspapers. On this particular day I was early for my meeting and was taking my time, absorbing the life of the city. A few blocks into my walk I came across a man lying against the newspaper boxes. He seemed to be sleeping on something, but it was hard to tell what. He had a few of his possessions around him. It was difficult to tell what was his clothing, his bedding or his body because he was incredibly filthy. His hair was matted and in disarray. I was moved when I encountered him, not only because he was dirty and seemed to have so little but also because he was lying on the side of the street and his butt was completely exposed.

As I was approaching the place where he was sleeping, my spirit was torn within me. I kept thinking of all of the verses that talk about feeding those who are without food and especially about James 2:16 that asks, what good is it if I say to him go and be well "but do nothing about [his] physical needs," but I was completely at a loss as to what to do. I thought of the passage that says to give my brother or sister the extra shirt I own (Lk 3:11), but I was wearing a suit—high heels, a skirt and a jacket that I am sure would not have done him any good. I thought about waking him up, but was fearful of what might happen if I aroused him from his slumber.

I thought about the good Samaritan who saw the man by the side of the road and took him to an inn and paid for his stay. I looked across the street and there was an Omni Hotel right there. I then envisioned what a fool people would think me if I attempted to take this dirty and disheveled man into their posh hotel. I didn't care as much about what people would think—although the thought crossed my mind—but I continued to rationalize that the man lying there certainly would have rejected my kindness had I offered it. As I continued to walk, I knew in the depths of my being that God was stirring in me, and yet, even acknowledging his presence, I did nothing. I was immobilized. So, when I think about Jesus saying "whatever you do unto the least of these, you do unto me"—I know that on that particular day, I totally walked right by Jesus. I continue to think of that man: What has become of him? How might he have responded if I had acted differently? But, even more than that, I ask God to forgive me for the ways that my stupid pride and my world of excessive luxury keep me from responding to him in my daily encounters.

‡ *Spiritual reflection exercise.* Have there been times when God has placed something on your heart, but something impeded you from acting? What did you sense God was trying to communicate to you? How did he want you to respond? What was your response? If you had the opportunity to respond again, how might you do things differently? As you reflect on these questions, journal about your thoughts and experience.

## The Night Ministry

One experience that shaped my understanding of the homeless was with Night Ministry (www.thenightministry.org) in Chicago. I was introduced to the ministry through the Seminary Consortium for Urban Pastoral Education (SCUPE). Our class arrived and we spent the first hour or so learning about the ministry and statistics about homelessness in Chicago. The ministry works with street people by sending pastors and ministers to walk the streets on a nightly basis looking for those who have need. They provide at the very moment of need, offering medical care from the mobile health bus, invitations to their shelter and other supportive programs. After our orientation the ministry sent our class on the streets of Chicago two by two. Our task was to "pretend that we were homeless." We did not have any money and were supposed to find a place to stay and try to find something to eat.

My partner and I walked the streets. I could not believe the things that we noticed. One of the first things that came to my attention was that almost every single store in the community had signs posted "No Public Restrooms"—what were we supposed to do when we needed a bathroom? As we walked by restaurants I couldn't help but think of what it would be like looking in from the outside and knowing that I would never sit down at a place like that—with fresh table linens, sparkling water and cut flowers in a vase.

After about an hour, we decided to go to the Dunkin Donuts. We introduced ourselves to the manager and asked what he did with the donuts he didn't sell. He said he just threw them away. We asked him if we could have them, and since it was almost 10 p.m., he pulled out a box to put together a dozen for us. It might have helped that we were two young girls who were appropriately dressed. As he fixed the box, we asked him what he was going to do with the dozens of other donuts that were left over. Again, he said he was going to throw them away. I then asked him if we could have all of those too to take to our friends. He asked who our friends were. I told him the homeless on the streets. The change in his expression was as quick as lightning. He grimaced and then started to yell at us. Shaking his fists, he told us to get out of his store and to never come back again.

Later that evening, still walking, having had nothing to eat, we came upon a man who was leaning against a building, wrapped in blankets, playing the harmonica. We asked if we could join him. His name was Jim. We sat and talked to Jim for well over an hour. We heard that he used to have a well-paying job, but his wife kicked him out of the house because of his drinking problem. He had three grown kids, but they wanted nothing to do with him. He told us about his friend on the street who had died the week before, frozen to death in an alley. Jim taught me that night that even though you think alcohol will keep you warm, the exact opposite is the case. When you drink alcohol, it thins your blood, which makes your more disposed to hypothermia—especially on a cold winter night in Chicago. Jim told us of a couple of places where we could go to get a warm bed and a decent night's sleep. He told us to be careful and sent us on our way.

←* *Take action.* See if there are any ministries in your area that host opportunities for you to sleep on the street and catch a glimpse of what it might be like to be homeless. Be sure to do this with one or more people. It is best to have someone with you who knows the area. Reflect on what you have learned after your experience. Share your story with your friends, small group and church community.

## Habitat for Humanity

Founded in 1976 by Millard and Linda Fuller, Habitat for Humanity (www.habitat .org) does amazing work responding to housing needs. Through the work of Habitat, thousands of low-income families have found new hope. Churches, community groups and others join together to successfully tackle a significant social problem—decent housing for all. For the last quarter of a century, former President Jimmy Carter has partnered with Habitat to help bring worldwide visibility to the need for housing. Each year Jimmy and Rosalynn Carter give a week of their time—along with their construction skills—to build homes and raise awareness of the critical need for affordable housing.

*Blitz Build 2006.* "In everything I did, I showed you that by this kind of hard work we must help the weak, remembering the words the Lord Jesus himself said: 'It is more blessed to give than to receive.'" (Acts 20:35)

One of the most devastating things I

have ever witnessed was the aftermath of Hurricane Katrina during the fall of 2005. I had the privilege of leading a team of twenty-five staff members from Willow Creek Community Church to Waveland, Mississippi, a small town on the Gulf Coast. We saw firsthand that the storm was a great equalizer. During those first several weeks, the rich and the poor gathered together in the Kmart parking lot where we served hot meals and distributed clothing, basic groceries, hygiene items and even tents for shelter. Everyone had lost their home and their physical possessions. Many had lost family members and loved ones. The infrastructure of the community was completely destroyed.

Upon returning after the storm, there was no place to live, no place to shop, no recreation, no schools, no office buildings to return to work. For months and even years, things would not return to normal. The backbone of the community had been destroyed. I returned to the Gulf Coast several times, and about a year after the storm I had the opportunity to return with a larger team as a part of a project with Habitat for Humanity.

One of the great legacies that Axis, the twentysomething community at Willow Creek, brought to the greater church body was their leadership and participation in Blitz Build through Habitat for Humanity. Blitz Build was a gathering of more than one hundred people who gave up a week of their time to help build houses for underresourced families in partnership with Habitat.

In 2006 the location of the Blitz Build was in Waveland, Mississippi. Our team took three large buses on the eighteen-hour ride from Barrington, Illinois, to Mississippi. The buses were full of building supplies, tools for the trip and over two hundred volunteers. I had the privilege of serving on the leadership team and at one point was assigned to help with the roofing of one of the houses. We laughed about who made the decision for the trip to be in the middle of the Mississippi summer sun and heat. Working on a rooftop nailing shingles was certainly hot!

One of the things that I love about Habitat for Humanity is the expectation that new homeowners participate in and contribute to the building of their new home. All homeowners are required to put in numerous hours of labor and capital before the title of the property is handed over. One of the homeowners was a young single mom with a young son. She and her son would join us every night for dinner and worship services. After the first couple of days, she would come to our camp with a long stretch of tapestry material. She would carefully lay out the tapestry and pull out her paints—blues and greens. Then through smiles and hugs and great joy—she would wait patiently while all the volunteers (hundreds!) dipped their hands into the paint and put their handprints on the tapestry. She had every one of us sign our names. She told us that she wanted her living room wall to be covered with the names and hands of the people who had helped her to build her home.

As our buses were driving down the freeway toward home, that same woman had organized some of the other home owners to raise signs that said "Thank you for serving . . ." They cheered and waved goodbye to the departing buses. What an incredible gift she was to us! And how incredibly blessed we were to receive her affirmation and encouragement. Another reminder that we are the ones who receive when we give. What a glorious gift that is!

←❋ *Take action.* See if there is a Habitat for Humanity chapter in your community where you can volunteer and serve (www.habitat.org). Volunteer opportunities are available for people of different skill sets in local communities and around the world, and include global village trips, youth programs, recovery efforts in the Gulf Coast, women builds, disaster response, and more long-term serving opportunities.

**FOR FURTHER STUDY**

*The House That Love Built: The Story of Linda and Millard Fuller, Founders of Habitat for Humanity and the Fuller Center for Housing* by Bettie B. Youngs

Other ministries, such as Habitat for Humanity, have similar discount building supply stores around the country. Find a discount building-supply ministry near you. Spend some time getting to know the ministry to learn about where they need volunteer support. Contact builders in your area and see if they would be willing to donate materials to help bolster the ministry of the warehouse.

←❋ *Take action.* Support an organization like Engineering Ministries International (www.emiusa.org) by reading testimonies of how they are having an impact around the world, praying for their ministries, volunteering for a trip, serving as an intern and learning about their construction management program and how you can get involved. Technical professionals may join EMI's Association of Christian Design Professionals to support EMI and its initiatives.

**FOR FURTHER STUDY**

*Making Housing Happen: Faith-based Affordable Housing Models* by John Perkins and Jill Suzanne Shook

*Housing Policy in the United States: An Introduction* by Alex Schwartz

## HUMAN RIGHTS

Some of the worst human rights violations have been race related. As in the Tutsi massacre in Rwanda, many times human rights violations are race related. Following World War II, as the atrocities of Hitler's regime became apparent, there was an increased commitment by the world to intervene on behalf of human rights. On December 10, 1948, the United National General Assembly approved the Universal Declaration of Human Rights (UDHR), which began a movement to address global human rights issues.[176]

Another international code developed following the Nazi War Trials is the Nuremberg Code, which includes principles still in effect today that detail how the use of human subjects can be used in scientific experiments. They include principles such as informed consent and forbidding the use of coercion.[177]

Nearly a decade after the Rwandan genocide, the International Criminal Court (ICC) was established to prosecute genocide and other gross violations of human rights. Other human rights violations of the twentieth century include the more than one million people who were massacred during Armenian Holocaust, Hitler's extermination of six million Jews, twenty million Soviet citizens killed under Stalin's regime, the tens of millions of political enemies and peasant famine victims under Mao in China, and the massacre of two million Cambodians by Pol Pot.[178]

Today, "human rights" include the basic privileges all people are entitled to. The Bible takes a different perspective. It doesn't start with human entitlements but instead calls its followers to be mutually submissive to one another. Followers of Christ are to value and protect one another because of the love that Christ first showed us: "A new command I give you: Love one another. As I have loved you, so you must love one another" (Jn 13:34). Christian love compels the strong and privileged to protect those who have less access, privilege and power by advocating for life, liberty, and equality.

With the increased colonization of the world by the West, the human rights of indigenous people groups were and continue to be violated. Indigenous people groups include Native Americans, the Aborigines of Southeast Asia and Australia, and the Incas and the Mayans of Latin and South America. In the last few years the abuse of these people groups has been acknowledged on an international level. In 2007, after more than two decades of discussion, the General Assembly of the United Nations adopted a "Declaration on the Rights of Indigenous Peoples." The declaration promotes and protects human rights and fundamental freedoms for all, especially those who were colonized and forced to give up their cultures, traditions and land.

***Awareness exercise.*** Read a personal account of someone who lived through a genocide or some other human-rights violation. Consider *The Tears of My Soul: The Story of a Boy Who Survived the Cambodian Killing Fields* by Sokreaksa Himm. This is the story of a boy who lost most of his family at the hands of the brutal Khmer Rouge Cambodia. The book tell of Himm's personal journey as a survivor and the significant impact of his relationship with Christ. What feelings does this story provoke within you? How does Christian love compel you to respond?

←* ***Take action.*** Christian Solidarity International (CSI) is a human rights organization that works for religious liberty helping victims of religious oppression, victimized children and disaster victims. CSI has affiliates in several countries, including the Czech Republic, France, Germany, Hungary, Italy, South Korea, the Netherlands, Switzerland and the United States. Visit www.csi-int.org to find out how you can get involved.

←* ***Take action.*** There are hundreds of human rights organizations around the world.

## Evangelicals for Human Rights

Evangelicals for Human Rights was founded as an initiative of the National Religious Campaign Against Torture. Started by professors David Gushee, Ron Sider, Glen Stassen and four evangelical leaders in 2006, the organization is committed to raising evangelical awareness about torture and human-rights violations. Add your name to the Evangelical Declaration Against Torture and join their Action Alert Network at www.evangelicalsforhumanrights.org.

Amnesty International is a secular human-rights organization that strives to protect people wherever justice, freedom, truth and dignity are denied. Amnesty provides opportunities for people to act locally, respond on line, or get involved in other ways. Order an activist tool kit or research more opportunities at www.amnestyusa.org.

### FOR FURTHER STUDY

*Human Rights, Justification, and Christian Ethics* by Per Sundman

*Faith and Human Rights: Christianity and the Global Struggle for Human Dignity* by Richard Amesbury and George Newlands

*See also* "Bioethics" and "Genocide."

## HUNGER

On November 11, 1974, *Time* magazine published "The World Food Crisis," which began, "For nation shall rise against nation . . . and there shall be famines and troubles; these are the beginnings of sorrows—Mark 13:8." Now over thirty years later, hunger is still a great challenge. The March 14, 2008, *Washington Post* included an article titled "Food Crisis: Soaring Prices Are Causing Hunger Around the World." Between October 2007 and March 2008, food prices increased by 41 percent, pushing many people, as the *Post* describes it, "from poverty into privation or even hunger." According to Bread for the World, over 850 million people worldwide do not have enough to eat. And as many as two billion people lack food because they are poor.[180] The problem is less about the amount of food available and more about its worldwide distribution.

Transporting food to hungry people continues to pose problems in the twenty-first century. Some of the reasons for distribution difficulties include (1) isolated villages have few roads and airports, (2) resources supporting the functionality of the food distribution system is not sustainable, and (3) when food is donated to famine-affected regions, local food suppliers are devastated, making it harder for the community to recover from famine and other disasters.

Another problem is the lack of some basic foods. I was shocked in 2008 to see a kiosk set up next to the rice and grain section at Costco. Every person who purchased bulk rice had to register and was limited in their purchase of rice. Sam's Club also imposed limits on the purchase of bulk rice, only allowing customers to purchase four bags of imported jasmine, basmati and long-grain white rice. The price of rice increased about 70 percent in 2008 be-

## Tuskegee Syphilis Study

The "Tuskegee Study of Untreated Syphilis in the Negro Male" is an example of human-rights violations in the United States. The experiment was conducted between 1932 and 1972 on 399 poor and mostly illiterate African Americans. Tuskegee men suffered the painful consequences of untreated syphilis while researchers studied the disease's progression. The men were told that they were being treated for having "bad blood," and in return for participating in the experiment they were given free medical exams, free meals, and the cost of their burial. This experiment was not only a horrendous violation of the ideals of "informed consent," it also was racist. The U.S. Department of Health was informed of the experiments and supported them. In 1997, President Clinton apologized on behalf of the nation to the survivors and their families.[179]

### FOR FURTHER STUDY

*Tuskegee's Truths: Rethinking the Tuskegee Syphilis Study* by Susan Reverby

*Bad Blood: The Tuskegee Syphilis Experiment* by James Jones

cause of increasing demand and poor crop yields. Rice is the staple consumed by almost half of the world, and there is fear of severe shortages. There have been food riots in Pakistan, Haiti and Senegal as a result of increased food prices and decreased supply.[181]

Many poor people may have access to rice and other grains but not to vegetables and other necessary foods to prevent malnourishment. Malnutrition can cause eye diseases, scurvy and a lack of essential vitamins for growth and development. UNICEF estimates that one million children died between 1999 and 2001 from lack of vitamin A.[182]

Developing nations face a variety of problems in food production. Soil conditions are often poor and irrigation is difficult. Erosion, water pollution and natural disasters such as floods or droughts are devastating to communities. And in many communities, food storage and preservation is a major challenge.

*Spiritual reflection.* If there is any one place where the church should unquestionably be involved, it is in responding to those around the world who are without food. Do a search of the four Gospels to discover how many times the word *bread* is used. Jesus did not ignore the needs of the hunger of the people: "I have compassion for these people; they have already been with me three days and have nothing to eat. I do not want to send them away hungry, or they may collapse on the way" (Mt 15:32). Likewise, we are called to respond with compassion to those who are without food.

←⚞ *Take action.* Walk or run in an event to raise money for hungry children. For example, in Illinois, Bright Hope International's (www.brighthope.org) annual Run for Hungry Children 5K Run/3K Walk raises money to feed and educate children in some of the poorest places in the world.

←※ *Take action.* Host a letter-writing campaign at your school, work or church inviting people to write to Congress to ask for increased government support of global hunger. Bread for the Word is a collective Christian voice urging our nation's decision makers to end hunger at home and abroad. Bread for the World (www.bread.org) provides resources for an annual offering of letters.

←※ *Take action.* World Vision and other organizations provide programs for hunger awareness, like the youth-based program 30 Hour Famine (www.30hourfamine.org). Host an event like this and donate the money to an organization fighting world hunger.

←※ *Take action.* Participate in a solidarity challenge. In 2008 Willow Creek Community Church hosted "Celebration of Hope," which challenged people to participate in five days of solidarity with the hungry, eating as half of the world's population does, with meals of oatmeal, rice, beans and vegetables. The money that would have been spent on additional groceries was collected in a special offering to be used to combat hunger. Meal options included plain oatmeal; a tortilla, rice and beans; or rice with bits of fish or chicken and a vegetable. Portions were suggested in solidarity with the majority of the world as well. One cup or eight ounces is a generous portion. "Meat is a luxury, with the average African consuming about 3/4 ounce per day—the size of a small chicken nugget. Fresh fruit is rare, available only if locally grown and in season. While these meals seem meager by American standards, they actually represent diets in the broad middle of the world's

population."[183] If you do participate in a solidarity challenge, be sure to use discernment and be safe in determining your portion size. If you have medical conditions or concerns, you should consult your physician before participating in this type of activity.

←※ *Take action.* Heifer International (www.heifer.org) works with communities to end hunger and poverty and to care for the earth. Since 1944 Heifer International has assisted over four million families in 120 countries to become self-reliant through the gifts of income and food-producing animals and training. The amazing thing about this ministry is that families who have received support and become self-reliant then pass on the gift to others in need. A friend of mine who is an elementary school teacher sponsored a Heifer International project with her fifth grade class. All of the students were encouraged to participate and to ask their friends and family to sponsor them for a read-a-thon. Many of the donors agreed to pay $1 for every book that a student read. The class raised $2,250 and also had the opportunity to read great books!

←※ *Take action.* Start a community garden. Have participants contribute by playing a role in the planting and harvesting. Donate extra food and vegetables to a food pantry or other community group that serves meals to people who are hungry. Another version of this type of ministry is a gleaning ministry. If members of your community have fruit trees, ask if they would be willing to have someone come and pick the extra fruit to give away to the poor.

**FOR FURTHER STUDY**

*A Blueprint to End Hunger* by the National Anti-Hunger Organizations[184]

*Changing the Face of Hunger: The Story of How Liberals, Conservatives, Republicans, Democrats, and People of Faith are Joining Forces in a New Movement to Help the Hungry, the Poor, and the Oppressed* by Tony Hall

*See also* "Children" and "Poverty."

## IMMIGRATION

Recently, I was at the Chinese American History Museum in San Francisco. It was unbelievable how many of the questions and concerns surrounding the immigration of Chinese Americans during the nineteenth century are parallel to the current conversation around Hispanic immigration. Immigration is one of the most relevant social justice questions the evangelical church must wrestle with in the twenty-first century. It is necessary to understand how Christian theology and practice informs the treatment of people seeking to come into the United States, many of whom are poor. For example, in Exodus 22:21 the Lord says, "Do not mistreat or oppress a foreigner, for you were foreigners in Egypt."

In the last decade of the twentieth century, almost a million legal immigrants and close to 150,000 undocumented people entered the United States.[185] The majority of undocumented people are Hispanic and Asian, who make up close to 75 percent of all United States immigrants. Of the 28.4 million foreign-born residents in the United States in 2000, Latinos accounted for 14.5 million; 7.2 million were Asian.[186]

One of the major questions surrounding the debate around immigration is how the United States government should respond to the estimated 11 million undocumented people already living in the United States.[187] In 2005 the Boarder Protection, Anti-Terrorism, and Illegal Immigration Control Act (H.R. 4437) was passed in the House of Representatives, but was defeated in the Senate. The bill would have made it a federal crime to be an illegal immigrant in the United States. If the law had passed, millions of undocumented immigrants would have become felons. The bill also would have made it a crime for religious organizations and social service groups to open their doors or offer support to undocumented people. Bishop Thomas Wenski observes, "The so-called 'illegals' are so not because they wish to defy the law; but, because the law does not provide them with any channels to regularize their status in our country—which needs their labor: they are not breaking the law, the law is breaking them."[188]

***Spiritual reflection exercise.*** The Scriptures are wrought with passages that speak about God's desire for the treatment of aliens and foreigners. For example: do not wrong or oppress (Ex 22:21), treat workers fairly (Deut 24:14) and welcome strangers with hospitality (Mt 25:35). Look up these passages and others that address God's heart toward the stranger, alien and foreigners. What do the Scriptures have to say about these people groups? How does your study inform the conversation about the question of immigration in the United States? Spend time in prayer for men, women and children who are living in the United States as undocumented guests. Ask God to move your heart on behalf of immigrants.

*Awareness exercise.* Gather some friends to watch the movie *A Day Without a Mexican* (2004).[190] The movie is a comedy about what California would be like if one day all of the Mexicans disappeared. As you watch the movie, consider what legitimate points are being made about undocumented workers and the questions surrounding immigration. More information about the movie is available at www.adaywithoutamexican.com.

*Awareness exercise.* Read about the Religion and Immigration Project at the University of San Francisco. The project does research on the role of religion as a part of the immigration experience in San Francisco and California. In the past the project has hosted conferences in which participants presented the result of their research on the ways immigrants adjust to life in the United States. The program gives diverse groups a voice in the conversation surrounding immigration. Familiarize yourself with The Religion and Immigration Project at www.usfca.edu/TRIP.

*Awareness exercise.* Study with friends what Scripture has to say about immigration—the strangers and the aliens. Sojourners

(www.sojo.net) has a four-week discussion guide available called *Welcoming the Stranger: Christians and Immigration* that is designed to spark discussion about how to live out God's call for justice in the world. Visit the Sojourners website for more information.

←* *Take action.* Enter into an immersion experience with BorderLinks (www.borderlinks.org), a ministry committed to raising awareness and inspiring action at the Mexico and United States border. BorderLinks programs focus on cross-border relationships, formation of community, economic development and social justice. Join a Borderlinks guided experiential delegation that focuses on education, service and action. Delegation programs last anywhere from one day to two weeks and are available for both individuals and groups. BorderLinks also offers academic programs for college students, a children's food security program and a women's co-op.

←* *Take action.* Partner with Esperanza USA (www.esperanza.us), the largest Hispanic faith-based community-development

## Tierra Neuva

Tierra Neuva (New Earth) is "an ecumenical ministry in Burlington, Washington, that seeks to share the Good News of God's liberation in Jesus Christ with migrant farm workers, new immigrants, and permanent Hispanic residents."[189] The People's Seminary, an affiliate ministry of Tierra Neuva, offers classes in theology on three levels: to people on the margins, to

congregations and pastors, and to seminarians, interns, and researchers. The ministry of Tierra Neuva also offers opportunities for spiritual reflection, prayer, renewal, advocacy and prophetic ministry. Consider attending an event, joining a prayer group or taking a class offered through the seminary. Go to www.tierranueva.org or www.peoplesseminary.org.

corporation in the country. Consider attending the National Hispanic Prayer breakfast in Washington, D.C., or partnering with Esperanza in one of their development programs through capacity building, workforce development, education, community development, health initiatives and *Mujeres de Esperanza* (Women of Hope).

←⚓ ***Take action.*** Work alongside of an organization like Justice for Immigrants (www .justiceforimmigrants.org) and help educate the public about issues surrounding undocumented persons. Support positive public dialogue about immigration reform, be a proponent of legislative and administrative reforms, and participate in the greater network of Christians advocating on behalf of this issue. Download a parish kit for more ideas about what positive advocacy can look like.

### FOR FURTHER STUDY

*Border of Death, Valley of Life: An Immigrant Journey of Heart and Spirit* by Daniel Groody

*Welcoming the Stranger: Justice, Compassion and Truth in the Immigration Debate* by Matthew Soerens and Jenny Hwang

*A New Christian Manifesto: Pledging Allegiance to the Kingdom of God* by Bob Ekblad

*See also* "Racial Reconciliation" and "Racism."

## INCARCERATION

As of December 2007, 2.3 million men, women and children were held in United States federal or state prisons and county jails.[191] One newspaper article wrote of the prison situation in the United States: "we tend to use incarceration as an indirect answer to many social problems: drug addiction, mental illness, poverty."[192] The prison crisis in California is so severe that the state is exploring how to export prisoners to other states because there is not enough room to house all of those who are incarcerated within the state. According to the New York times, "The United States has less than 5 percent of the world's population. But it has almost a quarter of the world's prisoners."[193] The United States has the highest percentage of inmates per capita of any nation in the world. Of this phenomena, James Whitman, a specialist in comparative law at Yale says, "Far from serving as a model for the world, contemporary America is viewed with horror."[194]

Leading the prison ministry at Willow Creek Community Church, I was exposed to several different facilities throughout the state of Illinois. We were involved in more than one juvenile detention center, in jails around the state and in a few prisons that were scattered throughout Illinois. I became a chaplain at Cook County Jail, and one of my highlights of the Christmas season was preaching the gospel to men struggling with addictions. Somehow those who are behind bars worship about the freedom that comes from Christ with a vigor that is not often experienced outside in the "free world." As I continued to have my heart turned toward the incarcerated, the prison ministries volunteer leaders kept putting pressure on me to take a trip to Angola. No, not Angola, Africa—Angola, Louisiana.

The Louisiana State Penitentiary is most commonly referred to as Angola. The prison got its name because in the early nineteenth century it was a slave-breeding plantation—a place where slaves from Angola, Africa, were brought to be bred and then sold in the slave market in the Southern states. The plantation was bought by the state in 1901 and was eventually converted into a facility for inmates. You may be familiar with the prison, because in the 1950s and 1960s it became known as the "bloodiest prison in America." For years, the inmates were guarded by themselves (with weapons) and the conditions behind the walls of the facility are truly hard to comprehend. At one point dozens of inmates, in an attempt to call national attention to the conditions of hard work and brutality in the prison, cut their Achilles tendons as a cry for help for the world to intervene. They became known as the "Heel String Gang." Since then the prison has experienced major reforms. In the past ten years, under the leadership of Warden Burl Cain, a professing Christian, the incidence of inmate-to-inmate violence (anything from a small infraction like spitting at someone to a more violent offense) has decreased to under one hundred incidents a year.

I first went to Angola in 2006, and since then my world has not been the same. I had heard about this place where convicted felons served time for heinous crimes—murder, rape, abuse, molestation, drugs and violence. In all truthfulness I had no desire to go! There are over five thousand inmates at Angola, and the majority of the population will die behind the walls of the prison. Louisiana strictly enforces their sentences, and I have often been reminded that there "Life means life." Close to 80 percent of the inmates have life sentences and will die behind the prison walls from illnesses, old-age or the death penalty.

My leadership team for the prison ministry at Willow Creek had visited Angola in

years past and had been introduced to the Christian community that existed in the prison. They wanted me to experience firsthand how the lives of the men had been transformed by faith in Christ. When I finally received permission to take a small team, my main reason for going was that I did not believe that the stories could be true. By that point I had experienced enough "jail time religion" to last a lifetime, and I wasn't about to be manipulated into believing that a vibrant Christian community could exist behind the walls of a place like Angola. So I decided to check this place out for myself. It is hard to describe in a brief account the ways that I experienced God and witnessed his presence when I was in Angola.

Since Angola is an active farm with over eighteen thousand acres, there are many things for the inmates to do. The prison has well-developed programs; some of the inmates have earned significant privileges to be able to participate in the biannual rodeo, take classes, make crafts and other enjoyable activities. There is a seminary on the facility, where students are being trained and discipled to study and learn to teach and preach the Word of God. Some of the inmates have become pastors and are the leaders of the Christian community in the different buildings on the facility. Other inmates have taken their call to Christian ministry so seriously they have asked to be transferred to other prison facilities that have less privileges and activities in order to be missionaries to the men there.[195] I saw glimpses of profound faith in many of the men that I encountered during our visit.

One of the greatest gifts I've received is

## Justice Fellowship

Partner with Justice Fellowship (an arm of Prison Fellowship) to work for national reform in the prison system. Justice Fellowship is a nonprofit online community of Christians working to reform the criminal justice system to reflect biblically based principles of restorative justice. Justice Fellowship works to recognize the needs of crime victims, hold offenders accountable and involve communities. Visit www.justicefellowship.org to see how you and your community can get involved through merchant accountability boards, neighborhood watch programs, community policing, community-based resolution centers, community reparation boards, victim-offender reconciliation programs (VORP), family group conferencing or community justice conferencing and sentencing circles.

the way my Angola brothers in Christ challenged my theology. In a worldly sense I believe the men and women behind bars have done something (or many things) wrong. Most of them are guilty of some crime, and according to the laws of our land they deserve to be punished. But my visits to Angola forced me to ask how God sees men and women who are behind bars. What does the call to Christian forgiveness and the commandment to forgive seventy times seven mean for those who have repented and turned from their ways? The greatest theological implication, however, is the depth and power of the blood of Christ. Jesus died for each one of the men at Angola. If they have truly repented of their sins and have confessed with their mouths and believed in their hearts that Jesus is Lord (Rom 10:9), I truly believe that Jesus' blood is enough for them to be forgiven.

I returned to Angola in 2007 and took a small group of people from Hillside Covenant Church in Walnut Creek, California, to lead services and visit with the inmates. I felt like I was returning to fellowship with true brothers in the faith. One of the members of my team remarked that he had never witnessed so much freedom in Christ before meeting the Christian men at Angola.

"The LORD looked down from his
    sanctuary on high,
   from heaven he viewed the earth,
to hear the groans of the prisoners
    and release those condemned to
    death."
So the name of the LORD will be
    declared in Zion
   and his praise in Jerusalem.
(Ps 102:19-21)

### FOR FURTHER STUDY

Visit Louisiana State Penitentiary at Angola's prison website at www.doc.louisiana.gov/LSP

*Cain's Redemption: A Story of Hope and Transformation in America's Bloodiest Prison* by Dennis Shere

←❊ *Take action.* Start a pen-pal ministry to inmates with members of your church. This is a great way for individuals and the community to take a first step toward getting involved in prison ministry. Contact prison fellowship for more information at www.pfm.org.

←❊ *Take action.* Start an Angel Tree (www .angeltree.org) program in your church that will provide gifts to boys and girls whose parents are incarcerated.

←❊ *Take action.* Consider volunteering at your local prison or jail to bring the message of the Gospel to the men, women and youth behind bars. If you have a special skill or talent, like singing or music, work with the chaplain of the facility to see if you can receive permission to perform for the inmates. Singing Christmas carols during the holiday season is a wonderful way to encourage the inmates and to provide a less threatening opportunity for volunteers to be exposed to prison ministry. If there is no chaplain at the facility where you would like to minister, contact the volunteer coordinator.

←❊ *Take action.* Get involved in an organization that advocates on behalf of prison reform. Research the prison and jail situation in your state. Find out what ministries are already working to transform the system, and explore how you might partner with them. Meet with your state and federal congresspersons in order to find out what types of prison policies and legislation they support.

←❊ *Take action.* Join Awana Lifeline Prison Ministry and volunteer their Returning Hearts Celebration at Angola. The celebration is an annual event held at U.S. prisons that seeks to restore relationships between fathers and their children through a special day of fun, reconciliation and bonding. Visit www.awana.org/lifeline to find out more.

**FOR FURTHER STUDY**

*Setting the Captives Free! Relevant Ideas in Criminal Justice and Prison Ministry* edited by Don Smarto

*God Behind Bars: The Inspiring Story of Prison Fellowship* by John Perry

*See also* "Capital Punishment," "Prison Entrepreneurship Program" ministry profile, "Race" and "Race—Incarceration."

# MALARIA

Each year, there are 350-500 million cases of malaria around the world, with some one million of those cases resulting in death.[196] Africa accounts for 90 percent of malarial deaths, and African children account for over 80 percent of malaria victims worldwide.[197] Malaria was eliminated from the United States in the mid-twentieth century.[198] During that same time there was a major push worldwide to eradicate the disease. These efforts were largely successful in industrialized nations but not in most of the developing world.

My perceptions of malaria have been largely misinformed. I knew that it had something to do with mosquitoes. I thought it was a tropical disease. I had heard of people coming back from the mission field because of exposure, but was not aware of the symptoms and effects, and was certainly ignorant of the number of deaths that malaria still causes: every thirty seconds an African child dies of malaria. Worldwide, approximately three thousand children die each day die of the same disease.[199]

Infection is caused by a parasite carried by mosquitoes. Symptoms of malaria include fever, shivering, vomiting and convulsions. It can cause cognitive impairments and brain damage, severe headaches and renal failure. It is especially dangerous for children because of their vulnerability during child development. Depending on the strand, an active malaria infection can require hospitalization. Other types of infections can be treated on an outpatient basis through supportive measures and antimalarial drugs. One of the main ways to prevent the spread of infection is through indoor residual spraying. Full mosquitoes digest their blood meal by resting on nearby surfaces. When the walls of dwellings have been coated with insecticides, resting mosquitoes are killed by the insecticide before they are able to bite another victim and spread the disease. Another major way to prevent the spread of malaria is through the use of insecticide-treated nets. Bed nets decrease the risk of infection by over 70 percent.[200] In malarial regions of Africa, only one out of every twenty people owns a bed net.[201]

The cost of fighting this disease around the world is incredibly high. In Africa, it is estimated to cost $12 billion a year.[202] In 2005 President George W. Bush started the President's Malaria Initiative (PMI) to save lives in Africa by wiping out the disease. He pledged to increase U.S. malaria funding by more than $1.2 billion over five years to reduce deaths due to malaria by 50 percent in fifteen African countries and challenged other donor countries, private foundations, and corporations to help reduce the suffering and death caused by this disease. President Bush proclaimed:

Americans are a compassionate people who care deeply about the plight of others and the future of our world, and we can all be proud of the work our Nation is doing to fight disease and despair. By standing with the people of Africa in the fight against malaria, we can help lift a burden of unnecessary suffering, provide hope and health, and forge lasting friendships.[203]

↤ *Take action.* Buy a bed net. Many organizations provide bed nets as a comprehensive solution to control malaria in impoverished nations. Malaria No More (www.malariano more.org) is an organization whose mission is to end deaths due to malaria. They receive donations for bed nets that cost $10 per net.

↤ *Take action.* World Malaria Day, April 25, was established and approved at the 60th World Health Assembly in March 2007. It replaces "Africa Malaria Day," which has been commemorated every year since 2001 and will henceforth be celebrated annually, in order to provide education and understanding of malaria as a global scourge that is preventable and a disease that is curable. Download the World Malaria Day Button and post it on your website to help raise awareness. Visit www.mobil ising4malaria.org.

**FOR FURTHER STUDY**

*World Malaria Report 2008*, available at www .malaria.org

*The Making of a Tropical Disease: A Short History of Malaria* by Randall Packard

*See also* "AIDS," "Health Care—Global" and "Tuberculosis."

## MICROFINANCE

Arguably, microfinance has become one of the most effective ways of mobilizing the poor out of poverty. Microfinance, also called microenterprise or microcredit, provides loans to poor people without them having to put up any collateral. Typically microfinance programs also provide training or support. Most of these loans are made to woman in the developing world. The World Bank has a program in which participants can receive small loans, but the requirements are relatively rigid and there is little freedom for those who are poor to propose how they could start a business or use their funds, because of the strict control.

Muhammad Yunus, author of *Creating a World Without Poverty: Social Business and the Future of Capitalism,* received the 2006 Nobel Peace Prize for his work in Bangladesh offering microcredit in the form of small loans with the Grameen Bank (Village Bank). Yunus's model is that the impetus for how the loans should be used must come from the individual's inspiration, desires and needs. As of May 2008 the Grameen Bank has had 7.5 million borrowers, 97 percent of whom are women. According to the Bank's May Report, as of April 2008, Grameen Bank has distributed $7.04 billion in microcredit loans.[204] The philosophy of Grameen Bank is almost the exact opposite of conventional banks, who work from the philosophy that the more resources or money that you have, the more you get, because there is less risk in loaning to you.

> Grameen Bank starts with the belief that credit should be accepted as a human right, and builds a system where one who does not possess anything gets the highest priority in getting a loan. Grameen methodology is not based on assessing the material possession of a person, it is based on the potential of a person. Grameen believes that all human beings, including the poorest, are endowed with endless potential.[205]

What is so amazing about microfinance is that it gives the poor the opportunity, through work and savings, to progress out of poverty. With the Bangladeshi participants in the Grameen Bank program as an example, the effects of the microcredit industry are amazing. According to the Bank:

> It is estimated that the average household income of Grameen Bank members is about 50 percent higher than the target group in the control village, and 25 percent higher than the target group non-members in Grameen Bank villages. The landless have benefited most, followed by marginal landowners. This has resulted in a sharp reduction in the number of Grameen Bank members living below the poverty line, 20 percent compared to 56 percent for comparable non-Grameen Bank members.[206]

Some argue that the opportunity for the poorest of the poor to invest and make a living through their own work is the only sustainable model to ending poverty worldwide.

←≪ *Take action.* Consider investing in a bank that provides microcredit to the poor. MicroPlace, now a subsidiary of eBay, was started by Tracey Pettengill Turner, a MBA graduate from Stanford University, who traveled to Bangladesh to work with the Grameen Bank. After seeing the effectiveness of mi-

## Opportunity International

Opportunity International (www.opportunity.org) is a Christian organization committed to providing people in chronic poverty the opportunity to transform their lives. Their commitment is motivated by Jesus Christ's call to serve the poor. In June 2008 Opportunity International reported a 98 percent repayment rate on their microloans. Since 1992 Opportunity's Women's Opportunity Network has raised more than $7 million to benefit poor women around the world. Ways to get involved include becoming a member of Opportunity's Board of Governors, becoming an Opportunity Partner with the Poor, joining telephone focus groups, opening your home to international visitors and staff members, and helping with volunteer projects like mailings and newsletters.

croenterprise, she returned to the United States and started MicroPlace, an organization committed to help alleviate global poverty by enabling everyday people to make investments in the world's working poor. MicroPlace (www.microplace.com) is unique because one can partner with them by investing resources with the expectation of a return, while at the same time helping provide loans for the world's poor.

### FOR FURTHER STUDY

*Creating a World Without Poverty: Social Business and the Future of Capitalism* by Muhammad Yunus

*God Is At Work: Transforming People and Nations Through Business* by Ken Eldred

*Christian Microenterprise Development: An Introduction* by David Bassau and Russell Mask

*See also* "Capitalism," "Global Economy" and "Work."

## MULTIETHNIC CHURCHES AND COMMUNITIES

Revelation describes a picture of worship around the throne of God in heaven of a multilingual and multiethnic community where people from every country and nation will be gathered in worship of the Creator and Lord of the universe.

> After this I looked, and there before me was a great multitude that no one could count, from every nation, tribe, people and language, standing before the throne and in front of the Lamb. They were wearing white robes and were holding palm branches in their hands. And they cried out in a loud voice:

> "Salvation belongs to our God,
>    who sits on the throne,
> and to the Lamb." (Rev 7:9-10)

A growing trend in the twenty-first-century church is ministry in a multicultural setting. More churches are actively pursuing multiethnicity within the United States. Nonetheless, according to the Hartford Institute for Religion Research, Sunday mornings in churches in America are still "the most segregated hour in America."[207]

A church is considered multiracial if more than 20 percent of the congregation are of a different ethnicity than the majority group. According to sociologist Michael Emerson, only 7 percent of churches in the United States are multiracial.[208] In 2005, according to Scott Thumma, also a sociologist, the percentage of megachurches that claim to be multiethnic is higher than the national average at 35 percent.[209] More than half of U.S. megachurches claim to be intentionally pursuing multiethnicity.[210]

God calls his church to be united regardless of skin color, cultural heritage or social class. The apostle Paul said, "I appeal to you, brothers and sisters, in the name of our Lord Jesus Christ, that all of you agree with one another in what you say and that there be no divisions among you, but that you be perfectly united in mind and thought" (1 Cor 1:10). In order to be obedient to its true calling, the church must be willing to work through cultural differences and to experience the great benefits of multiethnic community.

Multiethnic communities living out the biblical ideal of shalom (peace) is a wonderful way to combat racism. Models of healthy multicultural Christian communities are starting to pop up all around the United States. Consider Bridgeway Community

## Bridgeway Community Church

David Anderson committed his life to Christ at the age of eighteen and never looked back. Growing up in the suburbs of Washington, D.C., he had not experienced the realities of city life until moving to Chicago to attend Moody Bible Institute. While in Chicago, he had the opportunity to become the assistant pastor at Near North Baptist Church in Cabrini Green, one of the public housing developments known for drugs, gang violence and other terrible conditions. Through his ministry experience in the projects of Cabrini Green, David's heart began to break over the pain of inner-city poverty.

After graduation David became a pastoral intern at Willow Creek Community Church, where he became exposed to the leadership of Bill Hybels and ministry in a megachurch. In 1992, encouraged by leaders and friends from Willow Creek, David founded Bridgeway Community Church (www.bridgewayonline.org) in Columbia, Maryland, hoping to establish an evangelistic community that was welcoming to people of all racial backgrounds. Now more than two thousand people gather to worship at Bridgeway and to carry out their vision "to become a multicultural army of fully devoted followers of Christ, moving forward in unity and love, to reach our community, our culture, and our world for Jesus Christ."

### FOR FURTHER STUDY

*Multicultural Ministry: Finding Your Church's Unique Rhythm* by David Anderson

*Gracism: The Art of Inclusion* by David Anderson

Church, a multicultural congregation in Columbia, Maryland, under the leadership of David Anderson, author of *Multicultural Ministry: Finding Your Church's Unique Rhythm.*

*Awareness exercise.* Attend a multiethnic leadership conference to learn more about challenges and benefits of ministry in a multicultural setting. One example is the "Coming Together" conference that "brings together experienced practitioners to give Biblical inspiration for churches ministering in multicultural settings." For information about dates and speakers of Coming Together visit www.comingtogethertc.org. Another example is the Ethnic America Summit (www.ethnic-america.net) that sponsors networking opportunities around the country for people committed to sharing the love of Christ in a multicultural setting.

*Awareness exercise.* Look for articles about multicultural churches that address many different issues surrounding interracial ministry. Consider the *Journal for the Scientific Study of Religion* 47, no 1 (March 2008), where several articles are present. You can also google "multicultural ministry" as another resource for articles. What did you learn from your reading? What did you discover that was different from what you expected? What benefits are there to being in a multicultural community? What challenges?[211]

*Awareness exercise.* Gather a group of people to have a book study on one of the "For Further Study" suggestions that follow. There are many wonderful resources available for those considering starting up a multicultural worship community. Invite people to join your study who are from different racial or cultural backgrounds.

←❧ *Take action.* Consider getting involved as a member, volunteer or leader with the Mosaix Global Network (www.mosaix.info) and embrace the seven core commitments of a multiethnic church: (1) embrace dependence, (2) take intentional steps, (3) empower diverse leadership, (4) develop crosscultural relationships, (5) pursue crosscultural competency, (6) promote a spirit of inclusion, and (7) mobilize for impact.[212] Host a multiethnic summit at your church or attend a conference hosted by the Mosaix Center.

---

**FOR FURTHER STUDY**

*One Body, One Spirit* by George Yancey

*One New People: Models for Developing a Multiethnic Church* by Manuel Ortiz

*Against All Odds: The Struggle for Racial Integration in Religious Organizations* by Brad Christerson, Michael Emerson and Korie Edwards

*People of the Dream: Multiracial Congregations in the United States* by Michael Emerson with Rodney M. Woo

---

## PHYSICAL DISABILITIES

People who experience physical and developmental challenges are amongst those the most overlooked in society.[213] In 2008 there were over six hundred million people around the world with some type of disability.[214] Those with physical infirmities, debilitating diseases, inherited defects and other disabilities are often viewed as being without value and having little to contribute. In different parts of the world, men, women and children with disabilities are discarded, neglected, and even viewed as less than human. In some countries, children who are born with deformities are left with little or no attention, limited access to education and developmental oppor-

## Sarah Ago

Sarah Ago is the Director of Children's Ministry at Hillside Covenant Church in Walnut Creek, California, where I currently serve. She has a brother with Down syndrome and I asked if she might be willing to share part of her story. It is a powerful example of the way that Jesus reveals himself through the lives of those who are disabled.

### *My Journey into Disability Ministry*
by Sarah Ago

My world changed when I was just short of my eleventh birthday. On June 21, 1990, Jacob Bascom was born into our family. At his birth it was discovered my brother had Down syndrome and a heart defect. Shortly after his birth Jacob survived an operation to thread a catheter into his heart in order to open up a valve that was closed. During the surgery our church prayed, and the procedure was successful.

Jacob came home after three weeks in the neonatal intensive-care unit. It took him many weeks to show significant weight gain. As he continued to grow, new health problems arose. In 2008, by Jacob's eighteenth birthday, he had experienced several health complications, including immune-deficiency, thyroid issues, an enlarged heart and digestive/bowel problems. Jacob has had twelve surgeries, ranging from operations on his heart to correcting double vision. He has had nearly every health problem possible for a person with Down syndrome.

My brother's pain and the challenges that came with caring for him have greatly shaped me. More than that, Jacob's joy and purity have opened my eyes to God in a way that I would have missed had he not

been in my life. Jacob has a smile that lights up a room. He is not easily frustrated, nor is he fearful or mean. His endurance is stronger than anyone I know.

Jacob loves Jesus wholeheartedly. He cannot speak in long sentences, but he sings entire songs in praise to God! The highlight of his life is going to "Night of Praise" to worship with songwriter and vocalist Dennis Jernigan. Jacob's most prized possessions are his collections of Bibles.

Jacob's presence in my life built great compassion and depth into my heart. The same year that Jacob was born, I learned about the plight of orphans in other countries. I knew that I needed to do something about their situation. My heart broke while watching a journalist's report of the orphanages in Romania. I heard God speak to my heart that I could make a difference for children like them.

I began taking mission trips to countries such as Mexico, Albania and Romania. I visited orphanages on the latter two trips and felt God confirm what my heart had heard years before. I saw children in Romania who became needlessly disabled due to a lack of attention and basic childcare. The sight of children rocking themselves back and forth in their cribs was almost too much for an eighteen-year-old girl to comprehend. Yet it fueled me to share their plight. I spoke about my experiences with churches and youth groups upon my return home. I handed out the names of the orphans I had visited and asked people to commit to pray for them.

Soon after my trip to Romania, I met a missionary couple who had returned from serving in China. They told me about the horrors of abandoned baby girls in China. They also told me about an organization that rescued abandoned children and cared for the disabled. That organization is now called International China Concern.

I wrote to the director of programs at International China Concern (www.chinaconcern.org) and was placed on their mailing list. As I read about the children in the orphanage, I saw that everyone of them had special needs. There are very few resources for these children and their parents in China. As a result, many are brought to orphanages. International China Concern takes these children in and provides medical care, emotional support and loving group homes and foster care. I was deeply impressed by the organization from the start and have sponsored a child there for eight years. It was my joy to lead a team to work with the children at International China Concern in 2008. That was a trip that changed and affected us deeply.

←⊷ *Take action.* Consider sponsoring a child through International China Concern or participating in a two-week short-term trip, becoming an international volunteer, or getting involved through some other volunteer opportunity.

tunities, and severe limitations on opportunities for life and prosperity. As a result, in some institutional facilities for the disabled, the lack of regular human contact and physical stimulation leads to the loss of life. According to a joint press release by The International Labour Organization, Disabled Peoples' International, and Irish Aid, no more than 10 percent of people with disabilities in the developing world (particularly the Asian Pacific region) have access to advancement opportunities.[215]

The history of the treatment of people with disabilities is one of great shame and horror. Historically, people with disabilities were regarded as abnormal and were considered freaks. In the United States and Europe during the nineteenth century, people with mental and physical abnormalities were exhibited for entertainment at circuses, fairs and exhibitions.[216] Even in the twenty-first century, there are few public mandates for sharing basic information about the facts, realities and experiences of those who are disabled. This type of exploitation deeply grieves the heart of God. Jesus said:

> When you give a luncheon or a dinner, do not invite your friends, your brothers or sisters, your relatives, or your rich neighbors; if you do, they may invite you back and so you will be repaid. But

when you give a banquet, invite the poor, the crippled, the lame, the blind, and you will be blessed. (Lk 14:12-14)

The twentieth century marked great reforms in the United States on behalf of the disabled. In 1975 the Education for All Handicapped Children Act was passed, which guaranteed that all people with disabilities would be ensured the right to free, appropriate public education.[217] In 1990 the Americans with Disabilities Act (ADA) was passed, addressing former stereotypical treatment of people with disabilities by barring discrimination in the workplace, public services, public accommodations and telecommunications.[218] Opportunities for community living for the disabled has increased exponentially in the United States during the twentieth century. Between 1977 and 1998 the number of disabled individuals living in community environments increased from 20,409 to 237,796.[219] In 2008 Congress made amendments to the ADA by expanding its application to more broadly define *disability*, which would significantly expand the scope of the 1990s legislation.[220]

There are numerous reasons why disabilities exist. Many people are disabled through abuse, war, poverty or disease. According to the World Health Organization, approximately one-fourth of all disabilities result from injuries and violence.[221] Injuries that cause disabilities include traffic accidents, falls, burns, war and conflict, youth violence and child abuse.[222] These often result in neurotrauma, paralysis due to spinal cord trauma, partial or complete amputation of limbs, psychological trauma, sensory disabilities such as blindness and deafness, and

other physical deformations.[223] But the vast majority of disabilities are the result of congenital or birth defects.

In the United States forty-nine million people live with some level of disability. According to Joni and Friends, only 5 percent of them attend church.[224] People with disabilities worldwide are the third largest unreached people group. Marriages are also deeply affected by the challenges that arise when someone within a family has a disability. The divorce rate for couples with children who have special needs is significantly higher than the national divorce rate. Some statistics claim that up to 80 percent of marriages with disabled children end in divorce. The church and Christians around the world must face this reality and get involved to offer support and encouragement to people and their families who are affected by disability.

If bars are more accessible than altars, if theaters are more welcoming that churches, if the producers of PBS are more sophisticated about communication access than our liturgists, if the managers of department stores know better how to appeal to those with disabilities than our church leadership, if the publishers of popular magazines are more knowledgeable about alternative formats than those who produce religious materials, then we have failed to meet Christ's challenge to us all.[225]

*Awareness exercise.* Befriend someone with special needs. If you don't know of anyone, visit a group home. As you grow in your relationship, ask your friend to share his or her story with you and to talk about he or she has experienced God. Ask your friend what you should know about people who have disabilities and their contributions to the church community. Consider volunteering for an organization like Little City (Palatine, Ill.); visit www.littlecity.org.

←* ***Take action.*** Support your church's ministry to people with disabilities. If it does not have a ministry with the disabled, start one! Receive and make room for the contributions of people with disabilities. Minister *with* them, not just *to* them. The entire community of believers misses out if people with disabilities are not welcomed and embraced in the local church.

←* ***Take action.*** Spend time developing re-

### Joni and Friends

Joni and Friends International Disability Center is committed to the cause of Christ and has the vision of accelerating Christian ministry in the disability community. In 1967 seventeen-year-old Joni Eareckson (now Eareckson Tada) became a quadriplegic as the result of a diving accident. After two years of rehabilitation, Joni learned how to paint with a brush between her teeth. She created many fine-arts paintings and prints that are prized throughout the world. She wrote her biography, *Joni*, to tell the story of her experience and conviction to use her personal trauma on behalf of helping others.

In 1979 Joni founded Joni and Friends with the hope of sharing the gospel of Christ and offering encouragement to the disabled community around the world. Since then she has personally visited more than forty-five countries, spoken to over one million people each week on her radio program, served hundreds of families through twenty "Family Retreats" around the United States, refurbished more than fifty-two thousand wheelchairs through the support of inmate volunteers, written more than thirty-five books, served as a presidential appointee to the National Council on Disability, and worked with the U.S. State Department and Condoleezza Rice as a member of the Disability Advisory Committee on policy and programs that affect disabled persons in the State Department and around the world.

←* ***Take action.*** Extend the love of Christ to those affected by disability through joining the efforts of Joni and Friends. Programs that require volunteer support include family retreats, radio ministry, church relationships, wheelchair outreach, daily devotionals and visitation ministry. For more information about how you can serve go to www.joniand friends.org.

**FOR FURTHER STUDY**

*Joni* by Joni Eareckson Tada

*Hope . . . the Best of Things* by Joni Eareckson Tada

*A Lifetime of Wisdom* by Joni Eareckson Tada

lationships with families who have a disabled member. Listen, and offer support and encouragement. If there are several families in your church community, consider gathering together for a meal for fellowship and mutual encouragement. Ask how the church can come alongside these families, being attentive to their needs while encouraging them to fully participate in your community. Call a mom or dad and offer to spend an afternoon with their disabled child.

←❋ *Take action.* Invite a person with disability to speak before your congregation and to minister to your community. Seek to create a culture where people with disabilities feel welcomed and accepted rather than feared or misunderstood.

←❋ *Take action.* Pay attention to the architecture of your church building. What does it say about who is welcome? Could a disabled preacher enter your pulpit? Is it physically possible? Where would someone in a wheelchair sit? Look at the materials that are used in your church. Are they suitable for the blind or deaf?[226]

←❋ *Take action.* Special Olympics (www .specialolympics.org) is an organization that is "dedicated to empowering individuals with intellectual disabilities to become physically fit, productive and respected members of society through sports training and competition." Visit a Special Olympics event or volunteer to train or coach a special athlete. Watch the joy on the faces of those who participate. Have a part in empowering and encouraging them.

←❋ *Take action.* Host a respite night at your church to support individuals and families who are affected by disability. At our church, respite nights are a part of our "Room at the Inn" ministry, which is devoted to encouraging those who are most affected by disability. During respite nights, volunteers spend a few hours watching children with disabilities so their families can have some time without the responsibility of providing immediate care. Families are grateful for the care their children receive through respite ministries.

**FOR FURTHER STUDY**

*Autism and the God Connection* by William Stillman

*Sundays with Scottie* by Marlton Jones

*A Committed Mercy: You and Your Church Can Serve the Disabled* by Stan Carder

## POLITICS

How people should be involved in the public square has been the topic of political theory since ancient times. According to the philosopher Aristotle, the role of the politician is to contribute toward the governance of the state by playing the role of lawgiver and helping to determine the customs, the moral education and the institutions of the state.[227] How Christians should engage in politics is likewise worth our reflection.

The potential for effective change in the United States through the influence of the government is substantial. Reinhold Niebuhr remarked, "Man's capacity for justice makes democracy possible, but man's inclination to injustice makes democracy necessary."[228] Christians cannot afford to isolate themselves from political discourse, but rather must be willing to engage in the public square. One of most critical questions for Christians in that context is whether the ruling or legislative body of the state should mandate morality. Some Christians believe that the moral ethics outlined in Scripture should be instituted into law. Other Christians believe that laws do not exist to establish moral guidelines, but rather to protect the liberty of individuals. Christians must enter the conversation respectfully while being open to the experience and perspective of others of different faith traditions (see "Christianity in the Public Square" in chap. 3).

←⊷ *Take action.* Meet and dialogue with a friend of a different race, whether Republican, Democrat or of some other political persuasion, and ask about his or her views of politics and faith. How does your friend think faith should inform engagement in the political system? What is his or her perspective on the 2008 presidential election, in which the first African American, Barack Obama, was elected to the highest political office in the United States? How was this occasion significant? Listen to your friend's stories and hear his or her heart. Empathize with what is felt and enter into your friend's joy or despair. Not doing so will communicate that you don't care about your friend's feelings, culture, advances in history and significant events that affect his or her entire family.[229]

←⊷ *Take action.* Host a voting-registration campaign at your church, office or school. The goal is to raise people's awareness of their power and contribution toward the direction of government and political decisions by exercising the right to vote.[230]

**FOR FURTHER STUDY**

*Jesus and Justice: Evangelicals, Race, and American Politics* by Peter Goodwin Heltzel

*Jesus and Politics: Confronting the Powers* by Alan Storkey

*The Myth of a Christian Nation: How the Quest for Political Power is Destroying the Church* by Gregory Boyd

*The Great Awakening: Reviving Faith and Politics in a Post-Religious Right America* by Jim Wallis

*See also* "Christianity in the Public Square" (chap. 3).

## POVERTY—BIBLICAL PERSPECTIVES

Poverty is mentioned over two thousand times in Scripture. Yet the meaning of poverty can be elusive. Throughout the Old Testament the people of God had clear mandates about how to respond to the poor: "There will always be poor people in the land. Therefore I command you to be openhanded toward those of your people who are poor and needy in your land" (Deut 15:11). God did not want the Israelites to merely perform their religious duties but also to respond to the needs the poor. About the type of fasting he desires he asks:

> Is it not to share your food with the
>     hungry
>   and to provide the poor wanderer
>     with shelter—
> when you see the naked, to clothe
>     them,
>   and not to turn away from your
>     own flesh and blood? (Is 58:7)

The people of God had clear laws about how they were to provide for those living in poverty.

Physical poverty is concrete, observable and for the most part measurable. In speaking of material poverty, Gustavo Gutiérrez, a Peruvian theologian and Dominican priest wrote: "Concretely, to be poor means to die of hunger, to be illiterate, to be exploited by others, not to know that you are being exploited, not to know that you are a person. It is in relation to this poverty—material and cultural, collective and militant—that evangelical poverty will have to define itself."[231] Christians must ask what should be done about this kind of poverty.

Jesus had a lot to say about material poverty. He cared not only about his followers' internal righteousness but also about those who were considered the least of society. Jesus' ministry begins by calling attention to his role in fulfilling all righteousness (Mt 3:15). When he was tempted by Satan in the wilderness, he reminds his tempter that physical bread is not the source of life. "People do not live on bread alone, but on every word that comes from the mouth of God" (Mt 4:4). The juxtaposition in this passage of the pursuit of righteousness (obedience to every word that comes from God) and human's physical need for sustenance and food (bread alone) reminds us that our connection and intimacy with God is more important than our physical needs.

The most important needs that a human has are deeply spiritual. The moment that spiritual needs are ignored in the midst of material poverty, the battle has been lost. We must never neglect the spiritual well-being of souls while meeting physical needs. Nonetheless, Jesus calls us to address the physical needs that we see around us. Responding to "the least of these" is equivalent to respond-

## AJ

My husband and I have the great privilege of opening our home to urban kids whose family may not have a home or are not able to care for them.

Our first intimate encounter was with a little boy named Anthony. We called him AJ for short. A social worker dropped AJ off at our house around seven one evening. He had a dirty diaper and was sweaty and tired. AJ was only a year and a half old. He had severe asthma and had been living on the streets with his mother, who was a drug addict. She had given up custody of AJ and said that she didn't want him anymore. When the social worker brought in all of AJ's belongings, they fit in a small grocery bag. There was one extra diaper, one bottle and enough medicine to fill up half of our dining room table. AJ could barely breathe and wasn't able to play like other little boys; his asthma was severe.

Over the next several months my husband and I learned what it meant to love a little boy with ailing health. We took him weekly to the doctors and on occasion to the emergency room. All of his medical care was provided by Lawndale Christian Health Fellowship. We were so thankful to have a place to take him where we

ing to his needs (Mt 25). James expands on this, "Suppose a brother or sister is without clothes and daily food. If one of you says to them, 'Go in peace; keep warm and well fed,' but does nothing about their physical needs, what good is it? In the same way, faith by itself, if it is not accompanied by action, is dead" (Jas 2:15-17).

Paul tells us, "For you know the grace of our Lord Jesus Christ, that though he was rich, yet for your sake he became poor, so that through his poverty you might become rich" (2 Cor 8:9). The Lord has been abundantly gracious to the world. In light of his kindness and mercy, people must not close their eyes and ignore the horrors going on in the world, but engage and work to solve them. Rick Warren says, "I found those 2,000 verses on the poor. How did I miss that? I went to Bible college, two seminaries, and I got a doctorate. How did I miss God's compassion for the poor? I was not seeing all the purposes of God."[232] Christians must work to make a difference one small step at a time by loving those who are poor and walking alongside of those who have been rejected by society.

By living alongside the poor, Christians are a witness to Jesus' love to the world. In fact, Christ's followers are spiritually transformed through direct encounters with the poor. Through the lives, stories and experiences of the poor, Christ is revealed. Gutiérrez says it well:

> Christian poverty, an expression of love, is solidarity with the poor and is a protest against poverty. It is a poverty lived not for its own sake, but rather as an authentic imitation of Christ; it is a

knew he would get good treatment and we could afford the services.

We watched as AJ slowly came to life. He started to sleep through the night and soon was running around and getting into everything! It was as if, over the several months that he was with us, we watched God come to life within him. I have never seen such an amazing transformation—this little person who seemed so near to death, who could barely breathe, who didn't have any person immediately around him to love him and care for him.

Living with AJ was one of the greatest privileges of my life. We were able to meet his grandparents and to eventually assist them in the adoption process. It broke our hearts to see AJ go, but we had the opportunity during that year to experience life in a new way. We intimately encountered the way that poverty affected him, almost to the point of his death. And we were able to witness the love and mercy of Jesus as this little boy was given a second chance and came to life. It was wonderful to find out that AJ's grandparents had been looking for him and wanted to keep him, love him and raise him as their own. It was one of the greatest joys of our lives having AJ in our home, and we couldn't help but daily see Jesus shining through his little face.

poverty which means taking on the sinful human condition to liberate humankind from sin and all its consequences.[233]

**FOR FURTHER STUDY**

*God of the Poor: A Biblical Vision of God's Present Rule* by Dewi Hughes and Matthew Bennett

*Poverty on the Way to God: Thomas Aquinas on Evangelical Poverty* by Jan G. J. van den Eijnden

⚶ *Spiritual reflection exercise.* Henri Nouwen was a Catholic priest and author who wrote prolifically about the Christian life. In writing about poverty, Nouwen suggests that *our poverty is God's dwelling place:* "We are so inclined to cover up our poverty and ignore it that we often miss the opportunity to discover God, who dwells in it. Let's dare to see our poverty as the land in which our treasure is hidden."[234] Take some time to reflect on the following Scripture passages.

- Treatment of widows and orphans (Deut 10:17-18)

- The justice of God for children and the oppressed (Ps 72:1-4)

- The type of sacrifice that God requires (Is 58)

- Giving to those in need (Mt 6:1-4)

- The implications of living faith (Mt 25:31-46)

- The rich and the kingdom of heaven (Mk 10:17-23)

- Fulfillment of Isaiah's prophecy (Lk 4:16-21)

- The rich crop owner (Lk12:13-21)

- Invitations to a wedding feast (Lk 14:7-14)

- Expensive jar of perfume (Jn 12:4-11)

Where is there poverty in your life? Where do you experience lack—money, time, friendships, relationships? Where do you see poverty around you? How do you think God might be calling you to respond? Spend time in prayer. Ask God to give you the courage to take the steps that he is calling you to take.

## POVERTY—CAUSES

When we consider the global support for the eradication of poverty, we need to understand that the needs of the poor differ from nation to nation. The needs of the domestic poor in the United States are different than the needs of those in the developing world. Take water, for example. In 2007, 100 percent of people in the United States had access to clean and useable water. In Ghana only than 42 percent of the rural population has access to clean water.[235] For the poor in the United States, clean water is not an issue. However, access to computers for education plays a significant role in a child's ability to do well in school, get good grades and get into college. Limited opportunities in education could significantly influence a child's ability to get a good paying job later on in life. Domestic poverty is largely influenced by the following: the job market, education, housing, homelessness, the health care system and family structures.

One of the greatest challenges in understanding the causes of poverty are the roles of individual choices and personal responsibility for how people come to be in the situations they may find themselves. Certainly one's personal choices and decision making influence one's lot in life. Some people might look at examples like Ben Carson, a physician at Johns Hopkins Hospital, one of the greatest pediatric neurosurgeons in the world and the 2008 recipient of the Presidential Medal of Freedom.[236] Carson was raised by a single mother in intense poverty in urban Detroit. One might look at Carson and ask the question of why others can't follow his example and work themselves out of poverty. Carson grew up disadvantaged and, with so much going against him, if he can be successful, why can't the 15.89 million Americans living in abject poverty not do the same?[237]

Ben Carson, while growing up poor, had a lot going for him. One of the most influential factors in his success was his mother. She believed in him, encouraged him and provoked him to succeed. Not all children in poverty have the support of family and the fortitude to succeed in such limiting circumstances.

While it is true that individuals like Ben Carson are to be admired, millions of other Americans are subject to limited opportunities that continually discourage, burden, and oppress—limiting their chances of being successful and making the process of upward mobility nearly impossible.

*See also* "Education," "Family," "Health Care," "Housing," "Homelessness," "Poverty—Cycles," "Poverty—Domestic," "Poverty—Global," "Poverty—Statistics" and "Water."

## POVERTY—CYCLES

Poverty, whether domestic or global, is a vicious cycle in which many of the underresourced cannot escape. Dr. John Perkins, founder of the Christian Community Development Association, spoke of this on his work with the poor in Mississippi:

We saw that different aspects of poverty formed together into a cycle of destruction and dependence that winds itself down upon and around a person. That's the cycle of poverty . . . a continuous cycle of damage. Not enough food when young so that he can't think straight. No hope of education or personal development or family so she gets pregnant before she's fifteen. No education, poor jobs. Poor jobs, poor pay. Poor pay, bad housing and food. Bad housing and food, poor health. Poor health, poor performance on the job, less pay. A cycle, but at its center a captive, a mind so busy responding to the day-to-day needs that it has no time to think about the future or about those spiritual realities which give meaning to life.[238]

Cycles of poverty can affect every area of life: education, employment, income, health, housing, transportation, spiritual health, physical health, emotional needs and nutrition. Sometimes charity programs that have the best of intentions can help contribute to these cycles by creating dependency on their programs and on hand outs. Holistic responses must be employed that take into consideration (1) the depth of the problem, (2) the inherent dignity of the people involved, and (3) how Christ calls individuals and the church to be involved. Christians are called to be interdependent and therefore must seek solutions in which all are given a voice at the table so that possible solutions to poverty are not imposed on the poor. The gospel of Christ compels us, rich and poor, to love one another as we seek to make the world a better place.

**FOR FURTHER STUDY**

*Neither Poverty Nor Riches: A Biblical Theology of Possessions* by Craig Blomberg

*Passing the Plate: Why American Christians Don't Give Away More Money* by Christian Smith, Michael Emerson and Patricia Snell

*The Persistence of Poverty: Why the Economics of the Well-Off Can't Help the Poor* by Charles Karelis[239]

## POVERTY—DOMESTIC

Jim Wallis says, "The great crisis of American democracy today is the division of wealth."[240] Parts of the United States are so impoverished that if you saw them you would think you were in the developing world. Poverty is measured in the United States by what is known as the poverty threshold. The poverty threshold (or poverty line) is the minimum amount of money an individual or family needs to make in order to have a sufficient standard of living. Some people believe that the poverty threshold in the United States is too low and that some people who are above the line do not make enough money to make ends meet. The poverty threshold in the United States for one person is around $10,000 per year. For a family of four, the poverty threshold is just over $20,000 per year.[241]

Even within particular countries, wealth is not distributed evenly. In 2004 about one-tenth of one percent (i.e., 0.13) of the world's population controlled 25 percent of the world's financial assets.[242] Per person, Luxembourg is the richest country in the world.[243] However, the United States has the world's largest economy. In 2000 the United States had approximately 5 percent of the world's population and over 30 percent of the world's wealth.[244] The average American had a net worth of

$144,000, whereas the average Chinese (at the official exchange rate in 2000) only had a net worth of $2,600.[245] Even though a disproportionate percentage of the world's wealth is concentrated in the United States, domestic poverty still exists. In 2006, 36.5 million people in the United States were living in poverty.[246] With the 2008 financial crisis, that number has definitely increased. There is also great discrepancy in the United States between the percent of whites who are in poverty (about 8), the percent of blacks (about 24) and the percent of Hispanics (about 21).[247]

Children in the United States are among the most affected by poverty. In 2006, 12.8 million U.S. children were poor.[248] Many of these children have parents who work but have low-income jobs and thus struggle to make ends meet. Poverty can have a significant impact on children by contributing toward health, mental, physical, social and behavioral problems.

It is important to not compare the amount of pain and suffering that occurs in different parts of the world. Some people think that all of our resources, money and time should be used to fight global poverty because the poor in the United States "don't have it that bad." That would deeply grieve the heart of God! With this mindset, domestic poverty often gets the short end of the stick. The extreme poverty of the developing world is so severe that the relative poverty in developed nations is easily overlooked.

At the end of the first decade of the twenty-first century, the financial crisis that has struck the United States and developed countries around the world has caused many people to rethink their understanding of poverty and financial wealth. It is estimated that by October 2008, the United States lost $25 trillion in the value of the stock market; global markets were similarly affected.[249] As the United States has experienced the most home foreclosures in history—an estimated 405,000 households lost their homes in 2007—more and more people are unable to meet their financial obligations and are falling into poverty.[250] There is no better time for the church walk alongside the millions of Americans who are being affected by poverty.

Even in times of financial insecurity, the people of United States should not ignore the "least of these" in their own backyard. There are children who live only a few miles away who don't have enough to eat for dinner. Their mother is single and trying not to feel guilty about leaving her seven-year-old home to watch the infant while she goes out to work her second job. She can't afford a babysitter and the rent. She would pop her head into the neighbors to ask them to keep an eye on her son, but no one is home. How is the Christian community called to respond and to support her and her children? In these situations, we should remember Jesus' instruction to be his witnesses throughout Jerusalem, Judea, Samaria and to the ends of the earth (Acts 1:8). In our rush to care for those at the ends of the earth, we must not forget those who are at home in Jerusalem.

**FOR FURTHER STUDY**

*The Betrayal of the Urban Poor* by Helene Slessarev

*There Are No Children Here: The Story of Two Boys Growing Up in the Other America* by Alex Kotlowitz

*See also* "Children," "Housing" and "Work."

←⚒ *Take action.* With your friends, study what Scripture says about poverty. Sojourners has a four-week discussion guide, *Christians and Poverty*, which is designed to make us think about how to live out God's call for justice in the world. Visit store.sojo.net/category_s/136.htm for more information.

←⚒ *Take action.* Tech Mission (www.urbanministry.org) is a wonderful resource committed to connecting communities for social justice. Their mission is "to match hundreds of thousands of volunteers with urban ministries and short term urban missions opportunities." In 2005 faith-based volunteers made up 34.8 percent of the total volunteer base in the United States,[251] and their time was valued at $51.8 billion.[252] Search their volunteer website to find opportunities to serve in your local community on behalf of the domestic poor. If you are already involved in a Christian nonprofit, discover how to recruit volunteers for your ministry through this resource.

⚱ *Spiritual reflection exercise.* The Open Door Community in Atlanta seeks to be a voice for those who have no voice and to establish a sanctuary for the urban poor.

> Hospitality, sanctuary (the maintenance of safe space), discernment, and solidarity with poor people, homeless people, and prisoners are the primary gifts and disciplines that mark the distinctive spirituality of the community. . . . By naming and giving thanks to God and proclaiming Jesus as Lord in these spaces, the community seeks to disrupt business as usual.[253]

Think back on your story. When have you had direct encounters with the poor? Where have you experienced God in your encounters? Reflect about what it might mean to practice Christian hospitality to those in poverty. If you have not been in relationship with the poor, why do you think that is? Listen to hear God's heart.

> Never be lacking in zeal, but keep your spiritual fervor, serving the Lord. Be joyful in hope, patient in affliction, faithful in prayer. Share with the Lord's people who are in need. Practice hospitality. (Rom 12:11-13)

## POVERTY—GLOBAL

In 2008 the estimated world population was 6.55 billion people. Over five billion people lived in the developing world. Nearly half, almost three billion people, lived in moderate poverty, on less than $2 per day. Globally, over one billion people live in extreme (or absolute) poverty, that is, on less than $1 (USD) a day.[254] Extreme poverty only occurs in countries in the Third (or developing) World.[255] Those living in extreme poverty cannot meet their basic survival needs—food, water, shelter, health care. Those living in moderate poverty have their basic needs met, but just barely. Relative poverty is experienced when people's basic needs are met, but these individuals lack access to resources and upward mobility.

In his 2007 book *The Bottom Billion* Paul Collier addresses the problem of the one billion people who are stuck in extreme poverty. He says:

> This problem matters, and not just to

the billion people who are living and dying in fourteenth-century conditions. It matters to us. The twenty-first-century world of material comfort, global travel, and economic interdependence will become increasingly vulnerable to these large islands of chaos. And it matters now. As the bottom billion diverges from an increasingly sophisticated world economy, integration will become harder, not easier.[256]

Poverty is primarily an economic issue. Economics raise many questions about social justice and people's access to capital, resources and wealth. Wealth is not equally dispersed around the world. Parts of the world are overflowing with the poorest of the poor, and other parts of the world have concentrated wealth. For example, there are 380.6 million people in India who live on less than $1 per day. One third of India's population live in extreme poverty. To give you an idea of how vast that number is— the total combined populations of the United States, Canada and Australia do not add up to the amount of people living in extreme poverty in India.[257]

In terms of continents, Africa has the greatest proportion of people living in extreme poverty—more than 40 percent, or roughly 300 million people living on less than $1 a day.[258] (It is interesting to note that in Africa the majority of countries have only gained their independence in the last fifty years.) In South Africa alone, between 45-55 percent of the entire population and between 57-75 percent of children are living in poverty.[259]

Poverty is also dispersed among rural and

urban regions. Rural areas account for three-fourths of the people living on less than $1 a day, and a similar share of the world population suffering from malnutrition. However, urbanization is not necessarily the answer. Urban slum growth is outpacing urban growth by a wide margin.[260]

**FOR FURTHER STUDY**

*The Skeptic's Guide to Global Poverty* by Dale Hanson Bourke

*Rich Christians in an Age of Hunger* by Ronald J. Sider

*Millennium Villages Handbook: A Practitioner's Guide to the Millennium Villages Approach* (Version 1.0), available online at www.millenniumvillages .org/docs/MVP_handbook_complete_18jun08 .pdf.

## POVERTY—STATISTICS

Poverty exists all over the world. Travel to the slums of Tijuana, Mexico, and you will encounter children with little clothing running barefoot through heaps of burning garbage, trash, sharp objects and waste. Visit the urban ghettos of Naples, Italy, and the presence of gangs and violence will be clear. Spend time with AIDS orphans in Lesotho, Africa, who work as shepherds in the freezing mountains and run their households without access to the basic necessities of life. Play with a little boy from the projects of Westside Chicago whose brother, father and grandfather are incarcerated. Sit and talk with a young woman from Chiang Mai, Thailand, who was sold into the sex trade at the age of four and forced to work as a prostitute throughout her teen years. The stories are powerful and overwhelming. Statistics and facts help us better understand the true condition of the world today, but we must not forget that each one of these statistics represents the lives of people who are loved by God. As Joseph Stalin once said, "A single death is a tragedy; a million is a statistic."[261]

In 2007 our church, Hillside Covenant Church in Walnut Creek, California, hosted a Sunday service calling attention to the number of deaths of children that occur every day—29,000—because of hunger and other preventable causes. As an illustration, our youth group surrounded the sanctuary with a chain of 29,000 bright orange rings.[262] When we walked into the sanctuary on Sunday morning, the magnitude of those rings was enormous. We couldn't ignore it. We couldn't hide from it. In addition to the strands hanging all over the walls, there was a large box on the altar overflowing with strands of rings. Many found the service deeply moving, and I believe that some walked away with a more profound understanding of what it means when one child is lost because of poverty—let alone thousands. I hope that some people were provoked to get involved.

My fear is that we will get lost in the vast amount of information available. As I have researched, I have noticed that the numbers reported by different organizations differ. For example, in 2008 World Vision claimed that 29,000 children die daily because of hunger and preventable causes. But the World Bank says just over 30,000 children die daily from acute respiratory infections, diarrhea, measles, malaria and so forth. Global Issues claims that over 26,500 children died today from tragedy, poverty and other preventable causes. Does this mean that the data isn't credible? No. It shows it is very difficult to measure the daily effects of poverty, hunger and disease. And these organizations may have different definitions of *preventable* and may include children of different ages in their research.

As we explore this issue, we should verify our sources. At the same time, I would challenge us to allow the truth and the magnitude of these numbers to touch us deeply and to work their way into the theology and practice of our faith. Each number represents a person, a child, a human being who God created and loves. This is a part of the process of allowing our hearts to be broken for the things that break the heart of God.

*Awareness exercise.* Organize a poverty awareness event for your work, school, or church. Contact Christian organizations working with the homeless and low-income residents in your area and ask them to come and to share about their work and ministry. Organize the program so that a few of the ministry leaders could speak to share stories about their experiences and the problem of poverty in the communities where they work. Ask if participants in the program might be willing to share about their personal journey and how poverty has affected them. Have the poverty advocacy groups set up booths and bring materials to help raise awareness.

*Spiritual reflection exercise.* Mother Teresa quipped, "Our life of poverty is as necessary as the work itself. Only in heaven will we see how much we owe the poor for helping us to love God better because of them."[263]

Sometimes, activist believers are accused of trying to earn salvation and not rest in the comfort of knowing that we are saved by grace. Read Ephesians 2:1-20 and James 2.

What do these passages say to us about the source of our salvation? What do they teach about the way we should live our faith? How should we understand these two passages in light of one another? Spend time in prayer. Ask God to give you a deeper understanding of his Word and its meaning.

*Take action.* Join Jim Wallis and Call to Renewal (www.calltorenewal.org) to work toward ending poverty at their annual conference (typically in April) held in Washington, D.C. You will have the opportunity to rally, worship, learn, advocate, share and mobilize. The main sessions and workshops teach about the best practices of social justice ministries around the country. In addition, during lobbying day participants meet with their state representatives.

*Take action.* Host an information exchange with leaders in your community working as social justice advocates. Contact social justice leaders in your community who might be willing to meet with you and a small group of people to talk about their ministry in your area. Pray together. Seek ways that you can join forces in your efforts.

*Take action.* Call, write letters and use your voice to let your representatives know you care about the effects of poverty in the United States and around the world. Encourage your representatives to work to end poverty.

*Take action.* Join poverty-fighting ministries in your own community. If you are not sure where to start, look in the "Organizations" appendix for Christian and secular groups working for the eradication of poverty. Become a volunteer, policy advocate or community organizer.

---

**FOR FURTHER STUDY**

*Comfortable Compassion: Poverty, Power, and the Church* by Charles Elliott

*Cry of the Urban Poor* by Viv Grigg

---

See also "AIDS-Poverty," "Children," "Global Economy," "Health Care," "Homelessness," "Hunger," "Urban Decay" and "Work."

## PROSTITUTION

The perception that prostitution is a desirable and acceptable form of work is false. Consider the movie *Pretty Woman*, starring Julia Roberts. The movie tells the story of a young woman who became a prostitute because she felt there were no other viable options to support herself. One night she meets a wealthy businessman (played by Richard Gere), and he hires her to be his companion for the week. During their week together, they fall in love and the young woman finds there are other opportunities available for work.

Certainly some young women who watch *Pretty Woman* think prostitution is glamorous. Such false pictures make prostitution look safe, fun and appealing. But Melissa Farley and Vanessa Kelly set the record straight:

> For the vast majority of the world's prostituted women, prostitution is the experience of being hunted, dominated, harassed, assaulted, and battered. . . . In prostitution, demand creates supply. Because men want to buy sex, prostitution is assumed to be inevitable, therefore "normal." . . . Prostitution must be exposed for what it really is: a particu-

larly lethal form of male violence against women. The focus on research, prevention, and law enforcement in the next decade must be on the demand side of prostitution.[264]

Consider the following story told in *Prism* magazine.

In 2003, Melissa was 23 years old and had been arrested for prostitution 17 times since her 18th birthday. Melissa's father died before she started school; her mother remarried, then developed leukemia and later breast cancer. When Melissa was 11 her stepfather began sexually abusing her; her mother divorced him a couple of years later. No longer able to cope with her illness, mounting medical bills, and the care of her three children, Melissa's mother committed suicide. Melissa ended up living with an aunt in New Jersey for awhile, but was later thrown out. She was using drugs and in prostitution by age 15. In October 2003, she was the second-most-arrested prostituted woman in St. Petersburg and was facing a 10-year prison sentence because her previous arrests had increased her charges to felonies.[265]

Some might argue that Melissa wasn't forced into the sex trade; she began prostituting by her own volition. That is arguable considering her circumstances. Prostitution is one of the leading causes of the incarceration of women in the United States. In 2007 there was a record high of 103,000 women behind bars in state and federal prisons. In the decade between 1995 and 2005, the number of women

## Emmaus Ministries

Emmaus Ministries of Chicago, Illinois, is a Christian ministry that offers great hope to men who are a part of the prostitution industry. And as of March 2008, Emmaus—Houston has been birthed as a similar outreach ministry to men struggling with prostitution in Houston, Texas. Emmaus uses the three-tiered approach of evangelization, transformation and education to "make Jesus known on the streets among men involved in sexual exploitation." Emmaus's founder, John Green, is a graduate of Wheaton College who began the ministry in 1990 as a way to provide long-term care to men working as prostitutes and living on the streets. Emmaus has outreach programs, a drop-in center and a transitional living program. Volunteers can get involved by becoming interns, hosting events, serving on outreach teams, working as fundraisers and in numerous other ways. See www.streets.org for more information.

incarcerated in the United States increased by about 50 percent.[266] Many times, girls and young women are lured into the sex trade with the promise of a job, only to discover they are being forced into involuntary prostitution.[267] Visit an organization working with women who have come out of prostitution and listen to firsthand stories of their experiences.

There is some debate about how prostitution relates to sex trafficking. According to Donna Hughes, a leading international researcher on sex trafficking,

> Some people consider all prostitution as a form of sex trafficking, and others think there is a large difference. . . . Those who think we should work very hard to distinguish between prostitution and sex trafficking usually support legislation of prostitution and feel that prostitution is a legitimate form of work for women, and therefore they are invested in seeing them as very distinct.[268]

Regardless of your spiritual beliefs, selling one's body for sex is incredibly damaging—both for those offering services and for their customers. The Bible teaches that the body is the temple of the Holy Spirit and should be used to honor God (1 Cor 6:19-20). God did not intend our bodies to be used as commodities. And human intimacy is to be practiced in the context of marriage.

As Christians address prostitution, it is important that we are compassionate, merciful and gracious. Men and women who have engaged in prostitution may already be experiencing personal judgment and self-condemnation. Christ's love compels the church to address the injustice of prostitution by offering compassion and hope.

***Awareness exercise.*** In September 2008, the American Baptists through the Green Lake Conference Center and International Ministries (www.internationalministries.org) cosponsored the International Christian Conference on Prostitution in Green Lake,

## DIGNITY

DIGNITY is a subset of Catholic Charities that provides a comprehensive diversion and rehabilitation program that helps women and girls involved in prostitution gain the skills, support and education needed to make a successful break from prostitution. Visit www.catholiccharitiesaz.org/dignity.aspx.

Wisconsin. See if there might be a similar conference that you could attend. Invite friends and people from your church to join you as you learn more about the problem of prostitution and about ministry experiences from leaders working in the field.

←ж *Take action.* Use the wisdom and experience of a ministry like the National Christian Alliance on Prostitution (www.ncapuk.org) to start an awareness campaign in your community. Invite an expert in the field to teach a Bible study or small group at your church. Explore what it might be like to start an advocacy group in your congregation to work toward ending prostitution in your city, region and beyond. As you get more involved, consider if God might be calling you to become a speaker, advocate and educator about prostitution.

### FOR FURTHER STUDY

*Sex Work: A Risky Business* by Teela Sanders

*Love for Sale: A World History of Prostitution* by Nils Johan Ringdal

*International Approaches to Prostitution* edited by Geetanjali Gangoli and Nicole Westmarland

*Sex, Gender, and Christian Ethics* by Lisa Sowle Cahill

*See also* "Women" and "Sex Trafficking."

## RACE—DEFINITION

Discrimination is not limited to class or socioeconomic status but also extends to the view that one race is superior to another. Race is a human construct that claims people groups can be separated by characteristics. Some characteristics are visible, such as skin color, cranial features or hair texture; others are not visible and include things such as self-identification. Dave Unander observes:

> Race is a myth. There is only the human race, from every perspective: biological, historical, and in God's Word, the Bible. For the past five hundred years, Western society has been playing out a role in a drama written by the Enemy of our souls, the myth of the master race, and every act has been a tragedy. It's time to change the script.[269]

As early as the 1700s, race has been mentioned in scientific literature. Swedish botanist Carolus Linnaeus wrote, "The idea of humanity being broken into races, as different as different species, was picked up throughout European cultures."[270] Africans were identified as the lowest form of the human race, and white supremacy took hold.[271] In the United States it became illegal to hold a white slave, so dark skin denoted who could potentially be a slave.[272] The consequences for African Americans, who were told they were inferior or even less than human, are impossible to articulate. Fredrick Douglass, who personally experienced slavery, wrote, "Where justice is denied, where poverty is enforced, where ignorance prevails, and where any one class is made to feel that society is an organized conspiracy to oppress, rob and degrade them, neither persons nor property will be safe."[273]

The devastating effects of racial prejudice have been seen throughout the world, including apartheid in South Africa, Germany during World War II, the Balkan Wars and in more recent times the genocides in Darfur and in Rwanda.

*Awareness exercise.* Read what the American Anthropological Association has to say about race in their exhibit *RACE: Are We So Different?* (www.understandingrace .com). The exhibit focuses on race from the perspectives of history, science and experience. The message is clear: race is a recent human invention; race is about culture, not biology; race and racism are embedded in institutions and everyday life. Take the virtual tour of the website. Check the schedule to see when the exhibit will be coming to a city near you. Gather friends, family and others to attend the exhibit when it comes to your area.

## George Forrest

When I was growing up, I attended Saint Mary's Ryken High School in rural southern Maryland. The vice principal was George Forrest, an African American retired Lt. Colonel from the U.S. Army. As a young officer Forrest participated in the Battle of the Ia Drang Falley during the Vietnam War, which was depicted in Mel Gibson's movie *When We Were Soldiers* (2002). As a company commander during that battle, Forrest displayed conspicuous gallantry and saved the lives of many U.S. soldiers under his command. He was awarded the Bronze Star for Valor twice and the Republic of Vietnam Cross for Gallantry three times.[274]

I spent many of my lunch hours visiting with Mr. Forrest and listening to his stories. One particular day he was recounting some of his Vietnam experiences. I will never forget the agony that he expressed as he talked about the young men lost during that war, some of them under his own command. He told me he had the power to change many things when he was in Vietnam. He had real power and authority. Then, with tears in his eyes, he pinched the skin on his hand and said, "I have power to change a lot of things, but I will never have the power to change this. No matter what I do, this will never change."

**FOR FURTHER STUDY**

*The African American Experience in Vietnam: Brothers in Arms* by James Westheider

*Free at Last: The Gospel in the African-American Experience* by Carl F. Ellis Jr.

**FOR FURTHER STUDY**

*Shattering the Myth of Race: Genetic Realities and Biblical Truths* by Dave Unander

*From Every People and Nation: A Biblical Theology of Race* by J. Daniel Hays

*Race in North America* by Audrey Smedley

*See also* "Genocide" and "Human Rights."

✷ *Spiritual reflection exercise.* In the Yellow Pages or online, find a church where you would be in the racial minority and whose primary language isn't English. Attend one of their services or Bible studies. Talk to people who are there about their faith and culture. Reflect on what you noticed, experienced and observed. How did the experience make you feel? What made you comfortable or uncomfortable? How might this experience influence the way that you treat others who find themselves in similar situations.

## RACE—INCARCERATION

One of the most alarming race statistics is the percentage of people of color, particularly African Americans, in the prison system. In 2005 there were 2.1 million people behind bars in the United States—ten times the number thirty years earlier.[281] By 2007 those numbers had grown to 2.3 million people. Less than two hundred thousand of the incarcerated are women.[282] The vast majority are men—black men.

In the United States in 2007, 4.6 percent of the black male population was behind bars. The percentage of the Hispanic male population who were incarcerated was significantly less, 1.7 percent, and less than 1 percent (0.77 percent) of the white population.[283] The rea-

sons for this vast discrepancy among the races are highly debated. Nonetheless, in addition to individual responsibility, it is obvious that race plays a part. I have spent a significant amount of time ministering to children, women and men who are a part of the prison system, and I am convinced that people of color are disadvantaged in many ways—both in terms of why they are incarcerated and when being restored back into a right relationship with their communities.

↩✷ *Take action.* The Centre for Justice and Reconciliation is the criminal justice reform arm of Prison Fellowship International, an association of nongovernmental organizations active in more than one hundred countries. The Centre's mission is to promote the use of restorative justice so that one day it is the normal response to crime throughout the world. For more information about the Centre and to get involved go to www.pficjr.org.

**FOR FURTHER STUDY**

*Prison Ministry: Understanding the Prison Culture Inside and Out* by Lennie Spitale

*Why Are So Many Black Men in Prison* by Demico Boothe

*See also* "Death Penalty" and "Incarceration."

## RACE—POVERTY

There is a correlation between race and access to resources. One of the most significant resources that is unequally distributed across racial lines is that of capital. We see this in the income statistics of people who live in the United States. In 2005 the median income for all adults over age twenty-five was $40,000. For men, Asian/Pacific Islanders and whites

## The Youth Behind Bars

My first encounter with youth in the penitentiary system was at the Illinois Youth Center for boys in St. Charles, Illinois. I was a newly hired pastor at Willow Creek Community Church and in my new role I inherited prison ministry. As I began my ministry at the Youth Center, I didn't have much context except that the team leader of the ministry had been serving for over ten years leading a Bible study for the boys on Friday evenings. The kids who attended the meetings came by choice and were only allowed to come if they had good behavior and had stayed out of trouble during the proceeding week. Of the two dozen kids who attended, most were kids of color—African American and Latino—only two or three were white.

I went to the Bible study and engaged in active dialogue, story telling and conversation. One young man told me that his father, brother and grandfather were incarcerated. He shared with me his fears that once he got out of "juvie" he would be right back in an environment where he had no choice but to continue in the activities that got him put away in the first place. Another young man told me he was raised by a single mother who was never around because she was always at work trying to make ends meet. He was the primary caretaker for his younger siblings and said he couldn't take all of the pressure. Yet another young man shared how he had to carry a weapon to protect himself on the street; otherwise he would be killed. Some of the stories I heard were very difficult to relate to, but I couldn't help feeling that these young men were just kids! Kids who were trying to make it in the world and had made bad decisions. I was struck by how overwhelming their circumstances were, which predisposed them to act out in harmful ways.

Can you imagine being the third generation of your family to be incarcerated? Should we expect things to be any different? As I left the Youth Center, I started to weep. I felt I was leaving part of my family behind the chain-linked fence and security gates. I was overwhelmed by how little support and encouragement those kids were receiving in their homes. How will these young men make it without family support? How will they get good legal representation when their families can't afford to keep food on the table? I am not saying that they shouldn't face the consequences of their poor decisions. Some of them have done terrible things. Nonetheless, as I encountered bits and pieces of their stories I left with a firm conviction that God has called the church to stand in the gap where friends, family and society have failed.

What would it look like for the church to walk alongside young men and women in detention centers and speak words of hope, encouragement and affirmation while also offering practical tools, support and programs to help them effectively transition back into society? There are no easy answers, but the church does not have the luxury of sitting back and not responding. May Christ's love compel us to get in the game and extend his mercy and grace to the young men and women behind bars.

In addition, we must question systems that keep young people in situations where it is virtually impossible to succeed. For example, most of these young people attend schools that don't have adequate recreational and after-school programs to keep them off the street. Many

of their communities don't have grocery stores that sell healthy products to keep their families' diets nutritionally balanced. The few grocery stores close early because the community isn't safe. The lawyers who represent the poor have hundreds of cases a year, no exaggeration. The social workers who come along these young men to offer them alternatives are overworked and have limited resources. These issues lie at the root of the problem and help us understand why so many urban kids become a part of the prison system.

had the highest median incomes: $50,000 and $49,000 per year, respectively. Women of the same ethnic groups had incomes of $38,000 and $35,000, respectively. Blacks had an annual income of $30,000, whereas Hispanics and American Indians and Alaskan Natives had the lowest annual income of $26,000.[275] In other words, Hispanics made almost half as much as white or Asian men in 2005. Poverty rates in 2006 were statistically unchanged for non-Hispanic whites (8.2 percent), blacks (24.3 percent) and Asians (10.3 percent) from 2005. The poverty rate decreased for Hispanics (20.6 percent in 2006, down from 21.8 percent in 2005).[276]

Why is there so much differentiation across racial lines? Michael Emerson and Christian Smith addressed this question in *Divided by Faith*. According to their study, most white evangelicals felt that blacks have less economic resources because of one of two things: limited ability and lack of motivation. Most African Americans suggested

it's due to discrimination and the fact that blacks don't have the chance for the education that it takes to rise out of poverty.[277]

Numerous studies have shown that whites have far more access to resources than other races do. (See the example of the Chicago Public School system in "Education—Domestic"). In summary, Emerson and Smith say, "Access to economic resources strongly shapes life experience, life chances, and the ability to maximize children's life chances. The racial gap in occupational status, income, employment rates, labor force rates, and wealth is substantial."[278]

A great example of the differences in access to economic resources is the "Servicemen's Readjustment Act" of 1944, more commonly known as the GI Bill. The GI Bill was designed to provide education or housing loans for veterans when they returned from the war. The loans required zero down payment and provided very low interest rates for servicemen. Millions of American families, because of this opportunity, could afford to move out of urban centers and into the suburbs (where the wealthy and upper class lived). Black servicemen were technically eligible for these loans, but most suburban communities and real estate brokers used racial segregation tactics to keep them out of the white communities.[279] White families built significant capital when they purchased homes at such an advantage. Many families today still have wealth and resources because their fathers or grandfathers were able to purchase a home using the benefits of the GI Bill. African Americans were not given this opportunity and thus did not build up the collective assets and wealth that would have come had they been treated equally.

Desmond Tutu says, "If you are neutral in situations of injustice, you have chosen the side of the oppressor."[280]

←❋ *Take action.* Take someone of a different race out for lunch and ask them if they would be willing to share their thoughts, ideas and experiences about race. Ask them if they have ever witnessed or experienced discrimination on account of race. Ask them what they think the answer is to how you can make a positive difference. Enter into the conversation with a listening posture and create room in your heart to really hear what they have to say.

←❋ *Take action.* See if there is a Christian community-development organization in your area. Use the Christian Community Development Association (www.ccda.org) as a resource. Get involved in addressing the systemic needs that have perpetuated poverty around the area where you live.

**FOR FURTHER STUDY**
*With Justice for All* by John Perkins
*Restoring At Risk Communities* by John Perkins

*See also* "Capitalism," "Global Economy" and "Racism."

## RACIAL RECONCILIATION

Thousands of books have been written about racial reconciliation. As *Divided by Faith* makes clear, the good intentions of individual white people have failed and will continue to fail:

> White evangelical solutions to racialization are thus limited and, by themselves, ultimately doomed to failure. Although laudable for bringing in necessary components missing from policy-oriented, structural solutions— personal responsibility, repentance and forgiveness, interpersonal interaction . . . the white evangelical prescriptions do not address major issues of racialization.[284]

Several years ago in Chicago, I was sitting around a table surrounded by the generation of leaders who had gone before me addressing the problem of race. Wayne Gordon, the president of Christian Community Development Association and founder of Lawndale Christian Church and Lawndale Christian Community Development Association, sadly declared that his generation had failed when it came to racial reconciliation. He told the story of a multiracial church with a white pastor and a black pastor that had started on the west side of Chicago. They had high hopes of living out the reconciliation that

Christ calls us to. The church failed and ultimately died. The distance to be bridged was too great. Gordon is hopeful that the next generation will produce better results.

In addition to the strife between whites and people of color, there is also significant tension between people of color. For instance, tensions exist (1) within the Hispanic community, often depending on countries of origin; (2) between Chinese Americans and Japanese Americans and among other Asian American communities; and (3) between African Americans and Hispanics. Reconciliation must be pursued not just between blacks and whites, but between all races and people groups.

The answer to racism must go beyond good intentions and personal relationships; we must work to correct unjust systems. The challenge of racial injustice is pervasive around the world—from the injustices in Sudan to the treatment of those living in poverty around the United Sates. Christians must come together, consolidate our resources and persistently pursue the justice toward which God has called.

So from now on we regard no one from a worldly point of view. Though we once regarded Christ in this way, we do so no longer. Therefore, if anyone is in Christ, the new creation has come: The old has gone, the new is here! All this is from God, who reconciled us to himself through Christ and gave us the ministry of reconciliation: that God was reconciling the world to himself in Christ, not

## The Heart of Racial Justice

Brenda Salter McNeil and Rick Richardson introduce a new model for reconciliation in their book *The Heart of Racial Justice*. Rather than espousing simply an interpersonal model or a strictly institutional model to combat racism, they propose the "healing model." They write, "Understanding that racism and ethnic strife are ultimately spiritual problems that demand spiritual solutions, we want to offer an alternative model, not as a replacement but as a compliment to the present models, so that we can minister more effectively to the emergent culture."[285] Richardson and Salter McNeil offer a model of reconciliation that is deeply rooted in the reconciliation that we experience through Christ, on both an individual and a corporate level.

Learn more about Brenda Salter McNeil's ministry at Salter McNeil and Associates (saltermcneil.com), which is committed to partnering with Christian leaders who will transform organizations into reconciling communities through speaking, training, leadership development, diversity assessments, strategic planning, consulting and executive coaching. Learn more about Rick Richardson (www.wheaton.edu/evangelism/faculty/richardson) through his work at Wheaton College as an associate professor and the director of the master of arts in evangelism (www.wheaton.edu/evangelism/majors).

counting people's sins against them. And he has committed to us the message of reconciliation. (2 Cor 5:16-19)

---

### FOR FURTHER STUDY

*Reconciliation: Restoring Justice* by John de Gruchy

*Reconciliation Blues: A Black Evangelical's Inside View of White Christianity* by Edward Gilbreath

*God's Neighborhood: A Hopeful Journey in Racial Reconciliation and Community Renewal* by Scott Roley with James Elliott

---

*See also* "Journey Toward Racial Righteousness" ministry profile.

## RACISM

Racism is often understood as prejudice plus power. Prejudice is making negative assumptions about another person or group without understanding the truth or taking into consideration relative facts. Power is strength, might, force or privilege. People with less power are often at a disadvantage because of their lack of access to resources, financial and otherwise. Those with money, education, positional authority and other types of privilege exercise power over the less fortunate. Prejudice is sometimes unconsciously expressed by those in positions of influence.

Consider the Tuskegee syphilis experiments mentioned in the section on human rights. The participants needed the medicines available through the study, thus the researchers had power over them. The scientists also had the power of information—knowing that they weren't treating many of the patients.

---

### Divided by Faith

I have heard Bill Hybels, senior pastor of Willow Creek Community Church, say many times that the book *Divided by Faith* is the second most influential book he has ever read (the Bible is the first). The authors, Michael Emerson and Christian Smith, look at the role of white evangelicalism in black-and-white relationships. They conducted a national survey and held hundreds of face-to-face interviews with contemporary evangelicals to determine what role religion plays in racism. The results of their study should be deeply troubling to the white evangelical community. Summarizing the result of their study, the authors concluded: "Evangelicals desire to end racial division and inequality, and attempt to think and act accordingly. But, in the process, they likely do more to perpetuate the racial divide than to tear it down."[287]

I urge you to buy the book. Read it with an open mind. As we delve into racism in America, whites will be put into a defensive posture, but we must press on. I pray that God will break through our stubborn white pride and show us face to face the ways that we have perpetuated racism overtly and covertly, individually and corporately. We have benefited from a system that has unfairly treated people of color and those who are not a part of the dominant culture.

## Racism and Apartheid in South Africa

Apartheid is an unjust system that perpetrated the abuse of people of color in South Africa for close to half a century. Apartheid was rooted in the colonization of South Africa and was a system of laws, practices and policies based strictly on racial lines. Many blacks suffered brutality and abuse under apartheid. Nelson Mandela spent twenty-seven years in prison as an opponent of the apartheid regime. He was released from his incarceration in 1990 and became the president of South Africa in 1994. He presided over the dismantling of apartheid and return of South Africa's political structure back to the people of color. He won the Nobel Peace Prize in 1993 and is known around the world for his advocacy and work on behalf of reconciliation.

Another Nobel Peace Prize winner from South Africa is Bishop Desmond Tutu, the Anglican archbishop of Cape Town, South Africa. Tutu won the award in 1994 and is known by many as the "moral conscience" of South Africa. He urged states and corporations to divest in South Africa, and he staged peaceful protests throughout the time of apartheid, which ultimately brought down the regime. Bishop Tutu has worked for church reform and has spent his life fighting against injustice and other devastating problems, such as the HIV/AIDS crisis, war and conflict. He says,

> When we look squarely at injustice and get involved, we actually feel less pain, not more, because we overcome the gnawing guilt and despair that festers under our numbness. We clean the wound—our own and others'—and it can finally heal. [288]

Today some people, including former president Jimmy Carter, claim that the treatment of Palestinians in Israel is a form of apartheid. Read more about the Israeli and Palestinian relationship in his book *Palestine: Peace Not Apartheid*.

**FOR FURTHER STUDY**

*Long Walk to Freedom* by Nelson Mandela
*God Has a Dream* by Desmond Tutu

Prejudice was clearly involved because it was acceptable to treat poor black men in a way that would never have been acceptable with white men. To fight racism, we need to understand what it looks like and stand up against it when it rears its ugly head.

This type of prejudicial thinking appeared in the aftermath of Hurricane Katrina in New Orleans. One of the most powerful images I saw in the news after the storm was a picture of a group of white people lugging bags of food and other grocery items. The newspaper identified the whites as having "found bread and soda from a local grocery store." Another picture showed a young black man holding some food items close to his chest. The caption read: "A young man walks through chest deep water after looting a grocery story in New Orleans."[286] This is an example of how racism is still prevalent in our thinking today.

*Awareness exercise.* One of the first exercises I was asked to do by Alvin Bibbs at Willow Creek Community Church was to pick up a copy of Chicago's two leading newspapers every week: the *Chicago Sun-Times* and the *Chicago Tribune*. Every morning he told me to read the papers and to compare articles about the same subject. I couldn't believe the difference between the two papers! One of the papers very clearly described the effects of the news on minority groups in the city of Chicago. The other paper covered the very same events in a different light, largely ignoring the effects on lower-income communities of color. Consider this exercise in your own community. This is a great way to expose different perspectives on race and how they shape our thinking.

**FOR FURTHER STUDY**

*Racism: A Short History* by George M. Frederickson

*Dismantling Racism: The Continuing Challenge to White America* by Joseph Barndt

*Set Free: A Journey Toward Solidarity Against Racism* by Regina Shands Stoltzfus

*Beyond Racial Gridlock: Embracing Mutual Responsibility* by George Yancey

*See also* "Human Rights."

## RACISM—FEAR

White flight is another component of the African American experience in the United States. During the riots and chaos surrounding much of the 1960s, white people fled from racial-minority suburbs and urban areas.[289] The fear that precipitated this massive movement remains hidden in the minds of many people who lived through that era. Recently, a white Christian told me that he had seen a

black person walking in his neighborhood. He thought it was odd because his neighborhood is all white and no people of color live there. He called the police. For him, the presence of a black person walking at dusk "where he didn't belong" was out of the ordinary and suspicious. Motivated by fear? Ignorance? Racism? What does that man's perception of the situation say to the black man about his freedom, worth and identity?

I am aware that the suburbs are becoming increasingly diverse. I would argue that suburban communities are still, for the most part, monocultural. In addition, the luxuries of the suburbs (free parking, paved sidewalks, cleaning crews, landscaping) isolate people from one another and especially from the poor. The first time my husband and I ever spent the night in Barrington, a wealthy suburb of Chicago, we were amazed that over a three-day period we did not see one person of color. Living in urban Chicago, our overnight adventures in the 'burbs were culture shock! While the suburbs seemed so *perfect*, the needs of people in my community in Chicago were readily apparent: homeless on the street, unattended children, the unemployed hanging out in the local park.

The suburban middle class have the luxury of being able to ignore poverty because they don't encounter it face to face. People can't pretend that poverty doesn't exist just because it is not present in their immediate community. Christians especially must open their eyes and get involved in the lives of the poor domestically and abroad.

*Awareness exercise.* Gather a group of friends and watch the movie *Crash* (2004).[290] After the movie discuss your thoughts and feelings. Who exhibited fear in the movie? Where did fear come from? What perceptions of different racial groups were expressed? *Christianity Today* created a study guide with questions that might be helpful in guiding your discussion. Go to www.christianity today.com/movies/reviews/crash.html.

**FOR FURTHER STUDY**

*The Suburban Christian: Finding Spiritual Vitality in the Land of Plenty* by Albert Hsu

*The Urban Christian: Effective Ministry in Today's Urban World* by Ray Bakke and Jim Hart

## RACISM—INDIVIDUAL

*Divided by Faith* reports that the vast majority of white Americans consider racism to be an individual problem. The vast majority of blacks think it's an institutional problem; that is, established systems oppress the nondominant culture. One of the other discrepancies that amazes me is the difference between white's, black's and other ethnic group's perspectives on racism. If I were to ask any one of my friends of color, they would say racism is undoubtedly present. Yet even in this past year I have had white colleagues—leaders in the community, intelligent and successful people—ask me with all seriousness: "Does racism still exist?"

Other discrepancies exist based on how whites and people of color respond to the question of why inequalities are so present between whites and other racial groups. When white evangelicals were asked, "On average blacks have worse jobs, income, and housing than white people. Why do you think that is?" most said it was because of the ability and motivation of blacks.

Even though Asian Americans experience racial profiling and discrimination because of their racial background, they are often considered the "model minority." In 2007, a report was issued in the United Kingdom that determined blacks and Asians were twice as likely to live in poverty as their white counterparts.[291] Many whites fail to acknowledge outside factors that contribute to the success or failure of minority groups. Whites usually identify individualistic reasons as the causes of racism. In other words, whites believe the problem lies with the individual, not with any outside influences. "Because most white evangelicals perceive racism as an individual-level prejudice and discrimination, and do not view themselves as prejudiced people, they wonder why they must be challenged with problems they did not and do not cause."[292]

*See also* "Poverty—Causes" and "Solutions to Injustice."

*Spiritual reflection exercise.* Complete a life line or history of your experiences as they relate to race. What is your first memory of different ethnicities or people of color? What feelings do those experiences evoke? Meet with a friend to talk through your experience. What do you think God would say about those encounters? How do you see or witness institutional racism in systems around you? How might God be calling you to get involved?

*Awareness exercise.* Gather a group of people with more than one race represented. Watch the movie *Color of Fear* (1994). Commit to praying together. Give yourselves from time and space, then come back together a week later. Discuss your feelings about the movie. Have someone facilitate your conversations if that would be helpful. There are facilitator instructions with helpful insights about how to discuss the movie at the College of New Jersey website (www.tcnj.edu/~kpearson/color/packet.html).

**FOR FURTHER STUDY**

*Letters Across the Divide* by David Anderson and Brent Zuercher

*More Than Equals* by Spencer Perkins and Chris Rice

*My First White Friend* by Patricia Raybon

## RACISM—INSTITUTIONAL

John Rawls said, "Justice is the first virtue of social institutions, as truth is of systems of thought."[293]

It is important to address individual racism, but it's even more important to overturn unjust institutions and systems that promote racist practices. White evangelicals must learn from our brothers and sisters of color that the world works through more than our individual contributions. Systems, powers and institutions contribute greatly to the success and failure of individuals and entire people groups. Systems like the education system and health care are inextricably linked to race.

In order to be positive advocates of change, Christians must recognize the way institutions—economic, political, educational, social and religious systems—systemically oppress individuals and groups not of the dominant race. Reconciliation and love on the individual level are critically important, but so is advocacy for structural changes within unjust systems.

*Awareness exercise.* Inspired by the 2001 United Nations World Conference against Racism, Racial Discrimination, Xenophobia, and Related Intolerance (www.un.org/WCAR), the Community Summit on Eliminating Racism was hosted in 2003 in Dayton, Ohio. Research when additional conversations about racism will occur in your community or beyond. Attend the event with some people you know and discuss how you might be advocates against racism in your home community.

← *Take action.* Join a Christian community organization or church that is actively fighting institutional racism. Consider working with leaders such as Rev. Rufus Johnson and Betty Johnson, who lead First Light Christian Fellowship (www.firstlightchristian.org) in Iowa. They are committed to Christian ministry while working to overcome racial conflict.

← *Take action.* Partner with secular organizations working to end racism in your neighborhood, town and beyond. Consider an organization like Partners for a Racism-Free Community, based in Grand Rapids, Michigan (www.prfc-gr.org). These types of relationships provide a great opportunity for relational evangelism in addition to working against institutional racism.

← *Take action.* Speak up when you witness or observe institutional racism. Write letters to the editor of your local newspaper. Call or write to your local, state and federal representatives. Do not be silent; use your voice on behalf of others.

**FOR FURTHER STUDY**

*An Amazing Journey: The Church of England's Response to Institutional Racism* by Glynne Gordon-Carter

*Institutional Racism: A Primer on Theory and Strategies for Social Change* by Shirley Jean Better

## REFUGEES

Refugees are defined by the Department of Homeland Security as individuals who are "unable or unwilling to return to his or her country of origin because of persecution or well-founded fear of persecution on account of race, religion, nationality, membership in a particular social group, or political opinion."[294] In 2007 the United States received over forty-one thousand refugees from all over the world, but primarily from Somalia, Russia and Cuba.[295] Midway through 2008, over twelve thousand Iraqi refugees came to the United States.[296] Thousands more had escaped to other parts of the world. The Bible is clear in how we are to respond to those who are misfortunate, displaced or foreigners in our midst—they are to be welcomed, given provisions of food and clothing, and loved.

> For the LORD your God is God of gods and Lord of lords, the great God, mighty and awesome, who shows no partiality and accepts no bribes. He defends the cause of the fatherless and the widow, and loves the foreigners residing among you, giving them food and clothing. And you are to love those who are foreigners, for you yourselves were foreigners in Egypt. (Deut 10:17-19)

***Awareness exercise.*** Order the Refugee Highway Map (www.e-w-s.org/html/refu gee_highway.html) to learn where many refugees come from. The map also includes information about the travels of refugees and which countries are final destination places. Study the map to learn more about the experience of refugees. Maps can be ordered for a suggested donation of $1 plus shipping and handling.

←« ***Take action.*** Consider getting involved with an organization like Exodus World Services (www.e-w-s.org) to respond to the needs of refugees. Host an interactive refugee assimilation program that allows participants to experience what it is like to be forced from your home country for a new land. Learn how individuals and groups can help refugee families. Invite a refugee to speak at your church. Host a special meal (perhaps Thanksgiving) when refugee families can spend time with your family.

←« ***Take action.*** Celebrate World Refugee Sunday in June, which is sponsored by Refugee Highway Partnership (refugeehighway .net). The Refugee Highway Partnership is a community of people seeking to be the global church by welcoming and serving refugees, bringing hope along the highway.

**FOR FURTHER STUDY**
*Entertaining Angels* by Exodus World Services[297]
*Beasts of No Nation* by Uzodinma Iweala

*See also* "Human Rights" and "Immigration."

## RELIGIOUS PERSECUTION

Religious persecution of Christians and other religious groups continues unabated around the world. Over the past decade the persecution of Christians in Iraq has grown. During the fall of 2008 more than a dozen Christians were killed in the city of Mosul and more than two thousand Christian families fled the city for their safety.[298] In 2008 thousands of Christians in Orissa, India, fled their homes because of ongoing violence and threat of death.[299] In December 2008 the Vatican issued a statement that at least twenty Catholic church workers were killed during the year because of their faith.[300]

In 1998 the United States passed the International Religious Freedom Act in order to give policy recommendations to the U.S. government in regard to the "status of freedom of thought, conscience, and religion" in the international community.[301] Every year the United States Commission on International Religious Freedom issues a report on religious freedom that identifies countries of particular concern and where violations are occurring in regard to religious liberty. In 2008 the "countries of particular concern" were: Burma, China, Eritrea, Iran, Iraq, North Korea, Pakistan, Saudi Arabia, Sudan, Turkmenistan, Uzbekistan and Vietnam.[302]

In 2004 the Organization for Security and Cooperation in Europe (OSCE), which includes all of Europe, the former Soviet Union, Canada and the United States, identified the following two primary concerns: (1) the religious freedom of minority Muslim populations, and (2) growing anti-Semitism.[303] The Christian treatment of the Muslim community is one that attracts significant media attention. A 2002 *New York Times* article cited a Southern Baptist pastor who "incited cries of intolerance."[304] Christians should be deeply concerned with the way that other religious communities are treated. The expression of compassion and love toward other religious groups does not imply renunciation of the Christian faith. Rather, Christian hospitality expresses love and grace as it invites others to enter into the dialogue about the person of Jesus and what the Scriptures teach about his role in the salvation of those who choose to believe in him.

← *Take action.* Prayer is one of the most powerful and effective strategies on behalf of the persecuted church around the world. Organize a prayer night that meets one time or regularly to pray on behalf of Christians around the world—especially in communities that are experiencing persecution on behalf of their faith.

← *Take action.* Go to the website for International Christian Concern (www.persecution.org) and help fight the global persecution of Christians by signing their petitions. Officials in different countries care about their relationship with the United States and the international community. Use your voice to advocate for the end of religious persecution.

← *Take action.* Join in the online dialogue about the importance of religious freedom at charterforcompassion.com. The Charter for Compassion is an online discussion for people of all religious faiths, backgrounds and beliefs. It is important for the Christian community to engage the public square and to have a voice among the international community of faith.

← *Take action.* In writing or through a

phone call, contact an international embassy and ask them to treat Christians and other communities of faith in their country fairly and without persecution. Research the history of the treatment of Christians and other religious groups in their country before establishing contact or writing your letter. A list of international embassies in the United States is available at www.embassy.org.[305]

←⚓ *Take action.* Christian Solidarity Worldwide is a Christian organization based in the United Kingdom. Their bimonthly magazine, *Response*, is full of action items and next steps that can be taken to encourage religious freedom for Christians and others around the world. Christian Solidarity Worldwide also provides profiles with basic information about different countries' religious freedom, demographics and other helpful information to keep you informed in your prayer life and advocacy efforts. Visit their resource library at www.csw.org.uk/resourceslibrary.htm.

**FOR FURTHER STUDY**

*Operation World: When We Pray God Works*, 21st Century Edition, by Patrick Johnstone and Jason Mandryk

*In the Name of Heaven: 3000 Years of Religious Persecution* by Mary Jane Engh

## SEX TRAFFICKING

Sex trafficking and commercial sex exploitation is one of the most horrendous violations of women. According to International Justice Mission, "Sex trafficking is the recruitment, harboring, provision or obtaining of a person in order that a commercial sex act can be induced, often by force, fraud or coercion."[306]

More than one million children around the world are being exploited annually in the multibillion-dollar sex trade.[307] Human trafficking is so prevalent that it generates approximately $12 billion *per year* worldwide.[308] The total global market of sex trafficking is estimated to be more than $32 billion. Of the people who make up this number, 50 percent are minors and 80 percent are women.[309]

The FBI estimates that in the United States well over one hundred thousand children and young women are presently forced into the trafficking industry. They range in age from nine to nineteen years old, with the average age being eleven.[310]

The sex industry in San Francisco includes street prostitution, strip clubs, bars, adult entertainment theaters, pornography emporiums, massage parlors, escort services and rent-by-the-hour hotels. The industry on the West Coast goes back to the mid-1800s and includes the longstanding trafficking of Asian women into Chinatown for sexual exploitation and domestic labor. In the city of San Francisco, thirty of seventy licensed massage parlors are suspected of being centers for prostitution.[311] San Francisco is considered one of the major ports through which international women are brought into the United States for the sex trade.

On December 10, 2008, the United States Congress passed the William Wilberforce Trafficking Victims Protection Reauthorization Act of 2008 (TVPRA), a bill that reaffirms the United States' antitrafficking policy and commitment.[312] The primary function of TVPRA was to secure appropriations for the fiscal years 2008-2011 for the Trafficking Victims Protection Act of 2000, which helps protect victims of trafficking and strives to bring an end to the global trafficking of humans. HumanTrafficking.org gives updates on the most recent legislation and initiatives working against global trafficking.

Forced intimacy takes a toll on women—physically, emotionally and spiritually—which is a great travesty. Christians must find ways to reach out to and embrace women (and men) trapped in the trafficking industry. The church must welcome these people into the body of Christ by showing them compassion and love.

*Awareness exercise.* Take the human trafficking quiz available online through Stop the Traffik at www.stopthetraffik.org/downloads/stt-quiz.pdf. How did you do? Research the questions you got wrong so you will be more informed about the international problem of human trafficking.

*Awareness exercise.* Gather a group of people to watch a documentary or short film like *Born into Brothels: Calcutta's Red Light Kids* (Ross Kauffman and Zana Briski) or *Fields of Mudan* (Stevo Chang). After watching the film, discuss the things you learned and ways you can get involved to help end global trafficking. Amnesty International has created a companion curriculum for *Born Into Brothels*, which is available at www.takingitglobal.org/images/resources/tool/docs/1177.pdf.

←*⚞ Take action.* Use the educational materials and resources provided by International Justice Mission (www.ijm.org) to raise awareness and teach people about trafficking. They offer curricula for student ministries as well as for adults. Commit to praying with them as they work to bring justice to those who are oppressed.

←*⚞ Take action.* NightLight (www.nightlightbangkok.com) is a Christian organization committed to bringing light to women and children in Bangkok, Thailand. NightLight seeks to provide viable economic alternatives by providing life skills to girls rescued from the sex trade. They are committed to raising public awareness by educating the public (both in Thailand and around the world) of the physical, psychological, legal and economic consequences of prostitution and sex trafficking. One of the best ways to support NightLight is to throw a party to raise awareness about sex trafficking in Thailand and to sell jewelry that will support their ministry. You can order a party kit online that will provide sample jewelry and a DVD about the ministry. Have a Thailand theme, eat Thai food, light some candles and pray for sexually exploited women in Thailand.

←*⚞ Take action.* Learn about the key signs that identify when and where sex trafficking occurs. Keep your eyes open and if you suspect that you may be aware of a situation where trafficking is involved, contact the National Trafficking Hotline at (888) 373-7888. The U.S. Department of Health and Human Services Administration for Children and Families has fact sheets available that provide information about human trafficking at www.acf.hhs.gov/trafficking/about/fact_human.html.

**FOR FURTHER STUDY**

*Terrify No More* by Gary Haugen

*Escaping the Devil's Bedroom* by Dawn Herzog Jewell

*Prostitution, Trafficking and Traumatic Stress* by Melissa Farley

See also "Prostitution," "Sexism," "Slavery" and "Women."

## SEXISM

*Sexism* is more than a politically correct term defining unacceptable behavior in the workplace. According to the *American Heritage Dictionary*, *sexism* refers to: "attitudes, conditions, or behaviors that promote stereotyping of social roles based on gender or discrimination based on gender." This may mean that women are treated condescendingly, unfairly or even violently. Desmond Tutu aptly observes:

> Sexism quite literally makes men and women into each other's enemies instead of each other's equals, instead of each other's sisters and brothers. It creates artificial divisions everywhere that tear apart God's family. . . . I cannot be opposed to racism, in which people are discriminated against as a result of something about which they can do nothing—their skin color—and then accept with equanimity the gross injustice of penalizing others for something else they can do nothing about—their gender. There can be no true liberation that ignores the liberation of women.[313]

Sexism is an injustice that does not fulfill God's call to live in biblical community: "Let us think of ways to motivate one another to acts of love and good works" (Heb 10:24 NLT). As the body of Christ, Christians must pursue justice across gender differences and help usher in community as it will be fully expressed in the kingdom of God.

***Awareness exercise.*** Observe women in the marketplace. How many women are in top executive positions in your company? Compare the salary of women to that of men in your industry. What are some of the challenges that women face in the marketplace? Research *Newsweek*, *The Economist*, *Business Week* and *Forbes* to see what articles have been written about women in business.

### FOR FURTHER STUDY

*Racism, Sexism, and the Media: The Rise of Class Communication in Multicultural America* by Clint C. Wilson II, Felix Gutierrez and Lena M. Chao

*The First Hundred Years AD 1-100: Failures and Successes of Christianity's Beginning: The Jesus Movement, Christian Anti-Semitism, Christian Sexism* by Daniel Walker

See also "Women."

## SEXUALITY

The Christian faith places a high value on moral choice and righteous living. Throughout the Scriptures there is an emphasis placed on holiness and purity. First Thessalonians 4:7 says, "God did not call us to be impure, but to live a holy life." The church must address how holiness is expressed in sexuality.

There are many Scripture passages that speak about sexuality in the context of a marriage relationship. Consider Hebrews 13:4: "Marriage should be honored by all, and the marriage bed kept pure, for God will judge the adulterer and all the sexually immoral." Premarital sex is incredibly culturally relevant in the twenty-first century. According to the 2007 Public Health Reports, by the age of nineteen, 70 percent of females and 65 percent of males have had sex. The vast majority of those adolescents are unmarried.[314] God's best is that the act of sexual intercourse would be reserved for couples who have entered into the covenant of marriage.

Homosexuality, the practice of sexual relations with someone of the same sex, continues to challenge the church. Scripture states that human sexuality is designed for a man and a woman in a monogamous marriage relationship. Consider 1 Corinthians 6:9-10:

> Do you not know that wrongdoers will not inherit the kingdom of God? Do not be deceived: Neither the sexually immoral nor idolaters nor adulterers nor male prostitutes nor practicing homosexuals nor thieves nor the greedy nor drunkards nor slanderers nor swindlers will inherit the kingdom of God.

Even though Scripture speaks directly to the question of homosexuality, it does not say much in terms of how the church should pragmatically address the issue. How does the church express hospitality, love and kindness while maintaining the integrity of Scripture? Historically, the church's treatment of homosexuals has been abhorrent. Some Christians believe homosexuality is the worst sin of all, which leads to the sin of judgment and hatred toward homosexuals. This type of response is not warranted and is certainly not found in the Scriptures.

For many years the church has used the motto "hate the sin, love the sinner." But the message the world hears from the church is condemnation and hate. The church is not called to hate one type of behavior and ignore all of the others. The Bible tells us "Do not judge, or you too will be judged" (Mt 7:1). In the same passage, people are told to pluck the plank out of their own eye before removing the speck out of someone else's (Mt 7:5). The Christian community's treatment of homosexuals is a justice issue. God cares deeply how *all* people are treated. He calls people to love him and to love one another.

Some conservative theologians have argued that if we give women equality in the home or the church, it will lead to the acceptance of homosexual practice.[315] This could not be further from the truth. The role of women in the home and church, and the question of how sexuality should be expressed must be looked at individually. The church has a lot of growth to do in terms of its treatment of both of these justice issues.

The church must hold on to the truths that are taught in Scripture and not compromise in terms of purity, holiness and righteousness. Nonetheless, Christians must fall before the altar of God and ask for forgiveness for the ways they have treated homosexuals and others. May the church be courageous enough to ask God to fill all believers with compassion and love toward all people, regardless of their sexual orientation.

*Awareness exercise.* Check your local newspaper for recent news articles about the dialogue between the homosexual community and the church. What adjectives would you use to describe the conversation? Has the church used its voice in a positive way to extend love to the homosexual community? Reflect on the things that you have read. How might God be calling us to respond in a different manner than what the news has reported? When has the church responded in ways that honor God?

← *Take action.* Consider volunteering for

an abstinence program through your public school system. This will give you the opportunity to encourage students to abstain from intimate relationships until marriage. Often Christian pregnancy centers have parallel abstinence programs that are in need of volunteer support and educators.

←‖ *Take action.* Look for ways to reach out and extend love to the homosexual community. Perhaps there is a Christian ministry in your area that ministers with and among those involved in same-sex partnerships. Emmaus Ministries in Chicago is one such ministry that offers hope to men involved in same-sex prostitution. (See the ministry profile in "Prostitution.")

**FOR FURTHER STUDY**

*Homosexuality and Christian Faith: Questions of Conscience for the Churches* edited by Walter Wink

*Authentic Human Sexuality: An Integrated Christian Approach* by Judith Balswick and Jack Balswick

*Biblical Perspective on Sexuality* by Linda L. Belleville

## SLAVERY

Slavery did not only exist during the seventeenth through the nineteenth centuries; it still exists today. Slavery is when people are "forced against their will to work under violence or threat of violence and are paid nothing."[316] Conservative estimates suggest that there are over twenty-seven million people in slavery today—more than any other period in history.[317] There are three main reasons for the resurgence of slavery at the beginning of the twenty-first century: (1) a global population explosion, (2) rapid social and economic change making financial opportunities less secure, and (3) government corruption around the world has allowed slavery to go unpunished. How should the church respond? Jesus began his ministry by saying, "He has sent me to proclaim freedom for the prisoners / and recovery of sight for the blind, / to set the oppressed free" (Lk 4:18).

↨ *Spiritual reflection exercise.* The New Testament book of Philemon is about a slave

### Call + Response

*Call + Response* (2008) is a "rockumentary" that uses the voices and music of actors and musicians to help raise awareness about the global problem of slavery. The film was directed by Justin Dillon, a songwriter and musician who advocates for the end of human trafficking and slavery. The film *Call + Response* features political and cultural leaders such as Madeline Albright, Cornel West, Daryl Hannah, Julia Ormond and Ashley Judd. Artists whose music and talents are highlighted in the film include Moby, Natasha Bedingfield, Cold War Kids, Matisyahu, Switchfoot and many others. All of the proceeds of the film are distributed to Response Projects, which include efforts to eradicate the world of labor slavery, sex slavery, child soldiers and child slavery. For more information about the film and how you can get involved go to www.callandresponse .com.

named Onesimus, who escaped from his master, Philemon. Paul says to Philemon: "Perhaps the reason he was separated from you for a little while was that you might have him back forever—no longer as a slave, but better than a slave, as a dear brother. He is very dear to me but even dearer to you, both as a fellow man and as a brother in the Lord" (Philem 1:15-17). Read the entire book of Philemon (it's only twenty-five verses!). How does Paul describe himself? How does he describe Onesimus? Is there much of a difference? What is Paul asking Philemon to do? What does this passage say to us about slavery. Is slavery overtly forbidden? Reflect on and pray about what you have learned from this study.

← *Take action.* Get educated about the reality of global slavery by reading books, documents or watching relevant movies. Spread the word and help raise others' awareness about what you have learned. Become a member of the movement. Adopt a liberator and help the heroes who risk their lives to free slaves. In 2008 it cost about $132 for a raid to free child slaves in India, who are then helped to recover and rebuild their lives. Visit www.freetheslaves.net.

← *Take action.* With your friends, study what the Scriptures have to say about the global slave trade. Sojourners (www.sojo.net) has a four-week discussion guide called "Christians and the Global Slave Trade" that is designed to spark discussion and thought about how to live out God's call for justice in the world.

← *Take action.* Free the Slaves (www

.freetheslaves.net) is a nongovernment organization based in Washington, D.C., that focuses on issues of modern slavery worldwide. Their mission is to end slavery worldwide. Free the Slaves liberates slaves around the world, helps them rebuild their lives and researches real world solutions to eradicate slavery forever.

← *Take action.* Use your economic power to purchase food, clothing and other items that are made with slave-free labor. For example, the majority of chocolate consumed in the United States is made by workers who are not even paid a subsistence wage and are required to work in poor conditions. Many are children who are denied access to education and are forced into slave labor.

A 2002 report from the International Institute of Tropical Agriculture stated that more than 284,000 children were working in hazardous conditions on cocoa farms in the Ivory Coast and other African countries.[318] Slave-free chocolate can be purchased at Whole Foods (www.wholefoodsmarket.com), Global Exchange (www.globalexchangestore. org) and Trade as One (tradeasone.com). For a more complete list of places where slave free chocolate can be purchased visit the Stop Chocolate Slavery Project, which is sponsored by the University of California—San Diego at vision.ucsd.edu/~kbranson/stopchoco lateslavery/main.html.

← *Take action.* Write to companies such as Nestle, Hershey's and Mars to demand that they only use chocolate that has been provided by fair-trade labor and not from farms where children are exploited.[319] Write to clothing companies and other retailers to ask what measurers they are taking to ensure that the cotton and other materials used in the manufacture of their products does not come from forced labor.[320] Be a conscientious consumer.

**FOR FURTHER STUDY**

*Let My People Go! The True Story of Present Day Persecution and Slavery* by Cal R. Bombay

*Ending Slavery: How We Free Today's Slaves* by Kevin Bales

*Be the Change: Your Guide to Freeing Slaves and Changing the World* by Zach Hunter

*See also* "Human Rights," "Racism" and "Sex Trafficking."

## STEM CELL RESEARCH

Stem cells are perhaps the most hopeful discovery in the field of regenerative therapies in recent history. According to the National Institutes of Health, stems cells are unique because they have the potential "to develop into many different cell types in the body" such as blood cells, muscle cells or brain cells.[321] Embryonic stem cells are derived from human embryos—which are four or five days old and are still in the blastocyst stage (a microscopic postfertilized, pre-implanted embryo of about 150 cells).[322]

Embryonic stem cells come from fertilized embryos that have been donated from reproductive clinics and will no longer be used for in vitro fertilization (IVF). Embryos, which are a human life form, are destroyed when used in embryonic stem cell research.

In 1995 Christopher Reeve, who acted in the *Superman* movies, was paralyzed in a horse-

riding accident. Reeve became one of the leading advocates for stem cell research in the hope that spinal chord injuries could be cured. Reeve and his counterparts argued that stem cell research was a necessary and vital component of furthering medical technology in order to alleviate the suffering of those who could potentially be cured. While the alleviation of suffering and the furthering of medical technology is certainly a desirable goal, it should not be pursued at the expense of a human life.

Although it appears there are some potential benefits from embryonic stem cell research, other viable options do not involve the termination of the embryo. Both the placenta and the umbilical cord have stem cells, and stem cells are present in adult fat cells, bone marrow and other places in the body.[323] Some organizations offer to bank (or store) placental and umbilical cord stem cells in case they could be used in the future (www.lifebankusa.com).

One of the main attractions to embryonic stem cell research is the ability of scientists to study the differentiation process. Some studies have shown that postnatal stem cells (i.e., those derived from the placenta and umbilical cord) have the same differentiating properties.[324] And research on postnatal stem cells does not involve the destruction of the embryo.

The sanctity of human life must be emphasized as scientific technologies develop. Scientific progress and advancement does not justify the destruction of potential human lives. Even if alternative types of stem cells were not available (and they are), stem cell research that destroys embryos would not be justifiable from the Christian perspective.

***Awareness exercise.*** Read about the public policy discussions surrounding the use of embryonic stem cells in medical research. What are the key issues? What are the current U.S. policies surrounding the use of embryos for the derivation of embryonic stem cells? Much of this information is provided in great depth through the National Institutes of Health—Stem Cell Information at stemcells.nih.gov/policy/defaultpage.asp. What did you learn from your reading? What are the key ethical and moral decisions at stake? How is this a justice issue?

**FOR FURTHER STUDY**

*The Stem Cell Controversy: Debating the Issues* edited by Michael Ruse and Christopher Pynes

*The Stem Cell Divide: The Facts, the Fiction, and the Fear Driving the Greatest Scientific, Political, and Religious Debate of Our Time* by Michael Bellomo

*Sacred Cells? Why Christians Should Support Stem Cell Research* by Ted Peters

See also "Assisted Reproductive Technologies," "Bioethics" and "Cloning."

## TUBERCULOSIS

Tuberculosis (TB) is a common and highly communicable disease caused by bacteria. One third of the word's population (over two billion people) is infected by TB, and new infections occur at a rate of one per second.[325] In the mid-1990s the World Health Organization declared TB a global health emergency because of the rising infections and deaths. In addition, drug-resistant strains of the disease emerged, making the problem even worse. Tuberculosis infections are on the rise in developing countries. Today, approximately fifteen million people have active tuberculosis and will eventually develop symptoms of the disease. Most cases start in the lungs. Symptoms include chest pain, coughing up blood and a cough lasting for more than three weeks. Because those infected with HIV/AIDS are so vulnerable to other infections, TB and HIV/AIDS are called the "terrible twins."[326] In 2005 tuberculosis killed over 1.6 million people.[327]

*Awareness exercise.* Visit the Center for Disease Control's Division of Tuberculosis Elimination www.cdc.gov/tb/faqs. What basic facts did you learn about the disease? What people groups are most affected by the disease? Is there a correlation between poverty and the spread of TB around the world?

*Take action.* March 24 is World Tuberculosis Day, which is set aside to raise awareness and educate the world about the disease and its effects on humanity. It commemorates the day in 1882 when Dr. Robert Koch discovered the bacteria *m. tuberculosis*, which causes TB. Use this day as an opportunity to strengthen collaborative networks committed to eradicating TB globally. Visit an organization like Stop TB USA (www.stoptbusa.org) or the global partnership committed to ending TB (www.stoptb.org) for action ideas.

*Take action.* Lobby for new and improved measures for testing and treating U.S. immigrants who are infected by TB. Partner with an organization such as the National TB Controllers Association (tbcontrollers.org) to find out more about how you can lobby for this type of action.

**FOR FURTHER STUDY**

*"Extrapulmonary Tuberculosis: An Overview"* by Marjorie P. Golden and Holenarasipur Vikram[328]

See also "AIDS," "Health Care" and "Malaria."

# Juanita Irizarry

Juanita Irizarry formerly served as director of the CCDA Institutes for the Christian Community Development Association. I first met Juanita in 2002 when she was working as the executive director for Latinos United and was bolstering its position as a leading nonprofit policy-and-advocacy organization. She was about to pursue graduate studies at the Kennedy School of Government at Harvard University. In 2007 she completed her Master's in Public Administration degree and upon graduation received the Littaeur Fellowship Award for Public Service, Academic Excellence, and Potential for Leadership. Juanita is a leading advocate for social justice within the Latino community and beyond. There is much to be learned from her story and experience. She is a devoted follower of Christ and is continuing to work on behalf of the gospel in the attempt to witness to God's kingdom in places of injustice, poverty and oppression.

## *God's Heart for Justice in the Hood*
by Juanita Irizarry

I grew up on the border of Humboldt Park and Logan Square in Chicago—a largely Latino area that was the heart of the Puerto Rican and Cuban communities at the time. My parents had relocated to inner-city Chicago to help with a Spanish language church my dad had helped start while he was a student at Moody Bible Institute. As a result, though I grew up in the "hood," I didn't have a sense of being trapped, as many poor, inner-city kids do. We never had much money because my parents' teaching income—mostly from Christian schools—was never large. But we often had more than our neighbors, and we were taught to be generous with others and to care for the poor.

My mom was always helping people—the developmentally disabled neighbor, the single mom, the lonely senior citizen, the troubled youth. And she always brought my brother and me in on the ac-tion of caring for others. It was just a natural part of our growing-up years.

As a bicultural kid, with a Nuyorican dad and a mom who is white (but thinks she is Latina), at a pretty young age I worked through issues related to how I wanted to identify myself. My "look" is quite white, but my heart is Puerto Rican through and through. I always wanted to be more Puerto Rican and to fit in. But I realized that much of my role would be as a bridge person. And I chose very early on to use the privilege that comes with my light skin to help my more marginalized brothers and sisters.

During my growing-up years in the 1970s, my neighborhood was plagued with arson fires, but at the time I didn't know they were set by arsonists. It was almost as if it were neighborhood entertainment to watch someone's house burn down. Years later, after college, I ran across a book that described the rampant arson fires on the near northwest side of Chicago. I learned that bank redlining in communities like mine had led to "management toward demolition" as homeowners couldn't get loans to fix up their buildings, and they couldn't sell them because no one could get loans to buy them. They paid up their fire insurance and then burned the houses down. Though gentrification in my neighborhood has now swallowed up most of the vacant lots left behind by this phenomenon, I still am reminded of those days as I walk past certain parking lots and community gardens where my neighbors' homes once stood.

I wouldn't have been able to articulate it at the time, but I grew up with an interest in the "built environment"—housing and other physical structures in the neighborhood. I remember visiting the homes of my father's colleagues (professors at Christian colleges) who lived in the suburbs. I asked myself why their neighborhoods and homes were so much nicer than ours. Though my parents taught us about a biblical basis for caring for the poor, there was no one in my life doing much systemic analysis about poverty, racism and oppression.

A couple of years after college I moved back to Chicago and my lifelong neighborhood for a job at the Olive Branch Mission, a homeless service center that included in its mission the priority of teaching people how to care for the homeless, the poor and the oppressed. While I did my job there of coordinating urban-plunge programs for Christian college students through the Mission's Christian Center for Urban Studies, I encountered the world of affordable housing and economic development, and ran across the writings of John Perkins, Ray Bakke, Bob Lupton, Ron Sider and others.

As I read David Claerbaut's *Urban Ministry,* I exclaimed, "He's explaining my life!" I had my big "aha" moment, as these authors provided me words to articulate the stirrings in my soul. And my continued exploration into Christian community development helped me find the professional field of urban planning and policy. Since then the Lord has led me down a path of secular affordable housing, economic development and public policy work through nonprofits focused on Chicago's Latino community. The lines between my professional world and my neighborhood activism have been very blurry as my lifelong community has fought for its survival in the midst of oppression by politicians, the police, unscrupulous and uncaring real estate industry professionals, and predatory lenders. Pastor Phil Jackson whispered in my ear one day after church at Lawndale: "It's time for a certain Puerto Rican sister to go back to Humboldt Park and apply her gifts at a church in her own community." It will be interesting to see how God uses me in that environment as I continue to speak of God's heart for justice around housing and community development issues.

**FOR FURTHER STUDY**

*Compassion, Justice and the Christian Life: Rethinking Ministry to the Poor* by Robert D. Lupton

*A Theology as Big as the City* by Ray Bakke

## URBAN DECAY

In the 1970s a new term was coined: *urban decay.* U.S. cities were beginning to show signs of severe disrepair. During the late 1900s, there were major changes in the global economy; high unemployment, fragmented families and political unrest contributed to this phenomenon.

Detroit is one of the cities where urban decay was the most apparent. After the civil rights movement of the 1960s, almost the entire white population of Detroit moved to the suburbs, leaving abandoned homes. Industries relocated as well, leaving few jobs in the city. Unemployment soared, which had devastating effects. In the past few years there has been an increase in industry in the downtown area and the population has begun to increase gradually. Nonetheless, the effects of the 1960s and 1970s are still visible a half of a century later.

*Awareness exercise.* See if there is a Christian nonprofit in a nearby urban center that works with people living in urban poverty. Get to know the leadership and volunteers and see if they would be willing to let you spend a few days with them—getting to know their work, the needs of the surrounding community and the people who are the most affected by the challenges of urban poverty. Journal about your experience and the things that you are learning. To get an idea of what a Christian organization working on behalf of the most vulnerable of their communities might look like, consider Grace Urban Ministries (www.gum.org) in San Francisco, California.

← *Take action.* The primary way to get involved in standing against injustice on behalf of the poor of the city is to be in relationship with them. Get to know those in your immediate area who have the least access to the resources of health care, housing and education. Find out what programs are available to offer support and encouragement to singles, parents and families struggling in poverty. If your community is far from a poor community in the city, find out those most in need of support and encouragement in your immediate surroundings. You can start by contacting social service organizations in your city or town.

FOR FURTHER STUDY

*Urban Injustice: How Ghettos Happen* by David Hilfiker

*Transforming the Slums by Relationships* by Simon Batchelor

*See also,* "Global Economy," "Housing," "Poverty" and "Work."

## WATER

In the first decade of the twenty-first century, approximately half the world's population lived in cities and towns. In 2005 one out of three urban dwellers (approximately one billion people) was living in slum conditions.[329] One third of children in the developing world are without adequate shelter.[330] One billion people live in slums and lack the basic necessities of life.[331] Over twice that number (2.6 billion people) in developing countries lack access to basic sanitation.[332] In 2007 one billion people lacked access to safe drinking water—one of the fundamental sources of life. It is hard to imagine what a million people might look like, let alone one billion.

Over the past twenty years, water is one of the areas where we have seen significant developmental progress worldwide. During the

## Hillside Covenant Church

When I first came to Hillside Covenant Church of Walnut Creek, California, in January 2006, I was so pleased to learn about the church's legacy of helping to provide water in needy places around the world. The congregation was first introduced to the desperate need for access to clean water by physician Lisa Hudson, who had traveled to Sudan in 1993 to assist a Red Cross team caring for victims of the civil war. Lisa tells of her experience:

> Displaced refugees, usually women and their children, walked daily up to 3 miles each way to a muddy stream for water. With it they brought death and disease, and they knew it. Their alternative was to dig down 12 feet through the sand to the water table, a task too big for their meager resources. At that time, as a young internal medicine doctor, I realized it was better to provide wells for clean water than to keep coming back again and again to deworm sick children.[338]

She came back to her home church and shared the need.

The church embraced the idea of getting involved. Starting with a well project in Ghana through World Vision, the church was soon educated about how diseases like guinea worm, typhoid fever and cholera claim the lives of one million African children each year. They learned that the burden of carrying water from distant watering holes falls to women and children, who often rise before dawn to fetch enough water for their households' daily cooking and cleaning needs. Almost every year since 1993, the church has participated in a well project somewhere around the world, including a fish farm in Chiang Mai, Thailand, a hospital in the Central African Republic, an orphanage in India, water systems in the Congo and Ghana, a well-drilling rig in northern Afghanistan, and twenty wells serving over ninety thousand survivors of the 2005 tsunami in remote villages on the Andaman Islands, off the coast of India. The church has committed to serving unreached people around the world with the gospel of Christ and with clean water. Lisa describes Hillside as a "water church" that is making a way for people to receive clean water with the hope that they might come to know God as one who provides "living water" (Jn 7:38). You can learn more about the compassion, justice and missions ministry at Hillside at www.hillsidecovenant.org.

1990s nearly one billion people gained access to safe water and as many to sanitation.[333] Although much progress has been made, in 2005 four hundred million children (one in five) did not have access to safe water.[334]

The majority of the earth's clean and purified water is consumed by a very small percentage of the population. A mere 12 percent of the world's population uses 85 percent of its water.[335] The United States is the most excessive consumer of all. About a third of the world's population (approximately two billion people) consumes around twenty liters of water per day and has a water source that is within one kilometer of where they live. In the United Kingdom the average person uses more than 50 liters (approx. 13 gals.) a day just to flush toilets, and a total use of about 150 liters (approx. 40 gals.) a day. In the United States the average person uses 600 liters (approx 158 gals.) a day.[336] This makes me want to cry; children all around the world are dying of dehydration because of diarrhea—some 1.8 million child deaths a year. Almost half of the people in the developing world suffer from a health-related illness caused by lack of water or sanitation. And I consume thirty times the amount of water that most people in the developing world have access to in a day!

←✴ *Take action.* Stop using as much water! Take shorter showers. You probably wonder, How—if I turn off the water (instead of letting it run) when I brush my teeth—does that water get to sub-Saharan Africa? Well, it doesn't exactly. But it does mean that there is more water available and that less energy needs to be spent replenishing the supply that you would have used.

It takes far less energy (and cost) to consume less water than to increase the supply by that same amount. In other words, when we conserve a gallon of water by flushing the toilet less, turning off the faucet when brushing our teeth or fixing slow leaks in our house, all that water is being added back into the system.

Here are more creative ways to consume less water: (1) install a rainwater tank and connect it to your toilet, laundry and garden hose; (2) install a more efficient showerhead—this can save up to 13,500 liters (approx. 3,566 gals.) of water per year; (3) turn off the tap water when brushing your teeth or shaving; (4) install a dual-flush toilet; (5) use efficiency appliances, such as a washing machine (or hand wash your dishes); and (6) make sure that your washing machine or dishwasher is full and use an economy setting.[337]

←✴ *Take action.* Living Water (www.water .cc) is committed to providing a cup of water in Jesus' name. Support this ministry by hosting an event or volunteering to get a chapter started in your area. There are opportunities to get your hands dirty: join them for a training and go on a drilling trip while serving the people of a village, hospital, school or orphanage. Join their Facebook cause and invite your friends to get involved in the $H_2O$ project.

←✴ *Take action.* Take the $H_2O$ challenge. For two weeks, make water your only beverage. Save the money that you would normally spend on sodas, coffees and sport drinks for two weeks. Donate the money to an organization that is committed to providing clean water to people around the world.[339]

**FOR FURTHER STUDY**

*Blue Covenant: The Global Water Crisis and the Coming Battle for the Right to Water* by Maude Barlow

*Troubled Water: Religion, Ethics, and Global Water Crisis* by Gary Chamberlain

*See also* "Consumerism," "Health" and "Poverty."

## Journey to Mosaic

The Journey to Mosaic (J2M) experiences are four-day trips offered by the Pacific Southwest Conference of the Evangelical Covenant Church. The trips are facilitated by Christian leaders who encourage dialogue and discussion about compassion, justice and racial reconciliation. Participants are paired with a person of a different race as the journey progresses through Asian American, African American and Hispanic American historical and cultural experiences in the United States. The trips also serve to help identify and raise awareness about white privilege. Krisann Jarvis Foss is a director of conference ministries for the North Pacific Conference of the Evangelical Church and was a leader on one of the Journey to Mosaic experiences.

### I Was There Too That Day
by Krisann Jarvis Foss

My dad worked his entire career for the government agency that oversaw the Columbia River Reclamation Project in the Pacific Northwest.[341] Growing up, I heard about how beneficial the Columbia River dams were for the nation, and especially for the Pacific Northwest, providing clean, cheap power. In researching and planning for the upcoming J2M trip, I was visiting the museum at the Yakama Nation. At the museum, I saw an exhibit for the fifty-year commemoration of the inundation of Celilo Falls, a traditional and ancient fishing ground and center of community for the tribes along the Columbia River since ancient times. The building of the Dalles Dam caused the sacred ground and the entire Native American community of Celilo Falls to be completely submerged. With its inundation went the oldest continuously inhabited settlement in North America and the entire Indian village of Celilo.[342] It was only as I was telling my parents about my research that my mom told me that she (seven months pregnant with me) and dad had been at the dedication celebration for the Dalles Dam, which caused the inundation of Celilo Falls.

In November 2007, while on our J2M experience, we heard from Annie Lou Alexander, a Native American woman, about her memories of growing up, fishing, playing, swimming and being part of the Native American community that gathered at Celilo each summer for fishing. It was very central to her life story. Annie Lou shared with our J2M group about being at Celilo the day it was swallowed up, and how she grieved with her people at the profound loss.

It wasn't until that moment that the full impact of the racial barrier I had been part of became real. My first realization upon seeing the exhibit at the museum of the injustice of Celilo had caused me sadness; but when it became flesh and blood in

Annie Lou's story, I realized we had been worlds apart until that moment. On one side of the river my people were celebrating the new dam and the progress it represented; Annie Lou's people were across the river grieving a monumental loss. The paths of our life stories had intersected in profound ways, but we were worlds apart.

"I'm sorry" seemed like a trite and hollow thing to say to Annie Lou, but it was the first step. I was nervous to share with Annie Lou and the group about my experience. We can't bring back Celilo Falls. And I can't even say that the dams shouldn't have been built, or that they haven't been beneficial to the nation as a whole. But the process was unjust and destructive toward a whole community of people. After mustering the courage, I said to Annie Lou and the group, "I was there too that day." I vowed to Annie Lou that my children and siblings would hear the other side of the story, and that I will work however I can to become aware, speak out and act in ways so that something like this won't happen again. It would be easy to say,

"What difference can I make?" But only one thing is sure—if I don't become aware of social injustice, speak out and act to take a stand against it, I certainly won't make any difference.

It was such a blessing to me, that when I finished speaking, Annie Lou responded by standing up and giving me a grace-filled, solid and sustained hug. We have stayed in touch, she continues to speak to our J2M groups, and I have told my children and my brother and sister about her story. I have also given them the book she has written, *Blood Is Red . . . So Am I,* so that her story will not be forgotten.

Journey to Mosaic (J2M) is a program sponsored by the Mosaic Center, a nonprofit ministry that is a part of the Pacific Southwest Conference and the Evangelical Covenant Church. To learn more about J2M trips and the Mosaic Center visit http://themosaiccenterpswc.org.

**FOR FURTHER STUDY**

*Blood Is Red . . . So Am I* by Annie Lou Alexander

## WHITE PRIVILEGE

White privilege is one of the major injustices that exists in most parts of the world. In most countries, the lighter your skin, the more privileges you receive. When I was living in Taipei, Taiwan, many of my Taiwanese friends would purposefully overexpose their film when it was being developed so that their skin would appear lighter. Today whiteness continues to be desired because of its many privileges.

Clearly, since the conception of the United States, whites have had advantages that people of other ethnic groups have been denied. The history of the GI Bill (see "Race—Poverty") is one example where whites were given privileges over other war veterans of color. Consider the idea of "separate but equal" that was practiced regularly throughout the first half of the twentieth century: whites were given the best, the front seat on the bus, the cool water from the fountain, the brand new text books; people of color were given the leftovers, had to sit at the back of the bus, used out-of-date study materials and suffered other inequalities. The civil rights movement challenged these inequalities and confronted the United States with the ways that people of color were being oppressed. John Perkins says:

> Never forget that equality is the first and last issue between black and white people in this country. Equality is the sun shining at the center of all the galaxy of other racial and poverty issues. You can talk about integration or fair housing or busing or voter's rights, but at the heart, your discussion turns around the meaning of equality as certainly as the earth turns around the sun.[340]

Equality and equal access is not only a problem between blacks and whites, but between all people of privilege and those with less access to resources. In the twenty-first century, privilege for whites is expressed in many ways. Whites are rarely expected to speak on behalf of their entire race. Whereas for a person of color, it is often assumed when a thought or idea is shared that it is representative of that person's entire race. Whites shop in department stores without the presumption they are going to shoplift. Whites can choose to spend time with only other whites most of the time. Whites can walk in neighborhoods not their own without provoking fear. Whites aren't stopped by the police as often, aren't given as many tickets and aren't put in jail as frequently as people of color. In terms of numbers, whites are fairly represented by the media. The list of white privileges

is enormous but is largely ignored or subconscious for most whites.

If the church is going to be able to truly advocate on behalf of justice, white privilege must be recognized and understood. Whiteness needs to be understood by not only whites but also people of color. The privileges of power, resources and wealth held by whites around the world cannot be ignored by Christians who desire to pursue social justice.

*Awareness exercise.* With a group of people you know watch the documentary *Mirrors of Privilege: Making Whiteness Visible* produced by Shakti Butler. After watching the film, use the study guide made available by World Trust Educational Services (www.worldtrust.org/videos/index.html) to guide your discussion. Reflect on and journal about your experiences. What did you learn about yourself? What did you learn about others? Although this is a secular film, what did the experience and discussion teach you about God?

*Awareness exercise.* Peggy McIntosh is associate director of the Wellesley College Center for Research on Women. When considering how many men are unaware of their privileges over women, she was confronted with her own lack of awareness about white privilege. She began to record whenever she encountered white privilege in her life. You can read the extensive list of the privileges that she observed in her article "White Privilege: Unpacking the Invisible Knapsack," which can be found at mmcisaac.faculty.asu.edu/emc598ge/Unpacking.html.

Over the next month or so, consider starting a privilege list to keep track of white privileges that you observe. Persons of color and whites will have significantly different lists. If you have a friend of a different race, do this exercise together, and at the end of the month compare your observations and what you have learned.

**FOR FURTHER STUDY**

*The Next Evangelicalism: Freeing the Church from Western Cultural Captivity* by Soong-Chan Rah

*Being White: Finding Our Place in a Multiethnic World* by Paula Harris and Doug Schaupp

*Enter the River: Healing Steps from White Privilege Toward Racial Reconciliation* by Tobin Miller-Shearer

*See also* "Human Rights," "Poverty" and "Racism."

## WOMEN

There is a multitude of evidence that women around the world are looked upon and treated as inferior to their male counterparts. My hope is that regardless of your view on the role of women in the family or the church, your eyes will be opened to their stories (see also "Women—Serving in the Church"). May the Scriptures guide the conversation as Christians wrestle with questions about the reality of the repression that women face in the twenty-first century.

> They caused the cry of the poor to
>    come before him,
>   so that he heard the cry of the
>    needy. (Job 34:28)

What is the condition of women in America today? According to the United Nations Development Program, 106 of 156 countries have a better ratio in the gender-related development index (GDI) than the United States. The GDI measures countries' build-ing capabilities for women as they related to three aspects of human development: (1) living a long and healthy life (measured by life expectancy), being educated (measured by adult literacy and enrollment at the primary, secondary and tertiary level) and having a decent standard of living (measured by purchasing power parity). The United States ranked fifteenth out of ninety-three countries for the gender-empowerment measure (GEM) that evaluates how many women are in government, management, professional and technical works, and gender disparity in earned income, all of which reflect economic independence.[343] I was surprised at the low levels for the most wealthy and, arguably, developed country in the world.

The next several issues that are addressed relate to women and challenges that they experience domestically and abroad: aging, body image, child bearing and family care, international leadership, poverty in the developing world, serving in the church, and work and job opportunities.

*See also* "Sexism" and "Sexuality."

## WOMEN—AGING

Elderly women are among the most vulnerable in society. The devastating effects of the care crisis on aging women in the United States was addressed in the "Health Care—Domestic" section of this handbook. Because men die at younger ages than women, many females spend the last years of their lives living alone. This brings emotional challenges (e.g., loneliness) and material challenges, because women who depended on their husbands may not know how to run a household or may not have independent income apart from their husbands.

The Bible clearly calls us to respect the preceding generations. It is good for the church to be reminded to be good stewards of the elderly. Older people are gifted by God and have great wisdom and experience to offer younger believers. Katie Funk Wiebe writes:

> To the end, older people remain human. They are still on a journey of faith, susceptible to falling into sin, but also able to receive renewed measures of God's grace. This in itself is probably one of the greatest truths we can learn from Scripture about older men and women. They are still pilgrims on the way to glory.[344]

**FOR FURTHER STUDY**

*Second Calling: Passion and Purpose for the Rest of Your Life* by Dale Hanson Bourke

## WOMEN—BODY IMAGE

Throughout the world, body image is a difficult issue for women. The expectations that are placed on women by society to look a certain way, wear a certain size and to be thin are virtually impossible to meet. The impact is devastating to many women and can lead to depression, eating disorders and even suicide. Regina Shands Stoltzfus, assistant professor of sociology at Goshen College writes about her own personal experience:

> Waiting in line at the grocery store, I gaze at the magazine display. Row after row of smiling women greet me, assuring me I can be slimmer, more organized, save money, create mouthwater-

ing meals—be perfect. The faces selling me these dreams are overwhelmingly white, blond, blue-eyed—perfect. They represent the ideal American women. I represent the other. We are brown or black, with dark hair that may be nappy, are the outsiders. Still.[345]

Regardless of whether women are old or young, white or not, rich or poor, people must learn to listen to others' stories. The expectations women face are usually created by men in positions of authority and power within society. History has been written by men and therefore women's perspectives were typically left out.

There are also historical reasons for divisions between women. For example, white male slave owners would often use their black female slaves to satisfy their sexual desires, which often was known by the slave owners' wives. While the white women were viewed as pure and holy, the black women were viewed as sexually promiscuous, even though the sexual acts were forced upon them.[346] This shaped white and black women's perspectives of each other: "White women have been perceived by people of color as cold and emotionless and not to be trusted, or as naïve and silly."[347] Yet many women of color experience regret not having the same privileges as their white counterparts. One of my girlfriends, who is African American, told me that when she was little, she used to scrub her face so hard that it would turn raw, in an attempt to rub off the color of her skin.

The church should create safe places where women can tell their stories—both in the presence of women and men. The entire community misses out when the body of Christ is not fully participating, fully using their gifts and fully engaged in ministry.

**FOR FURTHER STUDY**

*Eve's Revenge: Women and a Spirituality of the Body* by Lilian Calles Barger

*Mirror, Mirror: Reflections on Who You Are and Who You'll Become* by Kara Powell and Kendall Payne

## WOMEN—CHILDBEARING AND FAMILY CARE

Motherhood is one of the greatest joys of being a woman and also one of the greatest challenges. Cheryl Sanders observes:

> A mother's struggles for the well-being of her children in a world fraught with deception and death is a redemptive struggle. A mother who has suffered the pains of labor and delivery for the sake of bringing forth life is positioned to gain deeper insight into the sacrificial posture that Jesus assumed in life and in death. A mother who brings a loving spirit of servanthood to the many tasks involved in meeting the needs of children has hope to redeem even the most wayward, willful, underachieving child by the power of God.[348]

Raising children can be very difficult for poor women because of limited access to adequate food supplies and health care. Two percent of all deliveries in the developing world result in the death of the mother. Each year, more than 500,000 women die from treatable or preventable complications of pregnancy and childbirth. In sub-Saharan Africa, a woman's risk of dying from such complications in a lifetime is 1 in 16, compared to 1 in 2,500 in the United States.[349]

Fortunately, virtually all countries are now developing safe motherhood programs and are poised for progress.[350]

Mothers are essential to any society. However, women should not be defined *only* by the role of motherhood. Some Christians believe that motherhood is the primary and solitary role for which women were created. For example, Timothy Bayly, writing for the *Journal for Biblical Manhood and Womanhood*, states: "Not surprisingly in a culture that disparages motherhood, we see a decline of conscious preparation for this task by women making academic, financial, and other career decisions."[351] This view disparages women for pursuing financial stability, education and other developmental opportunities as if these are mutually exclusive from motherhood. In addition, society, and especially Christians, should not discriminate against women who are not able to have children or who make a conscious choice not to become a mother.

←❧ *Take action.* Partner with the organization Women Thrive Worldwide (www.women thrive.org), which gives women greater economic opportunity and helps lift entire families, communities and countries out of poverty. Women Thrive Worldwide develops, shapes and advocates for innovative U.S. policies that help women in poor countries earn income. Focusing on U.S. foreign assistance and trade policies, they work to remove the barriers that keep women and families poor, such as lack of access to credit and trade, unequal property rights, violence, and poor wages and working conditions. Because of this, their work has a ripple effect—often benefiting millions of women living in poverty at once.

**FOR FURTHER STUDY**

*Balancing Act: How Women Can Lose Their Roles and Find Their Callings* by Mary Ellen Ashcroft

*Great with Child: Reflections on Faith, Fullness, and Becoming a Mother* by Debra Rienstra

*See also* "Children," "Family," "Poverty" and "Work."

## WOMEN—INTERNATIONAL LEADERSHIP

One of the most encouraging things over the last century is the increasing number of women leaders in business, global politics and other positions of influence. The twentieth century saw a number of firsts for women in the United States, including Sandra Day O'Connor, the first female justice on the United States Supreme Court (1981); Janet Reno, the first female Attorney General (1993); Madeleine Albright, the first female Secretary of State (1997); and Nancy Pelosi, the first female Speaker of the House of Representatives (2007).

Around the world, women have led different countries through significant times of transition, growth and development. Indira Gandhi was the prime minister of India (1966-1977). Golda Meir was a founder and the fourth prime minister of the State of Israel (1969-1974). Juan Peron's widow, Isabel, was the first female head of state in the America's as the president of Argentina (1974-1976). Simone Weil of France was the first president of the European Parliament (1979).

Other women are leaders in the business world, showing that opportunities for women are expanding. Some of the most influential leaders include Indra Nooyi (PepsiCo), Anne Mulcahy (Xerox), Meg Whitman (eBay), Irene Rosenfeld (Kraft Foods), Susan Arnold (Proctor & Gamble), and Oprah Winfrey (Harpo Productions). Dale Hanson Bourke remarks, "Evidence shows that expanding opportunities for girls and women not only improves their position in society, but it also has a major impact on the overall effectiveness of development."[352]

Though the trends are encouraging, the number of women in positions of power are still few compared to their male counterparts. The success of top women leaders must be juxtaposed to the conditions of the rest of the women around the world (see "Women—Poverty in the Developing World").

**FOR FURTHER STUDY**

*My Life* by Golda Meier

*Women, Politics, and Power: A Global Perspective* by Pamela Paxton and Melanie Hughes

## WOMEN—POVERTY IN THE DEVELOPING WORLD

In order to live out biblical justice, we must have an accurate picture of the conditions of women around the world. One phenomenon is the feminization of poverty, which refers to the fact that an increasing percentage of women constitute the world's poor.[353] Higher poverty rates apply to women because they have less access to resources and often are responsible for taking care of children. Poverty is not the only issue that affects women. According to Sisters in Service, women and children make up over 80 percent of the world's unreached people.[354] The following are some truths about women around the world:

- Millions of women spend hours every day

collecting water, which limits their ability to spend time doing other things, including pursuing education, taking care of their children and working.[355] (See also "Water.")

- 90 percent of Afghan women cannot read the alphabet of their own language. (See also "Education.")

- 80 percent of all refugees are women and children. (See also "Refugees.")

- Every year, two million girls undergo female genital mutilation, and approximately half a million die every year as a result of the practice. (See also "Female Genital Mutilation.")

These statistics are overwhelming. Women around the world are among the least fed, least educated and least reached of any people in the world.[356] God's call to justice demands that the body of Christ get involved and work to make a positive difference in each of these areas.

←※ **Take action.** Sisters in Service (www.sistersinservice.org) is a Christian nonprofit committed to informing, mobilizing and equipping advocates to extend God's love to women and children through local partnerships in the least-reached places of the world. Get involved by becoming a Sisters in Service advocate or associate.

←※ **Take action.** Aglow International (www.aglow.org) is an international ministry that operates in 171 countries over 6 continents. Indigenous women lead Aglow's efforts around the world. Aglow seeks to "mobilize women around the world, to promote gender recon-

ciliation in the Body of Christ as God designed, and to amplify awareness of global concerns from a Biblical perspective." Get involved by participating in their online institute of learning or one of their other programs.

**FOR FURTHER STUDY**

*The Feminization of Poverty: Only in America?* by Gertrude Schaffner Goldberg and Eleanor Kremen

*Daughters of Hope: Stories of Witness and Courage in the Face of Persecution* by Kay Marshall Strom and Michele Rickett

## WOMEN—SERVING IN THE CHURCH

Throughout the New Testament, women partnered with the disciples in the ministry of the gospel. Out of their own means Susanna, Joanna and Mary Magdalene helped fund Jesus' ministry (Lk 8:1-3). Jesus not only allowed women to travel with his disciples, but he allowed Mary to sit at his feet as a disciple and to learn from his teachings (Lk 10:39). Jesus responded to the needs of the women just as he responded to the men (Mt 9:22; 15:28; Lk 8:50). Women were present in the upper room when the Holy Spirit descended on the believers (Acts 2:4). Paul esteemed Junia as outstanding among the apostles (Rom 16:7), as were other women who were serving in ministry alongside men. There is a preponderance of evidence in Scripture that God desires all people, regardless of race, class or gender, to use their gifts to help build up the body of Christ. "There is neither Jew nor Gentile, neither slave nor free, neither male nor female, for you are all one in Christ Jesus" (Gal 3:28).

The role of women in the church is a

highly debated topic in many evangelical circles, and it is beyond the scope of this book to wrestle through the details of the debate. However, there are two main sides to the conversation: egalitarianism and complementarianism. Egalitarianism holds to a notion of biblical equality, defined as

> the belief that all people are equal before God and in Christ. All have equal responsibility to use their gifts and obey their calling to the glory of God. God freely calls believers to roles and ministries without regard to class, gender, or race. We believe this because the Bible and Jesus Christ teach it to us.[357]

Complementarianism is the belief

> which affirms that men and women are equal in the image of God, but maintain complementary differences in role and function. In the home, men lovingly are to lead their wives and family as women intelligently are to submit to the leadership of their husbands. In the church, while men and women share equally in the blessings of salvation, some governing and teaching roles are restricted to men.[358]

A perspective that embraces biblical justice motivated by love believes that limiting women's use of their God-given gifts in the home, workplace, church and society is a violation of the commandments of God. Throughout Scripture there are verses that teach about the distribution of gifts—irrespective of gender:

> For just as each of us has one body with many members, and these members do not all have the same function, so in Christ we, though many, form one body, and each member belongs to all the others. We have different gifts, according to the grace given to each of us. If your gift is prophesying, then prophesy in accordance with your faith; if it is serving, then serve; if it is teaching, then teach; if it is to encourage, then give encouragement; if it is giving, then give generously; if it is to lead, do it diligently; if it is to show mercy, do it cheerfully. (Rom 12:4-8)

When a woman is gifted to lead, which clearly many women are, did God mistakenly give her that gift? Or is that gift limited to the home or child-rearing (which are worthy places to invest energy, but not the only places women are called to serve)?

Before I was allowed to graduate seminary, I had to take an assessment of my gifts. I scored higher in leadership "than most men do in that area which measures male giftedness," according to the counselor administering the test. I am comforted by Scripture that says God knew everything about me as he formed me (Ps 139:13-16). I believe that I was given the gifts that I possess not for my own glory or benefit but so I can use them to build up others and serve the church.

I hope that the church will become the community God intended it to be—advocating on behalf of the voiceless and the poor, and that in obediently spreading his Word and serving others, the kingdom of God will be manifest on earth.

*Awareness exercise.* Read several books about the role of women in the early church. First consider what the Scriptures teach about women in the early church. Then consider

## Christians for Biblical Equality

Christians for Biblical Equality (CBE) is a nonprofit organization of Christian men and women who believe that the Bible, properly interpreted, teaches the fundamental equality of men and women of all racial and ethnic groups, all economic classes, and all age groups, based on the teachings of Scriptures such as Galatians 3:28. Injustice is an abuse of power, taking from others what God has given them: their dignity, their freedom, their resources and even their very lives. CBE also recognizes that prohibiting individuals from exercising their God-given gifts to further his kingdom constitutes injustice in a form that impoverishes the body of Christ and its ministry in the world at large. CBE accepts the call to be part of God's mission in opposing injustice as required in Scriptures such as Micah 6:8. The role of CBE is primarily about educating the church through individual and church membership, hosting conferences and their publications, *The Priscilla Papers* scholarly journal and *Mutuality*, the award-winning egalitarian magazine. Become a CBE member and learn more about their ministry at www.cbeinternational.org.

other sources and histories that have been written about the role of women in church history. One possible study is on the use of the name Junia in and outside of the Scriptures. What did you discover in your studies?

←⚔ *Take action.* For the purpose of networking, encouragement and advocacy on behalf of women, consider attending an event offered by a church that is affirming and supportive of the full equality of women. For example, in 2008 Willow Creek Community Church sponsored a couple of intentional dialogues called "Gifted to Lead: The Art of Leading as a Woman in the Church," facilitated by Nancy Ortberg and Nancy Beach. These types of conversations are critically important for both men and women in the church. Visit www.willowcreek.com for more information about this event.

←⚔ *Take action.* Participate in the "Gifted for Leadership: A Community of Christian Women" blog (an Internet dialogue) for women in leadership sponsored by Christianity Today, Inc. This will give you an opportunity to dialogue with women about issues related to women and their roles, faith and leadership. Visit blog.christianitytoday.com/giftedforleadership.

←⚔ *Take action.* Advocate on behalf of women using their gifts in any context by inviting them to the table. Encourage your pastor and leaders to have women preach from the pulpit, teach Sunday school classes, be guest speakers at events, sign their names to petitions, participate in board leadership and play other important roles where they can contribute and use their gifts.

## Class Action Lawsuit Against Wal-Mart

Wal-Mart is loved and appreciated by many who benefit directly from their low prices and extensive merchandise. But by placing such a high value on low prices, the fair treatment of workers has been neglected.[360]

On June 19, 2001, six current and former female Wal-Mart and Sam's Club employees filed a class-action lawsuit in federal court in San Francisco called *Dukes v. Wal-Mart Stores, Inc.* Their claim is that Wal-Mart discriminates against its female employees in making promotions, job assignments, pay decisions and training, and retaliates against women who complain against such practices. The largest class-action lawsuit the United States has ever seen, the case applies to over 1.5 million current and former female employees of Wal-Mart. Over one hundred women from thirty states have prepared extensive declarations about their experiences at Wal-Mart. The majority of Wal-Mart's employees, 65 percent, are women, whereas only 33 percent of Wal-Mart's managers are female.[361] The following are some of the comments included in the declarations against Wal-Mart:

A female employee was a personnel manager who had access to payroll records. She noticed that men generally made more than women who had as much or more seniority. When she told the male store manager about her observations, he said:

"Men are here to make a career and women aren't. Retail is for housewives who just need to earn extra money." When she later inquired about a raise that a male employee had received, she was told, "He has a family to support." When she pointed out that she was a single mother, the assistant manager ignored her and walked away.[362]

Another woman said that when she sought a job in the hardware department, a male manager told her: "We need you in toys. You're a girl, why do you want to be in hardware?"[363]

This class-action lawsuit is not the only bias case filed against Wal-Mart. In February 2005, Wal-Mart settled a complaint concerning allegations toward immigrant workers, many of whom were employed as janitors for less than minimum wage and without basic protections. They were exposed to poisonous chemicals, made to work more than seven days in a row and subjected to other unfair labor practices. The complaint concerning these allegations was settled with the federal government for $11 million. A civil action lawsuit is still pending.[364]

It is interesting that Wal-Mart's beginnings were rooted in Christianity and strong religious values. In fact, many of Wal-Mart's shoppers are female conservatives. As a result, the store doesn't sell compact disks bearing parental-advisory labels and doesn't carry men's magazines like *FHM, Maxim* and *Stuff*. Wal-Mart also partners with Christian retailers to sell Christian music like *NOW* and books like Tim LaHaye's *Glorious Appearing*.[365] It is disconcerting that a corporation that embraces Christian values would not treat its workers fairly and with justice. The class-action lawsuit regarding the treatment of women is still pending and will take many years before it is settled.

**FOR FURTHER STUDY**

*Selling Women Short: The Landmark Battle for Worker's Rights at Wal-Mart* by Liza Featherstone

*The Case Against Wal-Mart* by Al Norman

**FOR FURTHER STUDY**

*Beyond Sex Roles: What the Bible Says About a Woman's Place in the Church and Family* by Gilbert Bilezikian

*Discovering Biblical Equality: Complementarity Without Hierarchy* edited by Ronald Pierce, Rebecca Merrill Groothuis and Gordon Fee

*Women & Christianity: From the Reformation to the 21st Century* by Mary T. Malone

## WOMEN—WORK AND JOB OPPORTUNITIES

Another social justice issue that affects women in the United States relates to economics. In the nineteenth century, women began working outside their homes in large numbers, notably in textile mills and garment shops. In poorly ventilated, crowded rooms women (and children) worked for as long as twelve hours a day. Great Britain passed a ten-hour-day law for women and children in 1847, but in the United States it was not until the 1910s that the states began to pass legislation limiting working hours and improving employment conditions of women and children.[359]

The United States' participation in both World Wars also created a demand for increased female laborers because so many men were deployed around the world. During the 1960s several federal laws improving the economic status of women were passed. Between 1950 and 1960, women earned on average 59 to 64 cents for every dollar that a man made.[366] The Equal Pay Act of 1963 responded to this wage gap and required equal wages for men and women doing equal work.[367] Now, over forty years later, the rate of pay of women to their male counterparts is only slightly improved. In 2006 the female-to-male earnings ratio was 0.77 on the dollar.[368] These statistics take into consideration the amount of hours worked, the position on the job and other variables that could contribute to the difference in pay. One example of the effects of unequal pay plays out in the story of Wal-Mart and its female employees.

## WORK—JOB TRAINING

One way to solve unemployment is through job training and education. Others have disagreed and suggested that the government has already spent too much money on job programs that have been ineffective: "We spent tens of billions of dollars on job

## Focus: HOPE

Focus: HOPE, a nonprofit ministry, has a very successful jobs programs based in Detroit. Cofounded in 1968 by Father Cunningham and Eleanor Josaitis, Focus: HOPE has the following vision:

> Recognizing the dignity and beauty of every person, we pledge intelligent and practical action to overcome racism, poverty and injustice. And to build a metropolitan community where all people may live in freedom, harmony, trust and affection. Black and white, yellow, brown and red from Detroit and its suburbs of every economic status, national origin and religious persuasion we join in this covenant.

The 1967 riot left metropolitan Detroit sharply divided along racial lines. By early 1968 shock had deepened into bitterness and hostility, which produced polarization, white backlash, black militancy and flight. The Focus: HOPE cofounders felt compelled to make a difference. They wrote a mission statement and inspired a movement. The material resources available to them were minimal. But the human resources—courageous and determined people from all walks of life dedicated to the ideal of brotherhood—proved abundant. Focus: HOPE was born, and it remains a movement of minds, hearts and wills committed to "intelligent and practical action to overcome racism, poverty and injustice."

I first met Eleanor when she was a guest speaker at Willow Creek Community Church's 2005 Leadership Summit. I had the privilege of hosting her for the weekend, and her passion, drive and unwavering desire to see those who are hurting find hope and relief was awe-inspiring. No one who encounters Eleanor is the same after meeting her. She is full of spunk and challenge, and has poured herself into life and ministry in the city of Detroit. Focus: HOPE now has nearly 350 colleagues and is supported by 51,000 volunteers and donors. The ministry partners with the Detroit auto industry and assures job placements for graduates who complete their Fast Track, Machinist Training Institute, Center for Advanced Technologies, and Information Technologies Center programs. Board members consist of some of the top business leaders in the community including the chief operating officer of Chrysler Financial, a retired president of Ford Motor Company and a vice president from General Motors North America.

Focus: HOPE offers comprehensive and holistic support for underresourced individuals, families and communities. The ministry responds to people's immediate needs by offering compassion through food distribution programs, daycare and child support initiatives, and job training and skills improvement. They seek social justice by working to change the institutionalized systems. For more information visit www.focushope.edu.

programs in the 1970s, and they failed even to dent the numbers of inner-city men who have dropped out of the job market," says Charles Murray, a former Bradley Fellow at the American Enterprise Institute in Washington, D.C.[369] Few would disagree with Murray's assessment. However, that does not mean job programs should be abandoned all together. These job programs have not been successful at supporting urban men's needs. For example, I have repeatedly heard stories of money being thrown into a program that is two hours away from decent public transportation. A program is launched, money is poured into it, but no one comes. In cases such as these, job programs have not been run effectively.

←** *Take action.* Partner with an organization that is advocating for the fair treatment of workers. In Chicago, Interfaith Worker Justice (www.iwj.org) partners with the Department of Labor and calls upon religious values in order to educate, organize and mobilize the religious community on issues that will improve wages, benefits, and working conditions for workers, especially low-wage workers.

←** *Take action.* Research what job programs are available in your community. What is their success rate at helping people to find employment? Consider volunteering some of your time in support of their work.

### FOR FURTHER STUDY

*When Work Disappears: The World of the New Urban Poor* by William Julius Wilson

*The Living Wage: Building A Fair Economy* by Robert Pollin and Stephanie Luce

*See also* "Global Economy," "Globalization," "Poverty," "Racism" and "Work."

## WORK—LIVING WAGE INITIATIVES

According to *Sojourners* magazine:

> Economic inequality in America is at its greatest point since the 1920s. The social consequences of inequality are best symbolized by the fact that two of the nation's biggest growth industries are prison construction (almost 2 million people behind bars) and the construction of gated residential communities (9 million households behind walls).[370]

Over the past decade, there have been many nonprofit organizations lobbying for economic reform by promoting the idea of a "living wage."

A living wage enables full-time workers to afford the basics of community living: housing, food, transportation, child care and health care. Studies have shown that living-wage initiatives do not increase the rate of unemployment, nor do they overly burden small businesses. On the other hand, the positive effects of living wages are extensive. Living wages allow families to move out of poverty. Other public policy programs like "make work pay" provide high-quality early care and learning experiences for children of low-income parents.[371] These initiatives create win-win opportunities. Low-income individuals are given the incentive to work, and the system benefits because those who work need less economic support.

←** *Take action.* Engage in some form of

political advocacy to encourage your representatives to support living-wage initiatives. For example, the "Let Justice Roll" initiative is an advocacy group of faith and community voices uniting to lobby for a living wage through federal policy changes. The ministry supports several events and an educational program designed to address the core issues surrounding living-wage initiatives. The motto of the ministry is "A job should keep you out of poverty, not keep you in it." Join the initiative and learn more about advocacy efforts at www.letjusticeroll.org.

**FOR FURTHER STUDY**

*"A Just Minimum Wage: Good for Workers, Business, and Our Future"* by Holly Sklar and Paul Sherry[372]

*The Case for the Living Wage* by Jerold L. Waltman

*See also* "Children," "Housing," "Hunger" and "Work."

## WORK—THE WORKING POOR

One of the greatest tragedies of twenty-first century America is the working poor. People often think that the poor who live on the streets of our cities are lazy, unprincipled good-for-nothings. Many of the over six million Americans who are considered the "working poor" have full-time jobs at minimum wage.[373] A forty-hour-per-week job at the federal minimum wage ($6.55 as of July 2008) equals $13,624 per year—hardly enough money for an individual, let alone a family, to function.

From the nineteenth century and well into the twentieth century, poverty was understood to be the consequence of physical misfortune or the inability to be able to make decisions.[374] The able-bodied poor

were believed to be slackers not willing to put forth the effort to hold down a job. Since the second half of the twentieth century there has been a shift in our understanding of the poor.

Currently, the poor are understood to suffer systemic or institutional oppression. Many argue that the U.S. welfare system fosters a type of oppression. For example, inner-city children raised on welfare are taught to be dependent on a system that continually replenishes their basic needs even when they don't work for them. It's not their fault; they are stuck in a poorly designed system.

We must overcome our misperceptions of the poor in the United States. All people do not have equal opportunities to work and be successful. We commonly think that if people just work hard enough, they will be able to work their way out. Mary Jo Bane of Harvard's Kennedy School of Government observes, "Welfare reform has not succeeded in addressing poverty; instead, our policy has merely 'turned the welfare poor into the working poor.'"[375] The social context is much more complicated than we might imagine.

The welfare system actually gives incentives for the poor to stay below the poverty line. If a single mother is working to support her family and breaks through just beyond the poverty line, she loses the government benefits and subsidies that would have been provided to her had she worked just a little bit less. There are no immediate benefits for her breaking the threshold of poverty.

In the 1990 article "For Welfare Parents, Scrimping Is Legal, But Saving Is Out," Robert Rose identified the problems that the welfare system causes by offering incentives for low-income families to stay below the poverty line.[376] It is disconcerting that many of the same issues are still being discussed some twenty years later. The *New York Times* has documented similar problems in the government's management of social services.[377]

The fathers of some poor families can't pay child support and are arrested, facing fines, possible jail time, or the loss of their driver's licenses. This impedes them from being able to make money with which to pay the child support. The child-support system is part of the welfare reform of the 1970s, which has the goal of recovering government costs for welfare. Experience, research and experts suggest that the current policy is counterproductive and has the effect of "driving fathers into the underground economy and leaving families more dependent on aid."[378]

One mother, suffering from lupus, was forced to move to the outskirts of Milwaukee because the apartment that she was renting was lost to foreclosure. Her experience of being caught in the system of trying to make a living to support her family is described by journalist Erik Eckholm: "Going to work . . . may have been a wash financially because her federal disability check and food stamps were reduced, as is her energy."[379]

←※ *Take action.* Volunteer as a case worker at a Christian ministry that provides services for the working poor. Develop relationships with the men, women and children affected by the lack of living-wage jobs. Consider how the welfare system encourages these individuals and families to remain in poverty. As you continue in your volunteer service, reflect about the things you have learned. What more can you do to help advocate on behalf of the working poor?

←※ *Take action.* Join or begin a community organizing effort in your area on behalf of the working poor. Community organizers work on behalf of social, political and economic justice. Encourage members of your congregation to get involved. Consider resources or partnership with a ministry like Christians Supporting Community Organizing (www.cscoweb.org).

**FOR FURTHER STUDY**

*Walking with the Poor: Principles and Practices of Transformational Development* by Bryant L. Myers

*A Framework for Understanding Poverty* by Ruby Payne

*See also* "Children," "Poverty" and "Women."

# Appendix 1

## ORGANIZATIONS

There are several organizations listed throughout this book under different subtopics and headings. They are not all repeated here in the appendix. The descriptions of the organizations that follow have been adapted from the organizations' websites or other marketing material.

**Across Sudan.** Across Sudan (www.across-sudan.org) is an interdenominational, international Christian organization focused on Sudan with an emphasis on training. It was founded in 1972 by four evangelical mission societies (AIM, SUM, SIM and MAF). Today it operates in partnership with Sudanese Evangelical Churches. Across emphasizes the development of Sudanese nationals through four strategic areas of ministry: capacity building of the church, education, health and media.

**Advent Conspiracy.** Advent Conspiracy (www.adventconspiracy.org) seeks to inspire churches, families and individuals to avoid being consumed by commercialism at Christmas. Starting with five churches in 2006, Advent Conspiracy has become a movement. Change your spending habits this Christmas, avoid commercialism and give relationally—the way Christ modeled for us, through the gift of himself.

**Agathos Foundation.** The Agathos Foundation (www.agathosfoundation.org) is a nondenominational organization that values the diversity of the Christian body while endeavoring to encourage the unity of the faith. The Agathos Foundation provides Southern Africa's AIDS orphans and elderly with a familial environment that allows them to achieve healthy, prosperous and fulfilling lives, by meeting physical, emotional and spiritual needs critical to their advancement. Agathos will accomplish its mission by building self-dependent villages, typically on or near a profitable farm, where children orphaned by AIDS can be raised, supervised, educated and provided a moral foundation for life using its five-step methodology: (1) emergency pastors conferences, (2) creating an orphan village site, (3) raising the orphans, (4) impacting the community, and (5) sponsoring the orphan villages.

**AIDS Orphan Bracelet Project.** The Aids Bracelet Project (www.aidsbracelets.org), founded by Dale Hanson Bourke, is a grassroots effort to help ordinary, caring people work together to make a difference in the lives of AIDS orphans. A simple bracelet—made by AIDS orphans in Africa or the women who support them—is a tangible expression of concern. Churches, schools and other groups offer these African bracelets to individuals for a donation of $20. Those who wear the bracelets are asked to tell one other person about the AIDS orphan crisis. The funds go to Opportunity International, World Vision, Compassion International and the Chikumbuso Widows and Orphans Project.

**Association of Evangelicals Relief and Development Organizations (AERDO).** Founded in 1978, AERDO (www.aerdo.net) represents a network of more than fifty of the major evangelical Christian relief and development agencies across North America. The board of directors is composed of a representative from each member agency. The vision statement of AERDO is: "Being compelled by the love of our Lord Jesus Christ, we work together with all believers in partnership with the poor and oppressed so together we become all God intended us to be."

**Africare.** A specialist in Africa, Africare (www.africare.org) is the oldest and largest African American-led charity in its field. In thirty-six African nations since 1970, Africare has delivered more than $710 million in aid to Africa to address AIDS, poverty and more. Nelson Mandela says, "I regard Africare as one of America's greatest gifts to Africa."

**Amnesty International USA.** Amnesty International's (www.amnestyusa.org) purpose is to protect people wherever justice, freedom, truth and dignity are denied. They work by investigating and exposing abuses, educating and mobilizing the public, and helping to transform societies to create a safer, more just world. They received the Nobel Peace Prize for their life-saving work.

**Bread for the World Institute.** Bread for the World (www.bread.org) is a collective Christian voice urging U.S. decision-makers to end hunger at home and abroad. By changing policies, programs and conditions that allow hunger and poverty to persist, they provide help and opportunity far beyond the communities in which we live.

**Bright Hope International.** Bright Hope (www.brighthope.org) serves the poorest of the poor and only works with communities where people earn less than $1 per day. Bright Hope partners with indigenous local church leaders and churches who understand their communities and are working to change lives in a holistic manner—spiritual, physical, educational and financial. Bright Hope has projects all over the world in the areas of crisis response and relief aid, orphans and vulnerable children, job creation, healthcare (including HIV/AIDS), education, agriculture, economic development, and church development.

**CARE USA.** CARE USA (www.care.org) fights root causes of poverty in the world's poorest communities. Special focus is placed on working alongside poor women because, equipped with the proper resources, women have the power to help whole families and entire communities escape poverty.

**The Center for Bioethics and Human Dignity.** The Center for Bioethics and Human Dignity (www.cbhd.org) exists to equip thought leaders to engage the issues of bioethics using the tools of rigorous research, conceptual analysis, charitable critique, leading-edge publication and effective teaching. The Center is a national and international leader in producing a wide range of live, recorded and written resources examining bioethical issues. Recognizing that biblical values have exercised a profound influence on Western culture, the Center explores the potential contribution of such values as part of its work.

**Center for Global Development.** Founded in 2001, the Center for Global Development (www.cgdev.org) is an independent, not-for-profit think tank that works to reduce global poverty and inequality by encouraging policy change in the United States and other rich countries through rigorous research and active engagement with the policy community. CDG is committed to education about broad and specific issues affecting the poor.

**CHAP International.** CHAP International (www.chapusa.org) was founded in 2002 as a Christian organization with the initial goal of providing humanitarian aid to the war-torn nation of Liberia in West Africa. CHAP currently provides humanitarian aid to Liberia with hopes of someday becoming a worldwide relief organization.

**Christ for the City International.** Christ for the City International's (www.cfci.org) mission is to send out multinational teams into the least evangelized cities of the world to present people the opportunity to develop a personal relationship with Jesus Christ. Ministries are built to meet the needs of the most desperate people in the world's cities—street kids, prostitutes, orphans, the homeless, the unemployed and the destitute. Through the work of long- and short-term mission teams, these people meet Christ's love and can begin healing.

**Christian Community Development Association (CCDA).** The roots of the Christian Community Development Association (www.ccda.org) stretch back to 1960 when John and Vera Mae Perkins relocated their family to the struggling community of Mendenhall, Mississippi, to work with the people there. The Perkinses devoted thirty-five years to the principles of Christian Community Development in Mississippi and California, leaving behind ministries and churches that are now headed by indigenous Christian leaders. In 1989, John Perkins called together a group of Christian leaders from across America who were bonded by one significant commitment, expressing the love of Christ in America's poor communities, not at arm's length but at the grassroots level. An association was formed, and CCDA held its first annual conference in Chicago in 1989. The mission of CCDA is to inspire and train Christians who seek to bear witness to the kingdom of God by reclaiming and restoring underresourced communities.

**Christians for Biblical Equality (CBE).** CBE (www.cbeinternational.org) is a nonprofit organization comprised of individuals and church members from more than 100 denominations, who believe that the Bible, when properly interpreted, teaches the fundamental equality of men and women of all ethnicities and economic classes. They base this on the teachings of Scripture as reflected in Galatians 3:28: "There is neither Jew nor Gentile, neither slave nor free, neither male nor female, for you are all one in Christ Jesus." CBE also has excellent resources in their online catalog.

**Churches Together.** Churches Together (churchestogether.com) is committed to helping North American churches join together to engage in grassroots African church-based ministry to African communities, families and individuals infected and affected by HIV/AIDS. The North American Churches Together churches partner with African churches and church networks and faith-based organizations or nongovernment organizations on African AIDS ministry under the guidance of the African churches.

**Compassion International.** In response to the Great Commission, Compassion International (www.compassion.com) exists as an advocate for children, to release them from their spiritual, economic, social and physical poverty, and enable them to become responsible and fulfilled Christian adults. Compassion works through child-focused projects that introduce children to Jesus, provide health care, learning opportunities and a safe haven for children. Programs include child sponsorship, a child survival program and a leadership development program.

**Conservation International.** Conservation International (www.conservation.org) aims to protect life on earth and to demonstrate that human societies will thrive when in balance with nature. For two decades, they have worked with their partners to protect life on earth. They have saved some of the most critical sites—more than 200 million protected hectares on land and at sea.

**Convoy of Hope.** Convoy of Hope (www.convoyofhope.org) mobilizes, resources and trains churches and other groups to conduct community outreaches, respond to disasters and direct other compassion initiatives in the United States and around the world. A nonprofit organization, Convoy of Hope serves in the United States and around the world providing disaster relief, building supply lines and sponsoring outreaches to the poor and hurting in communities. During a Convoy of Hope outreach, free groceries are distributed, job and health fairs are organized, and activities for children are provided. Since 1994 Convoy of Hope has affected the lives of nearly sixteen million people. In 2006 alone, they have been active in twenty-six countries, while holding forty-three outreach events in the United States. They have given away over $100 million worth of food and supplies to people in need.

**Cross International.** Cross International (www.crossinternational.org) was born out of the vision of two ministries with a heart for the poor—Christian Children's Charity and the Kielar Family Foundation. Founded in the 1990s, these organizations discovered that they shared a call to expand their vision to help the suffering poor worldwide. Now, Cross International will carry out this mission, with the added goal of rallying like-minded Christians to the cause.

**CrossRoads.** CrossRoads (www.crossroadslink.org) is a character-based strategy dedicated to help communities worldwide discover the hope, life and truth of Jesus Christ in the midst of devastating societal needs such as HIV/AIDS, addictions and violence. It is centered around the Life at the CrossRoads curriculum, a highly interactive program created by educational, medical and youth services professionals. The curriculum, which teaches life skills and character development, can be presented during the course of an average school semester. It can also be modified to fit within other settings or in the context of most cultures.

**DATA (Debt, AIDS, Trade, Africa).** DATA (www.data.org) is an advocacy organization dedicated to eradicating extreme poverty and AIDS in Africa. DATA calls on the governments of the world's wealthiest nations to keep their existing commitments to Africa and adopt new trade and aid policies that will help Africans put themselves on the path to long-term prosperity and stability.

**Earth Day Network.** Founded by the organizers of the first Earth Day in 1970, Earth Day Network (www.earthday.net) promotes environmental citizenship and year-round progressive action worldwide. Earth Day Network is a driving force steering environmental awareness around the world. Through Earth Day Network, activists connect, interact and have an impact on their communities, and create positive change in local, national and global policies. EDN's international network reaches over 17,000 organizations in 174 countries, while the domestic program engages 5,000 groups and over 25,000 educators coordinating millions of community development and environmental protection activities throughout the year. Earth Day is the only event celebrated simultaneously around the globe by people of all backgrounds, faiths and nationalities. More than a half billion people participate in their campaigns every year. Their mission is to grow and diversify the environmental movement worldwide, and to mobilize it as the most effective vehicle for promoting a healthy, sustainable planet. They pursue their mission through education, politics, events and consumer activism.

**Earth Print.** EarthPrint (www.earthprint.com) was launched in 1999 as the official online bookshop of the United Nations Environment Programme. Since then, other prominent international organizations have joined this initiative.

**Educational Concerns for Hunger Organization**. Networking global hunger solutions, Educational Concerns for Hunger Organization (www.echonet.org) is a nonprofit, interdenominational Christian organization that has been assisting a global network of missionaries and development workers since 1981, and is currently serving agricultural workers in 180 countries. ECHO helps those working internationally with the poor to be more effective, especially in the area of agriculture. ECHO is a support organization helping community development organizations and workers by providing education and training, problem solving and networking.

**EDGE OUTREACH.** EDGE OUTREACH (www.edgeoutreach.com) is a faith-based nonprofit in Louisville, Kentucky, that trains and sends people and organizations to deliver integrated water solutions where they are needed most throughout the world, hosts vision clinics for refugees and the poor, and networks with local agencies and volunteers to provide community needs. In September 2007, EDGE created SwimServe.com to train college students about the most efficient water solutions available and to mobilize them to install the systems overseas and train indigenous leaders in their use and maintenance.

**Emergent Village.** Emergent Village (www.emergentvillage.com) is a growing generative friendship among missional Christian leaders seeking to love the world in the Spirit of Jesus Christ. The dream of Emergent is to join in the activity of God in the world wherever we are able, partnering with God as God's dreams for our world come true. In the process, the world can be healed and changed, and so can we.

**Engineering Ministries International.** Engineering Ministries International (www.emiusa. org) is a nonprofit Christian development organization made up of architects, engineers and design professionals who donate their skills to help children and families around the world step out of poverty and into a world of hope. EMI designs facilities, including buildings, roads, clean water projects and more, that serve the poor in developing countries and directly impact communities by meeting physical needs and communicating God's love in a practical way. From offices around the world, over seventy staff and interns labor to bring the gospel to the poorest and least reached peoples on earth.

**Exodus World Services.** Exodus World Services (www.e-w-s.org) transforms the lives of refugees and volunteers. They educate local churches about refugee ministry, connect volunteers in relationship with refugee families through practical service projects, and equip leaders to speak up on behalf of refugees. The end result is that wounded hearts are healed, loneliness is replaced with companionship and fear is transformed into hope.

**Food for the Hungry.** Food for the Hungry (www.fh.org) is an international relief organization that answers God's call to meet the physical and spiritual needs of the poor in more than twenty-six countries. Founded in 1971 by Dr. Larry Ward, Food for the Hungry exists to help individuals reach their God-given potential. In developing countries on nearly every continent, Food for the Hungry works with churches, leaders and families to provide the resources they need to help their communities become self-sustaining. Programs include child development, church development, economic development, food security, health, HIV/AIDS, water and Future Hope Special Needs Children's Services.

**Genocide Intervention Network.** Genocide Intervention Network (www.genocide intervention.net) empowers individuals and communities with the tools to prevent and stop genocide. Members envision a world in which the global community is willing and able to protect civilians from genocide and mass atrocities. As part of the antigenocide movement, they raise both money and political will for civilian protection initiatives around the world.

**Global Call to Action Against Poverty.** Global Call to Action Against Poverty (www .whiteband.org) is an alliance of trade unions, community groups, faith groups, women and youth organizations, nongovermental organizations and other campaigners working together across more than one hundred national platforms. GCAP is calling for action from the world's leaders to meet their promises to end poverty and inequality.

**Global Exchange.** Building people-to-people ties, Global Exchange (www.globalexchange .org) is a membership-based international human rights organization dedicated to promoting social, economic and environmental justice around the world. The vision of Global Exchange is people-centered globalization that values the rights of workers and the health of the planet, that prioritizes international collaboration as central to ensuring peace, and that aims to create a local green economy designed to embrace the diversity of community.

**Global Movement for Children.** Global Movement for Children (www.gmfc.org) is the worldwide movement of organizations and people (including children) uniting efforts to build a world fit for children.

**GoGo Grandmothers.** *Gogo* is a common African term for "grandmother." Gogo Grandmothers (www.gogograndmothers.com) is a support program in which groups of grandmothers from America and the urban cities Zomba and Blantyre, Malawi, have formed prayer and caring networks to help their less fortunate sisters. Funds for blankets, school fees and food have been raised to give to the poor village grandmothers.

**Grameen Foundation USA.** Grameen Foundation USA (www.grameenfoundation.org) is dedicated to reducing global poverty among the poorest of the poor through microfinance. GFUSA partners with fifty-two microfinance institutions in twenty-two countries that provide financial services to empower the poor to start very small businesses to support themselves and their families.

**Habitat for Humanity.** Habitat for Humanity (www.habitat.org) is an ecumenical Christian ministry that welcomes to its work all people dedicated to the eradication of poverty housing. Some 250,000 Habitat homes now provide decent, affordable shelter to more than one million people worldwide.

**Heifer International.** Heifer International (www.heifer.org) envisions a world of communities living together in peace and equitably sharing the resources of a healthy planet. Their mission is to work with communities to end hunger and poverty, and to care for the earth. Heifer's global initiatives include agroecology, animal well-being, gender equity, HIV/AIDS, microenterprise, urban agriculture and Young People's Initiative.

**Hope 4 Kids International.** Bringing hope and necessary care to kids through dignity, health, joy and love, Hope 4 Kids International (www.hope4kidsinternational.org) is a Christian-based organization committed to four hopes: (1) through long-term projects and two-week trips they restore the dignity stripped from innocent children who are suffering from extreme poverty and disease; (2) providing relief to poverty-stricken villages caught up in the global AIDS crisis by building hospitals, medical and dental clinics and establishing an emergency medical fund, (3) bringing joy into the lives of abandoned and sick kids through education and hope of a greater future; and (4) love. They hope their teams exemplify God's unconditional love to every child served.

**HOPE International.** HOPE International (www.hopeinternational.org) is a global, faith-based, nonprofit organization focused on poverty alleviation through microenterprise development. HOPE serves people living in Afghanistan, China, the Dominican Republic, the Democratic Republic of Congo, Haiti, India, Moldova, Philippines, Romania, Russia, Rwanda, South Asia and Ukraine. HOPE's vision is to enable sustainable economic development that results in significant and lasting change, temporal and eternal, in the lives of many people living in poverty.

**InterAction (American Council for Voluntary International Action).** InterAction (www.interaction.org) is the largest coalition of U.S.-based international nongovernmental organizations focused on the world's poor and most vulnerable people. More than 165 members work to meet people halfway in expanding opportunities and supporting gender equality in education, health care, agriculture, small business and other areas. The U.S. public shows its support for this work through contributions to InterAction members totaling around $6 billion annually.

**International Aid.** Changing lives through the power of compassion, International Aid (www .internationalaid.org) is a Christian relief-and-development agency that responds to biblical mandates by providing and supporting solutions to health care. IA is a health ministry serving people in the United States and around the world. In a physical expression of the power of compassion, IA bridges the three components of health delivery systems—community health, clinical care and technology—with tangible projects of mercy and love that restore the physical, emotional and spiritual health of others.

**Jubilee USA Network.** Joining hands to break the chains of debt, Jubilee USA Network (www.jubileeusa.org) is an alliance of more than eighty religious denominations and faith communities, human rights, environmental, labor, and community groups working for the definitive cancellation of crushing debts to fight poverty and injustice in Asia, Africa and Latin America. Jubilee calls for a definitive cancellation of international debts and the restoration of right relationships between nations.

**Living Water International.** Providing a cup of water in Jesus' name, Living Water International (www.water.cc) exists to demonstrate the love of God by helping communities acquire desperately needed clean water, and to experience "living water"—the gospel of Jesus Christ—which alone satisfies the deepest thirst. In its sixteen-year history, LWI has completed nearly five thousand community water projects in twenty-six countries, which provide safe, clean water to seven million people every day.

**Make Poverty History.** Make Poverty History (www.makepovertyhistory.org) is the antipoverty campaign in the United Kingdom established in response to the 2001 conversations at the G8 Summit. Four years after the campaign began, Make Poverty History claims the "world was failing dismally to reach those targets." The year 2007 marked the approaching halfway point toward the 2015 commitments.

**Malaria No More.** Malaria No More's (www.malarianomore.org) mission is to end deaths due to malaria. Malaria No More works to raise the profile of the disease among the public, policymakers and businesses, while engaging the private sector to provide life-saving bed nets and other critical interventions to families in Africa.

**Medical Teams International.** The mission of Medical Teams International (www.medical teams.org) is to demonstrate the love of Christ to people affected by disaster, conflict and poverty around the world. MTI has programs in medical services and training, community health and development, HIV/AIDS, emergency medical services, disaster response, humanitarian aid, mobile dental, and children's ministry.

**Mercy Ships.** Mercy Ships (www.mercyships.org), a global charity, has operated hospital ships in developing nations since 1978. Following the example of Jesus, Mercy Ships brings hope and healing to the forgotten poor, mobilizing people and resources worldwide, and serving all people without regard for race, gender or religion. Mercy Ships welcomes volunteers who would like to give of their time, efforts and expertise to the work of bringing hope and healing to the poor. Short-term volunteers can participate from two weeks to a year with Mercy Ships, while others may choose to serve in a career capacity. Since 1978, Mercy Ships has performed more than 1.7 million services valued at over $670 million and impacting more than 1.9 million people as direct beneficiaries.

**Millennium Campaign.** Millennium Campaign (www.endpoverty2015.org) hopes to end poverty by 2015, which will fulfill the eight UN Millennium Development Goals (MDGs) and the promise of 189 world leaders made at the United Nations Millennium Summit in 2000 when they signed the Millennium Declaration. On October 16-17, 2007, over 43.7 million people, in 127 countries broke the Guinness Book of World Records (set in 2006 at 23.5 million people) for the largest number of people to "Stand Up Against Poverty and for the UN Millennium Development Goals" in twenty-four hours.

**Millennium Promise and Millennium Villages.** In partnership with Jeffrey Sachs, Millennium Promise (www.millenniumpromise.org) and Millennium Villages (www.millenniumvillages.org) work to make the UN Millennium Development Goals a reality. Millennium Villages are the flagship imitative of Millennium Promise. In 2008 there were eighty villages across ten countries in sub-Saharan Africa, practicing a comprehensive approach to addressing extreme poverty. By combining the best scientific and local knowledge, Millennium Villages address all the major problems simultaneously—hunger, disease, inadequate education, lack of safe drinking water and absence of essential infrastructure—to assist communities on their way to self-sustainable development.

**Mission Aviation Fellowship.** The passion of Mission Aviation Fellowship (www.maf.org) is to see individuals, communities and nations transformed by the gospel of Jesus Christ. This transformation is promoted by positioning Christ-centered staff in strategic locations worldwide utilizing aviation, communications, learning technologies, other appropriate technologies and related services. In accomplishing their mission, they collaborate with churches, subsidiaries, partners and networks.

**Mobilising for Malaria.** Mobilising for Malaria (www.mobilising4malaria.org) is a Malaria Consortium advocacy program mainly supported by GlaxoSmithKline's African Malaria Partnership. M4M works to combat malaria by raising people's awareness of the disease in Europe and Africa in order to bring greater resources to bear against the disease. M4M addresses the shortfall in resources and also recognizes the unique role and urgently needed contribution of civil society, including media, in the global malaria advocacy movement.

**National Center for Children in Poverty.** National Center for Children in Poverty (www.nccp.org) is a part of the Columbia University Mailman School of Public Health. NCCP is one of the nation's leading public-policy centers dedicated to promoting the economic security, health and well-being of America's low-income families and children. NCCP promotes family-oriented solutions at the state and national levels to ensure healthy child development.

**National Conference for Community and Justice.** The vision of National Conference for Community and Justice is "to make our nation a better place for all of us. Not just some of us." Formerly called the National Conference of Christians and Jews, NCCJ changed their name in the 1990s to be more inclusive. NCCJ promotes interfaith dialogues, provides workplace consultations, youth leadership development, seminarian and educator training. NCCJ conducts research and provides data and analysis to the evolving study of intergroup relations, and its public policy works with government leaders and advocates policies that promote understanding and respect. Use Google to find a chapter near you of the National Conference for Community and Justice.

**National Council of Churches in Christ—Eco-Justice Programs.** Seeking "justice for God's planet and God's people," the Eco-Justice Program (www.nccecojustice.org) office of the National Council of Churches works in cooperation with the NCC Eco-Justice Working Group to provide an opportunity for the national bodies of member Protestant and Orthodox denominations to work together to protect and restore God's Creation.

**OmniPeace.** OmniPeace-branded products( www.omnipeace.com) unite people throughout the world in an effort to end extreme poverty by 2025. OmniPeace donates 25 percent of its profits to Millennium Promise. Since its conception, OmniPeace has donated over $150,000 to Millennium Promise.

**One International.** One International (www.oneinternational.org) is a faith-based nonprofit organization that seeks to reconcile people of different ethnic groups, nationalities and religions while still respecting and promoting diversity. Their goal is to gather people together from different backgrounds to live in community in order to build peaceful friendships around the person and principles of Jesus of Nazareth. They offer two primary experiences: "Renewing Our Minds," an event that works to develop a new generation of leaders with integrity and renewed minds, and "Desert Encounters," an event which promotes peace between Israelis and Palestinians as demonstrated in the life and teachings of Jesus.

**One Million Witnesses.** One Million Witnesses (www.onemillionwitnesses.com) has set out to find one million people who will testify to God's work in their lives. Participants add their faith testimony to the website's wall and make a donation to help fund Living Water International wells in desperate communities.

**OneWorld.** OneWorld (www.oneworld.net) is a global information network developed to support communication media for everyone. Its goal is to help build a more just, global society through its partnership community. OneWorld encourages people to discover their power to speak, connect and make a difference by providing access to information and enabling connections between hundreds of organizations and tens of thousands of people around the world. The OneWorld network spans five continents and produces content in eleven languages, published across its international site, regional editions and thematic channels.

**Operation Blessings International.** Founded by Pat Robinson in 1978, Operation Blessings International (www.ob.org) has touched the lives of more than 202.7 million people in 105 countries and all 50 states, providing goods and services valued at more than $1.4 billion. OBI's mission is to demonstrate God's love by alleviating human need and suffering in the United States and around the world through Bless-A-Child, Disaster Relief, Microenterprise/Life Skills, Orphans Promise, Hunger Relief, Water Wells and Cisterns, and Medical Services.

**Opportunity International.** Since 1971 Opportunity International (www.opportunity.org) has been a leader in microfinance, helping the poor fight poverty through small business loans, other financial services, training and counsel. As the world's largest Christian microfinance organization, Opportunity serves over 1.1 million poor entrepreneurs in twenty-eight developing countries. OI's mission is to provide opportunities for people in chronic poverty to transform their lives through a strategy of creating jobs, stimulating small business and strengthening communities among the poor. The commitment of OI is motivated by Jesus' call to serve the poor.

**Oxfam America.** Oxfam America (www.oxfamamerica.org) helps poor and marginalized communities around the world harness economic opportunities and advocate for their rights (e.g., women's rights, labor rights, indigenous peoples' rights) through grant-making, campaigning and emergency assistance.

**Refugees International.** A powerful voice for lifesaving action, Refugees International (www.refugeesinternational.org) provides a voice for refugees and internally displaced persons throughout the world. It generates lifesaving humanitarian assistance and protection for displaced people and works to end the conditions that create displacement.

**Samaritan's Purse.** Samaritan's Purse (www.samaritanspurse.org) is a nondenominational evangelical Christian organization providing spiritual and physical aid to hurting people around the world. Since 1970 Samaritan's Purse has helped meet needs of victims of war, poverty, natural disasters, disease and famine with the purpose of sharing God's love through his Son, Jesus Christ. "Let my heart be broken with the things that break the heart of God"—Bob Pierce wrote these now-famous words in his Bible after visiting suffering children on the Korean island of Kojedo. This impassioned prayer is what guided him as he founded and led the ministry of Samaritan's Purse in 1970. After Pierce's death Franklin Graham became the president and chairman of the board of Samaritan's Purse. Through more than twenty years of earthquakes, hurricanes, wars and famine, Franklin has led the ministry in following the biblical example of the good Samaritan all across the globe.

**Salvation Army.** In 1865 William Booth, an ordained Methodist minister, and his wife, Catherine, formed an evangelical group dedicated to preaching among the "unchurched" people living in the midst of appalling poverty in London's East End. Booth's ministry recognized the interdependence of material, emotional and spiritual needs. In addition to preaching the gospel of Jesus Christ, the Booths became involved in feeding and sheltering the hungry and homeless, and in rehabilitating alcoholics. The Booths and their followers, originally known as The Christian Mission, became The Salvation Army (www.salvationarmyusa.org) in 1878, when the organization took on a quasi-military pattern. The Salvation Army is one of the few Christian organizations that insisted on the equality of men and women from its very beginnings. As of 2005 its outreach has been expanded to include more than one hundred countries, and the gospel is preached by its officers in more than 160 languages.

**Save the Children.** Founded in 1919 in England after World War I, Save the Children (www .savethechildren.org) is an independent organization working to create real and lasting change for children in need in the United States and around the world. It is a member of the International Save the Children Alliance, comprising twenty-eight national Save the Children organizations working in more than 110 countries to ensure the well-being of children.

**Seminary Consortium for Urban Pastoral Education (SCUPE).** Seminary Consortium for Urban Pastoral Education (www.scupe.com) offers experiential learning that allows the city to touch the heart and the heart to reach out to the city. Academic courses prepare individuals with information and skills to become effective agents of transformation in the urban world. SCUPE partners and collaborates with seminaries, universities, denominations, churches, organizations, community groups and individuals seeking ways to join God's mission in the world with their mission in the city.

**Shelter for Life International.** The mission of Shelter For Life International (www.shelter.org) is to demonstrate God's love by enabling people affected by conflict and disaster to rebuild their communities and restore their lives. SFL believes that sustainable communities are built through the shared involvement of local people who are empowered to be an integral part of the rebuilding process. This process begins through the physical reconstruction of the community: shelters, schools, clinics and infrastructure. SFL restores lives by integrating its reconstruction projects with community-development programs that are designed to enable independence and self-sufficiency. These grassroots programs focus on four key areas: community health, economic development, food security, community projects and capacity building.

**Sojourners/Call to Renewal.** Sojourners/Call to Renewal (www.sojo.net) is an ecumenical Christian ministry whose mission is to articulate the biblical call to social justice, inspiring hope and building a movement to transform individuals, communities, the church and the world.

**Stand Up and Take Action.** Stand Up and Take Action (www.standagainstpoverty.org) is a worldwide call to take action against poverty and inequality and for the Millennium Development Goals. During the twenty-four-hour period between October 16 at 9 p.m. and October 17 at 9 p.m. (Greenwich Mean Time), close to 44 million people broke the world record for "largest stand up" in an attempt to "break the record of broken promises" from governments who have committed to increasing aid toward poverty and global hunger.

**Target Earth.** Target Earth (www.targetearth.org) is a national movement of Christians who are committed to making a difference on the earth. It's a movement of individuals, churches, college fellowships and Christian ministries motivated by the biblical call to be faithful stewards of everything God created—to love our neighbors as ourselves and to care for the earth. Through the efforts of this movement's members, Target Earth is active in fifteen countries—buying up endangered lands, protecting people, saving the jaguar, sharing the love of Jesus, feeding the hungry and reforesting ravaged terrain. It's a movement marked by a spirited desire to live a life of value and believe that Christians have a unique role in today's world that is so pressed by poverty, destruction and violence.

**United Nations Children's Fund.** UNICEF (www.unicef.org) is a part of the global movement for children and focuses its work in child survival and development, basic education and gender equality, HIV/AIDS and children, child protection, and policy advocates and partnerships.

**UN Millennium Project.** The UN Millennium Project (www.unmillenniumproject.org) was commissioned by the United Nations Secretary-General in 2002 to recommend a concrete action plan for the world to reverse the grinding poverty, hunger and disease affecting billions of people. Headed by Professor Jeffrey Sachs, the Millennium Project was an independent advisory body and presented its final report, "Investing in Development: A Practical Plan to Achieve the Millennium Development Goals," to the Secretary-General in January 2005. The Millennium Project was then asked to continue operating in an advisory capacity through the end of 2006.

**Village Care International.** The vision of Village Care International (www.villagecare.com) is that vulnerable children in communities throughout Africa will be safe, healthy, in a loving home, in school and learning, and respected in their community. VCI reaches out to orphans and widows who are in distress as a result of the HIV/AIDS pandemic by mobilizing communities to care for their most vulnerable members and facilitating partnerships with villages and orphanages.

**World Bank.** The World Bank (www.worldbank.org) is a source of financial and technical assistance to developing countries around the world. The bank is made up of two unique development institutions owned by 185 member countries—the International Bank for Reconstruction and Development (IBRD) and the International Development Association (IDA). Each institution plays a different but supportive role in the World Bank's mission of global poverty reduction and the improvement of living standards. The IBRD focuses on middle income and creditworthy poor countries, while IDA focuses on the poorest countries in the world. Together, they provide low-interest loans, interest-free credit and grants to developing countries for education, health, infrastructure, communications and many other purposes.

**World Day to End Extreme Poverty.** Since 1992, October 17 has been officially recognized by the United Nations as the International Day to Eradicate Poverty. The World Day to End Extreme Poverty (www.oct17.org/en) was first celebrated in 1987 by thousands of participants at the Trocadero Human Rights Plaza in Paris, France.

**World Health Organization.** The World Health Organization (www.who.int/en) is the directing and coordinating authority for health within the United Nations' system. It is responsible for providing leadership on global health matters, shaping the health research agenda, setting norms and standards, articulating evidence-based policy options, providing technical support to countries and monitoring and assessing health trends.

**World Hope International.** World Hope International (www.worldhope.org) is a faith-based relief and development organization alleviating suffering and injustice through education, enterprise and community health. The core values of World Hope are transformation, empowerment, sustainability and collaboration.

**World Relief.** World Relief (www.wr.org) is a Christian relief-and-development organization focused on empowering the church to relieve human suffering, poverty and hunger worldwide in the name of Jesus Christ. World Relief believes that the church must be the "hands of Jesus," that local church congregations offer hope and life, and that the church offers the best context for working with the poor in overcoming their lack of opportunity. The local church, with its emphasis on restored relationships, can meet spiritual, social and physical needs. World Relief programs include disaster response, child development, maternal and child health, AIDS, agriculture, microfinance, refugee care, immigrant services and trafficking-victim protection.

**World Vision.** World Vision (www.worldvision.org) is a Christian relief-and-development organization dedicated to helping children and their communities worldwide reach their potential by tackling the causes of poverty. Relationships are the starting point and the end goal of World Vision's work. Through relationships with community leaders, World Vision's staff helps communities set goals that families can achieve by working together. World Vision serves through community development, disaster relief and by responding to global issues like AIDS prevention and care for widows, orphans, and vulnerable children with a compassionate Christian response.

# Appendix 2

## Books

Please note: Not all of the books mentioned in the "For Further Study" sections are included in this appendix.

Aboagye-Mensah, Robert. "The Church, Ethnicity and Democracy." In *The Church, Ethnicity and Democracy*. Edited by David A. Dortey and Vesta Nyarko-Mensah. Accra, Ghana: Christian Council of Ghana, 1995.

Alcorn, Randy. *Money, Possessions, and Eternity*. Wheaton, Ill.: Tyndale House, 2003.

Amoo, Sam G. *The Challenge of Ethnicity and Conflict in Africa. The Need for a New Paradigm*. Emergency Response Division, UN Development Programme, 1997. This booklet is not theological but contains a lot of wisdom from an African perspective.

Athyal, Sakhi. "Women in Mission." In *Doing Mission in Context*. Edited by S. Sumithra and F. Hranghkuma. Bangalore, India: Theological Book Trust, 1995.

Audi, Robert, and Nicholas Wolterstorff. *Religion in the Public Square*. Lanham, Md.: Rowman and Littlefield, 1997.

Bakke, Ray. *A Theology as Big as a City*. Downers Grove, Ill.: InterVarsity Press, 1997. A book from one of the key contemporary advocates of urban holistic/integral ministry in the United States.

Bartholomew, Craig, and Thorsten Moritz, eds. *Christ and Consumerism: A Critical Analysis of the Spirit of the Age*. Carlisle, U.K.: Paternoster, 2005.

Bassau, David, and Russell Mask. *Christian Microenterprise Development*. Oxford: Regnum, 2003. This handbook provides information to help Christian Microenterprise Development (MED) practitioners and donors better understand how to apply Christian MED in ways that build Christ's kingdom. The book draws from literature on secular MED and undertakes eight case studies of Christian MED programs from around the world. It then compares the findings from both to identify the strengths and weaknesses of Christian MED.

Batchelor, Peter. *People in Rural Development*. 2nd ed. Carlisle, U.K.: Paternoster, 1993. A beautiful book full of wisdom, grace and practical advice flowing from forty years' experience of working with the rural poor in Africa.

Batchelor, Simon. *Transforming the Slums by Relationships*. Tearfund Case Study Series, 1996. A case study showing Christian and non-Christian women fighting poverty in hostile circumstances.

Bauckham, Richard. "Human Authority in Creation." In *God and the Crisis of Freedom: Biblical and Contemporary Perspectives*. Louisville, Ky.: Westminster John Knox, 2002. A brilliant historical study of how Christians have viewed their relationship to the rest of creation and how the Christian view is related to the modern view. Shows the inadequacy of Lynn White's famous thesis that the modernist exploitation of creation has its roots in Christianity. The section on the evidence of love and respect for creation in the lives of the saints from the fourth to the fourteenth century is fascinating.

Bebbington, David. "Evangelicals, Theology and Social Transformation." In *Movement for Change: Evangelical Perspectives on Social Transformation*. Edited by David Hilborn. Carlisle, U.K.: Paternoster/ACUTE, 2004. Focused mainly on the United Kingdom, this is a good survey of the traditional evangelical approach to social transformation.

Belshaw, Deryke. "Poverty-Reducing Development Strategies: Accepted and Neglected Challenges." In *Markets, Fair Trade and the Kingdom of God: Essays to Celebrate Traidcraft's 21st Birthday*. Edited by P. Johnson and Chris Sugden. Oxford: Regnum, 2001. This chapter focuses on sub-Saharan Africa and contains a helpful bibliography.

Berry, R. J. *The Care of Creation*. Leicester, U.K.: Inter-Varsity Press, 2000.

Bilezikian, Gilbert. *Beyond Sex Roles: What the Bible Says About a Woman's Place in Church and Family*. Grand Rapids: Baker Academic, 2006. One of the most influential books in my personal journey in understanding God's heart for women.

Blomberg, Craig L. *Neither Poverty Nor Riches: A Biblical Theology of Possessions*. Downers Grove, Ill.: InterVarsity Press, 2001.

Blue, Kevin. *Practical Justice: Living Off-Center in a Self-Centered World*. Downers Grove, Ill.: InterVarsity Press, 2006.

Bono. *On the Move*. Nashville: W Publishing, 2007. Based on his 2006 National Prayer Breakfast speech, his inspiring words, combined with pictures from his travels in Africa makes this book a great introduction to the crisis of extreme poverty and getting involved.

Bragg, Wayne. "From Development to Transformation." In *The Church in Response to Human Need*. Edited by Vinay Samuel and Chris Sugden. Grand Rapids: Eerdmans, 1987.

Bridges, Jerry. *The Discipline of Grace: God's Role and Our Role in the Pursuit of Holiness*. Colorado Springs: NavPress, 1994.

Burger, Delores T. *Women Who Changed the Heart of the City: The Untold Story of the City Rescue Mission Movement*. Grand Rapids: Kregel, 1997.

Canales, Isaac. "Alien Nation: One Pastor's Perspective on the Immigration Debate—and Immigration Opportunity." *Leadership Journal* 28, no. 4 (fall 2007): p. 46 <www.christianityto day.com/le/2007/004/21.46.html>.

Carr, Jeff. "Justice for Immigrants." *Sojourners Magazine* 35, no. 7 (July 2006): p. 9 <www.sojo. net/index.cfm?action=magazine.article&issue=Soj0607&article=060741a>.

Cassidy, Michael. *A Witness Forever*. London: Hodder and Stoughton Religious, 1995.

Chester, Tim. *Good News to the Poor: Sharing the Gospel Through Social Involvement*. Leicester,

U.K.: Inter-Varsity Press, 2004. A powerful case for integral mission.

Claiborne, Shane. *The Irresistible Revolution*. Grand Rapids: Zondervan, 2006.

Cooper, Tim. *Green Christianity*. London: Spire, 1990. Detailed, scientifically credible, evangelical framework for engagement with ecological issues, including useful biblical engagement with other worldviews.

Crossan, John Dominic. *Jesus: A Revolutionary Biography*. New York: HarperCollins, 1995.

Day, Dorothy. *The Long Loneliness*. New York: HarperCollins, 1952.

Duncan, M. *Costly Mission, Following Christ in the Slums*. Monrovia, Calif.: MARC, 1996.

Easterly, William. *The White Man's Burden: Why the West's Efforts to Aid the Rest Have Done so Much Ill and So Little Good*. New York: Penguin, 2006. Easterly's response to Sachs's ideas. Presents arguments as to why the United States shouldn't increase the budget by 1 percent to help the world's poor.

Eaton, Jenny, and Kate Etue, comps. *The aWAKE Project: Uniting Against the African AIDS Crisis*. Nashville: W Publishing, 2002. Contributors include Nelson Mandela, Senator Bill Frist, Desmond Tutu, Jimmy Carter, Jeffrey Sachs, Jesse Helms, Kofi Annan, Out of Eden, Dikembe Mutombo, President George W. Bush and Danny Glover.

Elliott, Charles. *Comfortable Compassion: "Poverty," Power and the Church*. London: Hodder and Stoughton, 1987.

Engel, James F., and William A Dyrness. *Changing the Mind of Missions*. Downers Grove, Ill.: InterVarsity Press, 2000.

Evans, David, with Kathryn Scherer. *Creating Space for Strangers: Thinking Afresh about Mission and the Church*. Leicester, U.K.: Inter-Varsity Press, 2004. A book of inspiring stories showing how churches can affect their societies for good.

Evans, Mary J. *Women in the Bible*. Carlisle, U.K.: Paternoster, 1984. A biblical defense of the "Equal Status, Different Function, No Hierarchy" approach.

Friedman, Stan. "Church Comes to Aid of Abandoned Workers." Evangelical Covenant Church site, November 20, 2008 <www.covchurch.org/cov/news/item6714>.

de Gruchy, John W. *Reconciliation: Restoring Justice*. London, U.K.: SCM Press, 2002.

Gnanakan, Ken. *God's World*. London: SPCK, 1999. A study guide on creation and environment in the contemporary context with practical responses.

Gordon, Graham. *What If You Got Involved? Taking a Stand Against Social Injustice*. Carlisle, U.K.: Paternoster, 2003. "A practical book for those who want to go beyond merely having an opinion on injustice and want to do something about it."

Goudzwaard, B., and H. de Lange. *Beyond Poverty and Affluence*. Grand Rapids: Eerdmans, 1995.

Grigg, Viv. *Companion to the Poor*. Monrovia, Calif.: MARC, 1990. A challenging book based on the experience of living as a missionary in the squatter community of Tatalon, a slum district of Manila.

———. *Cry of the Urban Poor*. Monrovia, Calif.: MARC, 1992. Develops the main themes of

*Companion to the Poor*. The central thesis is that forming communities of believers in the slums is essential to addressing the injustices that keep the poor in the slums.

Hanks, Thomas. *For God So Loved the Third World*. Eugene, Ore.: Wipf & Stock, 2000.

Hanson Bourke, Dale. *The Skeptics Guide to the Global AIDS Crisis: Tough Questions*. Waynesboro, Ga.: Authentic Media, 2004.

————. *The Skeptics Guide to the Global Poverty*. Colorado Springs: Authentic Media, 2007.

Harris, Cynthia M. *Eleanor Roosevelt: A Biography*. Westport, Conn.: Greenwood, 2007.

Hauerwas, Stanley, and William H. Willimon. *Resident Aliens: Life in the Christian Colony*. Nashville: Abingdon, 1989.

Haugen, Gary. *Good News About Injustice: A Witness of Courage in a Hurting World*. Downers Grove, Ill.: InterVarsity Press, 2009. On the basis of strong biblical exposition and historical precedent, this book provides practical help with involvement in justice issues on the side of the weak and vulnerable.

Hertz, Noreena. *The Debt Threat: How Debt is Destroying the Developing World*. New York: HarperCollins, 2005.

Heltzel, Peter Goodwin. *Jesus and Justice: Evangelicals, Race, and American Politics*. New Haven, Conn.: Yale University Press, 2009.

Hughes, Dewi. *Castrating Culture: A Christian Perspective on Ethnic Identity from the Margins*. Carlisle, U.K.: Paternoster, 2002. The author argues "that ethnic identity is not the cause of violent conflict but rather a gift from our creative God that needs to be preserved and nurtured."

Hughes, Dewi, with Matthew Bennett. *God of the Poor: A Biblical Vision of God's Present Rule*. Carlisle, U.K.: OM Publishing, 1998. This book argues that the church, as the visible community of God, is given the task of blessing the poor. Asserting that what people do flows from what they believe, Hughes explores the place of religion in perpetuating poverty. From this foundation, kingdom principles are applied to the world of economics, politics, ethnic identity, population growth and gender.

Jacobsen, Dennis A. *Doing Justice*. Minneapolis: Fortress, 2001.

Johnstone, P. "The Kingdom in Relation to the Church and the World." In *Word and Deed, Evangelism and Social Responsibility*. Edited by Bruce Nicholls. Exeter, U.K.: Paternoster, 1985.

Jones, James. *Jesus and the Earth*. London: SPCK, 2003. A strong biblical case for the care of creation by the current bishop of Liverpool.

Kapolyo, Joe. "Social Transformation as a Missional Imperative; Evangelicals and Development since Lausanne." In *Movement for Change: Evangelical Perspectives on Social Transformation*. Edited by David Hilborn. Carlisle, U.K.: Paternoster/ACUTE, 2004. This chapter contains a sobering section on the problem of development that every nongovernmental organization should consider carefully. It argues that development often benefits the developer more than those that are perceived to be in need of development.

Karelis, Charles H. *The Persistence of Poverty: Why the Economics of the Well-Off Can't Help the*

*Poor.* New Haven, Conn.: Yale University Press, 2007.

Kessler-Harris, Alice. *In Pursuit of Equity: Women, Men, and the Quest for Economic Citizenship in Twentieth-Century America.* New York: Oxford University Press, 2001.

Kim, Sebastian C. H., and Krickwin C. Marak. *Good News to the Poor: The Challenge to the Church.* Celhi, India: CMS/ISPCK, 1997. The papers from a consultation specifically on holistic/integral mission convened by the Centre for Mission Studies of Union Biblical Seminary, Pune, India.

———. *The Grand Rapids Report, Evangelism and Social Responsibility.* Exeter, U.K.: Paternoster, 1982. Though not totally satisfactory this report stands as a very significant and historic document on the evangelical understanding of the relationship between evangelism and social responsibility.

King, Louis L. "Mother Whittemore's Miracles," *Alliance Witness,* January 21, 1987.

Klay, Robin K. *Counting the Cost: The Economics of Christian Stewardship.* Grand Rapids: Eerdmans, 1986.

Kreider, Carl. *The Rich and the Poor: A Christian Perspective on Global Economics.* Scottdale, Penn.: Herald Press, 1987.

Kuzmič, Peter. "The Church and the Kingdom of God." In *The Church, God's Agent for Change.* Edited by Bruce Nicholls. Exeter, U.K.: Paternoster, 1985.

Lloyd, Rhiannon, with Kristine Bresser. *Healing the Wounds of Ethnic Conflict. The Role of the Church in Healing, Forgiveness and Reconciliation,* 2000. This booklet is the content of a seminar run by Rhiannon Lloyd and partners that has brought healing and blessing to many people who have suffered as a result of ethnic conflict particularly in Rwanda and South Africa.

Magnunson, Norris. *Salvation in the Slums: Evangelical Social Work 1865-1920.* Grand Rapids: Baker, 1977.

Mangalwade, Vishal. *Truth and Social Reform.* London: Spire, 1989. A convincing argument for holistic/integral mission from an Indian who has been intimately involved in serving the poor in Christ's name.

Marak, Krickwin C., and Atul Y. Aghamkar. *Ecological Challenge and Christian Mission.* Delhi: ISPCK, 1998.

Martin-Schramm, James B., and Robert L. Stivers. *Christian Environmental Ethics: A Case Method Approach.* Ecology and Justice series. Maryknoll, N.Y.: Orbis, 2003.

Mbugua, Judy, ed. *Our Time has Come; African Christian Women Address the Issues of Today.* Grand Rapids: Baker, 1994. An excellent introduction written by African Christian women on the problems and opportunities they face.

McAfee Brown, Robert. *Speaking of Christianity: Practical Compassion, Social Justice, and Other Wonders.* Louisville, Ky.: Westminster John Knox, 1997.

McCloughry, Roy. *Men and Masculinity.* London: Hodder and Stoughton, 1992. Perceptive analysis of how men should react to the changing roles of women in society.

McCloughry, Roy, and Carol Bebawi. *AIDS: A Christian Response.* Cambridge: Grove, 1987.

Medecins Sans Frontieres. *In the Shadow of Just Wars*. Ithaca, N.Y.: Cornell University Press, 2004. A collection of essays that covers the international response to a dozen humanitarian crises—and the successes and failures of each response.

Menzel, Peter, and Faith d'Aluisio. *Hungry Planet*. Berkeley, Calif.: Ten Speed Press, 2007.

Metzger, Paul Louis. *Consuming Jesus: Beyond Race and Class Divisions in a Consumer Church*. Grand Rapids: Eerdmans, 2007.

Milburn Thompson, Joseph. *Justice and Peace: A Christian Primer*. Maryknoll, N.Y.: Orbis, 2003.

Myers, Bryant L. *Walking with the Poor: Principles and Practices of Transformational Development*. Maryknoll, N.Y.: Orbis, 1999. This is the most comprehensive attempt to date to marry a thoroughly evangelical theology to the best practice in development. A must for anyone wishing to understand contemporary development theory and how it can be utilized and critiqued by evangelicals working with those who are poor.

———. *Working with the Poor: New Insights and Learnings from Development Practitioners*. Monrovia, Calif.: MARC, 1999.

Myers, Ched. *The Biblical Vision of Sabbath Economics*. Washington, D.C.: Tell the World, 2002.

Nicholls, Alex, and Charlotte Opal. *Fair Trade: Market-Driven Ethical Consumption*. Thousand Oaks, Calif.: SAGE, 2005.

Nicholls, Bruce, ed. *In Word and Deed, Evangelism and Social Responsibility*. Exeter, U.K.: Paternoster, 1985. The papers of the World Evangelical Fellowship/Lausanne Committee for World Evangelization Consultation on the Relationship between evangelism and social responsibility held at Grand Rapids, Michigan, in June 1982.

Nicholls, Bruce J., and Christopher S. Raj. *Mission as Witness and Justice: An Indian Perspective*. New Delhi: TRACI, 1991. The volume is divided into three sections—"Mission and the Spiritual Realities," "Mission and Evangelism" and "Mission and Justice." Section three deals with issues such as shalom, power, human rights corruption and dowry.

Nicholls, Bruce J., and Beulah R. Woods, eds. *Sharing the Good News with the Poor: A Reader for Concerned Christians*. Carlisle, U.K.: Paternoster; Grand Rapids: Baker, 1996. An attempt to "discern the theology of evangelization that is expressed in the practice of Christian ministries among the poor." There are three sections to this multi-author volume: "The Poor in Biblical Story," "Reflections on Good News as Word and Deed" and "Sharing the Good News as Mission and Witness." Theoretical chapters are interspersed with case studies.

Payne, Michael W. "Mission and Global Ethnic Violence Transformation." *Transformation* 19, no. 3 (2002). Argues that the gospel is the way to transcend exclusive ethnicity, but leaves one wondering whether there is any meaning to an inherited identity—especially if one does not belong to the globalizing Anglo-American identity. Available at <www.ocms.ac.uk/transformation/results_authors.php?mm_aut=515>.

Perkins, John. *Beyond Charity: The Call to Christian Community Development*. Grand Rapids: Baker, 1993. An inspiring book by one of the great elder statesman of Christian social action in our day.

————. *A Quiet Revolution*. London: Marshalls, 1985. Contains a wonderful description of a holistic church coming into being in the midst of the black struggle for justice in the United States. Unfortunately out of print but appears in Amazon's used-book list.

————. *Resurrecting Hope: Powerful Stories of How God is Moving to Reach Our Cities*. Ventura, Calif.: Regal, 1995. A vision of the possible scope of holistic/integral mission in an urban context. The book reveals a link between holistic mission and church growth.

————. *With Justice for All*. Ventura, Calif.: Regal, 1982.

————. ed. *Restoring At-Risk Communities*. Grand Rapids: Baker, 1995.

Pierce, Ronald, Rebecca Merill Groothuis and Gordon Fee, eds. *Discovering Biblical Equality: Complementarity Without Hierarchy*. Downers Grove, Ill.: InterVarsity Press, 2004. The most comprehensive work on the egalitarian perspective.

Pilarczyk, Daniel E. *Bringing Forth Justice: Basics for Just Christians*. Cincinnati: St. Anthony Messenger Press, 1999.

Piper, John, and Wayne Grudem, eds. *Recovering Biblical Manhood and Womanhood*. Wheaton, Ill.: Crossway, 1991. A biblical defense of the "equal status, different function" approach.

Rude, Anna Elizabeth. *The Sheppard-Towner Act in Relation to Public Health*. Washington, D.C.: Government Printing Office, 1921.

Sachs, Jeffrey. *The End of Poverty: Economic Possibilities for Our Time*. New York: Penguin, 2005. Outlines the various issues that contribute to the poverty trap of the one billion people living on less than $1 a day, as well as some cheap and easy solutions to address the problem.

Samuel, Vinay, and Chris Sugden, eds. *The Church in Response to Human Need*. Grand Rapids: Eerdmans, 1987. The revised proceedings of a conference held at Wheaton in 1983 under the auspices of the World Evangelical Fellowship. The papers consider "whether the Bible indicates any method for ministry among the poor; the place of the poor in God's plan; God's purpose and the movement of human history; the nature of the gospel of the kingdom; and the interrelation of the gospel and human culture." It also contains the statement produced by the consultation titled "Transformation: The Church in Response to Human Need."

Schaeffer, Francis. *He Is There and He Is Not Silent*. Carol Stream, Ill.: Tyndale, 1972.

————. *Pollution and the Death of Man: The Christian View of Ecology*. Wheaton, Ill.: Crossway, 1992. A prophetic book that is yet to be surpassed in terms of the contrast it draws between Christian and non-Christian worldviews in relation to nature. It also contains useful articles on common non-Christian perceptions of the Christian attitude to nature.

Seaton, Chris. *Whose Earth?* Cambridge: Crossway, 1992. A popular and passionate introduction to Christian responsibility for the care of creation.

Sen, Amartya. *Development as Freedom*. New York: Anchor Books, 1999. Outlines the argument that civic and political freedoms are necessary for development to be sustainable.

Sider, Ronald J. *Good News and Good Works: A Theology for the Whole Gospel*. Grand Rapids: Baker, 1999.

———. *Rich Christians in an Age of Hunger*. 2nd ed. London, U.K.: Hodder, 1997. With over 250,000 copies sold, this is the classic statement of the case for integral mission.

———. *The Scandal of the Evangelical Conscience*. Grand Rapids: Baker, 2005. Addressed to the big and powerful born-again/evangelical constituency in the United States, this book should serve as a warning to the growing evangelical movement in the United Kingdom.

Sider, Ronald J., and Diane Knippers, eds. *Toward an Evangelical Public Policy*. Grand Rapids: Baker, 2005.

Sider, Ronald J., Philip N. Olson, and Heidi R. Unruh. *Churches that Make a Difference: Reaching Your Community with Good News and Good Works*. Grand Rapids: Baker, 2002. This book is based on a careful analysis of fifteen urban churches committed to holistic/integral mission. Most of the churches are in Philadelphia. Though the book is obviously American, many of the principles for helping a church to "move into a life-changing outreach of holistic ministry" can be applied anywhere.

Simon, Paul. *Tapped Out*. New York: Welcome Rain, 1998. The late Illinois Senator outlines the global water crisis and how it will affect us in the United States.

Sittser, Gerald. *A Grace Disguised: How the Soul Grows Through Loss*. Grand Rapids: Zondervan, 1998.

Sleeth, J. Matthew. *Serve God, Save the Planet*. Grand Rapids: Zondervan, 2007.

Slessarev, Helene. *The Betrayal of the Urban Poor*. Philadelphia: Temple University Press, 1997.

Smith, Stephen C. *Ending Global Poverty: A Guide to What Works*. New York: Palgrave Macmillan, 2005. Smith outlines the issues related to poverty and what readers can do to help overcome the crisis.

Stiglitz, Joseph E. *Making Globalization Work*. New York: W. W. Norton, 2006. Covers how Western governments and international financial institutions can reform to be more equitable to the rest of the world. Covers the concepts of debt, fair trade and more.

Storkey, Alan. *Jesus and Politics: Confronting the Powers*. Grand Rapids: Baker Academic, 2005. A substantial and convincing challenge to the idea that Jesus and politics have nothing to do with each other.

———. *Transforming Economics*. London: SPCK, 1986. A good introduction to some of the key economic issues from a Christian perspective.

Storkey, Elaine. *What's Right with Feminism?* London: SPCK, 1989. An analysis of the merits and problems of feminism from an evangelical perspective.

Stott, John. *New Issues Facing Christians Today*. London: Marshal Pickering, 1999. A magisterial volume on the many aspects of Christian social responsibility.

Thomas, Cal, and Ed Dobson. *Blinded by Might*. Grand Rapids: Zondervan, 1999.

Thomas, Jacob. *From Lausanne to Manila: Evangelical Social Thought: Models of Mission and the Social Relevance of the Gospel*. Delhi, India: ISPCK, 2003.

Thurman, Howard. *Jesus and the Disinherited*. Boston: Beacon Press, 1976.

Tripp, Linda. "A Voice for Women." *Transformation* 6, no. 2 (1992). A concise, accurate introduction.

Tutu, Desmond. *No Future Without Forgiveness*. New York: Doubleday, 2000.

Valerio, Ruth. *L Is for Lifestyle: Christian Living That Doesn't Cost the Earth*. Leicester, U.K.: Inter-Varsity Press, 2004. An A to Z of how we can consume in a way that is honoring to God.

Van Til, Kent A. *Less Than Two Dollars a Day: A Christian View of World Poverty and the Free Market*. Grand Rapids: Eerdmans, 2007.

Volf, Miroslav. *Exclusion and Embrace: Theological Reflections in the Wake of "Ethnic Cleansing."* Grand Rapids: Zondervan, 1994.

Wallis, Jim. *The Call to Conversion: Recovering the Gospel for these Times*. San Francisco: Harper, 1992. A prophetic book.

———. *Faith Works*. New York: Random House, 2000.

———. *God's Politics*. New York: HarperCollins, 2005.

———. *Living God's Politics*. New York: HarperCollins, 2006.

———. *The Soul of Politics, A Practical and Prophetic Vision for Change*. London: Fount, 1994. An attempt to find a biblically motivated political route that transcends the sterile conflict of Left and Right.

Wallis, Joy. *The Woman Behind the Collar: The Pioneering Journey of an Episcopal Priest*. New York: Crossroad, 2004.

Westlake, David, and Esther Stansfield. *Lift the Label: The Hidden Cost of Our Lifestyle*. Milton Keynes, U.K.: Spring Harvest/Authentic, 2004. A biblical, passionate case for economic living in obedience to God.

Wheeler, Sondra Ely. *Wealth as Peril and Obligation*. Grand Rapids: Eerdmans, 1995.

Wilson, William Julius. *When Work Disappears*. New York: Vintage Books, 1996.

Whittemore, Emma M. *Records of Modern Miracles*. Toronto: Missions of Biblical Education, 1947.

Wolffe, John. "Historical Models of Evangelical Transformation." In *Movement for Change: Evangelical Perspectives on Social Transformation*. Edited by David Hilborn. Carlisle, U.K.: Paternoster/ACUTE, 2004. Shows that evangelical social transformation has historically been affected by churches, committed Christian communities, individuals and panevangelical agencies.

Wright, Nicholas Thomas. *Evil and the Justice of God*. Downers Grove, Ill.: IVP Books, 2006.

Yamamori, Tetsunao, and René Padilla. *The Local Church, Agent of Transformation: An Ecclesiology of Integral Mission*. Buenos Aires: Kairos, 2004. A welcome translation of some of the excellent material on church and development/social transformation published in Spanish.

Yancey, Philip. *Disappointment with God: Three Questions No One Asks Aloud*. Grand Rapids: Zondervan, 1988.

———. *What's So Amazing About Grace?* Grand Rapids: Zondervan, 2003.

Yoder, J. Howard. *The Politics of Jesus*. 2nd ed. Grand Rapids: Eerdmans, 1994.

Yunus, Muhammad. *Banker to the Poor: Micro-Lending and the Battle Against World Poverty*. New York: PublicAffairs, 2007. 2006 Nobel Peace Prize winner's memoir about his experiences with microcredit with the Grameen Bank.

# Appendix 3

## Documentaries and Unrated Movies

Please note that many of the movies listed in this appendix (and the next) are about difficult subjects, and they may contain language, images of violence or other disturbing images. Additional documentaries and movies are listed in the text of this book.

*America Beyond the Color Line with Henry Louis Gates Jr.* Wall to Wall Television, 2002. Through numerous personal interviews, this TV miniseries documentary has professor Henry Louis Gates Jr. examining the past, present and future of black/white race relations in the United States.

*Attack on Terror: The FBI vs. the Ku Klux Klan.* Quinn Martin Productions, 1975. In this TV movie, after three civil-rights workers are murdered in Mississippi in 1964, a team of FBI agents is sent to find the killers.

*Bamako.* Dir. Abderrahmane Sissako. Louverture Films, 2006. A village in Africa puts on a mock trial against the World Bank for crimes against the village. Danny Glover produces. Starring Aissa Maiga, Maimouna Helene Diarra. Some parts are in a foreign language with English subtitles.

*Born into Brothels: Calcutta's Red Light Kids.* Red Light Films, 2004. This film won the Academy Award for the best documentary feature. It is a tribute to the resiliency of childhood and the restorative power of art. *Born into Brothels* is a portrait of several unforgettable children who live in the red-light district of Calcutta, where their mothers work as prostitutes. Zana Briski, a New York-based photographer, gives each of the children a camera and teaches them to look at the world with new eyes.

Breathe Compassion Video: *Changing the World One Woman at a Time.* Lynne Hybels hosts this new video, which I produced, while at Willow Creek Community Church from the 2005 Women's Conference. Three amazing women, Dale Hansen Bourke, Nancy Zirkel and Pearl Willis, tell their stories to inspire all. Dale has been an executive in the Christian publishing industry and has served on the boards of World Vision, International Justice Mission and other major humanitarian organizations. Nancy is a Willow Creek attendee who has developed a program (Hope Parties) that is implemented internationally through World Vision. She has also done amazing projects with the Promiseland ministry, such as raising almost $15,000 for kids in Africa. Pearl is the executive director of Roseland Good News Day Care, a daycare for high school, college and working moms in an impoverished neighborhood on the south side of Chicago. Visit www.willowcreek.com/wca_prodsb.asp?invtid=PR27369 to order the video.

*Chicano! History of the Mexican-American Civil Rights Movement.* Galan Productions, 1996. This four-part, TV-documentary series tells the story of the Mexican American Civil Rights Movement, one of the least studied social movements of the 1960s. It encompassed a broad cross section of issues—from restoration of land grants, to farm workers rights, to enhanced education, to voting and political rights.

*A Closer Walk.* Dir. Robert Bilheimer. Worldwide Documentaries, 2005. Full-length film on the global AIDS crisis. Explores the relationship between health, human rights and outlines the need for global action. Narrated by Glenn Close and Will Smith. Includes interviews with widely recognized figures such as the Dalai Lama and singer Bono.

*The Color of Fear.* Dir. Lee Mun Wah. 1994. A documentary about the pain and anguish that racism has caused in the lives of eight North American men of Asian, European, Latino and African descent. Out of their confrontations and struggles to understand and trust each other emerges an emotional and insightful portrayal into the type of dialogue most of us fear, but hope will happen sometime in our lifetime.

*Debt of the Dictators: How Multinational Banks Supported Dictators in DR Congo, South Africa, The Philippines, and Argentina.* INSIGHT, 2005. This film asks whether it is just that people in impoverished countries are asked to repay the debts of former dictators. Copies can be ordered from Jubilee USA for $12—contact Nathan@jubileeusa.org or 202-546-4470.

*The End of Poverty.* Dir. Philippe Diaz. Cinema Libre Studio, 2008. A discourse about why poverty exists when there is so much wealth in the world. It is helpful for understanding the U.S. economic system and the foundations of today's global economy. Featuring John Christentson, William Easterly, Martin Sheen and John Perkins among others.

*4 Little Girls.* Dir. Spike Lee. 40 Acres and a Mule Filmworks, 1997. A documentary of the notorious racial terrorist bombing of an African American church in Birmingham, Alabama, in 1963 during the civil rights movement. It tells the story of the four little girls who were killed; a single explosion rocked a community and awakened a sleeping nation.

*The Girl in the Café.* Dir. David Yates. BBC Wales, 2005. Two people meet in a café and attend the G8 Summit together, romance blooms. Their goals at the Summit are contradictory. Good movie for information on the Millennium Development Goals. Starring Kelly Macdonald and Bill Nighy.

*The Ku Klux Klan: A Secret History.* Bill Brummel Productions, 1998. Since the days following the Civil War, the Ku Klux Klan has preached a gospel of hate, intolerance and exclusion. This TV documentary tells the history of the KKK from the Reconstruction Era through the twentieth century.

*Let Freedom Sing: How Music Inspired the Civil Rights Movement.* Brainstorm Media Productions, 2009. For a brief moment in time, a few daring, innovative musicians stood at the crossroads of a revolution in music and culture. Across one of the most turbulent periods in American history—from the early civil rights era to Watergate—they brought music, medium and message together as never before, composing a soundtrack perfectly tuned to the tempo and pulse of its time.

*Life and Debt*. Dir. Stephanie Black. Tuff Gong Pictures, 2001. A documentary on the affects of the International Monetary Fund, World Bank and other international organizations work in Jamaica. Author Jamaica Kincaid narrates with Belinda Becker to a reggae soundtrack that includes songs by Bob Marley, Ziggy Marley, Mutubaruka and Peter Tosh. Starring Jamaica Kincaid and Belinda Becker.

*Save Our History: Voices of Civil Rights*. 2005. Tells the story of the foot soldiers during the civil rights movement and gives voice to participants from different parts of the country and from different perspectives.

*3 Needles*. Dir. Thom Fitzgerald. Bigfoot Entertainment, 2005. Documents the spread of AIDS in Asia, Africa and North America through the lives of three people affected by the disease. Starring Stockard Channing, Lucy Liu and Sandra Oh.

*Unfinished Business: The Japanese-American Internment Cases*. Dir. Steven Okazaki. 1986. During World War II, more than 110,000 Japanese Americans were interned within the United States. Three young men served jail sentences for violating laws aimed at Japanese Americans. For forty years, these men were imprisoned until their sentences were overturned.

# Appendix 4

## Mainstream Movies

*Amistad*. Dream Works, 1997. Amistad is about a 1839 mutiny onboard a slave ship that is traveling toward the northeast coast of America. Much of the story involves a courtroom drama about the slave who led the revolt. Rated R.

*Betrayed*. CST Telecommunications, 1988. The story of a woman getting to know a family with some deeply embedded secrets. As she gets to know them she discovers the horror of racism, beyond what she could even imagine, and she is forced to make a very difficult choice. Rated R.

*The Color Purple*. Dir. Steven Spielberg. Warner Brothers, 1985. This film follows the life of Celie, a young black girl growing up in the early 1900s. Rated PG-13.

*The Constant Gardener*. Dir. Fernando Meirelles. Potboiler Productions, 2005. A British man in Africa discovers shocking evidence of the horrible consequences of some of his country's actions in the country. Starring Ralph Fiennes and Rachel Weisz. Some parts have English subtitles. Rated R for language, some violent images and sexual content/nudity.

*Crash*. Dir. Paul Haggis. Bob Yari Productions, 2005. Several stories interweave during two days in Los Angeles involving a collection of characters: a police detective with a drugged out mother and a thieving younger brother; two car thieves who are constantly theorizing on society and race; the white district attorney and his irritated and pampered wife; a racist white veteran cop (caring for a sick father at home) who disgusts his more idealistic younger partner; a successful Hollywood director and his wife who must deal with the racist cop; a Persian-immigrant father who buys a gun to protect his shop; and a Hispanic locksmith and his young daughter who is afraid of bullets. Rated R.

*A Day Without a Mexican*. Eye on the Ball Films, 2004. One day California wakes up and not a single Latino is left in the state. They have all inexplicably disappeared; chaos, tragedy and comedy quickly ensue. Rated R.

*Eat, Drink, Man, Woman*. Central Motion Pictures Corporation, 1994. A senior chef lives with his three grown daughters; the middle one finds her future plans affected by unexpected events and the life changes of the other household members. Unrated.

*The Great Debaters*. Dir. Denzel Washington. Harpo Films, 2007. A drama based on the true story of Melvin B. Tolson, a professor at Wiley College, an African American college in Texas. In 1935 he inspired students to form the school's first debate team, which went on to challenge Harvard in the national championship. Rated PG-13.

*Guess Who's Coming to Dinner?* Columbia Pictures, 1967. An affluent Caucasian couple get very upset when their daughter brings home a fiancé who is black. Stars Spencer Tracey, Katherine Hepburn and Sidney Poitier. Rated PG.

*Hotel Rwanda.* Dir. Terry George. United Artists, 2005. The story of an ordinary man in Rwanda who uses the hotel he manages to save more than one thousand refugees. Starring Don Cheadle, Sophie Okonedo, Nick Nolte and Joaquin Phoenix. Some parts have English subtitles. Rated PG-13 for violence, disturbing images and brief strong language.

*The Hurricane.* 1999. Denzel Washington plays Rubin "Hurricane" Carter, a man in the prime of his boxing career who finds himself wrongfully convicted of murder. Sentenced to life in prison, Carter's published memoir, *The Sixteenth Round,* inspires a teenager from Brooklyn and three Canadian activists who believe in the truth, to join forces with Carter to prove his innocence. Their extraordinary efforts ultimately secure his release, leaving "Hurricane" to sum up his twenty years in prison for a crime he didn't commit by simply stating, "Hate got me into this place, love got me out." Rated R.

*To Kill a Mockingbird.* Brentwood Productions, 1962. Atticus Finch, a lawyer in the Depression-era South, defends a black man against an undeserved rape charge and his kids against prejudice. Rated PG.

*The Long Walk Home.* New Visions Pictures, 1990. Two women (black and white) in 1955 Montgomery, Alabama, must decide what they are going to do in response to the famous bus boycott lead by Martin Luther King Jr. Starring Sissy Spacek and Whoopi Goldberg. Rated PG.

*Malcolm X.* Dir. Spike Lee. 40 Acres and a Mule Filmworks, 1992. The biopic of the controversial and influential Black Nationalist leader Malcolm X. Starring Denzel Washington. Rated PG-13.

*Mississippi Burning.* Orion Pictures, 1988. Two FBI agents with wildly different styles arrive in Mississippi to investigate the disappearance of some civil rights activists. Starring Gene Hackman and William Dafoe. Rated R.

*Remember the Titans.* 2000. A black man is hired to coach a high school football team in Virginia during the early 1970s, a time when the school has just been integrated to allow blacks into the school. Racism is high, and many white players threaten to sit out until he is replaced. During training camp, the white and black players learn how to get along and even become friends. The Titans go undefeated through a season of turmoil and confusion. Just before the state championship, the captain gets in a car crash and can't play. Can they still win the match? Rated PG.

*Roots.* David Wolper Productions, 1977. A saga of African American life, based on Alex Haley's family history. Kunta Kinte is abducted from his African village, sold into slavery and taken to America. He makes several escape attempts until he is finally caught and maimed. He marries Bell, his plantation's cook, and they have a daughter, Kizzy, who is eventually sold away from them. Kizzy has a son by her new master, and the boy grows up to become

Chicken George, a legendary cock fighter who leads his family into freedom. Throughout the series, the family observes notable events in U.S. history, such as the Revolutionary and Civil Wars, slave uprisings and emancipation. Unrated.

*Slumdog Millionaire*. Celador Films, 2008. A Mumbai teen, who grew up in the slums, becomes a contestant on the Indian version of *Who Wants to Be a Millionaire?* He is arrested under suspicion of cheating, and while being interrogated, events from his life history are shown to explain why he knows the answers. Rated R.

*Snow Falling on Cedars*. Universal Pictures, 1999. Carl, a fisherman in the waters off Washington state, has been found dead, drowned in his own nets, but with a serious head wound. Was he murdered? Postwar anti-Japanese sentiments are still running high, and a murder suspect is found in the local Japanese American community: Kazuo, another fisherman, who had a grudge against Carl's family. Ishmael, the small town's newspaperman, may have the information that would acquit Kazuo, but can he put his jilted love for Hatsue (Kazuo's wife) aside? Rated PG-13.

*A Time to Kill*. Regency Enterprises, 1996. A young lawyer defends a black man accused of murdering two white men who raped his ten-year-old daughter, which sparks the rebirth of the KKK. From a novel by John Grisham. Rated R.

*Yesterday*. Dir. Darrell Roodt. Distant Horizon, 2004. A mother in an African village finds out she is HIV positive and struggles with how it affects her husband and daughter. Starring Leleti Khumalo and Lihle Mvelase. English subtitles. Rated R for pervasive, strong violence.

# Notes

### Introduction
[1]This book is not a "Willow Creek" handbook for social justice, but many of its ideas were birthed as a result of my ministry there.
[2]Much of the language used in ministry profiles and action exercises is taken directly from the website of the organization being highlighted.

### Chapter 1: God's Heart for Justice
[1]Theologically both work and faith are deeply related to action and righteousness, respectively, although they are not completely synonymous. Consider the verses in Scripture that talk about the relationship between faith and righteousness: "Abraham believed God" (i.e., had faith), "and it was credited to him as righteousness." (Rom 4:3). Consider also Hebrews 11:7 in regard to Noah: "By his faith he condemned the world and became heir of the righteousness that is in keeping with faith."
[2]There is substantial scholarship around the meaning of *mišpāṭ* in the Old Testament. Consider reading the perspectives voiced in Sylvia Huberman Scholnick, "The Meaning of Mispat in the Book of Job," *The Journal of Biblical Literature* 101, no. 4 (1982): 521-29.
[3]*The American Heritage Dictionary of the English Language*, 4th ed.
[4]"Diðkaiov," in StudyLight.org's New Testament Greek Lexicon <www.studylight.org/lex/grk/browse .cgi?letter=d&sn=201&pn=11>.
[5]The only time *dikaios* is translated as "justice" is in relation to the way that slaves should be treated. The holding of slaves is certainly a justice issue and is indirectly spoken against in the New Testament. The book of Philemon suggests the holding of slaves is not what God intended when he commanded us to love our neighbors as ourselves.
[6]Consider using the United Bible Society's *Greek New Testament*, 4th ed. Study aids like a lexicon and Greek dictionaries can be found online through StudyLight at www.studylight.org.
[7]John Perkins is a civil rights hero and Christian leader who founded the Christian Community Development Association (CCDA), as well as several other ministries that advance the gospel and care for the poor.
[8]John Perkins, *Quiet Revolution* (Waco, Tex.: Word, 1976), p. 141.
[9]This definition was created with the support of the social justice group that I led at Willow Creek in 2005.
[10]See Ched Myers, "God Speed the Year of Jubilee!" *Sojourners* 27, no. 3 (1998): 24-28.
[11]Mark Labberton, "Imagining Justice," *Prism*, March-April 2007, p. 27.
[12]Gary Haugen, *Good News About Injustice* (Downer Grove, Ill.: InterVarsity Press, 1999), p. 118.
[13]Jeff Reed, in a personal conversation on September 26, 2008.
[14]U.S. Census Bureau. The medium income per household member of those in nonfamily households was $29,083. See <www.census.gov/prod/2007pubs/p60-233.pdf>.
[15]Martin Luther King Jr., quoted in Stephen Oates, *Let the Trumpet Sound* (New York: Harper Collins, 1993), p. 84.
[16]Ibid.
[17]Nicholas Wolterstorff, "The Contours of Justice: An Ancient Call for Shalom," in *God and the Victim: Theological Reflections on Evil, Victimization, Justice, and Forgiveness*, ed. Lisa Barnes Lampman and Michelle D. Shattuck (Grand Rapids: Eerdmans, 1999), p. 113.
[18]Lowell Noble, *From Oppression to Jubilee Justice* (Jackson, Miss.: Llumina Press, 2007), p. 58.
[19]Lowell Noble, *The Kingdom of God Versus the Cosmos: Justice and Shalom Replace Ethnocentrism and Oppression* (Riceville, Iowa: Spring Arbor College, 1997), p. 28.
[20]Haugen, *Good News About Injustice*, p. 72.
[21]Perkins, *Quiet Revolution*, p. 181.
[22]Thomas Hanks, *God So Loved the Third World: The Biblical Vocabulary of Oppression* (Maryknoll, N.Y.: Orbis, 1983), p. 38.
[23]Paulo Freire, quoted in Chap Clark and Kara Powell, *Deep Justice in a Broken World: Helping Your Kids Serve*

*Others and Right the Wrongs Around Them* (Grand Rapids: Zondervan/Youth Specialties, 2007), p. 191.

[24]Lowell, *Kingdom of God Versus the Cosmos,* p. 2.

[25]The threefold sabbath structure is taken from Conrad Hopkins's sermon "Let Justice Roll Down: The Jubilee Years," preached at Hillside Covenant Church, October 14, 2007.

[26]Myers, "God Speed the Year of Jubilee!" pp. 24-28.

[27]Shane Claiborne, *Irresistible Revolution* (Grand Rapids: Zondervan, 2006), p. 171.

[28]The TNIV and several other translations say "seventy-seven times." The New Living Translation, King James Version and English Standard Version, among others, say "seventy times seven."

[29]Hopkins, "Let Justice Roll Down."

[30]Haugen, *Good News About Injustice*, p. 176.

[31]Excerpts taken from Mae Elise Cannon, "(All) The Good News," *Prism,* January-February 2007.

### Chapter 2: Social Justice

[1]Chuck Colson, "What Is Justice?" *Christianity Today*, August 2005, p. 80.

[2]J. Philip Wogaman, "The Social Justice Perspective," in *Church, State and Public Justice: Five Views*, ed. P. C. Kemeny (Downers Grove, Ill.: InterVarsity Press, 2007), p. 221.

[3]Chap Clark and Kara Powell, *Deep Justice in a Broken World: Helping Your Kids Serve Others and Right the Wrongs Around Them* (Grand Rapids: Zondervan/Youth Specialties, 2007), p. 10.

[4]This quote is commonly attributed to Thomas Aquinas in the public domain. Aquinas was a Dominican priest whose philosophy and theology has greatly influenced Christian thought. His influential writings include *Summa Theologica*.

[5]I first heard this anecdote many years ago from Mary Nelson, the founder of Bethel New Life in Chicago.

[6]Dan Schmitz, The Mosaic Center strategic planning retreat at the Mercy Center, Burlingame, California, June 8, 2008.

[7]Bono, National Prayer Breakfast, February 2, 2006, courtesy of DATA (Debt, AIDS, Trade, Africa). The entire transcript is available online at <www.usatoday.com/news/washington/2006-02-02-bono-transcript_x.htm>.

[8]Charles Dickens, *Martin Chuzzlewit* (1844), chap. 27.

[9]Clark and Powell, *Deep Justice in a Broken World*, pp. 15-16. Used by permission.

[10]Friedrich Nietzsche, *Human, All Too Human*.

[11]Brian Barry, *Theories of Justice* (Berkeley: University of California Press, 1989), p. xiii.

[12]"Introduction to Restorative Justice," Prison Fellowship International <www.restorativejustice.org>.

[13]See Dan W. Van Ness and Karen Heetderks Strong, *Restoring Justice: An Introduction to Restorative Justice* (Cincinnati: Anderson Publishing, 2006).

[14]See <http://reentrypolicy.org/resources/links>.

[15]David Plotz, "Charles Colson: How a Watergate Crook Became America's Greatest Christian Conservative," *Slate*, March 10, 2000 <www.slate.com/id/77067>.

[16]N. T. Wright, *Evil and the Justice of God* (Downers Grove, Ill.: InterVarsity Press. 2006), p. 124.

[17]Helen Douglas, "Redeeming the Wages of Sin: the Workings of Reparations," *Perspectives on Evil and Human Wickedness* 1 no. 3 (2003): 47.

[18]Haugen, *Good News About Injustice*, p. 71.

[19]"Statement by Permanent Representative of Israel to the United Nations, H. E. Ambassador Dan Gillerman," United Nations, January 27, 2008 <www.un.org/holocaustremembrance/2007/statements/gillerman.shtml>.

[20]Haugen, *Good News About Injustice*, p. 72.

[21]Kevin Blue, *Practical Justice: Living Off-Center in a Self-Centered World* (Downers Grove, Ill.: InterVarsity Press. 2006), p. 98.

[22]Ibid.

[23]Ibid.

[24]Lowell Noble, *The Kingdom of God Versus the Cosmos* (Riceville, Iowa: Spring Arbor College, 1997), p. 3, available through the Christian Community Development Association <www.ccda.org>.

[25]Ibid., p. 9.

[26]This exercise is based on Clark and Powell, *Deep Justice in a Broken World*, p. 117.

[27]See the International Justice Mission website at <www.ijm.org>.

[28]While approximately $10,000 is spent per year on a student in the Chicago Public School system, some of the suburban public schools spend over $20,000 per student.

### Chapter 3: A History of Christian Social Justice in the Americas

[1]See "Mexico," Microsoft Encarta Online Encyclopedia 2000 <encarta.msn.com/encnet/refpages/search.aspx?q=mexico>.

[2]John E. Bennett, "Should the California Missions Be Preserved? Part I." *Overland Monthly* 29, no. 169 (1897): 9-24.

[3]George Wharton James, *The Old Franciscan Missions of California* (1913). Project Gutenberg Ebook #13854.

[4]Steven Waldman, *Founding Faith: Providence, Politics, and the Birth of Religious Freedom in America* (New York: Random House, 2008), excerpt from National Public Radio on March 11, 2008.

[5]There is historical debate about whether or not the violence against Native Americans should be considered genocide, which was defined in 1948 by the United Nations as: "any of the following acts committed with intent to destroy, in whole or in part, a national, ethnical, racial or religious group, as such: killing members of the group; causing serious bodily or mental harm to members of the group; deliberately inflicting on the group conditions of life, calculated to bring about its physical destruction in whole or in part; imposing measures intended to prevent births within the group; [and] forcibly transferring children of the group to another group" ("The Convention on the Prevention and Punishment of the Crime of Genocide" United Nations: Office of the High Commissioner for Human Rights <www.unhchr.ch/html/menu3/b/p_genoci .htm>. David Cesarani argues that the Native American genocide exceeded that of the Jewish Holocaust (*Holocaust: Critical Concepts in Historical Studies* [New York: Routledge, 2004], p. 381).

[6]See *About North Georgia* <http://ngeorgia.com/history/nghisttt.html>.

[7]Some historians suggest Parker was not permitted to take the bar exam because he was an American Indian (see Brown, *Bury My Heart at Wounded Knee*). Others argue he was not permitted to take the exam because he was not a United States citizen (see Gerry Gilmore, "Seneca Chief Fought Greed, Injustice," U.S. Department of Defense, American Forces Press Service, October 17, 2000 < www.defenselink.mil/news/newsarticle.aspx?id=45504>.). American Indians were not considered citizens in the United States until the Indian Citizenship Act (1924).

[8]Gilmore, "Seneca Chief Fought Greed, Injustice."

[9]From <www.historynet.com/ely-parker-iroquois-chief-and-union-officer.htm>.

[10]Arthur Caswell Parker, *The Life of General Ely S. Parker* (Buffalo, N.Y.: Buffalo Historical Society, 1919), p. 97.

[11]From <www.nativeamericanindians.com/ElySamuelParker>. Accessed March 7, 2009.

[12]Joe Kalt, "Native Americans in the 21st Century: Nation Building I," Harvard University, January 16-19, 2007.

[13]Two and a half million people reported being only Native American or Native Alaskan (Stella Ogunwole, "The American Indian and Alaska Native Population: 2000," February 2002 <www.census.gov/ prod/2002pubs/c2kbr01-15.pdf>).

[14]Richard's story was taken from Wiconi International <www.wiconi.com>. Used with permission.

[15]From 1992 to 1996, the number reported was 124 violent crimes per 1,000 American Indians. See Lawrence Greenfield and Steven Smith, "American Indians and Crime," Bureau of Justice Statistics, February 1999, NCJ 173386 <www.ojp.usdoj.gov/bjs/pub/pdf/aic.pdf>.

[16]Ibid.

[17]"A 2008 Summary of Statistics," Mothers Against Drunk Driving, Irving, Texas.

[18]"Indian Country Drug Threat Assessment," National Drug Intelligence Center, June 2008 <www.usdoj .gov/ndic/pubs28/29239/index.htm>.

[19]Marvin Olasky, *The Tragedy of American Compassion* (Wheaton, Ill.: Crossway, 1992), p. 7.

[20]Ibid., p. 6.

[21]Steven Waldman, *Founding Faith: Providence, Politics, and the Birth of Religious Freedom in America* (New York: Random House, 2008), excerpt from National Public Radio, "The Relationship Between Government and Religion" on March 18, 2008.

[22]See Donald Grinde Jr. and Bruce Johansen, "Errand in the Wilderness (Roger Williams and 'Soul Liberty')," in *Exemplar of Liberty: Native America and the Evolution of Democracy* (Los Angeles: American Indians Study Center [UCLA], 1990).

[23]Waldman, *Founding Faith*.

[24]Eric Foner, "Forgotten Steps Toward Freedom," *New York Times*, December 30, 2007 <www.nytimes .com/2007/12/30/opinion/30foner.html>.

[25]Lerone Bennett Jr., *Before the Mayflower: A History of Black America* (New York: Penguin, 1993), p. 29.

[26]Ibid., pp. 29-30.

[27]The Emancipation Proclamation only declared slaves free within "rebellious states." Slavery in the border states was not affected.

[28]"The Mirrors of History," *Sojourners*, July 2008, p. 38.

[29]"Religion and the Founding of the American Republic: Religion in Eighteenth-Century America," Library of Congress <www.loc.gov/exhibits/religion/rel02.html>.

[30]Holly Reed, "Jonathan Edwards (1703–1758)," 2004 <people.bu.edu/wwildman/WeirdWildWeb/courses/ mwt/dictionary/mwt_themes_420_edwards.htm>.

[31]Olasky, *Tragedy of American Compassion*, p. 7.

[32]Ibid., p. 13.

[33]Ibid.

[34]See J. F. Hurst, *John Wesley the Methodist* (Whitefish, Mt.: Kessinger, 2003).

[35]Olasky, *Tragedy of American Compassion*, p. 21.

[36]Ibid., p. 100.

[37]Ibid., p. 16.

[38]Note that this was extended only to those who were considered "acceptable" by the Christian community. Individuals who did not adhere to the strict moral code were excluded from the benefits of community.

[39]Olasky, *Tragedy of American Compassion*, p. 135.

[40]Ibid., p. 24.

[41]Ibid., p. 56.

[42]Ibid., p. 29.

[43]Charles Murray, quoted in ibid., p. xv.

[44]Alexis de Tocqueville, quoted in Olasky, *Tragedy of American Compassion*, p. 22.

[45]Olasky, *Tragedy of American Compassion*, p. 130.

[46]For more about Lewis and Clark see Stephen Ambrose, *Undaunted Courage* (New York: Simon & Schuster, 1997).

[47]From the U.S. Census Bureau, see <www.civilwarhome.com/population1860.htm>.

[48]Foner, "Forgotten Steps Toward Freedom."

[49]See Don Fehrenbacher, *The Dred Scott Case: Its Significance in American Law and Politics* (New York: Oxford University Press, 2001).

[50]See "William Lloyd Garrison," International World History Project <history-world.org/william_lloyd_garrison.htm>.

[51]Jefferson Davis, "Inaugural Address as Provisional President of the Confederacy," Montgomery, Alabama, February 18, 1861 <www.religioustolerance.org/chr_slav.htm>.

[52]"Sojourner Truth: Abolitionist and Women's Rights Advocate," Christian History.net, August 8, 2008 <www.christianitytoday.com/ch/131christians/activists/sojourner.html>.

[53]Sojourner Truth, quoted in *The Yale Book of Quotations*, ed. Fred Shapiro and Joseph Epstein (New Haven, Conn.: Yale University Press, 2006), p. 771.

[54]"Sojourner Truth: Abolitionist and Women's Rights Advocate."

[55]Michael Emerson and Christian Smith, *Divided by Faith: Evangelical Religion and the Problem of Race in America* (New York: Oxford University Press, 2000), p. 35.

[56]Helen Kendrick Johnson, "Woman Suffrage and the Church," in *Women and the Republic: A Survey of the Woman's Suffrage Movement in the United States and a Discussion of the Claims and Arguments of Its Foremost Advocates* (1913; reprint, Jone Johnson Lewis, 2000), see <womenshistory.about.com/library/etext/bl_watr_ch09.htm>.

[57]The Fifteenth Amendment was ratified in 1870. Although black men had the legal right to vote, it wasn't until the 1965 Voting Rights Act that the law was put into effect.

[58]For more on the amendments to the U.S. Constitution go to <www.usconstitution.net>.

[59]Lerone Bennett Jr., *Before the Mayflower* (New York: Penguin, 1993), p. 215.

[60]Ibid., p. 216.

[61]This act by Congress extended to both freed men and women.

[62]Bennett, *Before the Mayflower*, p. 224.

[63]Ibid., p. 219.

[64]Ibid., p. 231.

[65]Charles Quarles, *Christian Identity: The Aryan American Bloodline Religion* (Jefferson, N.C.: McFarland, 2004), p. 68.

[66]Olasky, *Tragedy of American Compassion*, p. 127.

[67]For more on the Salvation Army see their website at <www.salvationarmy.org>.

[68]Olasky, *Tragedy of American Compassion*, p. 131.

[69]Ibid., p. 15.

[70]Ibid., pp. 60-61.

[71]Ibid., p. 125.

[72]Ibid., pp. 128-29.

[73]Ibid., p. 21.

[74]"Diamond Dust Socialite Lands on Skid Row; Emma Whittemore and Door of Hope" Glimpses of Christian History, March 2007 <www.chinstitute.org/GLIMPSEF/Glimpses2/glimpses196.shtml>.

[75]Olasky, *Tragedy of American Compassion*, p. 50.

[76]Ibid., p. 65.

[77]Ibid., p. 135.

[78]Ibid.

[79]Randall Herbert Balmer, "Emma Mott Whittemore," *Encyclopedia of Evangelicalism* (Louisville: Westminster John Knox, 2001), p. 636.

[80]See "Charles Loring Brace," *Columbia Encyclopedia*, 6th ed.

[81]Stephen O'Connor, *Orphan Trains: The Story of Charles Loring Brace and the Children He Saved and Failed* (Chicago: University of Chicago Press, 2004), p. 210.

[82]Olasky, *Tragedy of American Compassion*, pp. 37-38.

[83]Tim Stafford, *Shaking the System* (Downers Grove, Ill.: InterVarsity Press, 2007), p. 53.

[84]Ibid., p. 23.

[85]Douglas Linder, "State v. John Scopes ('The Monkey Trial')," a speech given on the seventy-fifth anniversary of the Scopes Trial, July 10, 2000 <www.law.umkc.edu/faculty/projects/ftrials/scopes/evolut.htm>.

[86]"The Scopes Trial (July 10-21, 1925)" <www.u-s-history.com/pages/h1438.html>.

[87]Joel Carpenter, "Fundamentalist Institutions and the Rise of Evangelical Protestantism, 1929-1942," *Church History* 49, no. 1 (March 1980): 64.

[88]Ibid., p. 63.

[89]Eva Goodwin, "Opposition to Modernism & Liberalism," Mount Holyoke College, fall 2004 <www.mtholyoke.edu/~edgoodwi/mainpage1.html>.

[90]Ernestine Van der Wall, "The Enemy Within: Religion, Science, and Modernism," Netherlands Institute for Advanced Study in the Humanities and Social Sciences, June 2007, p. 7.

[91]Olasky, *Tragedy of American Compassion*, p. 10.

[92]Walter Trattner, *From Poor Law to Welfare State: A History of Social Welfare in America*, 3rd ed. (New York: Free Press, 1984), p. 81.

[93]David Morgan, "Yale Study: U.S. Genetics Paralleled Nazi Germany," Reuters, February 15, 2000 <www.hartford-hwp.com/archives/45/302.html>.

[94]Woodward Dustin, "Black Tuesday—1929: Worst Day in Stock Market History," About.com <mutualfunds.about.com/cs/1929marketcrash/a/black_tuesday.htm>.

[95]"Suicide Time," *Time*, Monday, June 13, 1932 <www.time.com/time/magazine/article/0,9171,743807,00.html>.

[96]Willard W. Cochrane, *Farm Prices, Myth and Reality* (Minneapolis: University of Minnesota Press, 1958), p. 15.

[97]During this time of economic hardship, Germany turned into a despot state under the leadership of Adolf Hitler, setting the stage for World War II.

[98]Olasky, *Tragedy of American Compassion*, p. 150.

[99]"Paradigm Shift," PBS, August 1, 1996 <www.pbs.org/newshour/bb/welfare/august96/welfare_history_8-1.html>.

[100]Olasky, *Tragedy of American Compassion*, p. 152.

[101]Ibid., pp. 161-62.

[102]Stafford, *Shaking the System*, p. 23.

[103]Robert Ellis Thompson, quoted in Olasky, *Tragedy of American Compassion*, p. 129.

[104]June Hopkins, "The Road Not Taken: Harry Hopkins and New Deal Work Relief," *Presidential Studies Quarterly* 29, no 2 (June 1, 1999): 306-16.

[105]"Celebrating 100 Years of Social Science Research," Russell Sage Foundation, p. 3; and Olasky, *Tragedy of American Compassion*, p. 164.

[106]Olasky, *Tragedy of American Compassion*, p. 182.

[107]Ibid., p. 174.

[108]John Perkins, *A Quiet Revolution* (Waco, Tex.: Word, 1976), p. 97.

[109]Stafford, *Shaking the System*, p. 55.

[110]"Oh, Freedom," author unknown.

[111]*The Biography of Martin Luther King, Jr.—The Nobel Peace Prize 1964* <http://nobelprize.org/nobel_prizes/peace/laureates/1964/king-bio.html>.

[112]Martin Luther King Jr., "I've Been to the Mountaintop," delivered April 3, 1968, at the Mason Temple (Church of God in Christ headquarters) in Memphis, Tennessee.

[113]William Leuchtenberg, ed., "President's Commission on the Status of Women," Federal Records Collection of the John F. Kennedy Library, Boston, Massachusetts.

[114]Luetta Reimer, "A Christian Response to the Women's Liberation Movement," *Direction* 3, no. 1 (1974) <www.directionjournal.org/article/?100>.

[115]"Chinese American Contribution to the Transcontinental Railroad," Central Pacific Railroad Photographic History Museum <cprr.org/Museum/Chinese.html>.

[116]The term *yellow peril* was commonly used in newspapers during the early twentieth century. It was also the title of a popular (1911) book by G. G. Rupert, an influential religious figure in the United States.

[117]Bill Moyers, "Becoming American: The Chinese Experience," PBS, 2003 <www.pbs.org/becomingamerican/chineseexperience.html>.

[118]Dinitia Smith, "Photographs of an Episode That Lives in Infamy," *New York Times*, November 6, 2006.

[119]*Korematsu v. United States*, dissent by Justice Frank Murphy, footnote 12 <http://supreme.justia.com/us/323/214/case.html>.

[120]Smith, "Photographs of an Episode That Lives in Infamy."

[121]100th Congress, S. 1009 <www.internmentarchives.com/showdoc.php?docid=00055&search_id=19269&pagenum=4>.

[122]"2006 American Community Survey," United States Census Bureau.

[123]"2020 Introduction," Pacific Southwest Conference Annual Meeting 2008, Evangelical Covenant Church.

[124]"U.S. Census Press Releases," United States Census Bureau (2005-05-01).

[125]Lawrence M. Small, "Latino Legacies," *Smithsonian*, January 8, 2002.

[126]Judith Rodin, "Interview with Judith Rodin," interviewed by Judith Woodruff on Bloomberg TV, March 7, 2008 <www.rockfound.org/about_us/speeches/030708rodin_woodruff.pdf>.

[127]"Faith-Based and Community Initiative: Improvements in Monitoring Grantees and Measuring Performance Could Enhance Accountability," United States Government Accountability Office, June 2006.

[128]Sojourner's website <www.sojo.net>..

[129]"Faith and Politics," hosted by Soledad O'Brien, CNN, June 4, 2007. Participants included Reverend Jim Wallis, Hillary Clinton, John Edwards and Barack Obama.

[130]Nina Munk, "Jeffrey Sach's $200 Billion Dream," *Vanity Fair*, July 2007, p. 141.

[131]Sachs, quoted in ibid., p. 140.

[132]Bono, National Prayer Breakfast Remarks, February 2, 2006.

[133]The United Nations Millennium Declaration was adopted on September 8, 2000, by the UN General Assembly.

[134]See the ONE Campaign at <www.one.org>.

[135]See Anup Shah, "G8 Summit 2005," Global Issues page, July 10, 2005 at <www.globalissues.org/article/541/g8-summit-2005>.

[136]Jim Wallis, *God's Politics* (New York: Harper Collins, 2005), p. 82.

[137]Haugen, *Good News About Injustice*, p. 63.

### Chapter 4: Moving from Apathy to Advocacy

[1]Gary Haugen, *Just Courage: God's Great Expedition for the Restless Christian* (Downers Grove, Ill.: InterVarsity Press, 2008), p. 43.

[2]Gary Haugen, *Good News About Injustice* (Downers Grove, Ill.: InterVarsity Press, 1999), p. 67.

[3]4eccentricabby, "Apathy," February 11, 2007 <www.youtube.com/watch?v=FYjBqJJD_wM>.

[4]N. T. Wright, "Heaven Is Not Our Home," *Christianity Today*, March 24, 2008, pp. 36-39, excerpt from *Surprised by Hope.*

[5]Lynne Hybels. Used with permission. Lynne is a Christian activist and teacher who cares deeply about God's heart for justice. She is one of the founding members of Willow Creek Community Church and is the author of *Nice Girls Don't Change the World.*

[6]Mac Pier and Katie Sweeting, *The Power of a City at Prayer* (Downers Grove, Ill.: InterVarsity Press, 2002), p. 79.

[7]For example, today in my own spiritual journey I am going through the process of growing in awareness about the injustices that are occurring in the Palestinian-Israeli conflict.

[8]Tim Stafford, *Shaking the System* (Downers Grove, Ill.: InterVarsity Press, 2007), p. 29.

[9]Soong-Chan Rah, *The Next Evangelicalism* (Downers Grove, Ill.: InterVarsity Press, 2009), p. 161.

[10]"NPU Students to Bike the U.S. Raising Funds, Awareness," Evangelical Covenant Church, May 6, 2008 <www.covchurch.org/cov/news/item6269>.

[11]Mother Teresa, quoted in Shane Claiborne, *Irresistible Revolution* (Grand Rapids: Zondervan, 2006), p. 136. Mother Teresa was a Catholic nun and founder of the Missionaries of Charity. She spent much of her life working with the poor and destitute in Calcutta, India and received the Nobel Peace Prize in 1979.

[12]David Van Biema, "Mother Teresa's Crisis of Faith," *Time*, August 23, 2007.

[13]Eleanor Roosevelt, "My Day," Eleanor Roosevelt National Historical Site, February 16, 1946 <www.nps.gov/archive/elro/who-is-er/er-quotes?/

[14]The luncheon was sponsored by the of department of benevolence of the Evangelical Covenant Church as a part of their annual Midwinter Conference in Chicago.

[15]I should note that Allender does not claim that any of the abuse experienced is the victims fault, rather that in the victim's response to abuse, he or she must repent of the ways their sinful nature gets in the way of having God's heart toward their oppressors.

[16]Chap Clark and Kara Powell, *Deep Justice in a Broken World* (Grand Rapids: Zondervan/Youth Specialties, 2007), p. 27.

[17]It envisions every local congregation engaged in holistic ministry in their respective communities. Further,

it envisions these congregations actively connecting with one another, with community organizations and local governments to truly participate in community transformation.

[18]Catherine Cuellar, writing about Catherine Rohr in "Investing in Second Chances," *Sojourners*. July 2008. p. 23.

[19]Catherine Rohr, Leadership Summit Speaker's Videos <willowcreek.com/events/leadership/2008/speaker-CatherineRohr.html>.

[20]Ibid., p. 24.

[21]For information on the Prison Entrepreneurship program see <www.prisonentrepreneurship.org>.

[22]Statistics taken from <www.pep.org/who/story.aspx>.

[23]See other types of social advocacy mentioned in "take action" sections in part two.

[24]Francis of Assisi was a thirteenth-century monastic known for his life of simplicity and as the patron saint of animals.

[25]From Rick Law, "From the Heart," Rick Law's Elder Law Blog, December 22, 2008 <ricksblog.lawelderlaw.com/2008/12>.

[26]Cornel West, *Call & Response*, a 2008 documentary film <callandresponse.com>.

[27]This exercise was first introduced to me by Dick and Sibyl Towner over the course of personal discipleship.

## Chapter 5: Solutions to Injustice

[1]Marvin Olasky, *The Tragedy of American Compassion* (Wheaton, Ill.: Crossway, 1992), p. 4.

[2]Jud Scott provided this idea in a conversation we had on October 19, 2008.

[3]The idea and emphasis of the value and importance of individuals responding faithfully to the call of justice within the community arose from a conversation I had with Tom Yaccino on March 5, 2009.

[4]Arloa Sutter, personal interview on November 10, 2004.

[5]Chap Clark and Kara Powell, *Deep Justice in a Broken World* (Grand Rapids: Zondervan/Youth Specialties, 2007), p. 201.

[6]Rick Rusaw and Eric Swanson, *The Externally Focused Church* (Loveland, Colo.: Group, 2004), p. 17.

[7]Tim Stafford, *Shaking the System* (Downers Grove, Ill.: InterVarsity Press, 2007), p. 168.

[8]Jimmy Carter, "Jimmy Carter's Big Breakthrough," *Time*, May 10, 1976, p. 7 <www.time.com/time/magazine/article/0,9171,914159-1,00.html>. It is said that he took this quote from Reinhold Niebuhr.

[9]Munk, "Jeffrey Sach's $200 Billion Dream," p. 146.

[10]Bourke, *Skeptic's Guide to Global Poverty*, p. 34.

[11]Jenny Eaton and Kate Etue, comp., *The aWAKE Project* (Nashville: W Publishing, 2002), p. x.

[12]Jeffrey Sachs, quoted in Nina Munk, "Jeffrey Sach's $200 Billion Dream," *Vanity Fair*, July 2007, p. 146. Sachs is an economist working to end global poverty. He was the director of the UN Millennium Project and serves as the special adviser to the UN Secretary General Ban Ki-moon. He is the director of the Earth Institute and a professor of health policy and management at Columbia University. He is the author of *The End of Poverty: Economic Possibilities for Our Time*.

[13]Bread for the World <www.bread.org/take-action/offering-of-letterslresources/guide-to-the-federal-budget.html>.

[14]See <www.care.org/getinvolved/advocacy/budget_factsheet.asp>.

[15]Dale Bourke, *The Skeptics Guide to Global Poverty* (Colorado Springs: Authentic Publishing, 2007), p. 17.

[16]Jubilee USA Network <www.jubileedebtcampaign.org.uk/download.php?id=514>.

[17]Ibid.

[18]Paul O'Neill, "Speech from the Chris Hani Baragwanath Hospital, South Africa," *The aWAKE Project* (Nashville: W Publishing, 2002), p. 170.

[19]Bourke, *Skeptic's Guide to Global Poverty*, p. 34.

[20]O'Neill, "Speech from the Chris Hani Baragwanath Hospital, South Africa," p. 170.

[21]DATA, "Debt. AIDS. Trade. Africa," *aWAKE Project*, p. 180.

[22]African Growth and Opportunity Act <www.agoa.gov>.

[23]"Debt. AIDS. Trade. Africa," *aWAKE Project*, p. 180.

[24]Bourke, *Skeptic's Guide to Global Poverty*, p. 35.

[25]Morley Glicken, *Social Work in the 21st Century* (Thousand Oaks, Calif.: SAGE Publications, 2007), p. 69.

[26]Olasky, *Tragedy of American Compassion*, p. 144.

[27]Ibid., p. 146.

[28]Ibid., p. 145.

[29]Charles Murray, quoted in ibid., p. xiii.

[30]From a personal conversation with Nathan George in Walnut Creek, California, on June 16, 2008.

[31]This is a description taken from a CCDA brochure. For more information, see the Christian Community Development Association's website <www.ccda.org>.

[32]From the Christian Community Development Association (CCDA) Brochure <www.ccda.org/xm_client/

client_documents/pdf/CCDA_Brochure.pdf>.

[33]Wayne Gordon, *Real Hope for Chicago* (Grand Rapids: Zondervan, 1995), p. 60.

[34]From a report for "Leadership & Empowering Laity," a course at North Park Theological Seminary. This data was received in an interview with Willette Grant, the hospitality coordinator in 2004.

[35]John Perkins, *Quiet Revolution* (Waco, Tex.: Word, 1976), p. 78.

[36]Gary Haugen, *Good News About Injustice* (Downers Grove, Ill.: InterVarsity Press, 1999), p. 97.

[37]"Major Religions of the World Ranked by Number of Adherents" <www.adherents.com/Religions_By_Adherents.html>.

## Part 2: Social Justice Issues

[1]Michael Emerson and Christian Smith, *Divided by Faith: Evangelical Religion and the Problem of Race in America* (New York: Oxford University Press, 2000), p. 88.

[2]David Walls, "Women's Movement," Sonoma State University, 2008 <www.sonoma.edu/users/w/wallsd/womens-movement.shtml>.

[3]*Roe v. Wade*, 410 U.S. 113 (1973).

[4]"Anti-Abortion Violence Movement," Office of International Criminal Justice of the University of Illinois at Chicago <www.religioustolerance.org/abo_viol.htm>.

[5]Nancy Gibbs, "Why Have Abortion Rates Fallen?" *Time*, January 21, 2008 <www.time.com/time/nation/article/0,8599,1705604,00.html>.

[6]Rachel Jones, Mia Zolna, Stanley Henshaw, and Lawrence Finer, "Abortion in the United States: Incidence and Access to Services, 2005," Guttmacher Institute <guttmacher.org/pubs/journals/4000608.pdf>.

[7]Gibbs, "Why Have Abortion Rates Fallen?"

[8]Bourke, *Skeptic's Guide to the Global AIDS Crisis*, p. 17.

[9]From Bread for the World, "Hunger & Poverty Fact Sheet," information pamphlet distributed to churches, organizations and individuals (2007).

[10]Dale Hanson Bourke, *Skeptic's Guide to the Global AIDS Crisis* (Tyrone, Ga.: Authentic, 2006), p. 11; Franklin Graham, "President, Samaritans Purse," *The aWAKE Project* (Nashville: W Publishing, 2002), p. 191.

[11]2007 Human Development Report, United Nations Development Program, November 27, 2007, p.25.

[12]William H. Frist, "Taking Our Stand Against HIV/AIDS," *The aWAKE Project* (Nashville: W Publishing, 2002), p. 31.

[13]Saddleback Community Church, AIDS Summit, November 28-30, 2007, informational packet.

[14]Dale Hanson Bourke, *Skeptic's Guide to Global Poverty* (Tyrone, Ga.: Authentic, 2007), p. 53.

[15]Colin Powell was appointed to be Secretary of State in 2001 by the newly elected President George W. Bush. Until the 2008 election of Barack Obama, Powell was the highest ranking African American in the United States Government <www.aei.org/publications/pubID.20506,filter.all/pub_detail.asp>.

[16]"World Map," HIV/AIDS Caring Community <www.hivandthechurch.com/en-US/WorldMap/HIV_AIDS_map.htm>.

[17]Johanna McGeary, "Death Stalks a Continent," *The aWAKE Project* (Nashville: W. Publishing, 2002), p. 4.

[18]Bono, "Speaking Out on the Crisis," DATA site <www.amsa.org/global/aids/dataspeakout.pdf>.

[19]Bourke, *Skeptic's Guide to Global Poverty*, p. 53.

[20]See UNICEF's statistics on this website <www.avert.org/aidsorphans.htm>.

[21]Kofi Annan, quoted in Saddleback AIDS Conference Materials, November 2007.

[22]Bourke, *Skeptic's Guide to the Global AIDS Crisis*, pp. 11-12.

[23]This video is still available at the Willow Creek Association (www.willowcreek.com) and is called "The Breathe Compassion Video: Changing the World One Woman at a Time" <www.willowcreek.com/wca_prodsb.asp?invtid=pr27369>.

[24]See Bourke, *Skeptic's Guide to Global Poverty*.

[25]Hope Chu, "Watching and Waiting for Justice and Debt Cancellation," *Economic Justice News Online* 8, no. 1 (January 2005): 278 <www.50years.org/cms/ejn/story/250>.

[26]Frist, "Taking Our Stand Against HIV/AIDS," p. 33.

[27]Bourke, *Skeptic's Guide to Global AIDS Crisis*, p. 26.

[28]Jesse Helms, "We Cannot Turn Away," *The aWAKE Project* (Nashville: W Publishing, 2002), p. 61.

[29]Lynne Hybels, "Why Bother to Hope?" *The aWAKE Project* (Nashville: W Publishing, 2002), p. 101.

[30]Tony Campolo, "Introduction: Indifferent Christians and the African Crisis," *The aWAKE Project* (Nashville: W Publishing, 2002), p. xi.

[31]Bourke, *Skeptic's Guide to Global Poverty*, p. 56.

[32]"How to Sponsor Drug Therapy for HIV+ Mothers and Their Newborn Children," *The aWAKE Project* (Nashville: W Publishing, 2002), p. 242.

[33]Bourke, *Skeptic's Guide to Global AIDS Crisis*, p. 17.

[34]Bourke, *Skeptic's Guide to Global Poverty*, p. 53.

[35]Mae Elise Cannon Fisk, "The New Baby Boom: A Look at the Growing and Morally Complicated World of In Vitro Fertilization," *Covenant Companion*, October 2004, p. 10.

[36]Ibid., p. 11.

[37]Many reproductive clinics call this process "selective reduction," which is when one or more of the fetuses is aborted at the ninth to twelfth week of the pregnancy.

[38]"Laws and Regulations: Regulations and Assisted Conception Treatment," IVF-Infertility.com <www.ivf-infertility.com>.

[39]The original Nuremberg Code may be found in *Trials of War Criminals before the Nuremberg Military Tribunals under Control Council Law No. 10*, vol. 2 (Washington, D.C.: U.S. Government Printing Office, 1949), pp. 181-82.

[40]Death Penalty Information Center <www.deathpenaltyinfo.org>.

[41]Jim Wallis, *God's Politics* (New York: HarperOne, 2005), p. 307.

[42]See the Death Penalty Information Center's National Statistics on the Death Penalty and Race <www.death penaltyinfo.org/race-death-row-inmates-executed-1976>. The execution information is accurate as of March 5, 2009.

[43]U.S. Department of Justice, "The Federal Death Penalty System: Supplementary Data, Analysis and Revised Protocols for Capital Case Review," June 6, 2001 <www.usdoj.gov/dag/pubdoc/deathpenaltystudy.htm>.

[44]Pennsylvania Alternatives for the Death Penalty site, "Pennsylvania's Death Row Is the 4th Largest in the Nation, Just Behind California, Texas and Florida: Innocent Lives in the Balance" <www.pa-abolitionists.org>.

[45]"The Death Penalty in 2007: Year End Report," Death Penalty Information Center, December 2007 <www.deathpenaltyinfo.org/innocence-cases-2004-present>.

[46]"General Assembly Committee Backs Global Moratorium Against Death Penalty," UN News Center <www.un.org/apps/news/story.asp?NewsID=24679&Cr=general&Cr1=assembly>.

[47]"Growing Calls for End to Executions at UN," Amnesty International, December 18, 2008 <www.amnesty.org/en/news-and-updates/good-news/growing-calls-end-executions-un-20081218>.

[48]For a more comprehensive understanding of capitalism and its history read Adam Smith's *The Wealth of Nations*, Karl Marx's *The Marx-Engels Reader* and Max Weber's *The Protestant Ethic and the Spirit of Capitalism*.

[49]Bourke, *Skeptic's Guide to Global Poverty*, p. 36.

[50]James Doti, "Capitalism and Greed," *The Freeman* 32, no. 11 (November 1982).

[51]John F. Kennedy (1917-1963) was the thirty-fifth President of the USA. See <www.un.org/ga/president/61/statements/statement20061127.shtml>.

[52]James Doti and Dwight Lee, eds., *The Market Economy: A Reader* (Los Angeles: Roxbury Publishing, 1991) <www.ccsindia.org/ccsindia/lacs/17capitalism_and_greed.pdf>.

[53]David Hilfiker, "The Limits of Capitalism," lecture given at the Servant Leadership School, 2007 <www.davidhilfiker.com/docs/Economics/Limits%20of%20Capitalism.htm>.

[54]Bob Pierce <www.samaritanspurse.org/index.php/who_we_are/history>. Pierce was the founder of World Vision (1951) and Samaritans Purse (1970).

[55]Compassion International <www.compassion.com/about/aboutus.htm>.

[56]Justin McRoberts, private conversation, December 3, 2008.

[57]"Child Soldiers," 2007 One World One Promise <worldnet.scout.org/scoutpax/en/8/8_childsoldiers_en>.

[58]"What's Going on? Child Soldiers in Sierra Leone," The UN Works for Kids <www.un.org/works/going on/soldiers/goingon_soldiers.html>.

[59]Ishmael Beah, *A Long Way Gone* (New York: Sarah Crichton Books, 2007).

[60]The documentary *What's Going On?* can be purchased through the Social Studies School Service at <www.catalog.socialstudies.com/c/product.html?record@TF36922>.

[61]"Social Issues: Child Soldiers," 2007 One World One Promise <worldnet.scout.org/scoutpax/en/8/8_child soldiers_en.pdf>.

[62]Hillary Mayell, "India's Untouchables Face Violence, Discrimination," *National Geographic News*, June 2, 2003 Retrieved June 19, 2008 <news.nationalgeographic.com/news/2003/06/0602_030602_untouchables.html>.

[63]Mohandas Gandhi, *Mahatma Gandhi: Selected Political Writings*, ed. Dennis Dalton (Indianapolis: Hackett, 1996).

[64]"Country Profile: India," BBC News, June 19, 2008 <news.bbc.co.uk/2/hi/south_asia/country_profiles/1154019.stm>.

[65]"First Cloned Sheep Dolly Dies at 6," *CNN*, February 14, 2003 <www.cnn.com/2003/WORLD/europe/02/14/cloned.dolly.dies>.

[66]Ibid.

[67]"Legislative Updates: Cloning," Office of Legislative Policy and Analysis, December 22, 2008 <olpa.od.nih.gov/legislation/109/pendinglegislation/cloning.asp>.

[68]Ibid.

[69]Leon Kass, "The Wisdom of Repugnance," in John Arras and Bonnie Steinbock, *Ethical Issues in Modern Medicine*, 5th ed. (Mountain View, Calif.: Mayfield, 1999), p. 500.

[70]See Aldous Huxley's *Brave New World*.

[71]Dan Brock, "Cloning Human Beings: An Assessment of the Ethical Issues Pro and Con," in John Arras and Bonnie Steinbock, *Ethical Issues in Modern Medicine*, 5th ed. (Mountain View, Calif.: Mayfield, 1999), p. 491.

[72]Kass, "The Wisdom of Repugnance," p. 503.

[73]"Consumption for Human Development," United Nations Development Program <hdr.undp.org/en/reports/global/hdr1998>.

[74]Vic Cox, "US Consumption Deserves Appraisal," *Faculty & Staff Newspaper University of California at Santa Barbara*, 12, no. 5 (2001).

[75]"Celebration of Hope 2008," Willow Creek Community Church < www.willowcreek.org/coh/home/>.

[76]Shane Claiborne, *Irresistible Revolution* (Grand Rapids: Zondervan, 2006), p. 167.

[77]This information was provided by William Rees, University of British Columbia. See Ronald Sandler and Philip Cataro, *Environmental Ethics* (Oxford: Rowman & Littlefield, 2005), p. 200. A hectare is approximately 2.5 acres.

[78]"About Us," Alternatives for Simple Living <www.simpleliving.org/Default.aspx?tabid=375>.

[79]The five stages of disaster response were taught to me in 2005 by Bill Janus and Mark Smith of World Relief during my time as the Director of Development and Transformation at Willow Creek Community Church.

[80]Jan Sullivan, "Where Did I Serve You, Lord?" *Hurricane Katrina: A Call to Action* site, November 15, 2005 <wccc.blogs.com/hurricane/2005/11/index.html>.

[81]L. Heise, M. Ellsberg, and M. Gottemoeller, "Ending Violence Against Women," *Population Reports*, ser. L, no. 11 (1999).

[82]Regina Shands Stoltzfus, "A Black Woman's Voice," in *Women & Men: Gender in the Church*, ed. Carol Penner (Scottdale, Penn.: Mennonite Publishing, 1998), p. 77.

[83]Midwest Domestic Violence Center, Madison, Wisconsin.

[84]Tracking survey conducted for The Advertising Council and the Family Violence Prevention Fund by Lieberman Research Inc., July-October 1996 <endabuse.org/content/action_center/detail/754>.

[85]"Statistics Crime Data Brief, Intimate Partner Violence, 1993-2001," Bureau of Justice, February 2003.

[86]Steven R. Tracy, "Clergy Responses to Domestic Violence," *Priscilla Papers* 21, no. 2 (2007): 9-16.

[87]"Fact Sheet: What Faith Leaders Can Do," United States Department of Justice's Office on Violence Against Women <www.ovw.usdoj.gov/docs/fs-whatfaithleaderscando.pdf>.

[88]"Homelessness," Almanac of Policy Issues <www.policyalmanac.org/social_welfare/homeless.shtml>.

[89]Ms. Pearl's story is available on the Breathe Compassion video: *Changing the World One Woman at a Time*, from Breathe: the Willow Creek Women's Conference, 2005.

[90]Sanford Cloud Jr., "Achievement Gap," The National Conference for Community and Justice <www.kccjky.org/summaries/full_achieve.htm>.

[91]Supreme Court of the United States. *Brown v. Board of Education*, 347 US 483 (1954). Argued December 9, 1952. Reargued December 8, 1953. Decided May 17, 1954. See <www.nationalcenter.org/brown.html>.

[92]Cloud, "Achievement Gap."

[93]Ginger Reynolds Jr., "Bridging the Great Divide: Broadening Perspectives on the Closing Achievement Gaps," National Center for Education Statistics, *Viewpoints* 9 (December 6, 2002) <www.ncrel.org/policy/pubs/html/bridging/identify.htm>.

[94]Jennifer Laird, Matthew DeBell, Gregory Kienzl and Chris Chapman, *Dropout Rates in the United States: 2005* (Washington, D.C.: National Center for Education Statistics, 2007) <http://nces.ed.gov/pubs2007/2007059.pdf>.

[95]"Status Dropout Rates of 16- Through 24-Year-Olds, by Race/Ethnicity: October 1972-2006," Table 23-1, Student Effort and Educational Process Tables, National Center for Education Statistics. <nces.ed.gov/programs/coe/2008/section3/table.asp?tableID=900>.

[96]Cloud, "Achievement Gap."

[97]Mae Elise Cannon, "Chicago Public Schools: The Growing Divide in Equal Education," *HandsOnMag.org*, 18, no 2 (2008): <www.northpark.edu/umin/ho/vol18/issue2/articles/cps.html>.

[98]United Nations, "The Millennium Development Goals Report 2008" <www.un.org/millenniumgoals/pdf/The%20Millennium%20Development%20Goals%20Report%202008.pdf>.

[99]Chris Brazier, "State of the World Report," *New Internationalist* 287 (1997) <www.newint.org/issue287/keynote.html>.

[100]UNICEF, "The State of the World's Children," 1999 <www.unicef.org/sowc99/>.

[101]United Nations, "Women at a Glance," May 1997 <www.un.org/ecosocdev/geninfo/women/women96.htm>.

[102]Bread for the World, "Hunger and Poverty Fact Sheet" (distributed through a mailing from Bread for the World).

[103]Julius Nyerere, International Workshop on Education and Poverty Eradication Kampala, Uganda, July 30-August 3, 2001 <www.unesco.org/education/poverty/news.shtml>.

[104]International Workshop on Education and Poverty Eradication Kampala, Uganda, July 30-August 3, 2001 <www.unesco.org/education/poverty/news.shtml>.

[105]John Stott, introduction to *Under the Bright Wings*, quoted in Tri Robinson and Jason Chatraw, *Creation Care: An Introduction for Busy Pastors* by Evangelicals and Scientists United to Protect Creation, p. 8. To purchase the booklet see <www.creationcareforpastors.com/ccfp-kit>.

[106]"Global Warming and the Poor," a fact sheet by the Evangelical Environmental Network. Taken from Intergovernmental Panel on Climate Change (IPCC), 4th Assessment Report (AR4), Working Group Two (WG2), pp. 298-300, 334, 213 respectively.

[107]United Nations Millennium Development Report 2007, p. 45.

[108]See *Creation Care: An Introduction for Busy Pastors*, p. 17.

[109]Robert D. Orr, "The Physician-Assisted Suicide," in *Suicide: A Christian Response*, ed. Timothy Demy and Gary Stewart (Grand Rapids: Kregel, 1998), p. 62.

[110]See Edwin DuBose, *Physician Assisted Suicide: Religious and Public Policy Perspectives* (Chicago: Park Ridge Center, 1999), p. 10.

[111]John Feinberg and Paul Feinberg, *Ethics for a Brave New World* (Wheaton, Ill.: Crossway, 1993), p. 105.

[112]See Margaret Battin, *The Least Worst Death: Essays in Bioethics on the End of Life*.

[113]H. Hendin, C. Rutenfrans and Z. Zylicz, "Physician Assisted Suicide and Euthanasia in the Netherlands: Lessons from the Dutch," *Journal of the American Medical Association* 277, no. 21 (1997): 1720-22.

[114]Euthanasia World Directory <www.finalexit.org>.

[115]See John Locke's *On Liberty*.

[116]See John Locke's *Two Treatises of Government*.

[117]Hendin, Rutenfrans and Zylicz, "Physician Assisted Suicide," p. 1721.

[118]"Seventh Annual Report on Oregon's Death with Dignity Act," Oregon Department of Human Services, March 10, 2005 <www.oregon.gov/DHS/ph/pas/docs/year7.pdf>.

[119]Paul Ramsey, *The Patient as Person* (New Haven, Conn.: Yale University Press, 1970), p. 153.

[120]Wallis, *God's Politics*, p. 226.

[121]Olasky, *Tragedy of Compassion in America*, p. 13.

[122]"Family Structure and Children's Living Arrangements: Percentage of Children Ages 0-17 by Presence of Married Parents in the Household, and Race and Hispanic Origin, 1980-2006," Child Stats.gov <www.childstats.gov/americaschildren07/tables/fam1a.asp>.

[123]Wallis, *God's Politics*, p. 326.

[124]"New Study Shows Female Genital Mutilation Exposes Women and Babies to Significant Risks at Childbirth," World Health Organization, June 2, 2006 <www.who.int/mediacentre/news/releases/2006/pr30/en>.

[125]Bourke, *Skeptic's Guide to the Global AIDS Crisis*, p. 55.

[126]See Ellen Gruenbaum, *The Female Circumcision Controversy: An Anthropological Perspective* (Philadelphia: University of Pennsylvania Press, 2000).

[127]"New Study Shows."

[128]"Convention on the Prevention and Punishment of the Crime of Genocide," Office of the High Commissioner for Human Rights, United Nations <www.unhchr.ch/html/menu3/b/p_genoci.htm>.

[129]"In Full: George W. Bush's BBC Interview," BBC News, February 14, 2008 <news.bbc.co.uk/2/hi/americas/7245670.stm>.

[130]"Security Council Expands Mandate of UN Mission in Sudan to Include Darfur," United Nations Security Council (SC/8821), 5519th Meeting. Resolution 1706, August 31, 2006.

[131]"Triumph of Evil," *Frontline* <www.pbs.org/wgbh/pages/frontline/shows/evil>.

[132]King Kigeli V. Ndahindurwa was the ruling king of Rwanda from 1959 to 1961. He said this in a speech, "The Rwanda Genocide: The Most Preventable Tragedy of Our Time," given at Georgetown University in the Bunn ICC Faculty Lounge on Thursday, September 18, 1997.

[133]Organization of African Unity (OAV), quoted in United Nations, *Africa Recovery* 14, no. 2 (2000): briefs page. The entire commission report, "Rwanda: The Preventable Genocide," is available at <www.un.org/ecosocdev/geninfo/afrec/vol14no2/brief2.htm>.

[134]Philip Gourevitch, "Interviews from the Triumph of Evil," *Frontline* <www.pbs.org/wgbh/pages/frontline/shows/evil/interviews>.

[135]Ibid.

[136]Bourke, *Skeptic's Guide to Global Poverty*, p. 31. Gross Domestic Product refers to the total value of all of the goods and services produced in a country over a specific period of time.

[137]"1999 Human Development Report," United Nations Development Program <hdr.undp.org/en/reports/global/hdr1999/>.

[138]"1999 Human Development Report," United Nations Development Program, November 27, 2007, p. 25.

[139]"The Corporate Planet," *Corporate Watch*, 1997 <www.corpwatch.org>.

[140]Dee Yaccino, personal communication, December 8, 2008.

[141]These ideas about globalization were discussed by Professor Beth Slutsky, visiting lecturer in Women's Studies at the University of California, Davis, fall 2008.

[142]Bourke, *Skeptic's Guide to Global Poverty*, p. 32.

[143]United Nations Millennium Declaration 55/2, September 8, 2000.

[144]Lyndon B. Johnson, signing ceremony of the Medicare-Medicaid Act, July 30, 1965 <www.ssa.gov/history/lbjstmts.html#medicare>.

[145]United States Department of Health and Human Services <www.medicare.gov>.

[146]"Health, United States, 2007," Center for Disease Control and Prevention and National Center for Health Statistics <www.cdc.gov/nchs/data/hus/hus07.pdf>.

[147]See Bio-Medicine <news.bio-medicine.org/medicine-news-2/Questions-arise-as-more-older-Americans-outlive-driving-privilege-7451-1>.

[148]"A Profile of Informal and Family Caregivers," Care for Caregivers <www.eldercare.com/modules.php?op=modload&name=CG_Resources&file=article&sid=861>

[149]"Call to Action: Health Reform 2009," Senate Finance Committee Chairman Max Baucus, November 12, 2008 <finance.senate.gov/healthreform2009/finalwhitepaper.pdf>.

[150]"Long-Term Care, Caregivers, Settings, and Financing Alternatives," The American College <www.theamericancollege.edu/docs/154.pdf>.

[151]"Graying of America," *NewsHour with Jim Lehrer*, May 25, 2005 <www.pbs.org/newshour/bb/social_security/jan-june05/graying_5-25.html>.

[152]Rick Law, quoted in Mae Elise Cannon, "Who Will Defend the Widows?" *Prism*, November-December 2007, pp. 17-20. See particularly p. 18. Much of the material in this section is adapted from the above article. To see the full text of the article, go to <www.esa-online.org/Images/mmDocument/PRISM%20Archive/Features%202007/NovDec07WhoWillDefendWidows.pdf>.

[153]Ibid., p. 18.

[154]"90th Anniversary of the First Woman Elected to US Congress," Jeanette Rankin Foundation, November 2006 <www.rankinfoundation.org/press/news.php?n=21>.

[155]Administration on Aging, "Older Women" <www.aoa.gov/naic/may2000/factsheets/olderwomen.html>.

[156]Cannon, "Who Will Defend the Widows?" pp. 17-20.

[157]"President Signs S1932, Deficit Reduction Act of 2005," The White House, February 8, 2006 <www.whitehouse.gov/news/releases/2006/02/20060208-8.html>.

[158]Ibid.

[159]"Senate Vote on the Budget Belies the Nation's Divisions," News from the National Council of Churches <www.ncccusa.org/news/051222senatevote.html>.

[160]Cannon, "Who Will Defend the Widows?" pp. 17-20.

[161]Rick Law, "Action Idea: Ask Your Legislators About the 'Diagnosis Lottery,'" *Prism*, November-December 2007, p. 19.

[162]Bourke, *Skeptic's Guide to Global Poverty*, p. 41.

[163]ChildStats.gov, "America's Children: Key National Indicators of Well-Being, 2007" <www.childstats.gov/americaschildren/care1.asp>.

[164]Jim Wallis, "Hearts and Minds," Morally Unacceptable—Sojo Mail, October 4, 2007.

[165]"Overview of National SCHIP Policy," HHS.gov <www.cms.hhs.gov/NationalSCHIPPolicy>.

[166]Glenn Palmberg, quoted in Morally Unacceptable—Sojo Mail, October 4, 2007.

[167]"State of the World's Children, 2005," UNICEF.

[168]Nina Munk, "Jeffrey Sach's $200 Billion Dream," *Vanity Fair*, July 2007, p. 143.

[169]"Fast Facts," GlobalHealthFacts.org <www.globalhealthfacts.org>.

[170]"Homelessness in America," *News Hour Extra with Jim Lehrer*, December 11, 2002.

[171]"Homelessness," Almanac of Policy Issues <www.policyalmanac.org/social_welfare/homeless.shtml>.

[172]Ibid.

[173]Ibid.

[174]Jim Wallis, *Faith Works: Lessons from the Life of an Activist Preacher* (New York: Random House, 2000), p. 137.

[175]"Homelessness in America."

[176]See the Universal Declaration of Human Rights at <www.un.org/Overview/rights.html>.

[177]*Trials of War Criminals before the Nuremberg Military Tribunals Under Control Council Law No. 10*, vol. 2 (Washington, D.C.: U.S. Government Printing Office, 1949), pp. 181-82.

[178]Haugen, *Good News About Injustice*, p. 47.

[179]"U.S. Health Service Syphilis Study at Tuskegee," Centers for Disease Control and Prevention <www.cdc.gov/tuskegee/timeline.htm>.

[180]Bourke, *Skeptics Guide to Global Poverty,* p. 46.

[181]Marcus Kabel, "Citing Supply, Sam's Club and Costco Limit Sales of Rice," *Washington Post,* April 24, 2008, p. D1.

[182]Kofi A. Annan, "We the Children: Meeting the Promises of the World Summit for Children" (New York: UNICEF House, 2001), p. 28 <www.unicef.org/nutrition/files/pub_sgreport_adapted_en.pdf>.

[183]"Hunger: Celebration of Hope 08," Willow Creek Community Church <www.willowcreek.org/COH08/ whatcanIdo.asp>.

[184]*A Blueprint to End Hunger* can be found at <www.alliancetoendhunger.org/resources/blueprint>.

[185]Lois Ann Lorentzen, "No Longer Strangers," *Sojourners,* March 1, 2001, p. 15.

[186]Helen Slessarev-Jamir, "Looking for Welcome," *Sojourners,* March 1, 2001, p. 18.

[187]"Undocumented Immigrants Close to 11 Million," MSNBC, March 21, 2005 <www.msnbc.msn.com/ id/7255409>.

[188]Bishop Thomas Gerard Wenski, "The Catholic Campaign for Immigration Reform," Justice for Immigrants <www.justiceforimmigrants.org>.

[189]"Welcome to Tierra Nueva," Tierra Nueva <www.tierra-nueva.org/TNHome.html>.

[190]Please note: The movie is rated R for language and brief sexuality.

[191]"Prison Statistics," U.S. Department of Justice, Office of Justice Programs, Bureau of Justice Statistics <www .ojp.usdoj.gov/bjs/prisons.htm>.

[192]Matt Petryni, "Prison Statistics Call U.S.'s Priorities Into Question," *Daily Emerald,* March 4, 2008 <media .www.dailyemerald.com/media/storage/paper859/news/2008/03/04/Opinion/Prison.Statistics.Call.U.s.s . Priorities.Into.Question-3250021.shtml>.

[193]Adam Liptak, "Inmate Count in U.S. Dwarfs Other Nations'," *New York Times,* April 23, 2008 <www.ny times.com/2008/04/23/us/23prison.html>.

[194]James Q. Whitman, quoted in ibid.

[195]See Mae Elise Cannon, "Trading Knives for a Double-Edged Sword: Inmates at Louisiana State Penitentiary in Angola Train to Be Prison Missionaries," *Prism* (January-February 2009), pp. 12-16.

[196]Bourke, *Skeptic's Guide to Global Poverty,* p. 55.

[197]"2007 Human Development Report," United Nations Development Program, November 27, 2007, p. 25.

[198]Bourke, *Skeptic's Guide to Global Poverty,* p. 54.

[199]Ibid., pp. 55.

[200]H. Bachou, T. Tylleskar, D. H. Kaddu-Mulindwa and J. K. Tumwine (2006), "Bacteraemia Among Severely Malnourished Children Infected and Uninfected with the Human Immunodeficiency Virus-1 in Kampala, Uganda," *BMC Infectious Diseases* 6, no. 160 (November 2006) <www.biomedcentral.com/1471- 2334/6/160>.

[201]Bourke, *Skeptic's Guide to Global Poverty,* p. 49.

[202]Ibid., p. 55.

[203]George W. Bush, "Malaria Awareness Day Proclamation," April 24, 2007 <www.fightingmalaria.gov>.

[204]"GB at a Glance," Grameen Bank <www.grameen-info.org/index2.php?option=com_content&do_ pdf=1&id=26.>

[205]"Is Grameen Bank Different from Conventional Banks?" Grameen Bank, December 2008 <www.grameen-info.org/index.php?option=com_content&task=view&id=27&Itemid=164>.

[206]"Breaking the Vicious Cycle of Poverty Through Microcredit," Grameen Bank <www.grameen-info.org/ index.php?option=com_content&task=view&id=25&Itemid=128>.

[207]"Fast Facts about Churches," Hartford Institute for Religion Research, December 31, 2008 <hirr.hartsem .edu/research/fastfacts/fast_facts.html#multiracial>.

[208]Ibid.

[209]"Megachurches Today," cited in ibid.

[210]A megachurch by definition has more than 2,000 members in the congregation.

[211]The idea for this exercise was taken from <www.djchuang.com>.

[212]See Mosaix Global Network <www.mosaix.info/visitors/commitments.cfm>. These commitments are also found in Mark DeYmaz, *Building a Healthy Multi-Ethnic Church* (San Francisco: Jossey-Bass, 2007).

[213]The content from this section is in large part influenced by the contributions of Sarah Ago, Director of Children's Ministries at Hillside Covenant Church, Walnut Creek, California, October 10, 2008.

[214]This statistic is according to the World Health Organization (WHO), quoted at Barrier Break Technologies, "Disability Statistics: World" <www.barrierbreak.com/disabilitystats.php>.

[215]The International Labour Organization, Disabled Peoples' International and Irish Aid, "Press Release: Photograph Competition Launched to Mark United Nations Day of Disabled Persons," October 25, 2007 <www .un.or.th/presscentre/documents/071025_ILO_Photographcompetition_000.pdf>.

[216]Gary Albrecht, Katherine Seelman, and Michael Bury, eds., *Handbook of Disability Studies* (Thousand Oaks, Calif.: Sage, 2003), p. 37.

[217]Ibid., p. 47.

[218]Ibid., p. 50.

[219]Ibid., p. 49.

[220]"Congress Approves Legislation That Would Expand Americans with Disabilities Act," Medical News To-day, September 19, 2008 <www.medicalnewstoday.com/articles/122087.php>. The ADA Amendments Act of 2008 can be viewed at <www.govtrack.us/congress/bill.xpd?bill=h110-3195>.

[221]"Violence and Injury Prevention: Disability and Rehabilitation," World Health Organization Regional Office for Europe <www.euro.who.int/violenceinjury/20080519_1>.

[222]Ibid.

[223]"What Are the Most Common Causes of Disability?" Council for Disability Awareness <www.disability-canhappen.org/chances_disability/causes.asp>.

[224]Joni Eareckson Tada, quoted in Jane Johnson Struck, "Sweet Surrender," Today's Christian Woman 26, no. 5 (September/October 2004): 38 <www.christianitytoday.com/tcw/2004/sepoct/1.38.html>.

[225]This quote was shared with me by Sarah Ago, who heard it in a class, "Spiritual Issues in Chronic Illness and Disability," taught at Noah Park Theological Seminary by Mary Jane Owen, a philosopher, policy expert and disability rights activist who was involved in the passage of the Americans with Disabilities Act (1990) and is founder of Disabled Catholics in Action (2005).

[226]Several of these action items are influenced by Sarah Ago and a class she took at North Park Theological Seminary, "Spiritual Issues in Chronic Illness and Disability."

[227]"Aristotle's Political Theory," Stanford Encyclopedia of Philosophy <plato.stanford.edu/entries/aristotle-politics>.

[228]Reinhold Niebuhr, quoted in Lydialyle Gibson, "Elemental Obama," The University of Chicago Magazine, September-October 2008, p. 42.

[229]David Anderson, "How Should Evangelicals Celebrate Obama?" BridgeLeader Network, November 11, 2008 <bridgeleadernetwork.com>.

[230]This idea was proposed in an e-mail conversation with Gerry Blumberg, September 27, 2008.

[231]Gustavo Gutiérrez, A Theology of Liberation: History, Politics, and Salvation (Maryknoll, N.Y.: Catholic Foreign Mission Society of America, 2000), p. 164.

[232]Rick Warren, quoted in Timothy Morgan, "Purpose Driven in Rwanda: Rick Warren's Sweeping Plan to Defeat Poverty," Christianity Today 49, no. 10 (October 2005): 17.

[233]Gutiérrez, Theology of Liberation, p. 172.

[234]Henri Nouwen, Bread for the Journey: A Day Book of Wisdom and Faith (New York: HarperCollins, 1997).

[235]African Studies Center of the University of Pennsylvania, "Ghana: Economic Challenges, 1/13/09," Africa-Focus Bulletin, January 13, 2009 <www.africa.upenn.edu/afrfocus/afrfocus011309.html>.

[236]See the "General Information" section about Benjamin S. Carson Sr., M.D. at <http://carsonscholars.org/content/dr-ben-carson/general-information>.

[237]Amy K. Glasmeier, "The Nation We've Become," Penn State's Poverty in America site, February 26, 2007 <www.povertyinamerica.psu.edu>.

[238]Perkins, Quiet Revolution, p. 88.

[239]This book is intense. It's for readers who want to be challenged and can handle technical language full of economic theory. Karelis is the research professor of philosophy at George Washington University and was formerly the president of Colgate. He pushes against conventional arguments regarding poverty and attempts to show why public policy initiatives have been largely ineffective.

[240]Wallis, God's Politics, p. 264.

[241]In 2006 the poverty threshold for one person under the age of sixty-five was defined by the U.S. Census Bureau as $10,488. For those sixty-five and older, that same threshold was $9,669. For a family of two the poverty threshold was defined as $13,500 for householders under sixty-five and $12,186 for householders sixty-five and older. For a family of four living in the United States, the poverty threshold was $20,794 irrespective of the age of the householder (Carmen DeNavas-Walt, Bernadette D. Proctor, and Jessica Smith, "Income, Poverty, and Health Insurance Coverage in the United States: 2006," U.S. Census Bureau, August 2007, p. 43.

[242]Eileen Alt Powell, "Some 600,000 Join Millionaire Ranks in 2004," Associated Press, June 9, 2005.

[243]The Gross Domestic Product is being evaluated per person (per capita).

[244]Based on both the percent of the world net worth and percent of the world GDP (using exchange rates). Taken from Henry J. Steiner, Philip Alston and Ryan Goodman, International Human Rights in Context: Laws, Politics, Morals, 3rd ed. (New York: Oxford University Press, 2008), p. 7.

[245]Ibid.

[246]DeNavas-Walt, Proctor, and Smith, Income, Poverty, and Health Insurance Coverage, p. 11.

[247]Ibid., p. 11.

[248]Over 17 percent of children under eighteen in the United States lived in families below the poverty line (ibid.).

[249]Wim Naudé, "The Financial Crisis of 2008 and the Developing Countries," United Nations University, January 2009, p. 1. Available online at <www.wider.unu.edu/publications/working-papers/discussion-papers/2009/en_GB/dp2009-01/_files/80843373967769699/default/dp2009-01.pdf>.

[250]Les Christie, "Foreclosures Up 75% in 2007," CNN.com, January 29, 2008 <http://money.cnn.com/2008/01/29/real_estate/foreclosure_filings_2007/index.htm>.

[251]Allie Martin and Jenni Parker, "TechMission Launches Online Christian Volunteer Opportunity Directory," UrbanMinistry.org, January 9, 2007 <www.urbanministry.org/techmission-launches-online-christian-volunteer-opportunity>.

[252]"The Opportunity: TechMission Connects Resources to Needs," TechMission, January 2008 <www.techmission.org/cms/tm/opportunity>.

[253]Stanley Saunders and Charles Campbell, *The Word on the Street: Performing the Scriptures in the Urban Context* (Grand Rapids: Eerdmans, 2000), p. 9.

[254]The definitions of extreme (absolute), moderate and relative poverty come from the World Bank. Poverty is measured based on the equivalent of $1, which is not adequate to cover the costs of food, basic nutrition, health care, clean water, education or housing.

[255]Technically, because there are no longer Second World countries (communist countries in the developed world), the Third World no longer exists. It would be more accurate to say that extreme poverty only exists in the developing world. During the twentieth century, *Third World* typically referred to countries that were underdeveloped. *Second World* commonly referred to countries that were communist and under the influence of the former Soviet Union. *First World* was used to identify democracies with high standards of living and abundant technology.

[256]Paul Collier, *The Bottom Billion: Why the Poorest Countries Are Failing and What Can Be Done About It* (New York: Oxford University Press, 2007), p. ix.

[257]Earth Trends <www.earthtrends.org>. Population data used in calculating totals are 2005 population estimates from the following source: Population Division of the Department of Economic and Social Affairs of the United Nations Secretariat, 2003; and *World Population Prospects: The 2002 Revision* (New York: United Nations, 2002).

[258]Millennium Villages <www.millenniumvillages.org/aboutmv/index.htm>.

[259]Wallis, *God's Politics*, p. 25.

[260]"2007 Human Development Report," United Nations Development Program, November 27, 2007, p. 25 <hdr.undp.org/en/reports/global/hdr2007-2008>.

[261]Joseph Stalin <www.quotedb.com/quotes/3356>.

[262]This event was initiated and led by our pastor for students and children, Brian Gleason, and was a part of our 30 Hour Famine Experience in partnership with World Vision. For more information about this experience visit World Vision's website at <www.30hourfamine.org>.

[263]Mother Teresa, quoted in *Something Beautiful for God,* ed. Malcolm Muggeridge (New York: Harper & Row, 1971), p. 74.

[264]Melissa Farley and Vanessa Kelly, "Prostitution: A Critical Review of the Medical and Social Sciences Literature," *Women & Criminal Justice* 11 (2000) <www.prostitutionresearch.com/prostitution_research/000019.html>.

[265]Lisa Thompson, "Prostitution: Pathway to Incarceration for American Females," *Prism*, September–October 2007, p. 15.

[266]Ibid.

[267]"Teen Girls' Stories of Sex Trafficking in U.S.," ABC News, February 9, 2006 <abcnews.go.com/Primetime/Story?id=1596778>.

[268]Donna Hughes, "Traffic Stopper," an interview by Lisa Thompson, *Prism*, September–October 2007, p. 17.

[269]Dave Unander, *Shattering the Myth of Race: Genetic Realities and Biblical Truths* (Valley Forge, Penn.: Judson Press, 2000), p. 2.

[270]Carolus Linnaeus, quoted in ibid., p. 21.

[271]Unander, *Shattering the Myth of Race*, p. 21.

[272]Ibid., p. 27.

[273]Frederick Douglass, "Speech on the 24th Anniversary of Emancipation in Washington, D.C." <www.americanswhotellthetruth.org/pgs/portraits/Frederick_Douglas.html>.

[274]"Forrest to Speak on Leadership at Yale University and Booz Allen Hamilton," Board of Commissioners of St. Mary's County Maryland, February 11, 2003 <www.co.saint-marys.md.us/docs/press/releases/press release.asp?id=30>.

[275]"Status and Trends in Education of Racial and Ethnic Minorities," National Center for Education Statistics <http://nces.ed.gov/pubs2007/minoritytrends/ind_7_28.asp>.

[276]DeNavas-Walt, Proctor, and Smith, "Income, Poverty, and Health Insurance Coverage," p. 11.

[277]Emerson and Smith, *Divided by Faith*, p. 95.

[278]Ibid., p. 109.

[279]Herbold Hilary, "Never a Level Playing Field: Blacks and the G.I. Bill," *Journal of Blacks in Higher Education*, Winter 1994-1995, pp. 104-5, 107, 108.

[280]Desmond Tutu, "Desmond Tutu Quotes," ThinkExist.com <thinkexist.com/quotation/if_you_are_neutral_in_situations_of_injustice-you/200264.html>.

[281]Donna Willmott and Juliana van Olphen, "Challenging the Health Impacts of Incarceration: The Role for Community Health Workers," *Californian Journal of Health Promotion 2005* 3, no. 2, p. 38 <www.csuchico.edu/cjhp/3/2/38-48-willmott.pdf>.

[282]"Prison Statistics: Summary of Findings as of June 30, 2007," U.S. Department of Justice, Bureau of Justice Statistics <www.ojp.usdoj.gov/bjs/prisons.htm>.

[283]Ibid.

[284]Emerson and Smith, *Divided by Faith*, p. 132.

[285]Brenda Salter McNeil and Rick Richardson, *The Heart of Racial Justice: How Soul Change Leads to Social Change* (Downers Grove, Ill.: InterVarsity Press, 2004), p. 52.

[286]Courtesy of T. Armstrong, "In New Orleans White People 'Find,' Black People 'Loot,' " HungryBlues site, September 1, 2005 <www.minorjive.typepad.com/hungryblues/2005/09/in_new_orleans_.html>.

[287]Emerson and Smith, *Divided by Faith*, p. ix.

[288]Desmond Tutu, *God Has a Dream* (London: Random House, 2004), p. 68.

[289]Albert Hsu argues that the suburbs were not created by white flight, but instead predated this phenomena and were born largely to create space for veterans returning from World War II (*The Suburban Christian* [Downers Grove, Ill.: InterVarsity Press, 2006], p. 41).

[290]Note: *Crash* is rated R for language, sexual content and some violence.

[291]"In Britain, Blacks and Asians Are Twice as Likely to Live in Poverty Compared to Whites," Poverty News Blog, April 30, 2007 <povertynewsblog.blogspot.com/2007/04/in-britain-blacks-and-asians-are-twice.html>.

[292]Emerson and Smith, *Divided by Faith*, p. 89.

[293]John Rawls, *A Theory of Justice* (Boston: Belknap Press, 1971), p. 3.

[294]Kelly Jefferys, "Annual Flow Report: Refugees & Asylees: 2006," Department of Homeland Security Office of Immigration Statistics <www.dhs.gov/xlibrary/assets/statistics/publications/Refugee_AsyleeSec508Compliant.pdf>.

[295]Ibid.

[296]"United States to Welcome 12,000 More Iraqi Refugees in 2008," America.gov, February 6, 2008 <www.america.gov/st/peacesec-english/2008/February/20080206160027idybeekcm0.824032.html>.

[297]A six-week Bible study published by Exodus World Services is available at <www.e-w-s.org/html/study_guide.html>.

[298]"You Can Help Fight Persecution Through Signing Petitions," Persecution.org <www.persecution.org/suffering/petitions.php>.

[299]"Christians Under Attack in India," BBC News, October 14, 2008 <news.bbc.co.uk/2/hi/south_asia/7670747.stm>.

[300]Cindy Wooden, "Vatican Agency Says at Least 20 Church Workers Killed in 2008," *Catholic News Service*, December 30, 2008 <www.catholicnews.com/data/stories/cns/0806469.htm>.

[301]"Frequently Asked Questions," United States Commission on International Religious Freedom <www.uscirf.gov/index.php?option=com_content&task=view&id=337&Itemid=1#1>.

[302]"Countries of Particular Concern," United States Commission on International Religious Freedom <www.uscirf.gov/index.php?option=com_content&task=view&id=1456&Itemid=59>.

[303]"Annual Report on International Religious Freedom 2004," United States Commission on International Religious Freedom, October 6, 2004 <www.uscirf.gov/index.php?option=com_content&task=view&id=2025&Itemid=1>.

[304]Susan Sachs, "Baptist Pastor Attacks Islam, Inciting Cries of Intolerance," *New York Times*, June 15, 2002 <query.nytimes.com/gst/fullpage.html?res=9D0CE7D6133CF936A25755C0A9649C8B63>.

[305]The idea for this action item was taken from International Christian Concern at <www.persecution.org>.

[306]"Sex Trafficking Fact Sheet," International Justice Mission, October 29, 2007 <www.ijm.org/statistics&factsheets/viewcategory>.

[307]"Child Labor Facts," Compassion International <www.compassion.com/child-advocacy/find-your-voice/quick-facts/child-labor-quick-facts.htm>.

[308]"Injustice Today," International Justice Mission, <www.ijm.org/ourwork/injusticetoday>.

[309]Sex Trafficking Fact Sheet," International Justice Mission, October 29, 2007 <www.ijm.org/statistics &factsheets/viewcategory>.

[310]"Teen Girls' Stories of Sex Trafficking in U.S.," ABC News, February 9, 2006 <abcnews.go.com/Primetime/story?id=1596778>.

[311]Janice Raymond, Donna Hughes, and Carol Gomez, "Sex Trafficking of Women in the United States. International and Domestic Trends," Coalition Against Trafficking in Women, March 2001, p. 38.

[312]*H.R. 7311: William Wilberforce Trafficking Victims Protection Reauthorization Act of 2008* <www.govtrack.us/congress/bill.xpd?bill=h110-7311>.

[313]Desmond Tutu, *God Has a Dream: A Vision of Hope for Our Time* (New York: Doubleday, 2004), p. 48.

[314]Lawrence Finer, "Trends in Premarital Sex in the United States, 1954-2003," *Public Health Reports* 122 (January-February 2007): 74 <www.publichealthreports.org/userfiles/122_1/12_PHR122-1_73-78.pdf>.

[315]See Catherine Clark Kroeger, "Does Belief in Women's Equality Lead to an Acceptance of Homosexual Practice?" *Priscilla Papers* 18, no. 2 (2004): 3-10.

[316]"Slavery Still Exists: And It Could Be in Your Backyard," Free the Slaves, p. 2 <www.freetheslaves.net/document.doc?id=69>.

[317]"The Shackles of Slavery in Niger," *ABC News,* June 3, 2005 <abcnews.go.com/International/story?id=813618&page=1>.

[318]"The Bitter Truth About Chocolate," Team Treehugger, February 1, 2007, viewed on June 20, 2008 <www.treehugger.com/files/2007/02/the_bitter_trut.php>.

[319]This idea came from the action items offered by "Stop Chocolate Slavery." Forms and other helpful information are available on their website at <vision.ucsd.edu/~kbranson/stopchocolateslavery/takeaction.html>.

[320]An example of a letter to send to retail chains is provided by Anti-Slavery: Today's Fight for Tomorrow's Freedom at <www.antislavery.org/homepage/campaign/slaveryandwhatwebuy.htm>.

[321]"Stem Cell Basics," National Institutes of Health Resource for Stem Cell Research <stemcells.nih.gov/info/basics>.

[322]Ibid., <stemcells.nih.gov/info/basics/basics3.asp>.

[323]"Types and Characteristics," *Cell Medicine* <www.cellmedicine.com/types.asp>.

[324]Ibid.

[325]"Tuberculosis," World Health Organization, March 2006 <www.who.int/mediacentre/factsheets/fs104/en/index.html>.

[326]Bourke, *Skeptic's Guide to Global Poverty*, p. 56.

[327]"Deadly HIV-TB Co-Epidemic Sweeps Sub-Saharan Africa: Report," November 3, 2007 <www.healthdev.org/viewmsg.aspx?msgid=7e2d14b3-ff22-41ae-8c9a-7da687154891>

[328]Marjorie Golden and Holenarasipur Vikram, "Extrapulmonary Tuberculosis: An Overview," *American Family Physician*, November 1, 2005 <www.aafp.org/afp/20051101/1761.html>.

[329]"The Millennium Development Goals Report: 2007," United Nations <www.un.org/millenniumgoals/pdf/mdg2007.pdf>.

[330]"State of the World's Children 2005: Childhood Under Threat," UNICEF, p. 2 <www.unicef.org/sowc05/english/sowc05.pdf>. Of the 1.9 billion children in the developing world, over 640 million do not have adequate shelter.

[331]Bourke, *Skeptic's Guide to Global Poverty*, p. 35.

[332]Kevin Watkins, *Human Development Report 2006: Beyond Scarcity: Power, Poverty and the Global Water Crisis* (New York: United Nations Human Development Programme, 2006), pp. 6, 7, 35 <hdr.undp.org/hdr2006/pdfs/report/HDR06-complete.pdf>.

[333]World Heath Organization <www.who.int/water_sanitation_health/mdg1/en/index.html>.

[334]"State of the World's Children 2005."

[335]Maude Barlow, "Water as Commodity—The Wrong Prescription," *Backgrounder* 7, no. 3 (2001).

[336]"2006 United Nations Human Development Report," pp. 6, 7, 35.

[337]"7 1/2 Ways to Save Water," Our Water Future <www.ourwater.vic.gov.au/saving/home/7.5ways>.

[338]Lisa Hudson, "Fresh and Living Water," *Covenant Companion,* n.d.

[339]This idea comes from the Water Project at <www.water.cc>.

[340]Perkins, Quiet Revolution, p. 138.

[341]I initially heard this story recounted by Greg Yee, associate superintendent of the Pacific Southwest Conference (PSWC) of the Evangelical Covenant Church on September 29, 2008.

[342]William Dietrich, *Northwest Passage: The Great Columbia River* (Seattle: University of Washington Press, 1995), p. 52.

[343]"2007/2008 Human Development Reports," United Nations Development Program <hdrstats.undp.org/countries/country_fact_sheets/cty_fs_USA.html>.

[344]Katie Funk Wiebe, "Gender and Aging: Male or Female—What Difference Does it Make?" *Women & Men: Gender in the Church*, ed. Carol Penner (Scottdale, Penn.: Mennonite Publishing House, 1998), p. 93.

[345]Regina Shands Stoltzfus, "A Black Woman's Voice," *Women & Men: Gender in the Church*, ed. Carol Penner (Scottdale, Penn.: Mennonite Publishing House, 1998), p. 75.

[346]Ibid., p. 80.

[347]Ibid., p. 74.

[348]Cheryl Sanders, *Ministry at the Margins: The Prophetic Mission of Women, Youth, and the Poor* (Downers Grove, Ill.: InterVarsity Press, 1997), p. 50. Sanders is the Senior Pastor of the Third Street Church of God in Washington, D.C. She is also a professor of Christian ethics at Howard University.

[349]From the Woodrow Wilson International Center for Scholars. Available at <www.wilsoncenter.org/index .cfm?fuseaction=events.print&event_id=202481&stoplayout=true>.

[350]United Nations <www.un.org>, <www.undg.org/archives_docs/2542-Fact_Sheet_MDGs.doc>.

[351]Timothy Bayly, "Preparing for Motherhood: A Christian Response to the Cultural Attack on Domesticity," *Journal for Biblical Manhood and Womanhood* 4, nos. 2-3 (1999) <www.cbmw.org/Journal/Vol-4-No-2-3/ Preparing-for-Motherhood>.

[352]Bourke, *Skeptic's Guide to the Global AIDS Crisis*, p. 28.

[353]Bourke, *Skeptic's Guide to Global Poverty*, p. 95.

[354]Kay Marshall Strom and Michele Rickett, *Daughters of Hope: Stories of Witness and Courage in the Face of Persecution* (Downers Grove, Ill.: InterVarsity Press, 2003), p. 9.

[355]"2006 United Nations Human Development Report," pp. 6, 7, 35.

[356]Sisters in Service <www.sistersinservice.org/7reasons.asp>.

[357]Alan G. Padgett, "What is Biblical Equality?" *Priscilla Papers* 16, no. 3 (2002): 22-25 <www.cbeinter national.org/new/pdf_files/free_articles/PPWhatIsBiblical.pdf>.

[358]"About Us," Council on Biblical Manhood & Womanhood <www.cbmw.org/About-Us>.

[359]"Women's History in America," Compton's Interactive Encyclopedia <www.wic.org/misc/history.htm>.

[360]This idea came from a comment from Al Hsu, associate editor at InterVarsity Press.

[361]Steven Greenhouse and Constance Hays, "Wal-Mart Sex-Bias Suit Given Class-Action Status," *New York Times*, June 23, 2004 <www.nytimes.com/2004/06/23/business/Wal-Mart-sex-bias-suit-given-class-action -status.html>.

[362]Wal-Mart Class Website <www.walmartclass.com/walmartclass_declarationsummaries.html>.

[363]Greenhouse and Hays, "Wal-Mart Sex-Bias Suit."

[364]Liza Featherstone, *Selling Women Short* (New York: Basic Books, 2005), p. 265.

[365]Ibid., pp. 232-34.

[366]Borgna Brunner, "The Wage Gap: A History of Pay Equity and the Equal Pay Act," Information Please site <www.infoplease.com/spot/equalpayact1.html>.

[367]"Women's History in America," <www.wic.org/misc/history.htm>.

[368]DeNavas-Walt, Proctor, and Smith, "Income, Poverty, and Health Insurance Coverage in the United States: 2006," p. 6 <www.census.gov/prod/2007pubs/p60-233.pdf>.

[369]Charles Murray, quoted in Olasky, *Tragedy of Compassion in America*, p. xii.

[370]Chuck Collins, "Culture Watch: Restoring Labor's Voice," *Sojourners*, January-February 2000.

[371]National Center for Children in Poverty <www.nccp.org/about.html>.

[372]This report is available at <www.letjusticeroll.org>.

[373]"A Profile of the Working Poor," U.S. Department of Labor, Bureau of Labor Statistics, March 2002.

[374]In the 1800s the poor were typically people who were unable to work because of some type of physical limitation. In 1821 Josiah Quincy, the Massachusetts Chairman of the Legal Committee on Pauper Laws, identified the following categories of the poor: (1) mentally or physically disabled (i.e., not able to work) or (2) able in mind and body (notwithstanding psychological or social trauma) (Olasky, *Tragedy of Compassion in America*, p. 24).

[375]Mary Jo Bane, quoted in Jim Wallis, *Faith Works: Lessons from the Life of an Activist Preacher* (New York: Random House, 2000), p. 148.

[376]Robert L. Rose, "For Welfare Parents, Scrimping Is Legal, But Saving Is Out," *Wall Street Journal*, February 7, 1990, pp. A1, A11.

[377]See, for example, Erik Eckholm, "Mothers Scrimp as State Takes Child Support," *New York Times*, December 1, 2007 <www.nytimes.com/2007/12/01/us/01child.html>.

[378]Ibid.

[379]Ibid.

# Acknowledgments

Any errors in this work are my own, and I am certain that any meaningful contributions are because of the contribution of others in my life. I have been incredibly blessed to have amazing and wonderful people speak into my life from the time that I was small. I would like to thank some of those people.

My parents, from the time my mother brought home a black Cabbage Patch doll, have largely shaped my perspective on life: my father, through leading his business more faithfully and with more love than many pastors I know; and my mom, through working as an executive for Black Entertainment Television (BET). I am so proud! And I am very grateful for the sacrifices they made on my behalf.

Others have significantly influenced my journey as well. My childhood in southern Maryland was shaped by the tides of racism that are prevalent south of the Mason-Dixon line, and I want to express my love to those who led me through that time in my life—Sister Francis, Brother Romuald, Mrs. McIntyre, Mrs. Poe, Vaughn Evans, Sherry Momberger, Sally Ayres, George Forrest and Charles Gauthier. I hope to continue to learn from your examples.

Greg Jao was one of the first people in my life who gently walked me through the horrors of my own prejudices and opened my eyes to the richness of multiethnic community; he is a dear friend. Others have helped open my eyes and to call out my giftedness, including Daniel Hill, Sibyl Towner, Nancy Ortberg, Kazi Joshua, Alvin Bibbs, Paul Ackerman, Gilbert Bilezikian and John Perkins. I appreciate my friends and colleagues at Willow Creek—Anne Rand, Scott Pederson, Susan Demel and the volunteers who serve so faithfully—we certainly made some memories. I think, too, of the social-justice team, also from Willow, including Sarah Johnson, Allison Hosack, Brian Kammerzelt and Sandra Seitman.

There are so many people to whom I owe a great debt. I am thankful for the time and space to write afforded to me by Hillside and the greatest staff team ever! And to the people who walk alongside me now in my journey toward justice: Debbie Blue, Greg Yee and the Mosaic Center Board. I had the privilege of writing much of this manuscript in the Santa Cruz Mountains at Mission Springs in the home of Gaylon and Marla Patterson; thank you for the gift of quiet space. And then to the wonderful InterVarsity team, and to my editor, Al Hsu, who has had great patience in walking me through the process of book writing.

Finally, I wish to mention my family. To my extended family: Richard and Leslie, Mel and Dan, Laura and Tom, Jean and Ted—thank you for loving me. To the children in my life who have brought me great joy—Daniel, Sara, Josie, Jeffrey, Maggie, Sandy, AJ, Kimberly, DaShawn, Kate, Tori, Allie and Jenny—you have taught me many lessons. And to Roby, having sacrificed more than any person I know by being married to me, you have certainly earned your treasures in heaven!

May the Lord give each of us strength as we attempt to truly worship him. I have great faith that the person of Jesus we encounter in Scripture will continue to transform us into agents of his love and justice.

*I will sing of your love and justice;*
*to you, LORD, I will sing praise. (Psalm 101:1)*

## About BridgeLeader Books

BridgeLeader Books are produced through a partnership between InterVarsity Press and BridgeLeader Network, a nonprofit organization that helps churches, colleges, companies and other groups move toward multicultural effectiveness. Addressing such topics as reconciliation, diversity and leadership development, BridgeLeader Books contribute to a better understanding and practice of multi-ethnic ministry within the church and in the world.